A Race Against Time

New
Century
Books

A Race Against Time

Racial Heresies for the 21st Century

Edited by

George McDaniel

Foreword by

Jared Taylor

New Century Foundation

New Century Books
Box 527
Oakton, Virginia 22124-0527

Tel. (703) 716-0900
Fax (703) 716-0932

www.amren.com

ISBN 0-9656383-2-4
Library of Congress Control Number: 2003107725

Cover: Callanish stones on the Scottish island of Lewis in the Hebrides. The megaliths were erected 5,000 years ago to form a circle and several avenues. The tallest is just over 15 feet high. The stones were abandoned around 800 BC, and had nearly disappeared beneath the peat when they were excavated in the mid-19th century. Photo by Charles Tait.

Manufactured in the United States of America

To Glayde Whitney

1939 - 2002

Contents

Foreword ix

Preface xv

Current Events 1

The Racial Revolution 3

The Religion of Anti-Racism 13

Multiculturalism and the War Against White America 20

Race, Crime, and Violence 28

Hell on Wheels 51

White Man in a Texas Prison 58

The Myth of Diversity 66

Life Along the Fault Line 78

White Might, Black Fright 82

Pushing Out Whitey 86

The Past 96

Race, Nation and the Soldier 97

The War with Mexico 106

Forgotten Black Voices 111

The "Reparations" Hoax 113

Madison Grant and the Racialist Movement 121

Multiculturalism and Marxism 129

The Decline of National Review 135

Undue Process 145

Sowing the Seeds of Destruction 151

Integration . . . Disintegration 161

Selma to Montgomery, 30 Years Later 168

The Doctor in Spite of Himself 181

Science **186**

The Descent of Man 187

A New Theory of Racial Differences 192

Race and Psychopathic Personality 203

The Definitive Word on Intelligence 212

Why Race Matters 223

Philosophy **232**

Why Race Matters 233

The Morality of Survival 241

Race and the American Identity 255

The Evolution of Racial Differences in Morality 266

Is There a Superior Race? 272

The Future **281**

If We Do Nothing 282

Fairest Things Have Fleetest Endings 291

Closed Minds Are an Open Book 296

Towards Renewal and Renaissance 301

A Certain Trumpet 313

Twelve Years of American Renaissance 323

Foreword

by Jared Taylor

On March 10, 2003, two policemen died in a shootout at the Stapleton Houses in New York City. Grace Watkins, who lives in the virtually all-black housing project, explained that when people learned of the killings they said the policemen got what they deserved. "I think a lot of people out here weren't worried about [the shootings]," she explained, "because they thought they were white cops, but when they heard the cops were black, their attitude changed totally, and they started expressing concern for the police officers' families."[1]

Grace Watkins is 18 years old, which means she was born 20 years after the landmark civil rights legislation of the 1960s. Since well before the 1980s, every pillar of American society has passionately supported the goal of eliminating racial prejudice. For her entire life, people of Miss Watkins' race have not only been legally protected from discrimination but have benefited from the preference programs we call "affirmative action." Our country has invested more moral energy in the fight against "racism" than in any national undertaking since the Second World War. And yet, nearly 40 years after the crowning achievements of the civil rights struggle, Miss Watkins calmly tells a reporter that her black friends and acquaintances were unconcerned by the deaths of two men they assumed were white. The policemen became human beings in their minds only when they turned out to be black.

Miss Watkins' comments were just a touch of atmosphere to liven up a routine crime story. No doubt most readers soon forgot about her. But what Grace Watkins said—and the silence that greeted it—are symbols of the almost complete failure of the colossal effort our country has made to transform race relations. Grace Watkins does not live in the America the activists of the civil rights movement promised us. None of us does.

The goal of integration, of eliminating racial prejudice, of dismantling racial barriers was to build a society in which race would lose its significance. We were, in Martin Luther King's now almost scriptural terms, to judge each other by the content of our character and not by the color of our skin. Grace Watkins' friends certainly judge people by the color of their skin. Although whites do not usually express themselves quite so freely, they often do the same.

Americans still separate themselves by race. Residential neighborhoods are almost as segregated as they were in the 1960s. Church congregations are segregated. Generation after generation, school children fail the "lunch-room test" by sitting with friends of their own race. If they ever stop to think about it, Americans know that the constant cheerleading for integration and "diver-

---

[1] Douglas Montero, "Surprising Sympathy Dawns in Projects," *New York Post*, March 12, 2003.

sity" only masks deep divisions. Outside of a few pockets of self-conscious mixing, Americans generally live their lives among people like themselves.

Occasionally, the country goes through a spasm of self-righteousness, in which someone pretends to take the old civil-rights vision seriously. Does anyone remember President William Clinton's racial initiative? Launched with great fanfare during his second term, it was supposed to be the cornerstone of his legacy. It would set the country back upon the road to racial harmony and become the basis for building—to use the initiative's full name—"One America in the 21st Century."

The very fact of the initiative was a recognition that race relations are not as we had expected. Its name even implied that racial conflict threatens the idea of "one America." And yet, despite all the power and prestige of the White House, the initiative achieved nothing. Perhaps not even Mr. Clinton himself would claim it accomplished anything. What was to carve a president's name into history has disappeared without a trace. Like hundreds of other race initiatives, outreach programs, commissions, and blue-ribbon panels, it was a futile exhalation of hot air.

The only interesting thing about this failure was that, like so many before it, it in no way dimmed the official goal of establishing an America in which race does not matter. We still celebrate Martin Luther King Day, we still muster fury on an Inquisitional scale for blasphemers like Trent Lott,[2] we still mouth platitudes about the glories of "diversity"—but are there any real believers left? Does anyone still think blacks can be taught to do as well in school as whites, that the ghettos will become middle class, that whites will stay when blacks or Mexicans move in, that racial tension will disappear, or that the national unity we took for granted in the 1940s and 1950s can survive bilingualism, multiculturalism, and the reduction of whites to a minority?

We have become like the Soviet Union, where a classless utopia continued to be the official national goal, even though everyone knew it was impossible. Our racial myths may have been propounded with the best intentions but they are as mistaken and corrupting as Marxist economics. Nations cannot be built in pursuit of unobtainable goals, and on principles in which almost no one believes.

The authors represented in this book reject today's racial orthodoxy. A few never believed it. Most initially absorbed it without question, but finally accepted the evidence of their senses. They are all fully aware that what they

---

[2] On December 5, 2002, at a 100th birthday celebration for Strom Thurmond, Mississippi Senator Trent Lott said: "I want to say this about my state: When Strom Thurmond ran for president we voted for him. We're proud of it. And if the rest of the country had followed our lead, we wouldn't have had all these problems over all these years, either."

Mr. Thurmond was the 1948 candidate of the "Dixiecrat" Party, and ran on a segregationist, states'-rights platform. Mr. Lott's reference to this campaign was widely denounced as an endorsement of segregation. Mr. Lott apologized repeatedly, but the denunciations did not stop. He resigned from his position as Senate Majority Leader when the Republicans threatened to remove him.

propose in its place is no less a revolution than the one that rescued the Soviet Union and Eastern Europe from their own moribund orthodoxy.

This book is a collection of articles from a monthly magazine, *American Renaissance*, of which I am editor. During its 13 years of publication, the many contributors to AR have, I believe, laid the foundations of the only approach to race that is genuinely factual, historical, and moral. This book represents an unapologetic break with the assumptions and clichés of the civil rights era. The authors believe that when decades of experience do nothing but contradict the assumptions that underlie social policy, those assumptions must be reexamined. America has tried—as earnestly as a nation can try anything—to build a society according to a certain vision. Grace Watkins—and Grace Watkins is hardly alone—tells us we have failed. It is time to recognize failure, and stop blundering down a path that leads nowhere.

If we are not to keep repeating the same mistakes, we must accept at least the following propositions:

- Race is an important aspect of individual and collective identity.
- Most people have strong feelings of racial loyalty, and prefer the culture and way of life associated with their race.
- When people of different races come into contact there is friction.

These three statements are universally true, and are controversial only in a society determined to ignore the obvious. Even if they would not admit these principles openly, most Americans live by them.

In this book we go a little further than the obvious: Races are not identical or interchangeable in terms of average ability and capacity for high civilization. Any society that expects—or as ours often does, demands—equal outcomes by race is asking the impossible. Ultimately, given the reality of racial loyalty and racial differences in ability and behavior, separation comes more naturally than integration.

We go further still: Racial and ethnic groups have collective interests, and these interests often conflict. One example is "affirmative action." Blacks and Hispanics like it, because it benefits them at the expense of whites and Asians. Whites and Asians dislike it for the same reason. These are antagonistic interests that cannot be reconciled, and yet for decades whites who raise their voices against systematic racial discrimination against themselves have been accused of "racism."

Another example of conflict is the demographic transformation of America. Whenever census figures report increases in the numbers of Hispanics, Latino activists celebrate the political, cultural, linguistic, and economic gains that come with numeric gain. They make no secret that they want the country to become yet more Hispanic, to reflect their tastes, acknowledge their way of life, celebrate their holidays, and glorify their heroes.

Most non-Hispanics do not want their country to become more like Latin America, and there is no reason they should. Many would like to see the burgeoning Hispanic presence reduced. Like "affirmative action," this is yet another symmetrical, irreconcilable conflict: The country cannot become more Hispanic without harming the interests of those who liked it the way it was, and it cannot become less Hispanic without harming the interests of those who want it more Hispanic.[3] Is it unreasonable or immoral for those who built the country to prefer that it reflect their own heritage, to prefer to keep it for their own children rather than turn it over to strangers?

Perhaps the most controversial position taken in this book is that whites have the right to resist displacement by people unlike themselves. This is a fundamental right we recognize for non-whites everywhere. It is only whites—whether in Europe or North America or Oceania—who are expected to act as if it is a privilege to share their lands with aliens who arrive in ever-greater numbers, transforming everything they find.

Displacement is the group equivalent of death. Whites will only see their cultures and ways of life slip away if they continue to let their homelands fill up with immigrants of other races. On an individual level, whites show their distaste for racial transformation by moving away when their neighborhoods turn black or Mexican or Haitian—or, in Europe, when they turn Turkish, Pakistani, or Algerian. If whites refuse to accept this transformation at the local level, why should they welcome it at the national level?

George McDaniel, web page editor of *American Renaissance* and editor of this collection, has given it the title *A Race Against Time*. Whites are, indeed, in a race against time. If they do nothing, if they let themselves become minorities, their destiny will be taken out of their hands. The newcomers have their own ideas about government, religion, culture, law—and how to treat racial minorities. Once they have arrived in sufficient numbers, they will disregard the wishes of the founding stock, just as they already have in those parts of the United States, Germany, Britain or France where they have become local majorities. Whites have every right to resist dispossession, and if they fail to assert this right, if they lose the race against time, they will be brushed aside by others who do not hesitate to assert collective rights.

It is not too much of an exaggeration to think of this book as a collection of heresies against the state religion. It is a religion few people actually live by (If integration is such an important national goal why don't whites buy houses in black neighborhoods?) but it still has the power to dictate policy, and to terrify and punish scoffers. At its simplest, our heresy is this: Race is important, and whites have rights *as a race*.

Our country, and indeed whites everywhere, have taken a terrible wrong turn. The consequences of multiracialism are plain to see, whether in Los Angeles, Philadelphia, London or Milan. Everywhere it has been attempted,

---

[3] Needless to say, every American institution is entirely on the side of those who want the country more Hispanic. They say "diversity" is good for non-Hispanics. They would not, of course, take this position if the roles were reversed, and Americans were emigrating to and transforming other countries in the name of "diversity." Double standards of this kind are analyzed in detail in several of the articles that follow.

racial integration has produced friction. As soon as they arrive in sufficient numbers, immigrants cease to assimilate to their host countries and insist, instead, that the host country adapt to them. In the long term, adaptation means the disappearance of one way of life and its replacement by another.

The authors of this book and the movement we represent are entirely in earnest about the survival of our people and our culture. Unless whites shake off the teachings of racial orthodoxy they will cease to be a distinct people with a culture of their own. History, morality, biology, and generations of common sense justify our desire that our children should walk in the ways of their own people, that they should be the heirs to the culture and civilization of Europe, that their lives be shaped by their own history rather than by the demands of people unlike themselves. More and more whites are awakening to the crisis they face. They will eventually shake off their lethargy and secure for themselves that to which all men have a right: survival as a people.

Oakton, Virginia, July 2, 2003

Preface

by George McDaniel

The working title of this book was "The Best of *American Renaissance*." Although we eventually discarded it for the current one, it is that title that has symbolized our challenge throughout this project. Somehow, we had to pore through 13 years of work, almost 500 feature articles and reviews, and distill a collection of no more than about seven percent of the total.

Our first step was simply to get a grip on the task by getting out the back issues and having a look. There they were, more than fifteen hundred 8.5-by-11-inch pages, including 400 major articles and more than 100 book reviews, written by scores of authors from all over America and many countries around the world. The range of the contributors' occupations alone was astounding: from police and firemen to research scientists, historians to subway conductors to prison inmates to Catholic priests, those 1,500 pages represented contributions from people from all walks of life.

But before we decided how to make the difficult selections, we needed a plan. AR is a journal of ideas and not a news magazine. For that reason, we decided that a conceptual approach would be best.

The articles and reviews (each of which is essentially an article, with one or more books as a backdrop) fell into some fairly easily identifiable categories. Those that described events or situations were either current events, historical accounts, or extrapolations to the future. Most of the rest could be classified as either science or philosophy. So these became our categories. But which articles to use? We worked our way through the AR oeuvre, looking for signs of repetition and overuse, with an eye for stylistic quality and factual depth. We wanted a book that would be a statement of what AR has been about during its first 13 years and also a book that could stand alone, providing its readers with the very best work from a wide spectrum of experts in a variety of fields.

You now hold in your hands our "seven-percent solution" as we distilled it from those often heroic works. It contains contributions from AR stalwarts such as Sam Francis and Sam Dickson, leading-edge scientists like Richard Lynn, free-thinking philosophers like Michael Levin, bold commentators such as Michael Masters and Joseph Fallon, and some of the most cogent and hard-hitting work by AR editors James Lubinskas, and, of course, Jared Taylor.

This short preface would not be complete without heart-felt acknowledgment of one member of the AR community who will no doubt have a place in any future AR collection. Even the most casual reader of AR over the past few years knows the name of Stephen Webster and is familiar with his excellent work both inside and outside the pages of AR. I would like to acknowledge his very able assistance in creating this book.

In closing, readers familiar with AR might ask, what of those regular features of AR not represented here: the Letters section, those trademark AR line drawings, and, especially, the irrepressible "O Tempora, O Mores"? At least 700 letters have appeared in AR, from readers worldwide, most of them friendly, a few decidedly unfriendly, but each making its own contribution. None of these appears in the present volume, though a separate and very interesting volume all its own could be culled from them. As for OTOM, each month that unique, sardonic feature exposes the peculiar approach modern society has to race, ethnicity, and culture. We have published close to 3,000 of those little nuggets over the years, chronicling, in bite-sized chunks, the absurd results of our society's collisions with the truth, and of its desperate attempts to hide from the truth. How could we possibly publish a compilation that left them out altogether?

Well, we couldn't. So here—complete with trademark drawing—is just one of the 3,000 tiny gems from "O Tempora, O Mores!"

PC Gone Wild

The June 1995 *Reader's Digest* included the following short item:

From the Fresno, Calif. *Bee*: "An item about the Massachusetts budget crisis made reference to new taxes that will help put Massachusetts 'back in the African-American.'

"The item should have said 'back in the black.' "

CURRENT EVENTS

The Racial Revolution
by Jared Taylor

Everyone knows that during the last 50 years or so there have been fundamental changes in the ways Americans think about race. In fact, what has occurred is nothing short of a revolution, a complete rejection of what earlier generations of Americans—from Colonial times until perhaps the 1950s—took for granted.

Although contemporary racial thinking is so monolithic it has become hard to imagine how Americans could have thought otherwise, we can get a sense of how radical the change has been if we try to imagine equally far-reaching changes: What would it be like for America to reverse the sexual revolution completely and return to Victorian propriety in just a few generations? Or for a country suddenly to stop being deeply and universally religious and become atheist? Or to abandon the principle of private property and switch to hippy-style communal living?

The United States has gone through a revolution that is not only just as dramatic, but astonishing in another respect: What was once taken for granted about race has become not just outmoded but *immoral*. Only revolutions bring such sweeping, back-to-front moral changes.

Yesterday's Assumptions

The best way to gauge the extent of the revolution is to compare the present to the past. The contrast is staggering. Practically every historical American figure was by today's standards an unregenerate white supremacist.

Until just a few years ago virtually all Americans believed that race was a profoundly important aspect of individual and national identity. They believed people of different races differed in temperament and ability, and that whites built societies that were superior to those built by non-whites. They were repelled by miscegenation—which they called "amalgamation"—because it would dilute the unique characteristics of whites. They took it for granted that America must be peopled with Europeans, and that American civilization could not continue without whites. Many saw the presence of non-whites in the United States as a terrible burden.

Among the founders, Thomas Jefferson wrote at greatest length about race. He thought blacks were mentally inferior to whites, and though he thought slavery was a great injustice he did not want free blacks in American society: "When freed, [the Negro] is to be removed beyond the reach of mixture." Jefferson was, therefore, one of the first and most influential advocates of "colonization," or sending blacks back to Africa.

He also believed in the destiny of whites as a racially conscious people. In 1786 he wrote, "Our Confederacy [the United States] must be viewed as the nest from which all America, North and South, is to be peopled." In 1801 he looked forward to the day "when our rapid multiplication will expand itself . . . over the whole northern, if not the southern continent, with a people speaking the same language, governed in similar forms, and by similar laws; nor can we contemplate with satisfaction either blot or mixture on that surface." The empire was to be homogeneous.

Jefferson thought of the United States as only the latest outpost in the ever-expanding march of the Anglo-Saxon, the Saxon branch of which had originated in the Cimbric Chersonesus of Denmark and Schleswig-Holstein. He was thinking of the Saxons when he proposed a 1784 ordinance to create new states in the Mississippi valley, suggesting the name Cherronesus for the area between lakes Huron and Michigan. Its shape reminded him of Denmark. The race was not to forget its origins.

James Madison, like Jefferson, believed the only solution to the race problem was to free the slaves and send them away. He proposed that the federal government sell off public land to raise the huge sums necessary to buy the entire black population and ship it overseas. He favored a Constitutional amendment to establish a colonization society to be run by the President. After his two terms in office, Madison served as president of the American Colonization Society, to which he devoted much time and energy.

The following prominent Americans were not merely members but officers of the society: Andrew Jackson, Henry Clay, Daniel Webster, Stephen Douglas, William Seward, Francis Scott Key, Gen. Winfield Scott, and two Chief Justices of the Supreme Court, John Marshall and Roger Taney. As for James Monroe, the capital of Liberia is named Monrovia in gratitude for his help in returning blacks to Africa.

Abraham Lincoln considered blacks to be—in his words—"a troublesome presence" in the United States. During the Lincoln-Douglas debates he said:

". . . I am not nor ever have been in favor of making voters or jurors of negroes, nor of qualifying them to hold office, nor to intermarry with white people; and I will say in addition to this that there is a physical difference between the white and black races which I believe will for ever forbid the two races living together on terms of social and political equality. And inasmuch as they cannot so live, while they do remain together there must be a position of superior and inferior, and I as much as any other man am in favor of having the superior position assigned to the white race."

He, too, favored colonization and even in the midst of a desperate war with the Confederacy found time to study the problem and to appoint Rev. James Mitchell as Commissioner of Emigration. Free blacks were going to have to be dealt with, and it was best to plan ahead and find a place to which they could be sent.

Before Lincoln's time, no President had ever invited a group of blacks to the White House to discuss public policy. On August 14th, 1862, Lincoln did so—to ask blacks to leave the country. "There is an unwillingness on the part of our people, harsh as it may be, for you free colored people to remain with us," he explained. He then urged them and their race to go to a colonization site in Central America that his Commissioner of Emigration had investigated. Later that year, in a message to Congress, he even argued for the *forcible* removal of free blacks.

His successor, Andrew Johnson, did not feel differently: "This is a country for white men, and by God, as long as I am President, it shall be a government for white men . . . ." Like Jefferson, he thought whites had a clear mandate: "This whole vast continent is destined to fall under the control of the Anglo-Saxon race—the governing and self-governing race."

Before he became President, James Garfield wrote, "[I have] a strong feeling of repugnance when I think of the negro being made our political equal and I would be glad if they could be colonized, sent to heaven, or got rid of in any decent way . . . ."

What of 20th century Presidents? Theodore Roosevelt thought blacks were "a perfectly stupid race," and blamed Southerners for bringing them to America. In 1901, he wrote: "I have not been able to think out any solution to the terrible problem offered by the presence of the Negro on this continent . . . he is here and can neither be killed nor driven away . . . ." As for Indians, he once said, "I don't go so far as to think that the only good Indians are the dead Indians, but I believe nine out of ten are, and I shouldn't inquire too closely into the health of the tenth."

William Howard Taft told a group of black college students, "Your race is adapted to be a race of farmers, first, last and for all times."

Woodrow Wilson was a confirmed segregationist, and as president of Princeton prevented blacks from enrolling. He enforced segregation in government offices and was supported in this by Charles Eliot, president of Harvard, who argued that "civilized white men" could not be expected to work with "barbarous black men." During the Presidential campaign of 1912, Wilson took a strong position in favor of excluding Asians: "I stand for the national policy of exclusion. . . . We cannot make a homogeneous population of a people who do not blend with the Caucasian race. . . . Oriental coolieism will give us another race problem to solve and surely we have had our lesson."

Warren Harding's views were little different: "Men of both races may well stand uncompromisingly against every suggestion of social equality. This is not a question of social equality, but a question of recognizing a fundamental, eternal, inescapable difference. Racial amalgamation there cannot be."

Henry Cabot Lodge took the view that "there is a limit to the capacity of any race for assimilating and elevating an inferior race, and when you begin to pour in unlimited numbers of people of alien or lower races of less social efficiency and less moral force, you are running the most frightful risk that any people can run."

In 1921, as Vice President-elect, Calvin Coolidge wrote in *Good Housekeeping* about the basis for sound immigration policy: "There are racial considerations too grave to be brushed aside for any sentimental reasons. Biological laws tell us that certain divergent people will not mix or blend. . . .

Quality of mind and body suggests that observance of ethnic law is as great a necessity to a nation as immigration law."

Congressman William N. Vaile of Colorado was a prominent supporter of the 1924 immigration legislation that set policy until the revolution of the 1960s. He explained his opposition to non-white immigration this way:

"Nordics need not be vain about their own qualifications. It well behooves them to be humble. What we do claim is that the northern European, and particularly Anglo Saxons made this country. Oh yes, the others helped. But that is the full statement of the case. They came to this country because it was already made as an Anglo-Saxon commonwealth. They added to it, they often enriched it, but they did not make it, and they have not yet greatly changed it. We are determined that they shall not. It is a good country. It suits us. And what we assert is that we are not going to surrender it to somebody else or allow other people, no matter what their merits, to make it something different. If there is any changing to be done, we will do it ourselves."

Harry Truman is remembered for having integrated the armed services by executive order. Yet, in his private correspondence he was as separatist as Jefferson: "I am strongly of the opinion Negroes ought to be in Africa, yellow men in Asia and white men in Europe and America." In a letter to his daughter he described waiters at the White House as "an army of coons."

As recent a President as Dwight Eisenhower argued that although it might be necessary to grant blacks certain political rights, this did not mean social equality "or that a Negro should court my daughter." It is only with John Kennedy that we find a President whose public pronouncements on race begin to be acceptable by contemporary standards.

Politicians usually express careful, non-controversial views, and their sentiments were reflected by men of letters as well. Ralph Waldo Emerson, for example, believed that "it is in the deep traits of race that the fortunes of nations are written." Walt Whitman wrote: "Who believes that Whites and Blacks can ever amalgamate in America? Or who wishes it to happen? Nature has set an impassable seal against it. Besides, is not America for the Whites? And is it not better so?" Jack London was a well-known socialist, but he did not think socialism was universally applicable. It was, he wrote, "devised for the happiness of certain kindred races. It is devised so as to give more strength to these certain kindred favored races so that they may survive and inherit the earth to the extinction of the lesser, weaker races." Mark Twain, in an essay that no longer appears in popular anthologies, once described the American Indian as "a fit candidate for extermination."

There is essentially no limit to the "racist" quotations one could unearth from prominent Americans of the past, but views that are considered unacceptable by today's standards were so widespread that virtually anyone who said anything about race reflected those views.

Needless to say, this embarrasses today's guardians of orthodoxy. Most historians ignore or gloss over the racial views of prominent figures, and most people today have no idea Lincoln or Roosevelt were such outspoken "white supremacists." Some people deliberately distort the views of great Americans. For example, inscribed on the marble interior of the Jefferson Memorial are the words: "Nothing is more certainly written in the book of fate than that these people [the Negroes] shall be free." Jefferson did not stop there, but went on to say, "nor is it less certain that the two races equally free, cannot live under the same government"—which rather changes the effect.

Another approach to Jefferson is to bring out all the facts and then try to repudiate him. Conor Cruise O'Brien did this in a 1996 cover story for *Atlantic Monthly*. After describing Jefferson's views, he writes:

"It follows that there can be no room for a cult of Thomas Jefferson in the civil religion of an effectively multiracial America—that is, an America in which nonwhite Americans have a significant and increasing say. Once the facts are known, Jefferson is of necessity abhorrent to people who would not be in America at all if he could have had his way." Richard Grenier agrees, likening Jefferson to Nazi Gestapo chief Heinrich Himmler, and calling for the demolition of the Jefferson Memorial "stone by stone."

It is all very well to wax indignant over Jefferson's views 170 years after his death, but if we start purging American history of "racists" who will be left? If we demonize Jefferson we have to repudiate everything that happened in America until the 1960s—which is precisely what the revolution in racial thinking logically requires.

After all, until 1964, any employer could refuse to hire non-whites and merchants could refuse to do business with whomever they pleased. Until 1965, immigration laws were designed to keep the country white. In 1967, when the Supreme Court ruled them unconstitutional, 20 states still had anti-miscegenation laws on the books. State legislatures were unwilling to repeal laws that reflected the customs and ideals of generations of Americans.

The Revolution

So how does a society handle a revolution that turns the common sense of previous eras on its head? One thing that changes is language. Because the thinking of men like Lincoln and Wilson was so widespread, there was no need for a special term to describe it. Just as there is no word to describe only those days on which the sun rises—because it rises every day—there was no word to describe people who thought of race the way they did.

The word "racism," therefore, did not appear until the 1930s, and was a description not of American thinking but of Nazi ideology. Only in the 1960s did the word become common in its current usage, and as late as 1971, the *Oxford English Dictionary* had no entry for it. We managed to establish slavery, abolish it, establish Jim Crow, and abolish it too without ever using a word that today's newspapers find indispensable. When our ancestors wrote about race, they wrote of antagonism, kindness, hostility, admiration, hatred, and a host of other feelings, but never about "racism." The word does not appear even in so late and influential a book as Gunnar Myrdal's *An American Dilemma*, published in 1942 (see "Sowing the Seeds of Destruction" on page 151). Only in the context of mid-20th century assumptions did the word become necessary as a way to condemn what people had always taken for granted.

Even the word's predecessor, "racial prejudice," is a recent construction (it is the term Myrdal used). Whatever Abraham Lincoln or Theodore Roosevelt thought about other races, they would have been insulted to be told it was *prejudice*, that is to say, unreasonable preconceived judgment. "Racial prejudice" was a particularly clever coinage because it implied that white attitudes were a form of ignorance that could be cured with proper education. It managed to discredit while appearing to describe.

What Americans traditionally practiced was racial *discrimination*, that is, they made distinctions. Choice and freedom are impossible without discrimination, and a "discriminating man" is one who knows the differences between things and chooses wisely. Discrimination—the most necessary and natural thing people do—is now called "bigotry."

The very newness of terms like "racism" and "racial prejudice" is reason enough to be suspicious of them. To define a serious moral failing with words that did not even exist in the time of our grandparents is not a sign of normal social change. It is revolution.

The race revolution has been like the Russian revolution, which also stood common sense on its head. In the Soviet Union the profit motive, which had been the driving force of every economy in history, became a sin against the people, and new words had to be invented for new crimes. People who still believed in private property had a "petty bourgeois mentality." Those who wanted to keep what they made were "stealing from the state." Anyone who defended free markets was a "stooge of imperialism." After the fall of Communism common sense was rehabilitated, and all the new crimes and words to describe them disappeared.

Ironically, during the years that led to the return of common sense in the former Eastern Bloc, the reverse process continued in the West. "Racism" was such a success it inspired the discovery of all sorts of new crimes: sexism, lookism, ableism, speciesism, male chauvinism, homophobia, nativism, etc. One natural, healthy distinction after another was discovered to be a crime. It must be a uniquely 20th century experience for large numbers of people to be accused of crimes for which the very words to describe them have only just been invented.

Rules for Whites

So what is racism, anyway? For whites (and only for whites), it is anything that deviates from the following principles: Race is an utterly insignificant matter. It means nothing, explains nothing, and stands for nothing. The races are not only equal, they are interchangeable. Therefore, it makes no difference if the neighborhood turns Mexican or the nation turns non-white or your children marry Haitians. For whites, race is not a valid criterion for any purpose, and any decision they make on the basis of race is immoral. For whites to take notice of race at all is "racism."

Of course, this contradicts one of the current myths about America, that racial diversity is one of our great strengths. If the races are equivalent, how can racial diversity have any meaning at all? For racial diversity to be a strength (or a weakness or be noticed at all) race must have *some* kind of meaning, and to the extent that race stands for something why is it wrong for whites to take race seriously both in their personal lives and political views?

The benefits of racial diversity are now supposed to be so important that they justify "affirmative action," or racial discrimination against whites. If racial diversity is that valuable, race has to mean something significant. But if race is both real and important, why is it wrong to notice and care about these meanings? Why is it wrong for whites to find these differences not to their liking?

Presumably, the theory is that although races are essentially equivalent and interchangeable, blacks, for example, have had different experiences from whites, and whites benefit from contact with the different "culture" blacks have acquired. This doesn't explain why whites must be forcibly brought into contact with this "culture." And if it is so different from white culture that "affirmative action" must be resorted to in order to expose whites to it, some whites will find that they don't like it all, and decide they want nothing to do with it.

The real, unspoken explanation for why diversity is a strength is that race *is* in fact meaningful. Diversity is thought to expose whites to *superior* people and *superior* ways of thinking. After all, sermons about diversity are directed only at whites. Bringing non-whites onto campus or into the club is supposed to be improving and edifying for whites, not for non-whites.

In fact, the idea that whites are inferior, or at least deeply and uniquely flawed is the *one* distinctly racial idea whites are allowed to have about themselves. Outside the underground "racialist" press it is impossible to find whites portrayed in positive terms *as a race*. In the past 30 years, probably no mainstream public figure or commentator has expressed pride or satisfaction in being white or urged other whites to do so. On the contrary, in any discussion of race, it is obligatory to write disparagingly about whites, to remind them of past and present crimes, to make them ashamed to be white. Most of the time, whites are supposed to believe that race is simply an empty category, but if they are to have one explicitly racial sentiment about themselves, it is shame.

"The white race is the cancer of human history," says Susan Sontag. "Treason to whiteness is loyalty to humanity," says Noel Ignatiev of *Race Traitor* magazine. He wants to "abolish the white race—by any means necessary." Christine Sleeter writes that "Whiteness . . . has come to mean ravenous materialism, competitive individualism, and a way of living characterized by putting acquisition of possessions above humanity." This is presumably the sort of thing President William Clinton's daughter, Chelsea, was supposed to think about when her high school had her write an essay called "Why I am Ashamed to be White." The text book for teacher training reviewed in the previous issue of AR[1] is packed with creative ideas about how to make whites apologize for their race and for their very existence.

The black author James Baldwin once wrote that any white person who wants to have real dialogue about race must start with a confession that is nothing short of "a cry for help and healing." Perhaps columnist Maggie Gallagher was crying for help when she wrote that she thinks of herself as an American, a Catholic, and sometimes an Irish-American but added, "I hate the idea of being white. . . . I never think of myself as belonging to the 'white race.' Those who do, in my experience, are invariably second-raters seeking solace for their own failures. I can think of few things more degrading than being proud to be white."

For almost all whites, the only time they ever speak *as whites* is to apologize. President Clinton is typical. When he speaks as a white man it is to apologize for the Tuskeegee medical experiment that left black men untreated for syphilis or to apologize for slavery.

The celebration of Martin Luther King's birthday is a celebration of white apology. King spent his life telling whites they were wrong. This is now thought to be so valuable a role that it makes no difference that he was a plagiarist, adulterer, and communist sympathizer. For having succeeded in persuading so many whites that they were wicked he has now eclipsed George Washington as America's most honored son. Only King and Jesus Christ have national holidays on their birthdays.

The Final Solution

So where has the revolution brought us? Whites are to pretend that race is meaningless. They have no legitimate group aspirations. Racial diversity is a good thing if it comes at the expense of whites. Slavery is a crime for which we—and only we—must be forever guilty. The conquest of the continent was not the expansion of civilization but a rape and an abomination. We have no claim to this land, but must let in every band of Third-Worlders that wants to come. If we believe the propaganda of the last 50 years, we must rethink and abandon virtually everything about America. Whites are a uniquely flawed race, and the sooner we are reformed by virtuous non-whites the better.

Once more, we can rely on President Clinton to show us the way. He says that after independence from England and the War Between the States, the reduction of whites to a minority will be "the third great revolution of America." He looks forward to the challenge of seeing "if we can prove that we literally can live without having a dominant European culture."

Former Republican congressman Robert Dornan of California agrees. In 1996, while he was still in the House, he said, "I want to see America stay a

---

[1] See "The Religion of Anti-Racism," page 13.

nation of immigrants. And if we lose our Northern European stock—your coloring and mine, blue eyes and fair hair—tough!" In his next election, he lost to a Hispanic, Loretta Sanchez. This is exactly what Mr. Dornan's cheerfulness about immigration should have prepared him for—his constituency had rapidly become half Hispanic—but apparently it did not. He refused to concede defeat and charged Miss Sanchez' supporters with vote fraud. He has not, however, changed his position on the advisability of whites becoming a minority.

And it's not just Americans who look forward to oblivion. Gwynne Dyer, a London-based Canadian journalist, takes for granted that "ethnic diversification" is a good thing for white countries, but notes that Canada and Australia, which have opened their borders to non-white immigration, are trying to "do good by stealth." Politicians understand the advantages of diversity but think they must not let ordinary whites know what is happening: "Let the magic do its work, but don't talk about it in front of the children. They'll just get cross and spoil it all." Being reduced to a minority will be good for whites but the prospect must be kept secret from them for fear they might object. Mr. Dyer looks forward to the day when politicians can be more open about displacing their own people.

Pauline Hanson is the famous Australian politician who doesn't want whites to become a minority. Such a view is "racist," of course, and an Australian writing in the *Washington Post* describes the people for whom Miss Hanson speaks as "the beast," which is "alive and well, slimily squirming." No doubt these loathsome forces will be vanquished. The *Chicago Tribune* gave an article about Miss Hanson the sub-headline: "A new, anti-immigrant party appeals to some Australians who still harbor notions of remaining a Caucasian society." Fancy that: There are still a few Australians who "harbor the notion" that their country should stay white.

Of course, reducing whites to a minority is only a good first step; with enough interracial marriage, whites might be made to disappear completely. It has therefore become fashionable to propose miscegenation as the final solution to the race problem. "It would be a lot easier if each of us were related to someone of another color and if, eventually, we were all one color," writes Morton Kondracke in *The New Republic*; "In America, this can happen." "I think intermarriage may be the only way out [of our racial problems]," writes Jon Carroll of the *San Francisco Examiner*. Ben Wattenberg, noting the increase in interracial marriages writes happily, "Does all this mean that as we move into the next century race will be much less of an issue? That we will all end up bland and blended? That (as I believe) we will fulfill our difficult destiny as the first universal nation?"

Even "conservatives" think intermarriage is the answer. Douglas Besharov of the American Enterprise Institute says it may be "the best hope for the future of American race relations." In a recent book, Stephen and Abigail Thernstrom write that the "crumbling of the taboo on sexual relations between the two races [black and white]" is "good news," because that will make it impossible to draw racial distinctions.

John Miller is a reporter for *National Review*, which is thought to be the main "conservative" magazine in America. He thinks miscegenation is inevitable and could be the only way to end racial tension. "Perhaps the best way to undermine the ideology of group rights is to permit this natural process of assimilation to work its way down the generations as people of mixed background marry and have children." "In the future," he adds confidently, "everyone will have a Korean grandmother." This is the happy ending. As they become a minority, whites will dissolve into a glorious *café au lait*.

Not only was this the very reverse of what the founders had in mind, it was not even what the racial activists of just a few decades ago had in mind. The post-1965 changes in immigration policy were not supposed to upset the ethnic balance. The civil rights movement was supposed to usher in a new Camelot of racial understanding and harmony. Both predictions were dead wrong: the percentage of whites is shrinking and scarcely anyone pretends that race relations are good. What do we do? Just toss the whole country into a blender and do away with race entirely. Of course, this really means doing away with whites. Whites are only about 15 percent of the world's population and are having perhaps seven percent of the world's babies. No one is proposing the blender treatment for Africa or Asia.

The racial revolution has stripped whites of any intellectual defenses against this final solution. Race is a forbidden criterion—at least for *their* purposes—and whites are a vexatious bunch anyway. A people whose only collective sentiment is guilt might as well fade away. We have come a long way from Jefferson's vision of Europeans filling the Americas from north to south.

Pierre Vergniaud (1753-1793) was a French lawyer and revolutionary politician who, like so many others, ended up on the guillotine. It was he who said that the revolution "might devour each of its children in turn." Ours has been a revolution that, if left unchecked, will certainly devour our children.

However, revolutions that violate the laws of human nature eventually founder. Some day ours will collapse, as biology reasserts itself over sociology, and white racial consciousness reawakens. The Soviet Union staggered on for 75 years before its revolution collapsed under its own weight. The racial revolution has been in full swing for 50 years, and its absurdities and contradiction have never been more evident.

This article appeared in the May 1999 issue. Jared Taylor is the editor of American Renaissance.

━━━━◆━━━━

The Religion of Anti-Racism

Enid Lee, Deborah Menkart and Margo Okazawa-Rey (Eds.)
Beyond Heroes and Holidays: A Practical Guide to K-12 Anti-Racist, Muticultural Education and Staff Development,
Network of Education on the Americas,
1998, $27.00, 464 pp. (soft cover)

reviewed by Thomas Jackson

Most people know that teachers and professors are well to the left of most Americans—their loonier antics sometimes make it into the press—but few outsiders have any idea of the real designs "anti-racists" have on American children. *Beyond Heroes and Holidays* is a collection of 80-odd essays by "progressive" school teachers and education professors about how to use the classroom to fight "racism." It is supposed to be a guide for training teachers and instructing students—but is nothing less than a field manual for the subversion of American society.

This is a characterization many of the authors would not dispute. Anyone who can drag himself through the more than 450 large-format pages of this book soon learns that everything in America—including the economic system—will have to be revamped in order to eradicate "racism." The authors have a mentality exactly like that of doctrinaire Marxists. Although they never mention Marx or Communism, and they write about "transformation" rather than "revolution," they have the same totalitarian compulsion to control and reform every detail of our lives. They even have the equivalent of dialectical materialism. Just as Marxists used the dialectic to interpret reality, they use "critical thinking" to interpret everything—and I mean everything—in terms of "racism," "sexism," and a batch of other "isms." What the "crits" have established is a militant, secular religion, with schools as churches and children as compulsory congregations.

The central message of this religion is that every group difference is proof of exploitation, and every form of exploitation has been perfected by whites. The history of whites is an unending chronicle of rapine and despoliation, and only when these sins have been atoned for and all group differences eradicated will there be justice.

The "crits" do not yet control society but they control what they teach: "All aspects of the curriculum [must] integrate multicultural, critical thinking and justice concepts and practice." "Diversity and equity issues are integrated into all aspects of the teacher-training curriculum." This is necessary because, as one of the editors of the book puts it with breath-taking finality, "The purpose of education in an unjust society is to bring about equality and justice." Thus, "schools should be the place where students can analyze the forces which maintain injustice and develop the knowledge, hope and strategies needed to create a more just society for us all."

In short, education is indoctrination and its purpose is political: "Every student whom we help to read and write is being provided with tools to defend herself or himself. We are helping prepare them for the onslaught of antihuman practices that this nation and other nations are facing today: racism, sexism, and the greed for money and human labor that disguises itself as 'globalization.' "

Success is measured by how many students can be turned into anti-racist fanatics, and properly managed students can be made to unbosom grateful testimonials like: "I also learned that all the institutions in this country are *inherently* racist and exist for the purpose of maintaining the power and wealth of the dominant group." (emphasis added)

Curing Whites

Because whites are the world's biggest problem, the fight against "racism" begins with them. This book emphasizes over and over that "racism" is not just a matter of thoughts and acts. It is an entire way of being that permeates society, institutions, and whites as a group. We know most whites are openly, hopelessly "racist," but what about the ones who think they are not? They must be made to understand that "racism" is not something practiced by *other* whites but is in the very marrow of their bones. As one anti-racist expert explains, his job is to take well-meaning white naïfs and give them "a new recognition of themselves as race-privileged, capable of racist thoughts and behaviors." All whites are "racist" whatever their intentions, whereas no non-whites are "racist."

This goes without saying for most of the authors, but one or two try to explain it. As Peggy McIntosh of Wellesley, a celebrated proponent of this goofiness explains, inherent "racism" is all about something called "unearned privilege:"

"I can turn on the television or open to the front page of the paper and see people of my race widely represented." "I can if I wish arrange to be in the company of people of my race most of the time." "I can easily buy posters, postcards, picture books, greeting cards, dolls, toys and children's magazines featuring people of my race." "I can take a job with an affirmative action employer without having coworkers on the job suspect that I got it because of race." "I can choose blemish cover or bandages in 'flesh' color and have them more or less match my skin."

As Miss McIntosh explains, for non-whites these privileges are experienced as oppression. "Whiteness protected me from many kinds of hostility, distress, and violence, which I was being subtly trained to visit in turn upon people of color," she explains. Not recognizing and renouncing "privilege" is the same as oppressing non-whites.

Of course, nearly all the "privileges" Miss McIntosh describes are found just about everywhere. Japanese and Nigerians see people of their own race on television, too. A Frenchman living in Japan presumably suffers just like a black in America. There is the further implication that American whites gain some kind of stupendous advantage simply because non-whites live here. Having millions of poor, crime-prone, violent people among us gives us a great advantage over Norwegians, for example, who presumably don't experience "white skin privilege" ten times a day the way we do. It beggars the imagination how anyone could have thought of anything so stupid but, as Miss McIntosh explains, it is vital to open whites' eyes to how awful their country really is: "To redesign social systems we need first to acknowledge their colossal unseen dimensions."

This doctrine of inherent racism is so weird and implausible it takes a lifetime to master it: "Because the ideology of White racial superiority is so deeply embedded in our culture, the process of 'unlearnng racism' is a journey we [whites] need to continue throughout our lives." "Keep in mind that learning about racial identity and racism is a lifelong process." "Racism is *learned*, and it can be *unlearned*, but it takes a commitment to stay aware, to keep working and to accept the unlearning as a lifelong journey."

Start Early

The authors all agree that anti-racist education has to start just as soon as teachers get their hands on children. Even for pre-schoolers, we are to "integrate anti-bias issues into every theme," and put toddlers through "activism activities" that will teach them that "injustice is not overcome by magic or by wishes, but that people make it happen and that each one of them can make it happen."

Teachers must be ready to pounce whenever a child utters an act of oppression, and the book offers such improbable examples as: "People in wheelchairs can't be mommies and daddies," or (to a child with lesbian parents) "you can't have two mommies," or "she dresses like a Puerto Rican."

One recommended exercise is to get a box of bandages, put them on black children, and jeer at any company that would claim they are "flesh colored." Advanced subjects can be made to scratch out letters of protest to the company. Other lessons can be learned by getting children to designate parking spaces for handicapped people and having the children issue "tickets" to violators. Classroom walls should be covered with pictures that refute stereotypes: black doctors, white janitors, people in wheelchairs at the beach, etc.

Day care staff should rewrite children's books. The story of the three pigs, for example, implies that European-style brick buildings are superior to Third-World straw and stick houses. The wolf should be changed into an elephant that blasts water from its trunk. The Third-World house of sticks survives because it is on stilts while the brick house floods.

Another "teaching tool" is to get parents of toddlers to come to class and "share" experiences of "racism." But it is best to get children themselves on the march. Trot them down to greeting card stores to yell because there aren't "cards or decorations for non-dominant holidays." Or, says one author, pre-schoolers can be made to protest non-union fruit [!]. Better still, children can be put to work for the staff's own selfish interests. The book actually recommends that little ones be taught "why better wages are necessary for child care center staff," and be recruited to help teachers "working in their union to get smaller classroom sizes."

Once children are older, there are countless techniques for attacking "the dominant culture," and the book suggests particularly lively ways to take the stuffing out of whites. Children can pretend to be Congressmen debating the Indian Removal Act of 1830, or can try to think of all the evil motives for the Chinese Exclusion Acts of the 19th century. They should put on a mock trial of "the profit system" as the cause of the drug trade, as they consider "drugs as a weapon against the Black community." Students can draw cartoons about the "racism" they experience, or can collect tourist brochures about Hawaii and note that they fail to mention that whites seized the islands and raped the culture. They can discuss why Thanksgiving Day can be thought of as a day of mourning, or take turns answering the question: "What is your earliest recollection of being excluded because of your race or culture?" Whites can keep diaries of the unearned privileges they enjoy each day. Children can pretend to be Congressmen at the 1870s hearings on KKK violence. To learn about today's Klan, they should get anti-Klan activists— not Klan members—to speak to the class. Students should be trained in "critical literacy," which is the ability to detect oppressive messages in books, newspapers, and advertising. A very common theme is to get students to devise "action plans" for combating "racism" in their schools.

Clearly, the object is to rear up fanatical little busy-bodies who will be a kind of anti-racist Red Guard. It is important constantly to remind children of oppression, and never to let the favored groups forget they are victims. One workshop "to explore and celebrate what it is like to be a girl," was a success because participants later said things like, "I learned that too many young women are being disrespected by young men."

In one school, "activist" teachers got students to start a Let's-Stop-Racism-in-Our School campaign. (One complaint had been that a girl said a teacher told her to "prove others wrong and not get pregnant by the age of sixteen like all the other Puerto Rican girls.") At their first session, how did they prepare for the campaign? "Students reenacted the forced migration of over fifty million Africans brought to the Americas and sold into slavery, and the slaughtering of native Americans for land and gold."

Heroes and Holidays

The title of this book makes the point that tacking a few non-white heroes onto the curriculum or eating tacos on Cinco de Mayo is not good enough. Every lesson in every subject must be propaganda. Besides, whooping up the occasional distinguished black may give the false impression that talented non-whites can get ahead in America. In order to supplement the usual study of King and Harriet Tubman, the authors recommend that students look into 150 or so lesser-known "activists for social change." On the list are Angela Davis, Malcolm X, Che Guevara, Morris Dees, Marcus Garvey, and the two slave insurrectionists Nat Turner and Denmark Vesey. Chief Crazy Horse is identified as a "Native American rights activist." Still, the book warns that we should be careful with the idea of heroes because it gives the impression that individuals actually count for something, whereas we all know that it is groups that "empower."

"Heritage celebrations" also must be handled carefully. Making much of national costumes and unfamiliar food is wrong because it suggests foreigners are exotic and Americans are normal. Also, when food and pageantry are taken by themselves "they mask the obstacles that people of color have faced, [and] how they have confronted those obstacles . . . ." Lots of oppression must therefore be worked into all exercises of this kind, and they cannot be called "international" because that suggests things can be foreign to America.

Language is an important part of the multi-culti cult: "In our racist, sexist, classist and heterosexist society, our decisions about word usage are political decisions." For example, Irish peasants live in "cottages" but we have been trained to say Africans live in mere "huts." Likewise, to speak of "slaves" and "masters" implies that status is inherent. It is better to speak of "enslaved Africans," and really "transformative" people say "African people stolen from their families and societies."

One author notes that whites are only ten percent of the world population. In an American context, "use of the word 'minority,' therefore, obscures this global reality and reinforces racist assumptions." We are always to say "people of color," a term which "was borne out of an explicitly political statement that signaled a solidarity among progressive African Americans, Asian Americans, Latinos, Native Americans and Pacific Islanders."

Anti-racists agonize over black English. They would never say it is *bad* English, and instead complain about "the arbitrariness of designating one variety [of English] over another as 'standard.' " "On the other hand, it is equally important to understand that students who do not have access to the politically popular dialect form in this country . . . are less likely to succeed economically . . . . How can both realities be embraced?" The trick is to call black English a dialect and try to help blacks become "bi-dialectical." When a student asks "Who do dat?" you do not "correct" him; you encourage him to translate into the politically popular dialect.

We must have bilingual education for immigrants, because expecting them to learn English is "racist." One author writes that "in a moment of generosity" one could imagine that English-only advocates just want newcomers to assimilate and get ahead, but that would be wrong. As he points out, white women speak English as well as white men, but don't earn as much money. Therefore, since speaking English doesn't lead to equality, the English-only people can be shown to be the racist frauds they really are.

Thus, "language policy in the United States continues to be used as an effective tool to control access to social, economic and political resources."

Math classes must be indoctrination, too. Inequities in income, the number of blacks in jail, unemployment rates by race—studying these makes math "a tool to interpret and challenge inequities in our society." In the right hands, math can "uncover stereotypes, understand history, and examine issues of inequality." Pure science is harder to turn into propaganda but instruction can be "transformed to consider how science itself is conceptualized, valued and practiced by those who have traditionally been outside the scientific mainstream"—whatever that may mean.

The anti-racists hate free markets and world trade. The profit motive is a gruesome thing that "values property over people," but is beaten into all Americans: "Where do people learn the values of this system? Just think back to elementary school. Columbus, who killed hundreds of Native Americans in his search for gold, is touted as a hero." Here are some basic economic concepts:

"Wealthy countries became wealthy by exploiting the resources of the Southern countries."

"The colonial and capitalist systems, which grew up together, were also inherently and inescapably racist."

"The world financial system is a greater cause of hunger in Africa than is bad weather."

If teachers do their jobs they will be rewarded with student comments like:

"I had not previously understood that capitalism requires keeping a large group of people in extreme poverty, and is deliberately and purposefully racist, promoting divisions among people in order for the dominant group to maintain political, economic, and social power and control . . . ."

Oddly, none of this leads to outright advocacy of Communism, and neither Marx nor Mao is on the list of sainted "social activists." It is unclear what will replace capitalism in the anti-racist paradise.

Hating White People

Ultimately this brand of "anti-racism" shows its true colors as a religion—the religion of hating white people. It has a few other doctrines but they all derive from racism: "we must ask how sexism, classism, and linguicism [?] are part of this oppression called *racism*." (emphasis in the original) It is a religion that calls for total devotion. As one author explains, "We must grapple with both [individual and institutional "racism"] at every moment of our lives."

Like all fanatics, these people cannot see obvious contradictions. Over and over we hear that all children must have positive self-images and yet even science lessons must be stuffed with anti-white propaganda. There is incessant talk of fighting stereotypes—except for one: the wicked white man. America is a cesspool of "racism," but non-white immigrants are quite right to want to come. This book purports to promote multi-culturalism, but its myriad "celebrations" leave no room for Western Civilization. In fact, Western Civilization is just another name for evil "isms." As the authors say repeatedly, their goal is to transform *every institution* in the country. This is nothing less than an open declaration of war on Western Civilization—and a veiled declaration of war on the people who built it.

There are a few worthy whites—John Brown, Morris Dees, Andrew Goodman, Fidel Castro, Gloria Steinem—but every one is a radical critic of his own society and people. In the minds of these authors the only role left to whites as a group is that of demons to be routed by heroic non-whites. This book is full of photographs, but of the hundreds of faces in them, perhaps three percent are white.

White-hatred flows naturally from the doctrine of racial egalitarianism. So long as the "mainstream" denies racial differences, and insists that all group differences in achievement are caused by that blackest of all crimes, "racism," there will be anti-racist fanatics who will stop at nothing to eradicate this evil.

This review originally appeared in the April 1999 issue. Thomas Jackson is a frequent reviewer for American Renaissance.

Multiculturalism and the War Against White America
by Lawrence Auster

Underlying everything we have heard at this conference [the 1994 *American Renaissance* conference held in Atlanta] are two bedrock truths about race and race relations that go against everything we have been taught. The first truth is that there are significant differences in average intelligence between different populations, and that such gaps in intelligence cannot be closed by any known human means.

The second truth is that not all groups are equally assimilable to each other, in the sense of the ability to come to share a common outlook, identity and way of being. The greater the historical and racial differences between two peoples, and the greater the numbers involved, the harder assimilation is going to be, and the more likely it becomes that conflict between such different peoples will be permanent.

Today's liberal and conservative orthodoxies hold the opposite beliefs—first, that all racial groups are equal in inherent abilities, and second, that all racial groups in the world, no matter how different, are at bottom basically alike and equally assimilable into American culture.

The first belief, in the equality of abilities, leads to the notion that any actual differences in achievement between races must be due to discrimination, which is to be overcome by preferential racial quotas. The second belief, that everyone in the world is equally assimilable, has led to an immigration policy based on what are in effect racial quotas applied to the entire world. The continuing influx of over a million immigrants per year, 90 percent of them non-Europeans, combined with higher nonwhite birth rates, is steadily turning America into a multiracial, nonwhite country—a "mirror" of the entire world.

A good way to understand the impact of massive nonwhite immigration on American society is to compare it to the impact of preferential minority admissions in the university. As Dinesh D'Souza has described it in *Illiberal Education*, universities admit underqualified minority students, while assuring them that they are perfectly well qualified. When these students find themselves having academic difficulties, they blame "institutional racism," then they blame the curriculum itself, which they say is culturally alien to them.

The administration, not wanting to admit the truth, eagerly agrees with the minority activists that racism is at work. In effect, the administration makes the entire university community, especially the white students and the faculty, the scapegoat for a racial inequality *that was created by the administration itself* when it admitted unqualified minorities. The school then sets up coercive "anti-racist" programs and speech codes aimed at whites, and adopts multicultural curricula and intellectual standards that conform to minority cultures and "learning styles." When white students protest these things, the minorities, in D'Souza's words, "conclude that they have discovered the latent bigotry for which they have been searching."

In sum, the result of admitting large numbers of unqualified minorities into a university is that whites start to be demonized as racist and are systematically silenced, while their civilizational heritage is attacked as unrepresentative and illegitimate and begins to be systematically dismantled.

Now if all these things happen when you admit large numbers of nonwhite students into a predominantly white school, what happens when you admit massive numbers of nonwhite immigrants into a predominantly white society? The very same things. The failure of the nonwhite population to fit into the society is blamed *on the society itself*, rather than on the fact that they were admitted in the first place. The white majority starts to be demonized as racist and is systematically silenced, while its civilization is attacked as unrepresentative and begins to be systematically dismantled. The great irony is that the admission of nonwhites is supposed to prove that the society is nonracist and egalitarian, yet the more nonwhites are admitted, the more racist and unequal the society seems.

Impact on American Life

While the "delegitimizing" impact of unassimilable immigrants can be seen in many areas of American life, in no other field is it more obvious than in the arts. Cultural institutions in cities with large Third-World populations are rapidly abandoning the Western high culture tradition in favor of Third-World folk cultures. According to music critic Edward Rothstein writing in the *New Republic*, the new immigrants simply aren't interested in Western music:

"[S]trikingly in a city like New York, [classical music culture] is largely a racially stratified culture as well: there are almost no black or immigrant faces (aside from Asians) to be seen in concert halls. . . . My neighborhood arts organization, like many others around the country, has been unsuccessful in marketing Western art music to the new racial and international communities in the area. So instead they've begun presenting the folk musics of immigrant and black cultures."

The same applies to the theater. "The reason that Broadway appeals less to New Yorkers these days," writes theater critic Thomas Disch, "isn't just that Broadway has changed: so have New Yorkers. . . . [A] glance around the lobby at any Broadway show reveals who isn't there: any of the city's readily identifiable minorities: blacks, Hispanics, Asians . . . ."

Theatrical companies have tried to address the problem by introducing multiracial casts into Western plays, but have been disturbed to find that the audiences for such multiracial productions are still almost exclusively white. Evidently, Third Worlders are simply not attracted to Western theater, even when it has lots of nonwhites in the cast. Since changing the cast doesn't work, the only solution will be to give up the plays themselves. The irony is that these problems, are not seen as the result of nonwhites' lack of interest in Western culture, and therefore as proof of their non-assimilability; rather, Western culture itself is blamed for not appealing to nonwhites.

Artistic images of American history are also coming under attack. Rush Limbaugh recently noted that the state of Oregon, after commissioning a beautiful bronze statue of a 19th century pioneer family, had rejected the completed statue because the image of a white pioneer family was considered "racist" and "noninclusive." While Rush was unusually upset about this incident, it didn't seem to occur to him that it had anything to do with demographic change—i.e., that it is our society's increasingly nonwhite character that is making any "all-white" image seem unrepresentative and therefore illegitimate.

In 1993 there was an angry protest by black and Hispanic students at the University of Massachusetts who wanted the school to dump its official symbol, the Minuteman. The image of a "white man carrying a gun, they charged, was racist. For the time being the school has resisted this demand. But for how long? As the university's white population continues to decline, can we expect the Chinese and Pakistani students and administrators of the future to care enough about the image of the Minuteman to defend it against intimidating black and Hispanic protesters? Who will preserve the symbols of our Anglo-European national heritage after whites are gone?

Indeed, who will defend that heritage even now, while whites are still the majority? On Long Island this past spring, a school production of *Peter Pan* was canceled at the last minute, after six weeks of rehearsals, because the town's American Indian minority felt that the play's portrayal of Indians (which, remember, is simply a childlike fantasy taking place in Never-Never Land) was insulting to them. So, to accommodate multiracial America, this classic play that we all remember with fondness from our childhood is to be proscribed. The most significant thing about the incident was that no one in the town, including the parents whose children had their play taken away from them, seriously protested this outrage.

In an even more horrifying example of white surrender, an elite private school in New England was considering hiring a well-known multicultural curriculum consultant when it was discovered that the consultant—a Caribbean-born black woman based in Toronto—had admitted in a published interview that her approach would make white children feel intimidated and guilty. After some discussion, the school's board of trustees went ahead and hired her anyway.

These are examples of what is happening to our entire country and culture. As America becomes more and more nonwhite, everything we think of as the American culture and identity will be either censored, squeezed out or transformed into something else.

The response of establishment conservatives to these concerns is to say that such problems are created not by immigrants but by alienated white elites, as well as by the general moral decay of our society. "It is true that radical and liberal elites in education, government, and media appear to be doing everything they can to destroy whatever is left of traditional America, and they might well be doing so even if there were no immigrants at all." But we must understand that even if there were no "cultural revolution" going on in this country, the kind of massive demographic change we are experiencing as a result of immigration would still be enough, by itself, to destabilize and ultimately destroy our culture.

The list of horrors proving this point goes on and on: the dominance of Latin American mores and language in southern Florida; the transformation of southern California into an outpost of the Third World; multiracial juries unable to reach verdicts because jury members don't share any common understanding of reality; the exodus of hundreds of thousands of whites from immigrant-intensive areas every year; the booming population of Southeast Asian refugees that will make a town like Wassau, Wisconsin (which was 99 percent white 15 years ago) a Hmong-majority city in a generation; the Santeria animal sacrifice cult from the Caribbean; Muslim extremism and terrorism; expanding Chinese and other foreign-based criminal networks; the takeover by Dominican drug-dealers of upper Manhattan, where Dominicans marched with huge banners denouncing "500 Years of Genocide" after a Dominican drug dealer was killed by a police officer in self-defense.

These and many other disorders are occurring not because of cultural radicalism or affirmative action or middle-class moral decay. They are happening as the direct result of revolutionary changes in this country's ethnic and racial make-up.

The Weapon of "Race-neutrality"

What is it that prevents whites from protesting their own demographic and cultural dispossession? The most common explanation is that people fear being called racist. That is true, and it's not just political correctness. Deep in the American mind is the ideal of America as a country where advancement is open to anyone, where "it doesn't matter who your parents were." The fatal problem with that formula is that it can work only within certain limits—when you're speaking of individuals sharing a basic commonality. If you apply it *en masse* to radically diverse populations, it becomes absurd and dangerous. The ideal of "race-neutrality," applied to incommensurable groups, turns out to be not race-neutral at all, but becomes a weapon used by one race to dispossess the other.

I came across a remarkable example of this in the coverage of the South African election. Amidst all the media's joyous talk about a "nonracial" or "multiracial" democracy being born, *Newsweek* came out with a sensational cover with bold letters crying "Black Power!" So deep is the doublethink in which we live today, that I wonder if more than a handful of people noticed the gross contradiction of celebrating black power in what was supposed to be a "nonracial" election. But of course it's not a contradiction at all: What "nonracial" really means is that it is *whites* who are supposed to be indifferent to race, in order to help nonwhites advance *their* racial interests.

This same double standard and delusion works across the board. For example, the belief that all the peoples of the world are equal in intellectual abilities is thought to be a race-neutral or "nonracial" idea, since it is saying that race doesn't matter. But since the races are *not* equal in average abilities, this "nonracial" belief in equality turns out to be completely racial. It holds that blacks have far greater abilities than they in fact have, and invariably blames white racism for actual black inequality. It is therefore the duty of whites, until the end of time, to exhaust their wealth and spiritual energy in a hopeless effort to make blacks collectively equal to themselves. The "nonracial" belief in equality thus turns out to be a kind of black racialist mythology.

Similarly, our immigration policy, which is thought to be race-neutral, is in fact turning America into a nonwhite country, dispossessing white America and its culture. Yet it is considered "racist" to oppose this policy, and "nonracist" to support it.

Ultimately the pursuit of race-blindness (in anything more than a legal and procedural sense), leads to complete incoherence. Columnist Jon Carroll of the *San Francisco Examiner* once complained about the fact that we are supposed to respect everyone's differences, while at the same time we're supposed to treat everyone equally—which requires us not to notice differences at all. Carroll continues:

"One is required to deny the evidence of one's senses. I perceive that African American men are different from Caucasian men are different from Asian women are different from (what?) Ethiopian Jews. Can we compare these differences? No, we cannot. We may say for the record that these differences are beautiful, equally beautiful, precisely geometrically equally beautiful, but that's it."

And if we do begin to compare these differences, Carroll says, that leads us right back to value judgments about racial differences, which immediately devolve into "racism."

Paralyzed by these contradictions, as well he should be, Carroll concludes: "I think intermarriage may be the only way out . . . . Of course, we'd lose a lot of interesting specific cultures that way . . . ." What he means, of course, is that we'd lose a lot of interesting races that way, including our own.

Along the same lines, but with far more enthusiasm, Morton Kondracke in the *New Republic* wondered how America could overcome its racial inequalities, and concluded that racial intermarriage is the only solution: "It would be a lot easier if each of us were related to someone of another color and if, eventually, we were all one color. In America, this can happen." Racial intermarriage is even more aggressively championed by Ben Wattenberg, who sees it as the path to universal salvation.

I want to make the meaning of all this very clear. Modern liberalism told us that racial differences don't matter, and on the basis of that belief, liberals then set about turning America into a multiracial, integrated, race-blind society. But now that very effort has created so much race consciousness, race conflict and race inequality, that the same liberals have concluded that the only way to overcome those problems is to merge all the races into one. The same people who have always denounced as an extremist lunatic anyone who warned about "the racial dilution of white America," are now proposing, not just the dilution of white America, but its complete elimination. Race-blind ideology has led directly to the most race-conscious—and indeed genocidal—proposal in the history of the world.

This is the insanity that results from uncritically accepting the idea that race doesn't matter. And the moral paralysis of whites in the face of immigration comes from the terror or distaste that they feel at saying that race does matter. There is also whites' inability to face the fact that they are a civilizationally distinct group—comprising only 15 percent of the world's population—that is demographically threatened by the rest of the world's desire to live in the uniquely attractive societies that whites have created.

If whites continue to be open to nonwhites, as their race-blind moralism tells them they must, their societies will cease to exist; but if they exclude or disengage from nonwhites, that will require them to be "harsh," "unkind," "mean-spirited." It will require them to say that they care about the survival of their race vis-a-vis other races. To the contemporary white person, such an idea is utterly evil and unacceptable. But the funny thing is, there is really nothing evil or horrible about it at all. It turns out to be the most reasonable and commonsensical thing in the world. It's the current race-blind ideology that is insane.

So before we recoil in horror or embarrassment from speaking explicitly about race, let us remember that America's current politics is already a race-conscious politics, only it's a politics based on *lies* about race. It's a politics directed against whites and their civilization. And it pretends that it's not about race at all, but that it's race-neutral and universal. So instead of today's race-conscious politics, which is based on lies about race, let us have a race-conscious politics based on truths about race.

These truths include the following propositions:

• Long-term harmonious relations between a racial majority and racial minorities are possible only when the minorities do not exceed a certain percentage of the population.

• While individuals of different races living in the same society can get along on a basis of equality and mutual recognition, entire races, living in the same society, cannot.

• In the right circumstances, individuals or small groups of one people can be assimilated into a host culture of a different people, but there are limits to such assimilation. Certainly if the entire people associated with the host culture is displaced or swamped by a different people, the host culture will also disappear. Even smaller shifts in numbers can be enough to delegitimize the host culture and produce chronic cultural conflict.

• Therefore, the culture, identity and traditions of white America and Western civilization cannot survive in any community or institution that becomes multiracial or white-minority.

• Because of the greater attractiveness, prosperity and openness of white Western societies, nonwhites will keep moving into them as long as they can. Therefore white America can survive demographically and culturally only if it recognizes itself as a threatened ethnoculture; if it ceases or drastically reduces, on a national scale, all non-European immigration; and if it assures, on a local scale, communities where its own institutions may survive.

• The large and enduring differences in average intelligence between blacks and whites mean that blacks cannot in any foreseeable future be expected to achieve collective economic equality and other kinds of parity with whites. The forced attempt to achieve such collective equality, through affirmative action and through endless attacks on white racism as the supposed cause of existing inequalities, can only break down all the institutions and standards of society and lead to race warfare.

• There are therefore only two sane options for black-white relations in this country. Either blacks accept the above facts; accept a society where white Western standards of law, behavior and intellectual life are dominant and where advancement will be open for blacks only on an individual, not a collective basis; accept their status as an ethnic minority and be grateful to be living in a white society where they have goods and opportunities undreamed of in a black society; or else, if blacks are not willing to accept these things, then to avoid race warfare there must be peaceful separation between the races.

These propositions have nothing to do with any notions of race-hatred of the other, or of race-worship of one's own. White people are just as sinful and imperfect as any other people. Unlike ideologies such as Afrocentrism and Nazism, which are based on the deification of one's own people and the demonization of others, this new politics is based on a Christian recognition of our human limitations, namely that we do not possess the godlike power to create a perfect world where everyone is equal, and where differences don't matter. If there is any arrogance to be seen today, it is in our current immigration and affirmative action policies, which are among the greatest examples of hubris in the history of the world.

The irony is that whites are terrified that non-whites will hate them and even start a race war if whites stand up for themselves, while the truth is that many nonwhites will begin for the first time to respect whites. Currently minorities don't respect whites because whites have defined themselves ideologically as nothing while, in personal terms, they still try to protect their self-interest. Whites thus seem both weak and hypocritical and therefore despicable, and nonwhites just keep moving into the vacuum left by white surrender. But when whites begin to assert their own civilizational and racial identity and their desire to preserve it, not in a hateful way but in a calm, intelligent and firm way, then nonwhites will begin to see whites, not as the "oppressors" of left-liberal demonology, but as human beings who have the same basic interests and concerns for their people and culture that the minorities have for theirs.

At bottom, all we are doing is making an appeal to justice. The injustice and unacceptability of the current double standard will become obvious to any person of good will once it is pointed out. And that is why the principles I've described need to be at the center of an anti-multiculturalist, pro-Western civilization politics in this country. In my view, given current demographic realities, any conservative politics that lacks these principles cannot be a serious politics.

In *Deuteronomy*, Chapter 28, God pronounces the curse that will fall on the people of Israel if they fail to follow God's law:

"Your sons and your daughters shall be given to another people, while your eyes look on and fail with longing for them all the day; and it shall not be in the power of your hand to prevent it. A nation which you have not known shall eat up the fruit of your ground and of all your labors; and you shall be only oppressed and crushed continually; so that you shall be driven mad by the sight which your eyes shall see."

Unless America wakes up to the threat of demographic and cultural dispossession, and finds the will to resist it, the curse pronounced in *Deuteronomy* awaits us all.

This article is adapted from a speech given at the 1994 American Renaissance *conference, and originally appeared in the August 1994 issue. Lawrence Auster is a freelance writer living in New York City. He is the author of* The Path to National Suicide.

✦

Race, Crime, and Violence
by Jared Taylor

Who is committing crime in this country and against whom? How much crime do blacks commit? Are Hispanics as violent as blacks? What about Asians? How much so-called hate crime is there in the country and who is committing it? The US Department of Justice collects a huge amount of information on crime—enough to answer these questions—and indeed, there are substantial racial differences in crime rates.

Government statistics are essentially of three kinds: victim survey data, statistics on crimes reported to police, and arrest figures. The annual Department of Justice victim survey is important because it gathers information on many crimes that victims do not report to the police. Even more important, every few years it gathers information on the race of both victims *and* perpetrators of violent crimes. It is therefore the only information about interracial crime collected at the national level. The survey is about as accurate a picture as it is possible to get of crimes Americans say they have suffered.

Racial data are also included in Department of Justice figures on crimes reported to the police and the number of arrests made. Needless to say, these three kinds of information—crimes reported in surveys, crimes reported to police, and arrests—represent a steady decrease in volume. For example, in 1997, the most recent year for which there is complete information, the annual survey found there were 1,883,000 cases of aggravated assault (attacks that could cause serious injury or death). Only 1,022,000 cases were reported to police, and only 535,000 resulted in an arrest.

It is significant that the racial proportions for perpetrators as found in the survey data and the racial proportions for arrests are remarkably similar. Americans reported in the survey that close to 60 percent of all robberies are committed by blacks and, indeed, 57 percent of arrests for robberies in 1997 were of blacks. The proportions are close for other violent crimes as well, which means that the police are arresting people of different races at essentially the same rates at which the public is being victimized by them. Endless assertions that the police arrest non-whites because of "racism" are clearly false.

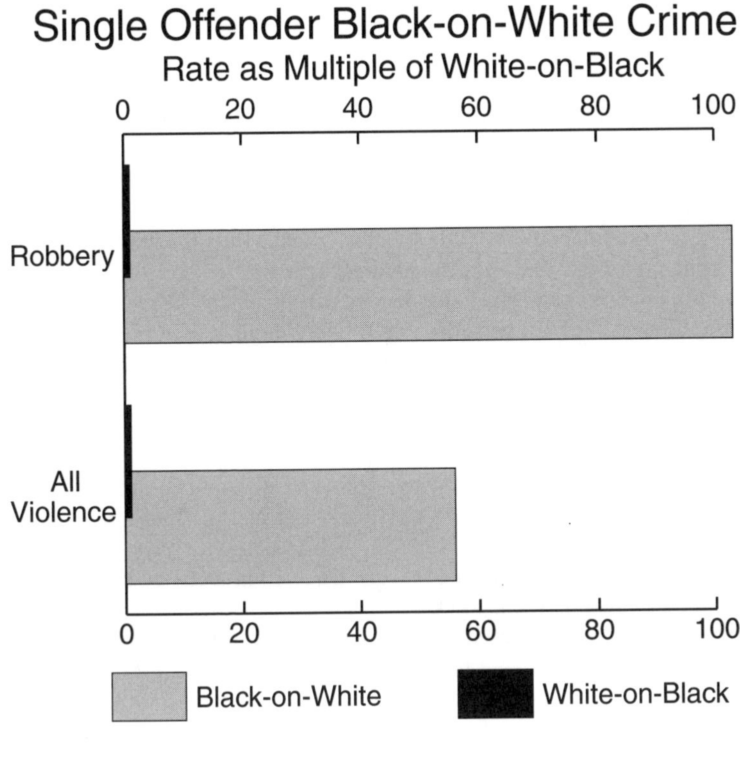

Graph 1

So who is committing the crime—and against whom? To start with the survey data on interracial violent crime, in 1994 (the most recent year racial data were gathered) there were about 1,276,000 single-offender crimes and 490,000 multiple-offender crimes. The survey categorizes victims and perpetrators only as "white," "black," and "other," but 89 percent of the single-offender and 94 percent of the multiple-offender interracial crimes are recorded as committed by blacks against whites.

These are astonishingly lopsided figures. One way to understand just how lopsided they are is to express them as *rates*. The frequency of crime is usually expressed as a rate per 100,000 people. In these terms, 3,494 blacks out of every 100,000 committed a violent crime against a white person in 1994 while only 63 whites out of every 100,000 committed a violent crime against a black. The black rate is more than 55 times the white rate, meaning that the average black was 55 times more likely to attack a white than vice versa. In the case of robbery, or "mugging," blacks were 103 times more likely to go victimize whites than the reverse. These figures are shown on Graph 1.

The numbers are even worse for group attacks. For overall group violence, the black-on-white rate is 102 times the white-on-black rate, and for robbery it is 277 times the white-on-black rate. It is very unusual to find multiples this great when comparing the behavior of different groups. If blacks are just two or three times more likely than whites to drop out of school or die of prostate cancer, it is considered a matter of national importance. But practically no one even knows that blacks are *50 to 200* times more likely than whites to attack someone of the other race. If whites were just four or five times more likely to attack blacks than the reverse, it would be considered a crisis that required national attention.

Some people have argued that blacks attack whites because whites are richer and more likely to be profitable robbery targets. However, fewer than 20 percent of all violent black-on-white crimes are robberies. The rest are assaults and rapes, which presumably do not have an economic motive. In 1994 more than 30,000 white women were raped by black men while only 5,400 black women were raped by whites (the latter figure is uncertain because the actual survey found too few actual white-on-black rapes to permit confidence in an extrapolation to the country at large). Blacks are thus approximately 40 times more likely to rape whites than vice versa. It is hard to avoid the conclusion that much of the violence committed by blacks against whites is motivated by racial hatred.

From the national survey data it is possible to tell how much violence is interracial and how much is not, and in fact there is more black-on-*white* violent crime than black-on-*black*. When blacks committed violent crime in 1994, they attacked whites 56.3 percent of the time, whereas when whites committed violence they attacked blacks only 2.6 percent of the time. This does not mean that blacks are victims of violent crime no more often than whites are. Even if blacks are victims of only about half of all black violence, that half is concentrated in the 13 percent of the population that is black. Therefore, blacks are still about five times more likely than whites to be victims of violent black criminals.

These findings from the national survey data are very important, but the data are limited to crimes of violence other than murder (you cannot survey a murder victim) and the racial breakdown of "white," "black," "other" tells us nothing about Hispanics or Asians. For information on other crimes and for better racial categories we can turn to arrest data.

Murder is, of course, the most spectacular violent crime but it is relatively rare. Of all violent crimes reported to police, fewer than one percent are murder. In 1997 there were 15,289 known murders in the United States, which represented a rate of 6.8 per 100,000 Americans. This is the lowest rate since 1968, and represents the fourth straight year of decline. The murder rate hit an all-time high of 10.2 per 100,000 in 1980.

Of the 15,289 Americans who were killed in 1997, 49 percent were black, 48 percent were white and the rest were "other" with a handful of "unknowns." More than half of those arrested for murder were black. Murder is the one crime for which the federal arrest data give some information about the race of both victim and criminal, and murder usually does not cross racial lines: Approximately 90 percent of murderers were the same race as their victims.

When murder is interracial, blacks are considerably more likely to be the offenders. There were approximately 1,100 whites killed by blacks and 480 blacks killed by whites, which means that a black was about 15 times more likely to kill a white than vice versa.

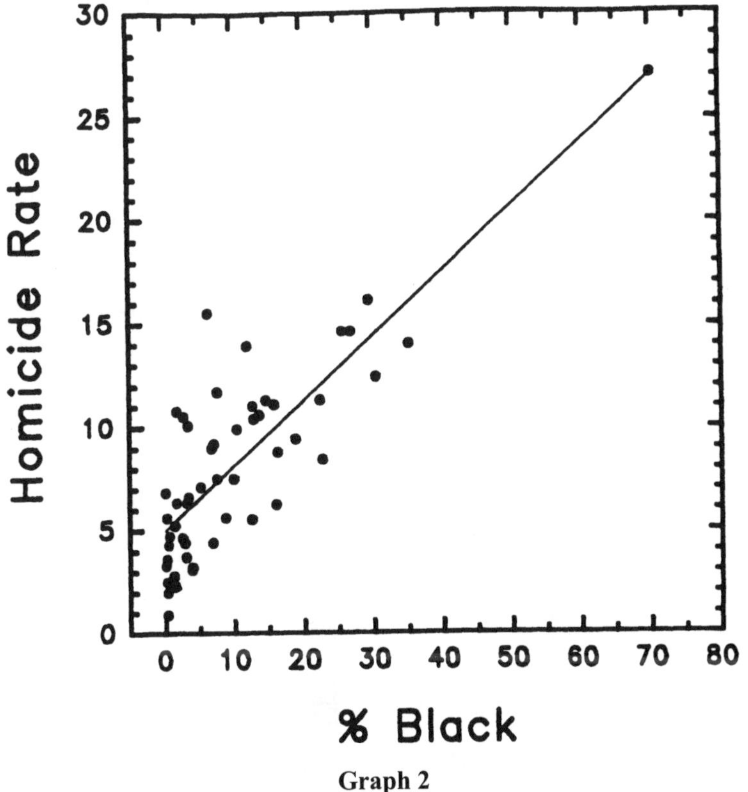

Graph 2

Because blacks are so much more likely to commit murder and robbery than any other racial group, the percentage of blacks in the local population is probably the best single indicator of the level of violence. Graph 2, compiled by the late Glayde Whitney of Florida State University, plots the murder rate against the black percentage of the population for the 50 states and the District of Columbia (which is the outlying data point at the upper right). The trend could not be much clearer.

Puerto Rico is not included in Prof. Whitney's data, but according to 1997 data, it had a murder rate of 18.9 per 100,000, which was three times the national rate of 6.8, and higher than that of any state. The murder rate was lower than that of the District of Columbia, however, which had a 1997 rate of 56.9. The states with the highest murder rates were those with the highest percentage of blacks: Louisiana (15.7 per 100,000) and Mississippi (13.1). The lowest murder rates are found in overwhelmingly white states like North Dakota (0.9), South Dakota (1.4), New Hampshire (1.4), and Vermont (1.5).

Needless to say, big cities with large black populations had the highest murder rates. In 1996, New Orleans came in first at 72 per 100,000 followed by Atlanta (47), Baltimore (46), St. Louis (44), Detroit (43) and Birmingham (42). By contrast, Seattle—mostly white—had a murder rate of seven per 100,000.

When arrest data for other crimes are compared by race, the results are as shown in Graph 3 and Graph 4. Here, arrest rates for different groups are calculated as multiples of the white arrest rate, with the white rate always set to one. The black rate of about nine for murder, for example, in the first graph does *not* mean that blacks committed nine time as many murders as whites, but that they were arrested for murder at nine times the white rate. Since there are about six times as many whites as there are blacks, it means that in absolute numbers, more blacks than whites were arrested for murder—in this case about 7,200 as opposed to 5,350.

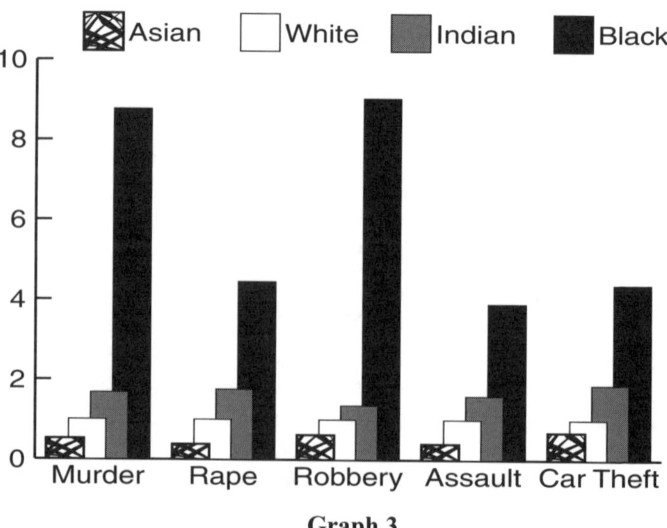

Graph 3

Graph 3 shows a very clear pattern: Asians are arrested at *lower* rates than whites, and American Indians and blacks are arrested at consistently higher rates. (The "Asian" category includes Pacific Islanders, some of whom are quite crime-prone. Tongans, for example, are much more violent than Chinese or Koreans. However, their numbers are small and do not distort crime rates very much. All the data in this article on Asians also include Pacific Islanders.) As we saw earlier, arrest rates are a very good indicator of actual crime rates. Blacks are the most dangerous, crime-prone group in America and Asians are the least dangerous. Only a few crimes break this pattern.

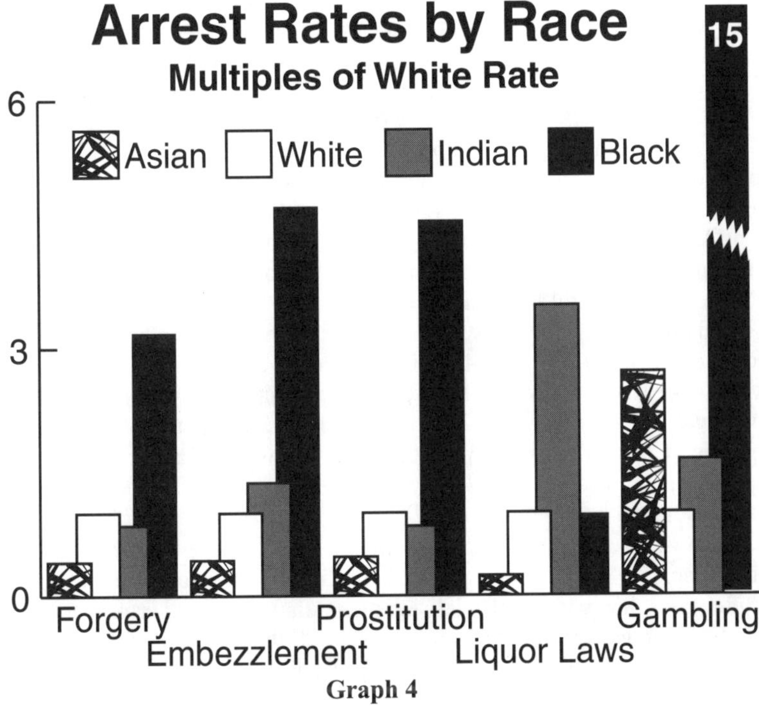

Graph 4

Graph 4 shows multiples of arrest rates for *atypical* crimes. Gambling, for example, is the only crime for which Asians are arrested at a higher rate than whites (blacks are arrested at a *much* higher rate). Alcohol offenses are unusual in that whites are arrested for them at essentially the same rates as blacks, while Indians—true to their reputation—are the worst offenders. For white-collar crimes like forgery, fraud, and embezzlement, blacks are arrested at about three times the white rate and Indians at something close to the white rate. For most crimes, however, the pattern is consistent, with blacks committing the most crimes, followed by Indians, whites, and Asians.

Hispanic Crime

What about Hispanics? The national arrest data give the impression that Hispanics are never arrested for anything. Hispanic criminals are, of course, included in the four obligatory racial categories for arrests: white, black, Indian, and Asian. How many in which categories? The US Census Bureau gives us a clue. Its official estimate of the 1997 population divides all 268 million Americans into the four standard racial groups, but adds that there were also 29 million Hispanics who "can be of any race." However, it also gives an estimate of *non-Hispanic* whites, *non-Hispanic* blacks, etc. Thus we find that according to the strictly racial classification there were 221 million whites in the country in 1997 but only 195 million *non-Hispanic* whites. When American Hispanics—approximately half of whom are Mexicans— are apportioned to the four racial categories, the Census Bureau thinks 91 percent are white, six percent black, one percent American Indian, and two percent Asian. This makes no sense—it would be more accurate to consider the majority of them American Indians—but as far as the US government is concerned, almost all Hispanics are white.

This makes for odd census results. For example, in 1990 it was not un- common to describe the 3,485,000 people of Los Angeles as 77 percent white, 14 percent black, and 9 percent Asian, which adds up to 100 percent. However, the city also had 1,300,000 Hispanics who could officially be "of any race," but most of them were counted as white. Take them out of the white population, and it suddenly plummets to about 37 percent—a more realistic figure.

What does this mean for crime rates? Since at least 91 percent—if not all—Hispanics are lumped in with "whites," if Hispanics commit crimes at higher rates than whites, official statistics inflate the white crime rate. Fortu- nately, some government jurisdictions can tell the difference between whites and Hispanics. The state of California, which has more Hispanics than any other, classifies its criminals as black, white, Hispanic, and other (it would be useful if it had a separate category for its large population of Asians). Graph 5, on the next page, shows California arrest rates for the major violent crimes. As expected, blacks are the most violent, and specialize in mugging. Hispanics are roughly three times more likely than whites to be arrested for violent crime.

There is another way to estimate Hispanic crime rates. In 1996 the De- partment of Justice calculated *incarceration* rates per 100,000 population for non-Hispanic whites (193), Hispanics (688), and non-Hispanic blacks (1,571). Expressed as multiples of the white rate, the Hispanic rate is 3.56 and the black rate is 8.14. These multiples are close to the multiples for the California arrest data and justify the conclusion that Hispanics are roughly three times more likely than whites to commit various crimes.

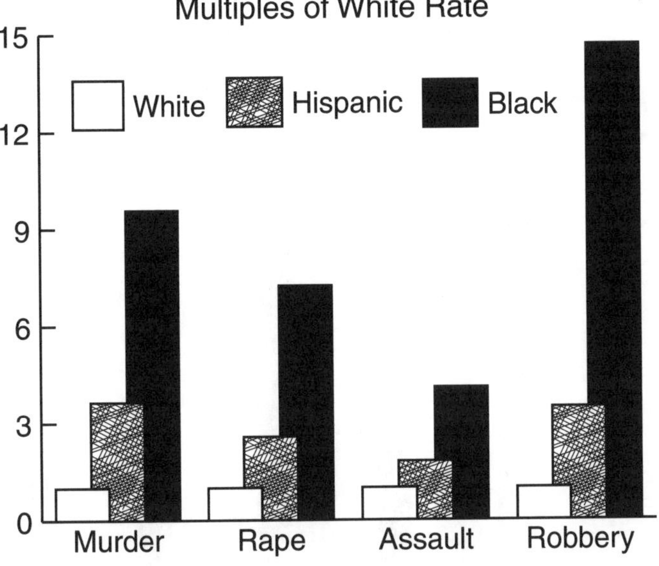

Graph 5

We can calculate more accurate racial arrest rates at the national level if we separate out the 91 percent of Hispanic criminals we can assume are classified as white when they are arrested. By doing so, the white arrest rate decreases by about 20 percent and the arrest multiples for other races increase proportionately (in some cases Asian rates begin to approach white rates). Graphs 6 and 7, on the following pages, show how arrest rate multiples change when Hispanics are treated separately. For lack of more precise information, the Hispanic multiple is set at three times the white rate for *all* crimes even though there is certain to be some variation. Both graphs are drawn to the same scale, with the white arrest rate set to one. They show at a glance how treating Hispanics as "whites" distorts racial comparisons.

It is worth noting that the survey data from which interracial crime data were extracted do not treat Hispanics as a separate category and probably include virtually all Hispanics in the "white" group. It is therefore impossible to know how many of the "whites" who were reported to have done violence to blacks (or against whom blacks did violence) were actually Hispanic. If Hispanics commit violent crimes against blacks at a higher rate than whites—and judging from their higher arrest and incarceration rates for other offenses this is likely—then the survey data inflate white crime rates. The true figures for interracial crime are probably *even more* lopsided than those reported in the survey.

Adjusted Arrest Rates
Multiples of White Rate

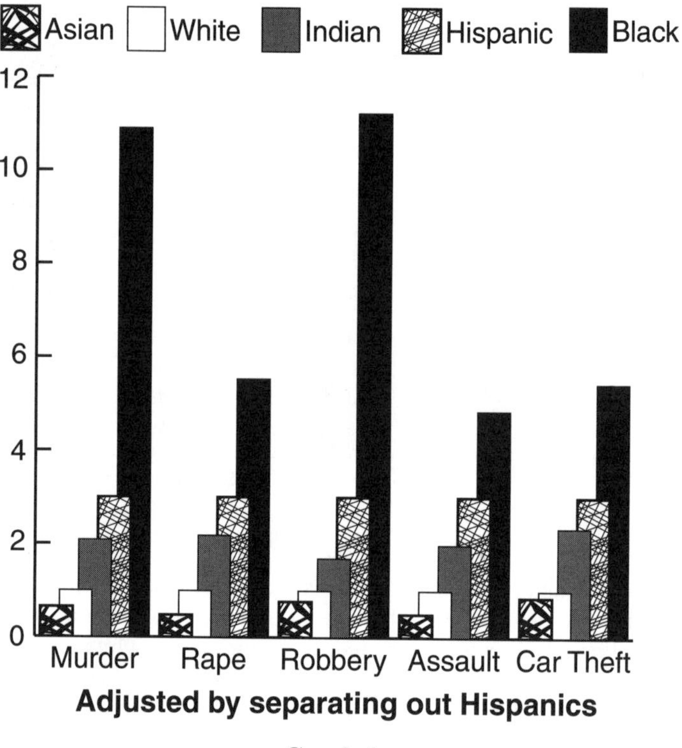

Graph 6

Disproportionate black crime rates have a seldom-discussed consequence: A lot of blacks lose the right to vote. In all but four states, felons
cannot vote. In twelve states, a felony conviction can mean disfranchisement
for life, but in most states, felons can reapply for the right to vote after they
are off probation. Lefties have been wringing their hands over this, unsure of
whether by calling attention to the number of blacks without the vote they
can fight "racism" or whether calling attention to staggering black arrest
rates will *promote* "racism." Human Rights Watch and the Sentencing Project have plumped for the former, and report that two percent of all American
adults are without the vote because of felony convictions and that among
black men the figure is 13 percent. In seven states—Alabama, Florida, Iowa,
Mississippi, New Mexico[1], Virginia, and Wyoming—a quarter of all black
men are *permanently* ineligible to vote.

---

[1] New Mexico rescinded the permanent ban on felon voting in 2001.

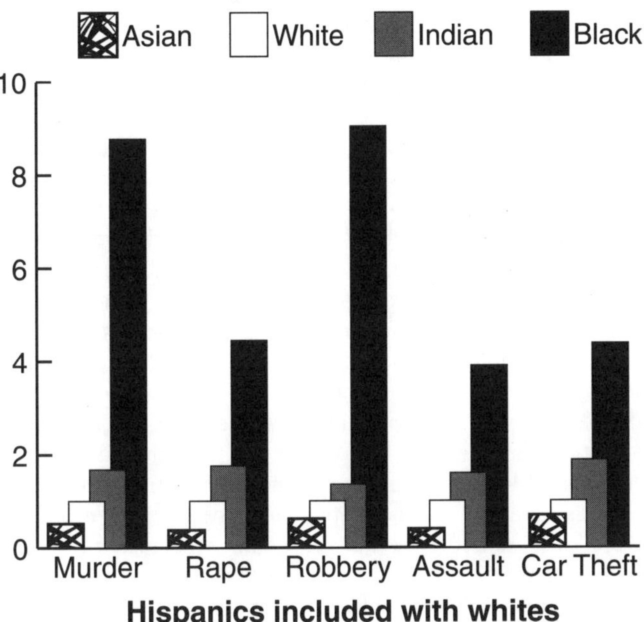

Graph 7

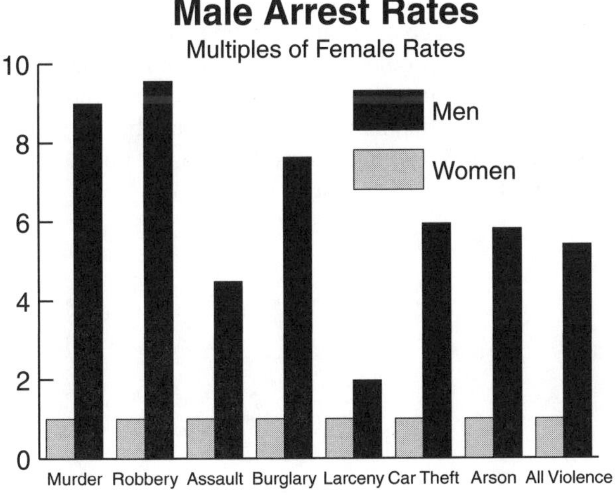

Graph 8

The lefties go on to point out that by 2020 about one third of all black men will probably have lost the right to vote. In the black parts of cities like Houston, Memphis, Miami, and New Orleans, as many as half the black men could be off the rolls. It causes the lefties great pain to imagine cities with black majorities but more white voters than black.

A very illuminating comparison can be made between arrest rates for blacks as compared to whites, and men as compared to women. We find that in terms of their likelihood to commit violent crimes, blacks are as much more dangerous than whites as men are more dangerous than women. Graph 8, on the previous page, shows arrest rates for men for various crimes as multiples of the arrest rates for women. The next three graphs (Graph 9, Graph 10, and Graph 11) compare the male-female arrest multiple to the black-white multiple. Blacks are as much more dangerous than whites as men are more dangerous than women—and these graphs are not even adjusted for the inclusion of Hispanics in "white" arrest figures.

Everyone knows that a group of unknown men is potentially more dangerous than a group of otherwise similar women. It is entirely reasonable to take precautions around men one would not take around women. From a statistical point of view, it is just as reasonable to distinguish between blacks and whites as carefully as one distinguishes between men and women. It would be foolish not to lock the car doors when driving through black neighborhoods.

Police, of course, know that blacks commit a great deal of crime, and this explains "racial profiling," the practice of stopping and questioning proportionately more blacks than people of other races. The police would be foolish not to. They also stop more men than women and more young people than old people. The police know from experience who the crooks are likely to be. If they spent as much time investigating old Asian ladies as they did young black men they would never get their jobs done. Everyone understands that men are more crime-prone than women, and understands why men are stopped more often than women. It is only because of racial hysteria that so many people at least pretend to believe the police stop blacks more often than whites because of "racism."

Graph 9

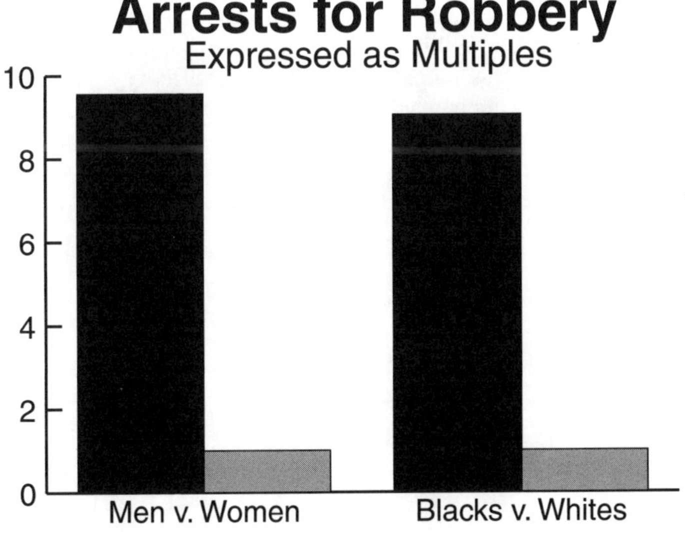

Graph 10

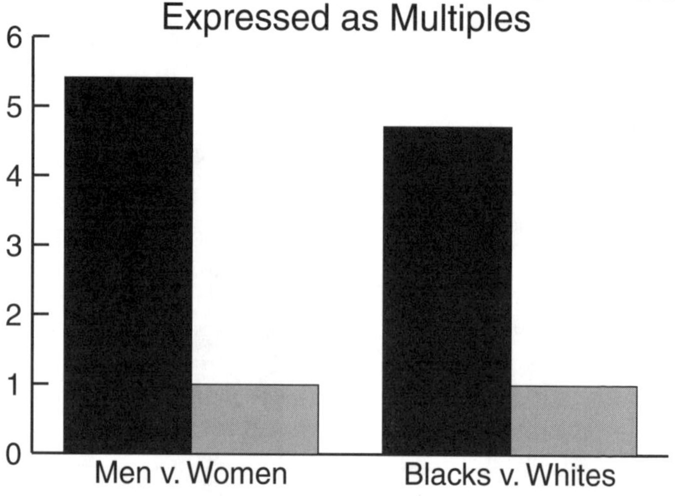

Graph 11

Why Crime is Down

Politicians and the press have made much of the fact that crime rates are inching down—and indeed they are. The rate of violent crime declined every year from 1991 to 1996 and decreased by a total of 12.7 percent during that period. However, violent crime rates were still *300 percent* higher than they were in 1960. President William Clinton likes to take credit for the recent decline, claiming that his initiative to spend federal money on a few thousand more police officers is what did the trick. Reality is not so kind. Crime rates are down because of the huge increase in the number of bad guys who are in jail. As the next graphs show, we have never had so many people in prison, and incarceration *rates*, in terms of prisoners per 100,000 population are at unprecedented highs.

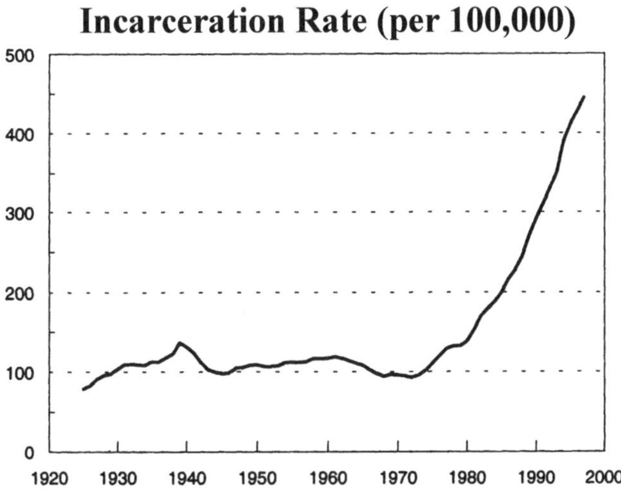

Incarceration Rate (per 100,000)

Graph 12

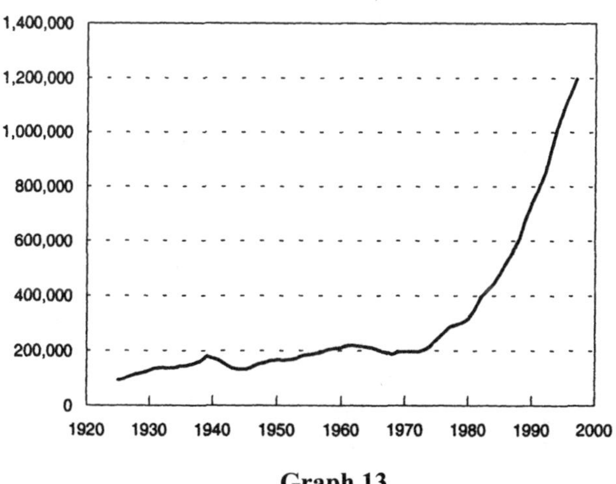

State and Federal Prisoners

Graph 13

As Graph 12 shows, America has traditionally had about 100 people in jail for every 100,000 citizens. In the decade of the 1960s there was a terrific increase in crime. Perhaps not coincidentally it coincided with the triumph of silly liberal views about crime: society rather than the criminal is to blame, imprisonment is ineffective, the police are brutal, blacks never get a fair shake, etc. And so, despite the surge in crime, prison sentences were reduced and incarceration rates actually went *down* during the decade. By 1970, however, the combination of more crime and less imprisonment had reached intolerable levels, and we started sending people back to jail: to the point that we now have 400 prisoners per 100,000 citizens—a four-fold increase in incarceration rates.

Current research suggests that every year of incarceration prevents 12 to 21 crimes. If we returned to our traditional incarceration rate of 100 per 100,000 it would require releasing nearly one million jailbirds—and would loose upon the country a crime wave that would drive every citizen into the arms of the National Rifle Association. The connection between falling crime rates and increasing incarceration rates should be clear to even the dimmest liberal; a crook who is doing time can't stick a knife in your ribs. And yet, the most common big-media reaction to the swollen prison population is to argue that it is caused by some kind of malicious "prison-industrial complex," and to worry that so many of the prisoners are black.

Because of the unprecedentedly large number of adults who are locked up and off the streets, juvenile arrest rates are a better indicator than adult arrest rates of real crime trends in the country. All children begin life *out* of jail, after all, so their crime and arrest rates are not held down by the fact that the worst of them are already locked up and out of circulation. And, in fact, the celebrated drop in adult arrest rates has largely passed them by. From 1991 to 1996, while adult crime rates were dropping steadily—as more and miscreants were put behind bars—juvenile violent crime was *rising* for all but one of those years. In fact, since 1987, juvenile violent-crime arrest rates have risen every year but one. There is every reason to think that this is the true crime trend in the United States.

Crime trends for girls have been even worse than for boys. In 1967, boys accounted for 92 percent of juvenile arrests for violent crime and girls for only eight percent. By 1996, girls were committing fully 25 percent of violent juvenile crime. From 1967 to 1996, violent crime arrest rates for boys increased 143 percent, but for girls the increase was an astonishing *345* percent.

It is often pointed out that immigration keeps the population young because immigrants have more children than natives. Most immigrants are non-white, so the American population is turning non-white most quickly at the younger ages. With the exception of Asians, non-whites commit considerably more crime than whites, so the demographic shift cannot help but produce more crime. Rising rates of juvenile crime—probably fueled largely by immigration—are reliable harbingers of rising rates of adult crime. Since the country does not seem likely to go through another 1960s-style period of soft-headedness about sentencing, we can expect the prison population to continue to grow at a good clip.

The prison population will also turn increasingly non-white—whites are already a minority. According to the Department of Justice, the 1995 racial breakdown in American prisons was as follows:

Total	1,126,287	
Black	544,005	48.3%
White	455,021	40.4%
Indian/Eskimo	10,176	.9%
Asian	6,483	.6%
Not Known	110,602	9.8%

110,000 Not Known? A footnote to the table warns that in California, Illinois, New Jersey, Nevada, Wyoming, and 15 other states, "some or all Hispanic prisoners [are] reported under 'not known' "! Footnotes also tell us that Montana considers all Hispanics to be white and that seven states—including big ones like Texas and Mississippi—just "estimate" the racial numbers. Once again, crazy bookkeeping makes it impossible to keep track of Hispanics, and impossible to know how many are lumped in with "whites." But even if we ignore all the "not knowns" and assume none of the "whites" is Hispanic, "whites" account for only about 40 percent of all prisoners.

In 1995 there were 100,250 federal inmates, of which 20 percent were non-citizens. The feds do not have any "not knowns," and report their prison population to be 36.9 percent black, 32.6 percent white, and 27.5 percent Hispanic, with Indians and Asians at 1.5 percent each. It is clear that an all-white America could make do with a much smaller prison system.

The dwindling minority of white prisoners—now likely to be controlled by non-white prison guards—will be increasingly vulnerable to rape, humiliation, violence, and extortion. More and more will seek protection by joining white-consciousness prison gangs. Already, in largely non-white prisons, it is whites who are members of "racist" gangs who maintain the best morale.

The large number of black and Hispanic prisoners has a significant but unquantifiable bearing on racial differences in rates of violent crime. According to the graph on page 40, blacks are about five times more likely than whites to be arrested for violent crime. Periodic Department of Justice surveys also find that Americans report blacks to be committing violent crime at about five times the white rate. It is worth noting that these figures apply only to blacks and whites *who are not already in jail*. To get a true indicator of genuine racial differences in violent or other criminal *tendencies* rather than just a record of criminal *behavior* for a given year, one would have to turn *all* the convicts loose and *then* compare crime rates. The 1997 black-white differential of 500 percent is large enough already, but it is substantially reduced by the fact that, proportionately, eight times as many blacks as whites are *already in jail* and are restrained from the violent acts they would certainly commit if they were free. A true black/white multiple of violence not distorted by existing differential incarceration rates would be considerably greater than five.

With the exception of Asians, the burgeoning non-white population presents a very significant threat to our safety and security. Crime considerations alone would justify a return to a much more selective immigration policy. So long as whites remain too timid to discuss the challenges they face, those challenges will never be met.

Police Bias? Says Who?

The "racist" police officer is practically a cliché. White cops all over the country are supposed to be shooting, beating, and arresting innocent blacks and Hispanics—or at least trying much harder to collar them than whites. Aside from some isolated incidents of racially motivated brutality, this is a false image. The police arrest blacks and Hispanics because they commit crimes.

The first line of evidence is the close correspondence between survey data and arrest data. If the public says half the muggers are black, and half the muggers the police arrest are black, it is unlikely the police are making "biased" arrests. Even more to the point, the police have essentially no discretion over whom they arrest for a violent crime. Except for murder victims, most people get a good enough look at an assailant to know if he is black or white. If the victim says a white man took his wallet, the police can't very well go out and arrest a black man even if they wanted to.

Police have much more discretion over whether to make an arrest in the case of non-violent crimes, such as violation of liquor laws. Unlike murder or rape, there is not a great deal of public pressure to make arrests, and the police can walk away from public drunkenness if they want to. Presumably, a "racist" officer would see a drunk on the gutter and make an arrest only if the drunk were black. In fact, drunk driving and other liquor offenses—in which police can make arrests or not largely as they choose—are the very crimes for which the black multiple of the white arrest rate is the smallest (see page 33). If "racist" cops are picking on blacks they are not doing a good job.

Finally, if the police are "racist," why are Asians arrested at consistently lower rates than whites? Wouldn't "racist" cops think of some way to snare Asians?

It is often argued that the large number of blacks arrested for drugs—particularly crack cocaine—is evidence of police bias. However, there is a completely independent indicator of who is using illegal drugs, which suggests that the police are arresting the very people they should. The Department of Health and Human Services keeps statistics on people admitted to emergency rooms because of drug overdoses. Blacks are admitted at 6.67 times the white rate for heroin and morphine, and no less than 10.5 times the white rate for cocaine (Hispanics are admitted at two to three times the white rate). What better evidence could there be that people of different races are using drugs at markedly different rates, and that the police are simply doing their job?

Like so many other destructive racial myths, the myth of the racist cop refuses to die.

Eye-opening crime facts from "the Sourcebook."

The Department of Justice collects an enormous amount of information in addition to arrest records and crime survey data. Some of the most interesting findings are summarized in a fat, annual volume called *Sourcebook of Criminal Justice Statistics*. The most recent edition generally reports data no later than for 1996, but it includes many interesting facts, which are presented here in no particular order.

We find, for example, that in 1996 Americans murdered 300 infants and about the same number of children aged one to four. Races of perpetrators and victims are not reported. In a rather chilling table we discover the number of children *under the age of ten* who were arrested in 1996 for the following crimes: Murder - 17, Rape - 61, robbery - 266, aggravated assault - 1,000, car theft - 199, forgery - 28, drunkenness - 103, weapons carrying - 600. Once again, it would be instructive to know the racial distribution of these arrests.

We also find that although during the 1970s, 120 to 130 police officers were killed in action every year, there has been a substantial decline since then, mainly because of the increased use of bullet-proof vests. In 1996, criminals killed only 55 police officers. Every year since 1979 (the first year for which data are given), no fewer than 80 percent of the slain officers have been white, and the figure has been as high as 91 percent. In 1996, blacks killed more officers than "whites" (including Hispanics) did—45 percent of killings v. 42 percent.

As of December 31, 1996, there were only 48 women on death row—1.5 percent of the total. Executions were halted in 1968 by a Supreme Court ruling but became constitutional again in 1976. Since then, there have been only 358 executions, with Texas killing the most (107) followed by Florida with 38 and Virginia with 37. Since resumption in 1977, 188 "whites" (there are no separate data for Hispanics) have been executed and 121 blacks.

Although it is not included in the standard government index of violence, suicide is a crime, so *Sourcebook* covers it. The very elderly have the highest suicide rates (around 22 per 100,000) but otherwise the most dangerous years are between ages 20 to 24 with a rate of around 16 per 100,000. At every age men are five to eight times more likely to kill themselves than women, and have grown more likely to do so over time. Male suicide rates have shown a steady increase from 9.3 in 1950 to 27.7 in 1995, though the rate has held steady in the mid- to high 20s since 1990. From 1950 to 1995, the suicide rate for women aged 20 to 24 has been as low as 2.9 and as high as 5.6 and was most recently 4.3. There is essentially no trend.

"Whites" are considerably more likely to knock themselves off than blacks. The white rate is about double the black rate at virtually all ages except for people 75 and over, at which point they begin to treble and quadruple. White men over the age of 85 are the most dangerous to themselves, with a suicide rate of 68 per 100,000. Black women at that age kill themselves at a rate of only 1.5 per 100,000.

Racial differences in suicide rates are seldom reported, though we can be sure that if blacks were killing themselves at two to three times the white rate it would be explained as a reaction to "racism."

The Sourcebook tells us that 1996 was a record year for deporting illegal aliens, which is different from catching them at the border. The feds bounced 50,000, which was a jump from 41,800 the previous year. About 33,000 had been convicted of crimes, which means that most illegals need to have a record before the feds bother to send them home.

In 1996 authorities eradicated more marijuana plants in Tennessee (1,113,000) than in any other state. California took second place with 632,000.

In 1997, counterfeiters passed 589,000 bogus banknotes with a total value of $31,750,000.

Only ten percent of rapists were complete strangers to their victims; the rest were at least acquaintances. Seventy-eight percent of robbers, however, were total strangers.

Every year there are about 25 times as many thefts from automobiles as there are incidents of pickpocketing or pursesnatching. Every year about 0.66 percent of all cars in the US. are stolen, or about one in every 150.

The Sourcebook also reports crime-related attitude surveys carried out by private organizations. There has been a steady increase in support for the death penalty. In 1965—perhaps the height of the society-is-to-blame era—only 38 percent of Americans supported the death penalty, but by 1997 that figure had grown to 75 percent. There are substantial racial differences, with 80 percent of whites in favor of capital punishment but only 46 percent of blacks. Seventy-two percent of Hispanics support it.

There are considerable racial differences in *reported* gun ownership, with 47 percent of whites, 17 percent of blacks, and 37 percent of Hispanics saying they have a gun in the house.

Religion does not seem to have a great influence on attitudes to crime and law enforcement except in the case of Jews. They are most likely to favor stricter gun control, least likely to own a gun, most likely to favor legalization of marijuana, and most likely to want to liberalize pornography laws.

In a rather surprising finding, *Sourcebook* reports that American attitudes toward legalization of homosexual acts between consenting adults have hardly budged in 20 years. In 1977, 43 percent favored legalization, 43 percent were opposed, and 14 percent couldn't make up their minds. In 1996, 44 percent favored legalization, 47 percent were opposed, and only nine percent were unsure. Public opinion has been remarkably impervious to the pro-homosexual movement.

The Great Hate Crimes Hoax

The idea of "hate" crimes and the increased penalties attached to them are a radical departure from traditional criminal justice in that they punish certain motivations more than others. Increased penalties are justified by pointing out that the law has always taken a criminal's state of mind into account: Was the killing deliberate or an accident? Was it planned in cold blood or done in the heat of the moment? However, these are questions of *intent*, and intent is, indeed, a factor in determining guilt. "Hate" crimes break new ground by considering *motive*. Traditionally the law does not care about motive. You are just as guilty of murder whether you kill a man because he stole your wife, blackmailed you, or stepped on your toe.

Hate crime laws require that the courts search for certain motives and add extra penalties if they find them. Therefore, if you punch a man in the nose because he took your parking spot or because he was unbearably ugly or because you just felt like punching someone that day, you are guilty of assault. If you say "nigger" and punch a black man you are guilty of a hate crime, and are punished more severely. Like almost all recent innovations in morals, what started with race has expanded to "sexual orientation" and even disabilities like blindness or feeble-mindedness.

Ever since 1990, when Congress passed the Hate Crime Statistics Act, the FBI has been charged with collecting national statistics on criminal acts "motivated, in whole or in part, by bias." The law does not force local police departments to supply this information but most do. In 1997, the most recent year for which data are available, the FBI received "hate crime" information from 11,211 local agencies serving more than 83 percent of the United States population.

That year, there was a total of 9,861 "hate crimes," of which 6,981 were based on race or ethnic origin. The rest were for reasons of religion (1,493—of which 1,159 were anti-Jewish), sexual orientation (1,375—of which 14 were anti-heterosexual), or disability (12).

The FBI reports 8,474 suspected offenders whose race was known—5,344 were white and 1,629 were black. Their crimes can be divided into violent and nonviolent offenses, and by calculating rates we find that blacks were 1.99 times more likely than whites to commit hate crimes in general and 2.24 times more likely to commit violent hate crimes. This over-representation of blacks in hate crimes—not just in race bias cases but in all categories—runs counter to the common impression that whites are the virtually exclusive perpetrators of hate crimes and are certainly more likely to commit them than blacks.

The real significance of "hate" crimes, however, is their small number. Of the 6,981 offenses based on race or ethnicity, only 4,105 were violent, involving murder, rape, robbery, or assault. The rest were such things as vandalism and intimidation. These numbers are almost insignificant compared to the 1,766,000 interracial crimes of violence (combining both single- and multiple-offender offenses) reported in the Department of Justice survey for 1994.

How important is the distinction between interracial crimes that are officially designated as hate crimes and those that are not? For a crime to be considered a hate crime, the perpetrator must make his motive clear, usually by saying something nasty. It is not hard to imagine that of the nearly two million interracial crimes committed in 1994, some—perhaps even a great many—were "motivated, in whole or in part, by bias" but the perpetrators didn't bother to say so.

Given the realities of race in the United States, would it be unreasonable for someone attacked by a criminal of a different race to wonder whether race had something to do with the attack, even if the assailant said nothing? Such suspicions are even more likely in the case of the 490,266 acts of *group* violence that crossed racial lines in 1994. A white woman gang-raped by blacks or a black man cornered and beaten by whites will think he was singled out at least in part because of race, even if the attackers only talked about the weather.

Hate crime laws assume that special harm is done to society when people are attacked because of race. But which does more damage to society: the few thousand violent acts officially labeled as hate crimes or the *millions* of ordinary interracial crimes of violence—90 percent of which are committed by blacks against whites? If race relations are so fragile they must be protected with laws that add extra penalties to race-related crimes, why not automatically add extra penalties to *any* interracial crime, on the assumption that it harmed race relations? The problem, of course, is that most of the people slapped with heavier penalties would be black.

Hispanics

Official thinking about "hate crimes" suffers from another crushing defect. As Joseph Fallon, who has written for AR (see page 86), has noted, the FBI reports hate crimes *against* Hispanics but not *by* Hispanics. In the forms the FBI has local police departments fill out, Hispanics are clearly indicated as a victim category but they are not an option as a perpetrator category when the FBI asks for "Suspected Race of Offender." The FBI therefore forces local police departments to categorize most Hispanics as "white" (see page 34). Official figures for 1997 reflect this. The total number of "hate crimes" for that year—9,861—includes 636 crimes of anti-Hispanic bias, but not one of the 8,474 known offenders is "Hispanic" because the FBI's data collection method doesn't permit such a designation.

If someone goes after a Mexican because he doesn't like Mexicans it is an anti-Hispanic crime. If the same Mexican commits a "hate crime" against a white, both the victim *and* the perpetrator are considered white. And, in fact, the 1997 FBI figures duly record 214 "white" offenders who committed anti-white hate crimes! The offenders were undoubtedly Hispanic, but the report doesn't say so. Some of the "whites" who are reported to have committed hate crimes against blacks and homosexuals are almost certainly Hispanic, but there is no way to be sure.

Hispanic perpetrators show up only if you investigate specific "hate" crimes. The FBI lists five cases of racially-motivated murder for 1997— three "anti-black" and two "anti-white." The report says nothing about the perpetrators or the circumstances of the killings, so AR got the details from local police departments.

Two of the anti-black killings took place in the same town, a mostly-Hispanic suburb of Los Angeles called Hawaiian Gardens. Hawaiian Gardens has a history of black-Hispanic tension that is so bad many blacks have cleared out. In one of the 1997 murders, a 24-year-old black man was beaten to death by a mob of 10 to 14 Hispanics who took turns smashing his head with a baseball bat. In the other, a Hispanic gang member challenged a 29-year-old black man's right to be in the neighborhood. A few minutes later he came back and shot the man in the chest. In both cases, the victims and killers did not know each other and the motivation appears to have been purely racial. These crimes are typical of what we think of as hate-crime murders, but because no Hispanics are identified as perpetrators in the FBI report, the killers were classified as white.

The third anti-black killing took place in Anchorage, Alaska. A white man, Brett Maness, killed his neighbor, a black man, Delbert White, after a brief struggle. Mr. Maness, who was growing marijuana in his apartment and kept an arsenal of weapons, had been shooting a pellet gun at Mr. White's house, and the black came over to complain. Interestingly, a jury found that Mr. Maness killed Mr. White in self-defense. The incident—which sounds rather ambiguous—was classified as a hate crime because Mr. Maness had shouted racial slurs at Mr. White in the past and because "racist" literature was found in his apartment.

The remaining two killings were classified as anti-white, but only one fits the usual idea of these crimes. Four white men were walking on a street in Palm Beach, Florida, when a car came to a stop not far from them. Two black men got out with their hands behind their backs and one said "What are you crackers looking at?" One of the white men replied, "Not you, nigger," whereupon one of the blacks brought a gun from behind his back and fired several times, killing one white and wounding another. Attackers and victims did not know each other, and the motivation appears to have been purely racial. The other anti-white killing involved a Texas businessman from India, Sri Punjabi, who shot his Mexican daughter-in-law because his son had divorced an Indian wife to marry her. Mr. Punjabi was furious because his son married someone who was not Indian. (Presumably, this crime could have been classified as anti-Hispanic rather than anti-white.)

These five "hate crime" murders reported for 1997 do not exactly fit the media image of whites brutalizing non-whites. In fact, only one perpetrator, the Alaskan, was "white" in the usually accepted sense. What was the nature of the thousands of other officially-reported hate crimes? Without examining all 9,861 of them it is impossible to say.

It is clear, though, that the FBI report gives a false impression of what is going on. It inflates the number of hate crimes committed by "whites" by calling Hispanics white, and suggests that Hispanics never commit "hate crimes." Every year, the press duly reports this nonsense. No one, apparently, ever bothers to ask why hundreds of whites are reported to be comitting hate crimes against other whites. By leaving out Hispanics and blaming their crimes on whites, the FBI report paints a picture of race relations in America so distorted it is worse than useless.

This article appeared originally in the July 1999 issue.

———◆———

Hell on Wheels
by Daniel Attila

I was born in Hungary, from which I escaped in 1982 at age 18. I settled in New York in 1984 with the intention of becoming an artist, but after nearly a decade of struggle I realized I might never make it. In 1993 I enrolled in the City University of New York, while I supported myself for four years as a conductor on New York City subway trains. There can be only a few jobs that so quickly introduce an immigrant to the realities of multiracialism. Beneath the streets of New York I have seen and done things that very few whites will—I hope—ever see or do.

Conductors operate the doors of trains, make announcements, give information to the passengers, and oversee the safety of people on trains and platforms. Most of the time they stay in a small compartment, or cab, in the middle car of the train. There are many cities that operate subways with only a driver, but New York City is a challenging place, where putting only one person on the train would expose the system to violence and chaos.

Attending college while working under ground is not a dream come true, but conductors are well paid. The starting salary is $30-40,000 a year, with a top salary of $40-50,000, which that can be reached in three years. Conductors who become drivers can earn $50-70,000 a year, depending on overtime. The high salaries are a result of the monopoly the Transit Authority (TA) enjoys over city transportation. The union is a mostly-black workforce, which cannot be tampered with by any politician who wants a career in New York. Even as far back as the 1930s, the all-powerful TA got through the depression without laying off a single employee.

I went to a high school in China Town to take the civil service exam for the job. Once inside, I noticed that I was the only white person there. Except for an Asian-Indian woman who sat in front of me, I saw only black people, even though there were at least 40 of us taking the test. "How come I'm the only white person here?" I wondered. "Don't white Americans want a job that pays $40-60,000 a year and doesn't even require a high-school education?" Perhaps in answer, one of the blacks in front of me turned around and gave me a bizarre, hate-filled look—a look I would often encounter in the years ahead.

The test was easy—surprisingly so—and I wondered if it was possible for anyone over the age of six not to pass it. I clearly remember one of the questions; I find it impossible to forget:

> If you are a bus driver and find that a kid jumped onto the back of the bus, traveling on the outside, what are you going to do?
>
> a) I will suddenly break, then accelerate, repeating this process until the kid falls off and learns a lesson.

b) I will just ignore the kid and keep on driving as if unaware of the problem.

c) I will stop the bus and personally make sure that the kid gets off.

As part of the test, we also had to find various places in the city, such as the Empire State Building, the Brooklyn Bridge, and the United Nations, with the help of a city map provided to us. This is similar to having Parisians find the Eiffel tower with the help of a map. Needless to say, the test went well and I congratulated myself for having settled in a country where well-paying jobs are so easy to get.

I began learning about the reality of America's racial dilemma right at the beginning of my training program at the Transit Authority. There was a huge black fellow in our class who had the habit of physically bumping into me at every opportunity. I could feel that he did this intentionally, trying to make it hurt more than an accidental collision would, but not enough to make it look like an assault.

The class consisted of about 80 people, with only a half dozen whites. Most of the training was given by an old white veteran who kept telling us funny and scary stories about transit workers on duty. We were told to watch out for assaults by passengers. "Every one of you will be spat at," he insisted repeatedly, "I guarantee it." After the class training, which lasted about four weeks, we spent two weeks on trains, operating under the supervision of experienced conductors. Right on the first day, a strong black man who stood on the platform, whose right arm was bigger than both of my thighs put together, made a sudden attempt to punch me in the face as I leaned out the window to observe the platform. The conductor who supervised me assured me that such things are very dangerous and happen every day.

Also during the break-in period, I saw a horrible incident in the East New York section of Brooklyn. A horde of black teenagers descended upon a black boy who was sitting quietly by himself. Within seconds, they beat him from head to toe, then quickly fled before the doors closed. We tried to talk to the boy, who was in bad shape, asking him if he wanted medical help or the police. When he said he didn't want either, we asked about the attack. It turned out he was on his way to the first day on a job. The gang beat him up because they didn't want him to work.

After the break-in period, I was qualified as a conductor and began to operate without supervision. It didn't take long for our instructor's prediction to come true. I was conducting a "D" train in the Bronx when I noticed a large group of black men gathered on the platform, just outside the conductor's window. I felt their threatening presence instinctively, but the rules require that the conductor lean out the window and look down the platform in both directions before he closes the doors. I had no choice but to open my window and take the risk. As soon as I opened it, one of the men spat right into my eyes. I was wearing safety goggles but still got some of the saliva on my skin—regulations require that goggles be worn primarily to protect against passenger assaults.

Throughout the four years I spent as a conductor, blacks and Latinos would hide behind posts or other cover and spit at me—with astonishing power and accuracy. Other times they would throw things at me, try to punch me, or yell vile and sometimes inarticulate things at me.

One attack involved a black man of about thirty, who threw a large, glass bottle at my face. I managed to close the window just as the bottle struck—it hit with such force, a pieces of glass stuck in the acrylic window of my cab all the way to the end of the trip. As we came into the terminal, I spotted a black supervisor on the platform and couldn't help asking: "What am I supposed to do when someone attacks me as I operate, and the attack is really nasty?" "If you have an injury, you pull the cord and call command to send for the police and the ambulance," was the reply. "But what if you have no injuries? What if he almost killed you but you lucked out?" I continued. "Then there is no problem," said the supervisor, "you keep on going."

On another occasion, when conducting a "D" train in the Bronx, a boy in a crowd of high-school students threw a heavy stone right at my face with great accuracy and force. I instinctively held up my hand to shield my face and was injured severely enough to go to the emergency room. At the hospital, the nurse told me that a bus driver, also injured in an assault, had just been treated and released a couple of hours earlier.

When operating during the "school hours," the early afternoon when students come home from public schools, rowdy students—none of whom was ever white or Oriental—would routinely disable the trains. They would break windows, pull the emergency break, and tear open the seats so they could cut out electric switches. If the train crew couldn't fix the problem, we would discharge the passengers and transfer the train to the storage yard for repair. When we discharged trains, black and Latino passengers would threaten violence, accusing us of deliberately disabling trains so that we could "go home early."

My ordeal did not end with the work-day. The commute home was just as agonizing as time on the job. In the late hours, when I usually made my way home, the trains were largely bereft of normal, working people. Often there were gangs of "youths" roaming the trains, walking from car to car, jumping on seats, starting fights, and harassing passengers. I often locked myself in the conductor's cab, as I did on the job.

One night, after work, as I was climbing the steps from the subway platform in my own neighborhood, a tall black man came running the other way and crashed into me. He was so badly dressed he looked like a bum. He was carrying a box of Chinese take-out food, which he dropped when he slammed into me. There went his dinner. Although the collision was entirely his fault, he began threatening me, cursing me, and demanding money. I looked around to see if there was anybody else in the station—not that one can expect help from whites in situations like this—but there was no one.

I don't know how long we argued, but it seemed like an eternity. Keeping him from attacking me took all the energy I had. I finally managed to break away and run home. Exhausted, I collapsed on the floor and began crying, in a way I don't remember doing since I was a small child. What broke me down was not so much this particular incident but the sum of all the assaults and humiliation that took place before it—the attacks, the spitting, the name calling, and, ultimately, my complete inability to do anything about it. Violent self-defense would certainly cost any white transit worker his job.

New Horizons

My job offered me the opportunity to see parts of New York whites seldom see. The United States may be the only country that has never been attacked, but still has places that look as though they went through a war. This once-glamorous cultural capital has neighborhoods, the size of cities, that look like Stalingrad or Yokohama right after a carpet bombing.

The job also acquainted me with blacks I would never otherwise have known. My black colleagues never seemed upset by the behavior of our "customers," nor did they try to avoid working in horrible neighborhoods. One reason was that although they were not entirely safe, they did not face attacks of the same severity or frequency, let alone attacks with racial overtones.

In their off hours, the blacks often held little parties in our filthy, stuffy, underground crew rooms, where they celebrated birthdays or Kwanzaa with cheap cake and fast food. Non-blacks were ordered to leave the room before such events; most blacks believed that segregation on equal terms was better than integration.

The blacks also talked about what a scandal it was that the schools do not teach that Jesus Christ and the ancient Egyptians were black. Every day, during lunch breaks, I witnessed heated debates about such topics. I also learned that anything wrong in black neighborhoods is the fault of whites. My colleagues believed that slavery caused illegitimacy and welfare dependency, and that the government simply refuses to spend money on neighborhoods where they live. "When are they going to take the money and clean up the Bronx, Brooklyn, and upper Manhattan?" they would ask.

Whites never engaged in open debate about such things, preferring to scribble their opinions on the walls of the bathrooms provided for transit workers. "Kill all Niggers," was the harshest sentiment I ever saw, along with such admonitions as "Do your country a favor, kill a liberal!" Working underground seemed to degrade everyone.

In addition to the pressures of the job, I was forced to put up with the anti-white atmosphere of City College. One of the most anti-white teachers was an otherwise intelligent English professor named Hannah Rogers. After a few classes filled with insults to whites, Prof. Rogers made a little speech that went something like this:

"In the beginning, before the white man came along, the colored peoples who once owned this land lived here peacefully, cohabiting with each other, with nature, and with the animals. Then came the Europeans, who killed the people and the animals, and destroyed nature. Now, however, the people of color are beginning to reclaim the land that belongs to them, and there will come a day when the colored masses rise up, and the white people who managed to enslave every other race will be destroyed. The land will be taken back so that the people to whom it belongs can return to living in peace and harmony with each other, and nature. I only hope," she concluded, "that when that day comes, the whites who were good will be spared."

I was offended and shocked, but I learned something I had never suspected. I always thought "liberals" are the way they are because they live in white ghettos and don't realize what is happening around them. Not so. At least some of them believe a civil war is on the horizon. They hope for it, they encourage it, and may even expect to gain from it.

East New York

Perhaps the most dreadful incident of my career at the TA was in the summer of 1993, while I was working on the A line. This is one of the lines that goes into the worst neighborhood of the city, the East New York section of Brooklyn. I never operated there for a single day without being assaulted or humiliated in some way.

On one hot afternoon, as I opened the doors at the Ralph Avenue station, I heard what sounded like gunshots. They were a lot quieter than in movies, and at first I thought it was just some noise coming from the equipment. However, I was unnerved to see a couple of blacks, wearing face masks, rush out of the last car, up the steps, and disappear.

There was no way to misunderstand the situation; an incident had taken place in the last car, and the rules required the conductor to investigate. No experienced conductor would ever go back to the last car in a situation like that, no matter what the rules say, but I was not very experienced. After making some announcements to the passengers, I gathered all my courage and walked back to the last car, pretending to be calm.

There were people standing in every door shouting about the delay. In the last car, I found a man lying on the floor with bloody wounds in his legs. I used my portable radio to tell the train operator what had happened, and began to walk back to the center of the train to my position. The train operator made a loud announcement requesting that all passengers leave the train, and I was to make sure that all the cars were empty before we closed the doors to wait for the police.

I was the only white person in the station. As the passengers got off, they stayed on the platform and began to form a row close to the train. I walked toward my position, fenced in by the train on the left and by the row of people on the right. I passed three cars and had two more to go, to reach the only position from which I could close the doors. I was supposed to walk all the way to the front, passing all ten cars, to make sure that no passengers remained in them. I sensed that I could not make it to the front of the train, and tried only to get back to my position.

As I advanced, the people seemed to move closer to the train, gradually narrowing the path until it became too narrow for me to pass without touching them. "Who got shot, black or white?" I heard a young man shout. Then I saw hands reaching out to grab me and fists aimed to punch me. Just as I was about to pass the third car, one of the punches hit my shoulder. At this point I realized there was a real chance that I could be—well, lynched—before the police arrived.

My heart pounding, I jumped into the car and began running inside the train, trying to reach my position. I no longer cared about any passengers remaining in the cars; I just ran. There were two more cars to cross, each separated by a pair of heavy, steel doors that open slowly. I wrenched them open with all my might. Meanwhile, the crowd seemed about to follow me into the train. I finally reached my position and, without any announcements or sticking my head out to observe the platform, shoved my key in and hit the door close buttons. The lights indicated that half the doors had not closed, meaning that people were holding them. When this happens, normally the conductor opens them again to let people in or out, but I refused to open up. After several tense minutes, people stopped holding the doors and they finally closed.

I hid in my cab for perhaps as long as half an hour until the police finally arrived. "What kind of people did you see running in masks?" asked a black bureaucrat dressed in a business suit. I refused to answer, for fear that mentioning blacks could get me in trouble. He seemed to be familiar with this attitude on the part of whites, because he calmly and understandingly said, "They were black, right?" He nodded his head in answer to his own question, and made a note on a piece of paper.

Later, as we were slowly moving into the service yard, accompanied by a police escort, I reflected on the incident. I recalled how many times I have heard liberals claiming that 99 percent of the blacks who live in these neighborhoods are "hard working and law abiding," with only a tiny one percent who cause trouble. Perhaps I'm prejudiced, but among the hundreds of people on that platform who looked as though they were ready to lynch me, I didn't see many who looked hard working or law abiding.

During the same summer, there was another incident, while passing Kennedy Airport. I heard something that sounded like an explosion. I investigated but didn't find anything that could have caused it, though the sound seemed to come from nearby. Then, as we pulled into the next station, I was notified over the radio that my train operator, a black woman, had had her windshield broken out by a stone block, the size of a child's head, thrown from somewhere on the airport's property. I then realized, that what I had heard was the sound of another stone smashing between the two cars, just missing my cab window. One of these rocks is heavy enough to kill a person easily. The train operator was lucky to be alive.

It is hard to believe, but I worked for two more years in the subway before I finally turned my back on that hellish job, in the summer of 1995. I now live in a privately policed community in Manhattan. I ride the subways only if an emergency requires it.

This article appeared originally in the January 1999 issue. At the time of publication, Daniel Attila was a junior at Columbia University.

White Man in a Texas Prison
by D. Zatukel

Demographers predict that some time around 2050 whites will become a racial minority in the United States. This status has already arrived for many of the several hundred thousand whites who have the least control over their lives: prisoners. They are forced to live in the most intimate contact with a class of blacks and Hispanics whom most whites have carefully arranged their lives so as to avoid completely. Forced integration has produced racial animosity in society at large; the even more intensive integration in prisons creates even greater animosity.

Prison administration is also a classic example of judicial dictatorship. At least in Texas, prisons are operated according to the desires of liberal judges, desires that would never be ratified by voters.

New Wave Texas Prisons

I am 39 years old, and have served 10 years of a 55-year sentence for aggravated robbery. For seven years I was confined in minimum- and medium-security prisons, but in 1992 I was shipped, without explanation, to the maximum-security McConnell Unit in Beeville, Texas. I believe that this was because I had been subscribing to racialist publications and was therefore wrongly classified as a "gang-related" prisoner.

Since this transfer I have been living in a "new wave" Texas prison that meets the standards established in the early 1980s by federal judge William Wayne Justice. The McConnell Unit is spacious, comfortable, and was incredibly expensive to build. It houses a maximum of 2,880 inmates but cost an astonishing $65 million—more than $22,500 per prisoner. The McConnell Unit and others like it are anything but penitentiaries. They are "resorts" for men who might otherwise be living in squalor. They are "recreation centers" where prisoners can practice sports and play games, and they are schools where inmates can study any number of academic and vocational subjects.

Judge Justice put great emphasis on sports, and the McConnell Unit shows it. The general population—that is to say, all but the 500 or so prisoners who are in solitary confinement, now known euphemistically as "Administrative Segregation"—live in four cell block buildings and two dormitories. Each dormitory houses about 300 inmates and is for "minimum custody" prisoners. The four cell block buildings, for higher custody prisoners, each house about 430 men.

For these six buildings there are four gymnasiums, each with a basketball court and a "universal" weight machine. Each cell block building also has an outdoor recreation area with a basketball court, weight machine, and two handball courts. There are other sports facilities at McConnell, so that the 2,400 men in the general population have a total of nine full-court and two half-court basketball courts, ten handball courts, ten "universal" machines, a softball field, and two full sets of "free" weights. This is a lavish complement of equipment even by the standards of fancy health clubs.

Many inmates, especially the blacks, devote themselves to physical conditioning. Many spend hours each day playing basketball and lifting weights; they are bulging with muscles and are an intimidating presence for inmates and guards alike.

In the day-rooms of the dormitories and cell-blocks, men can watch television or play chess, checkers, scrabble, or dominoes. These facilities are also lavish. For example, a day-room set aside for 60 men has two color television sets, eight four-man game tables, and seven three-man benches, and can therefore seat 53 men at once.

Anyone interested in education has an enormous variety of classes from which to choose, from remedial reading up to Master's degrees. There is vocational training in computers, electronics, drafting and a host of other professions. Until September first of this year, when a new policy came into effect, all courses were free—crime opened the door to unlimited education. Now prisoners will be required to reimburse the state for anything other than high school-equivalency courses or low-level vocational training.

Discipline

Criminals are in jail because they are rule-breakers, and a jail cannot be run without rules. Traditionally, there have been both "official" and "unofficial" ways to keep order. The official way is through formal disciplinary charges that can result in loss of status or privileges. For example, a prisoner may be denied commissary privileges, which means he cannot buy coffee, food, radios, sneakers, ice cream, etc. This is not much of a hardship. Ever since the ban on smoking in Texas prisons, the "store" no longer sells tobacco, which is what prisoners want most.

A more serious penalty is a reduction in class. There are seven status levels or classes in Texas prisons, including four categories of trusty. A reduction in class can mean that a trusty may no longer work unsupervised; a reduction to the lowest class means a man forfeits "good time," or periods of good behavior that can lead to earlier release. For prisoners facing a long sentence, this means very little. Even administrative segregation, or "ad-seg," is not much of a threat. A cell of one's own is luxurious privacy. Also, ad-seg units are the only ones with air conditioning; Beeville gets very hot and humid in the summer, so the worst discipline cases live in the best conditions!

The formal penalty system often does not work. It involves paperwork, which is a bother. Punishment usually goes into effect long after the infraction, and there are some men on whom it simply has no effect. Therefore, Texas prisons traditionally had an informal discipline system as well as the formal one. A popular way to handle an unruly inmate used to be to have him "stand on the wall" or stand in one place for a long time with his toes and nose touching the wall. There were occasional beatings and the threat of beatings. All this is now forbidden, and guards can never punish prisoners physically and may use force against them only if guards are, themselves, in clear danger of attack.

Guards therefore have very little real control. Take the case of the dormitories. They are supposed to be less restrictive housing for better-behaved prisoners but affirmative action has been at work here: blacks must be assigned to them in proportion to their numbers in the prison population. If 45 percent of the prisoners are black, 45 percent of the men in the dormitories must be black, so many aggressive, hostile blacks are assigned to low-security areas. The six-foot five-inch, 260-pound black who recently became my neighbor was quite surprised to be assigned to a dormitory; he was in close custody just before his move.

A white officer is making the rounds of a 55-man dormitory unit at 11:00 p.m. to conduct a head count. All prisoners are supposed to be in their bunks after 10:30, so he doesn't expect to find much activity, but he is wrong. Many blacks are up and carousing. Two are in the showers, some are at the latrine, others are visiting friends' quarters.

"Get to your houses or get an out-of-place case [Go to your bunks or face a citation for being where you are not supposed to be.]," orders the officer.

The order triggers shouts of "Suck a d**k, mother f****r!" "F**k you, whore!" "Get your bitch ass outta here, whore!" The officer says nothing as he waits for the inmates to get to their bunks. They deliberately move slowly. They repeatedly call the officer "bitch" and "whore."

One muscular black inmate blatantly ignores the officer's order and struts to the latrine. "Looky here, can't I take a piss?" he says.

"It's count time," says the officer.

An argument develops. The dorm resounds with shouts of "bitch!" "whore!" and "motherf****r!" The officer knows he faces the possibility of a riot and a serious beating at the hands of men who would love to hurt him. He backs down and lets the inmate use the latrine. His authority has been successfully challenged, he has been humiliated, his count has been disrupted, and his work has been delayed.

These are the well-behaved blacks. Officers face even more danger and abuse in the "medium" and "close" custody areas. These prisoners are discipline problems and have already lost most of their privileges and "good time." They have little else to lose. They may have jobs assigned to them but work seldom, if at all. Instead, they lift weights, work out, watch "rap" music on MTV, and play dominoes.

They know the restrictions on physical punishment as well as the officers do. They do not hesitate to get into an officer's face, shout abuse at him, and dare him to strike or touch them. Verbal attacks of the vilest kind are not sufficient cause for a guard to strike a prisoner, and any who do so are fired. Racial abuse of the guards is standard fare, though whites are now "bitches" and "whores" rather than "honkies" or "red-necks."

Because there is so little that can be done to punish them, prisoners in high-security areas exact special privileges from a system that has adopted a de facto policy of black appeasement. "Problem" prisoners are quietly allowed to ignore rules that forbid beards and long hair, and that require them to be fully clothed in the TV-game rooms. Known trouble-makers get more food than well-behaved prisoners because officers want to avoid trouble. For the same reason, officers rarely inspect the living areas of problem inmates—they don't want trouble. By contrast, men assigned to dormitories may not put up so much as a pin-up because it might offend female officers.

Race

What is it like to live in close quarters with underclass blacks? One of the greatest torments is constant noise. Blacks are always shouting at each other, banging around, making a din. The TV-game rooms, for example, are oftentimes scenes of pandemonium. Blacks congregate around domino games and yell at each other while the players slap their dominoes on the table as hard as they can. This combination of yelling and domino-slapping goes on for hours at a time: "C'mon, nigger!" BAM! "You ain't got nuthin,' nigger!" BAM! "Give me ten, nigger!" BAM! . . . . The racket and incessant shouting of blacks is so loud that many whites and Hispanics (and a few blacks) *wear earplugs 24 hours a day.*

Because blacks, as a group, are more aggressive than whites or Hispanics, they generally get their choice of exercise facilities or television programs. In any TV-game room with more than one television set, one set is constantly tuned to sports programs, which is what blacks want. Since blacks have rioted when they were not able to watch what they wanted, they have essentially been given their own television sets.

Whenever an important sporting event is broadcast, groups of blacks set up an ear-splitting din yelling at the television set. The noise is so loud it is painful to be in the room, and the yelling carries throughout the building. During the spring of 1994, the "sports only" televisions carried basketball play-offs until 1:00 a.m., seven days a week, for about two weeks. The policy of black appeasement meant that prisoners were shouting at the television late into the night, making it impossible for others to sleep.

Before Judge Justice rewrote prison rules, inmates were not allowed to talk in the chow halls. Inmates must now be permitted to talk at a "low level" but this restriction is ignored. Groups of blacks yell to each other across the length and breadth of the chow hall just as they do in cell blocks and dormitories. Meal times are a constant racket, and in the commotion, many inmates slip back into the chow line to eat again. Most officers will not confront an inmate who goes through the line twice, especially if he is black; other blacks would immediately take his side and there could easily be a riot. Perhaps as many as half of the black prisoners eat twice or more during each meal.

Since racial integration is official prison policy, it is difficult for a white prisoner to get a white roommate for his two-man cell. Over the years I have had four black, three Hispanic, and three white cell-mates. Even if a black or Hispanic "cellie" is well behaved, there is always tension in this unnatural integration. Generally blacks are provocative and make terrible cellies. About the only way for a white to get a "whites only" designation for cellies is to have inflicted serious violence on a black for racial reasons—and the punishment for this makes it a costly strategy.

Blacks and Hispanics have much greater racial loyalty than whites. Even most white criminals are racially passive and endure racial insults without reacting. I do not permit blacks to insult me, but if I were to fight every time I heard someone called "white boy" I would never get out of lock-up. Typically, whites are greatly outnumbered, and to make a stand for racial loyalty would be suicide. Some whites do develop a racial consciousness, however, and begin to look out for each other.

For Hispanics, the racial bond has an added dimension in that they normally speak Spanish to each other. In the old days they were required to speak English, but Spanish is now a civil right. Nevertheless, whites and Hispanics tend to have a lot in common and share a similar temperament. Hispanics appear to be a bit more emotional than whites, but blacks are very emotional and aggressive. Whites and Hispanics share an antipathy towards blacks and will work together when faced with a black threat. There is only a small amount of fraternization across racial lines and most prisoners would clearly prefer the old segregated system.

Race riots are common in integrated prisons. They generally start when whites or Hispanics get fed up with being pushed around by blacks. Tension builds up between the races until it explodes in a riot.

In one "close custody" unit (a high-security building for prisoners with discipline problems) there has been an ongoing war between blacks and Hispanics that started soon after the unit opened in October 1992. The Hispanics got very annoyed at black rudeness, yelling, domino slapping, and at blacks who would masturbate when Hispanic female guards were in the area (see below).

One Friday evening, groups of blacks and Hispanics were watching a televised boxing match between a black and a Hispanic. Words were exchanged and a fight broke out. The fight quickly spread as blacks and Hispanics began rumbling throughout the whole building. The fighting overflowed into the recreation yard and soon over a hundred inmates were hammering each other.

Dozens of officers converged on the area, wearing crash helmets and wielding shields and batons. They broke up the riot, herded the men back to their cells (and the badly injured to the hospital) and locked them down. As punishment for the riot the inmates were locked down for about three months. This means they had to stay in their cells for 24 hours a day, except for showers, and were given sack lunches, which they ate in their cells.

Shortly after they were let out, there was another race riot and the prisoners were locked down again. This cycle of race riots has repeated itself endlessly in this unit. The obvious solution would be racial segregation, but this would violate prison policy.

Riots with white prisoners are unusual because most whites are passive. However, there was one serious black-white incident during the basketball play-offs mentioned earlier. A dozen whites were watching a television movie but were told by a guard that they would have to let blacks watch the play-off instead. As usual, the guard was placating the group most likely to make trouble, but this time he got it wrong. As the blacks filed in to watch the game, one of the whites, angry at not being allowed to watch the end of the movie, pulled the plug on the television. There was a free-for-all with about a dozen men on each side, but the fisticuffs were soon broken up by officers. The incident could have been much, much worse.

One of the worst kinds of racial assault is homosexual rape—usually blacks gang-raping a white. This is known to happen in the McConnell Unit, but it takes place in maximum- and medium-security areas, about which I have little direct knowledge.

"Killing"

It may be a surprise to people on the outside to learn that Texas prisons are rife with public masturbation. Masturbation is now such a problem that prison trousers *no longer have flies or pockets*. Men used to cut holes in the front pockets so they could masturbate with their pants up.

Affirmative action means that there are now many female prison guards, and prisoners—mostly black—sometimes masturbate as they follow women around the cell block. Blacks have a special term for this: "killing." Practitioners of this lewdness are "gunslingers" or "snipers" and engage in "drive-by-shootings." White women are the preferred targets but any woman will do. Many killers drape a coat or shirt over themselves but some blacks expose themselves any time, any place, to anyone!

Until recently, a favorite perch for snipers was a set of benches beside the entrance to the administration building, where the secretarial pool works. Killers would take up positions on these benches and open fire on the secretaries as they walked by. It finally occurred to someone to move the benches.

The women's reactions to "killing" vary enormously. Some do not tolerate it and write offense reports for it. This can mean a loss of commissary privileges and, sometimes, a reduction of class. As explained above, if a man is destitute and is doing a long sentence, this means nothing. Most of the time, the women simply tell the offender to stop. Ordinarily this works. When the killing continues despite a warning, the offender is usually locked up in isolation for a short time. Again, this means nothing to a man who has nothing to lose. There are some women who ignore killing and do not react to it at all.

One attractive Hispanic woman who worked in the prison law library had a real problem. She was stuck at her workplace and, throughout the day, blacks would come into the library, stare at her and masturbate. She wouldn't stand for it, but was soon swamped with paperwork, filing offense reports. The unit warden eventually told her not to bother writing up reports, that he preferred less troublesome, "verbal" solutions.

Sometimes, if a female guard finds a prisoner attractive she will quietly encourage him to kill on her. Women like this to be done discreetly, in a cell or some other place where the two will not draw attention to themselves.

The ostentatious lewdness of blacks creates a lot of racial tension in an integrated prison. White and Hispanic inmates must endure the crudest racial/sexual taunting by blacks when white or Hispanic women come through the area. Blacks will put their hands down their pants and play with themselves or take off their clothes and decide to take a shower. Some will go to their cells and call to the women to come watch them masturbate—all of this in the presence of white and Hispanic prisoners. In the lax atmosphere of today's Texas prisons, there is no way to stop this disgusting behavior.

This is Prison?

The McConnell Unit is certainly a disagreeable place for a white man; life at close quarters with hostile, loud, masturbating, white-hating blacks is punishment enough. But for many blacks, a stint in a "new wave" Texas prison is about as close to country-club living as they are likely to get. They live in clean, well-maintained buildings. They get three square meals a day. They can work out, play basketball, and watch as much television as they like. They can humiliate white prisoners with impunity and even shout the most inflammatory racial insults at uniformed white officers. They cannot have sexual intercourse, but they get the thrill of exposing themselves to white women and taunting white men as they do it. Even the most drastic disciplinary measure—solitary confinement—means a transfer to air-conditioned housing. For a poor, black youngster from Houston, a stay in the McConnell Unit is a vacation. Who can be surprised to learn that more than half of the convicts released from Texas prisons are back within a year? Or that the Texas inmate population has grown 400 percent since Judge Justice's "reforms"?

And what about the guards? In what other profession must a man submit every day to constant racial slurs and insults—insults that would instantly yield huge civil-suit awards if the victim were black and this happened on the outside? In what other profession must women put up with men who follow them around masturbating and mumbling obscenities? This, too, on the outside is grounds for enormous compensatory damages. In today's prisons it is the inmates who punish the guards.

The kid-glove approach to prisoners means that the meanest, most refractory men—mostly blacks—get better treatment rather than worse. Since guards have so few meaningful ways to punish offenders, violations are ignored—essentially rewarded—rather than punished. Because everyone knows that blacks are likely to riot, even the guards see to it that they get their way over better-behaved whites and Hispanics. Wrong-doing and the threat of violence bring special treatment. One of the abiding lessons that an inmate learns in prison is that the authorities can be treated with the utmost contempt.

Federal control of the Texas prison system has been a complete though almost entirely unreported disaster. Unless the state manages to free itself from the tyranny of federal judges, prisoners will continue to laugh at the prospect of a jail sentence. Today, the central feature of a Texas prison is the basketball court. Some day, when Texans regain control, it may once again be what it was in the old days: the chapel.

This article appeared in the October 1995 issue. Mr. Zatukel works in the law library of the McConnell Unit. He has been supplying information on prison conditions to state legislators who are trying to take control back from the federal government. Mr. Zatukel will be eligible for parole in the year 2004.

The Myth of Diversity
by Jared Taylor

The idea that "diversity" is one of the country's great strengths is now so firmly rooted that virtually anyone can evoke it, praise it, and wallow in it without fear of contradiction. It has become one of the great unassailably American ideas, like democracy, patriotism, the family, or Martin Luther King.

The President of the United States glories in diversity. In May 1995, in a message recognizing the Mexican holiday, Cinco de Mayo, William Clinton said, "The Fifth of May offers all of us a chance to celebrate the cultural diversity that helps to make our nation great." A few days later, when he designated May as Asian/Pacific American Heritage Month, he said, "With the strength of our diversity and a continued commitment to the ideal of freedom, all Americans will share in the blessings of the bright future that awaits us." In his 1996 speech accepting the nomination for President, he asked the audience to look around the hall and take heart in how varied the Democratic party was.

In his 1996 Columbus Day proclamation, he said, "The expedition that Columbus . . . began more than 500 years ago, continues today as we experience and celebrate the vibrant influences of varied civilizations, not only from Europe, but also from around the world. America is stronger because of this diversity, and the democracy we cherish flourishes in the great mosaic we have created since 1492."

Appeals to diversity are not just for domestic consumption. In a 1996 speech before the Australian parliament, President Clinton noted that both the United States and Australia were becoming increasingly diverse, and added, "And, yes, we [Australia and America] can prove that free societies can embrace the economic and social changes, and the ethnic, racial and religious diversity this new era brings and come out stronger and freer than ever."

Hillary Clinton feels the same way. In February 1995, she spoke to the students of her former high school in the Chicago suburb of Park Ridge. She noticed there were many more non-whites among the students than when she was a student, 30 years earlier. "We didn't have the wonderful diversity of people that you have here today," said Mrs. Clinton. "I'm sad we didn't have it, because it would have been a great value, as I'm sure you will discover."

Diversity has clearly become one of those orotund, high-sounding sentiments with which politicians lard their speeches. Of course, the idea that diversity—at least of the kind that Mr. and Mrs. Clinton are promoting—is a great advantage for America is one of the most obviously stupid propositions ever to see the light of day.

Nevertheless there is one kind of diversity that *is* an advantage. A contractor, for example, cannot build houses if he hires only electricians. He needs carpenters, plumbers, etc.—a diverse work force. However, *functional* diversity of this kind is not what the Chief Executive is on about. He is talking about largely non-functional differences like race, language, age, sex, culture and even whether someone is homosexual. One might call this *status* diversity.

What advantages would a contractor get from a mixed work force of that kind? None. What are the advantages the United States gets from a racially mixed population? None.

The idea that status diversity is a strength is not merely a myth, but a particularly transparent one. Explaining why diversity is *bad* for a country is a little like explaining why cholera is bad for it; the trick is to understand how anyone could possibly think it was good.

In fact, diversity became a strength *after the fact*. It became necessary to believe in it because skepticism would be "racist." Otherwise intelligent people began to mouth platitudes about diversity only because of the blinding power of the race taboo. After diversity began to include sex, mental disabilities, and everything else that was alien or outlandish, to disbelieve in the power of diversity was to show oneself to be "intolerant" as well as "racist."

Of course it is only white societies—and white groups within multiracial societies—that are ever tricked by diversity. Everyone else recognizes the Clinton-Harvard-*New York Times* brand of diversity for exactly what it is: a source of weakness and dissension.

Immigration

Despite President Clinton's view that "diversity" started with Columbus, for most of its history the United States was self-consciously homogeneous. In 1787, in the second of *The Federalist Papers*, John Jay gave thanks that "Providence has been pleased to give this one connected country to one united people, a people descended from the same ancestors, speaking the same language, professing the same religion, attached to the same principles of government, very similar in their manners and customs . . . ."

This is not exactly a celebration of diversity, nor was Jay an eccentric. Benjamin Franklin, Thomas Paine, and Thomas Jefferson were all explicit about wanting the United States to be a white country, and in 1790 the first federal naturalization law required that applicants for citizenship be "free white persons." Until 1965, it was very difficult for non-whites to immigrate to the United States and become citizens (an exception being made for the descendants of slaves). Immigration law was explicitly designed to keep the United States a white nation with a white majority. It was only in the 1950s and 60s that the country turned its back on nearly 200 years of traditional thinking about race and began its long march down the road to nowhere.

Once the country made the mistaken assumption that race was a trivial human distinction, all else had to follow. Congress abolished not only Jim Crow and legal segregation but, with the Civil Rights Act of 1964, put an end to free association as well. The Immigration and Nationality Act Amendments of 1965, which abolished national origins quotas and opened immigration to all nations, was a grand gesture of anti-racism, a kind of civil rights law for the entire world.

As has been pointed out in such books as Lawrence Auster's *The Path to National Suicide* and Peter Brimelow's *Alien Nation*, the backers of the immigration bill were at pains to explain that it would have little effect on the country. "Under the proposed bill," explained Senator Edward Kennedy, "the present level of immigration remains substantially the same. Secondly, the ethnic mix will not be upset. Contrary to charges in some quarters, it will not inundate America with immigrants from any one country or area." The senator suggested that, at most, 62,000 people a year might immigrate.

When President Lyndon Johnson signed the bill into law, he also downplayed its impact: "This bill that we sign today is not a revolutionary bill. It does not affect the lives of millions. It will not reshape the structure of our daily lives, or really add importantly to either our wealth or power."

The point here is not that the backers were wrong about the bill—even though in 1996, for example, there were a record 1,300,000 naturalizations and perhaps 90 percent of the new citizens were non-white. The point is that "diversity" of the kind that immigration is now said to bless us with was never even hinted at as one of the law's benefits.

No one dreamed that in just 20 years ten percent of the entire population of El Salvador would have moved to the United States or that millions of mostly Hispanic and Asian immigrants would threaten to reduce whites to a racial minority in California by 1998.[1] In 1965, before the discovery that "diversity is our strength," most people would have been shocked by the thought of such population changes.

Today, the intellectual climate is different, but in entirely predictable ways. "Racism" looms ever larger as the greatest moral offense a white person can commit, and anyone who opposes the arrival of yet more non-whites cannot but be "racist." There is therefore no longer any moral basis for opposing the prospect of minority status for whites, and what would have been an unthinkable prospect before 1965 must now be seen as an exciting opportunity. Thus did diversity become a "strength," despite the suspension of disbelief required to think it so.

This is a perfect example of an assertion, for purely ideological reasons, of something obviously untrue. Like the equality of the races, the equivalence of the sexes, the unimportance of heredity, and the insignificance of physical or mental handicap, the strength of diversity is one of a whole series of fashionable absurdities.

Having started with race, diversity now includes just about anything. Feminists, angry people in wheel chairs, AIDS patients, militant homosexuals, and people who would rather speak Spanish than English have all taken

---

[1] According to the US Census Bureau, non-Hispanic whites made up just 46.7 percent of the population of California in 2000.

much of their style and impetus from the civil rights movement. Demands for "inclusiveness" almost always include the language of grievance and compensation pioneered by blacks. Fat people fight discrimination, ugly people struggle against "lookism," and at least one local government has required that the stage set for a strip tease show be wheel-chair accessible. Anyone who opposes the glorification of the alien or abnormal can expect to be denounced with much fanfare and finger-pointing. The metastasis of diversity is a fascinating story, but the disease began with race.

Occasionally a mainstream author sniffs around the edges of the population problem. At some risk to his professional respectability, columnist Scott McConnell of the *New York Post* has pointed out that if it will be such a good thing for whites to become a minority, there is no reason to wait until the mid-2000s. We could throw open the borders right now and become a minority in just a few years. "Why deny ourselves and our children the great benefits of Third Worldism that we are planning for our grandchildren?" he asks.

Advantages of Diversity

On those rare occasions when people actually attempt to defend diversity, the one claim they make with any semblance of conviction is that its advantages will become evident as the world becomes more "international." It will be a great thing to have citizens from all around the world as nations have more and more contact; specifically, our "international" population will boost American exports. Of course, since this view is based on the assumption that people communicate better with people like themselves, it is an argument against national diversity. If it takes a Korean to deal with the Koreans, how are Americans supposed to get along with the Koreans who live in America?

If anyone really thought a diverse population is good for trade, we would presumably be adjusting the mix of immigrants in accordance with trade potential. There would be no point in admitting Haitians, for example, since Haiti is a pesthole and never likely to be an important trade partner. After Canada, Japan is our largest trading partner. Does this mean we need more Japanese? No one *ever* talks about immigration this way, because no one really believes immigration has anything to do with promoting exports.

The example of Japan in fact shows just how little racial diversity has to do with international trade. Japan is one of the most racially homogeneous nations in the world. By American standards, Japanese are hopeless "racists," "homophobes," "sexists," and "nativists." They even eat whales. Here is a country that should therefore be a complete failure in the international economy—and yet it is probably the most successful trading nation on earth.

Taiwan and Korea are close behind, with China now recording huge trade surpluses with the United States. These countries are even more closed and exclusionist than Japan. If they could ever be made to understand the American notion of diversity, Asians would politely wait until we had left the room and then double up with laughter. Germany is likewise one of the world's great exporting nations. Who would dream of thinking this was due to the presence of Turkish *Gastarbeiter*?

The fact that millions of Mexicans now live in the United States does not make our products more attractive to anybody—certainly not to Mexico, which already has plenty of the things Mexicans know how to make. "Diversity" adds nothing to our international competitiveness.

Racial diversity is also supposed to bring cultural enrichment, but what are its real achievements? The culture of ordinary Americans remains almost completely untouched by the millions of non-white immigrants who have arrived since 1965. Perhaps they have now heard of the *Cinco de Mayo* festival, but even if they live in California or Texas how many Americans know that it commemorates a Mexican military victory against the French?

Immigrants do not teach us about Cervantes or Borges or Lady Murasaki and it would be silly to think they did. Chinese stowaways do not arrive with a curator's knowledge of Ming ceramics and copies of the *Tao-te Ching* in their pockets. The one cultural artifact immigrants bring with them is their language—which increasingly becomes an Americanized farrago that would astonish their countrymen—but the so-called "culture" of immigrant settlements is a tangle of peasant folkways, Coca-Cola, food stamps, T-shirts with writing on them, and truculence.

High culture and world history cross borders by themselves. Who in America first learned of Tchaikovsky or the Mayans from an immigrant? Nearly every good-sized American city has an opera company but it is not necessary to have a large Italian community in order to state Verdi or Puccini.

What, in the way of authentic culture have Miami's dwindling non-Hispanic whites gained from the fact that the city is now nearly 70 percent Hispanic? Are the art galleries, concerts, museums, and literature of Los Angeles improved by the fact that its population is now nearly half Hispanic? How has the culture of Washington, D.C. or Detroit been enriched by majority-black populations? If immigration and diversity bring cultural enrichment, why is it that the neighborhoods now being the most intensively enriched are the places where whites least want to live? Like the trade argument, the "cultural enrichment" argument collapses with a pinprick.

It is true that since 1965 more American school children have begun to study Spanish, but fewer now study French, German, or Latin. How is this an improvement? People can, of course, study any language they want without filling the country with immigrants. Virtually all Norwegians speak excellent English, but the country is not swarming with Englishmen.

Any discussion of the *real* advantages of ethnic diversity usually manages to establish only one benefit people really care about: good ethnic restaurants. Still, probably not even William Clinton would claim that getting an authentic Thai restaurant in every city is a major national objective.

Public Services

At a different level, it is now taken for granted that public services like fire and police departments should employ people of different races. The theory is that it is better to have black or Hispanic officers patrolling black or Hispanic neighborhoods. Here do we not have an example of one of diversity's benefits?

On the contrary, this is merely the first proof that diversity is a difficult burden. If all across America it has been demonstrated that whites cannot police non-whites or put out their fires it only shows how divisive diversity really is. The racial mix of a police force—touted as one of the wonders of diversity—becomes necessary only because officers of one race and citizens of another are unable to work together. The diversity that is claimed as a triumph is necessary only because diversity does not work.

The same is true of every other effort to diversify public services. If Hispanic judges and prosecutors must be recruited for the justice system it means whites are incapable of dispassionate justice. If non-white teachers are necessary "role models" for non-white children it means that inspiration cannot cross racial lines. If newspapers must hire non-white reporters in order to satisfy non-white readers it means people cannot write acceptable news for people of other races. If blacks demand black television newscasters and weathermen, it means they want to get information from their own people. If majority-minority voting districts must be set up so that non-whites can elect representatives of their own race, it means elections are nothing more than a racial headcount. All such efforts at diversity are not expressions of the inherent strength of multiracialism; they are admissions that it is a source of tension, hostility, and weakness.

Just as the advantages of diversity disappear upon examination, its disadvantages are many and obvious. Once a fire department or police force has been diversified to match the surrounding community, does it work better? Not if we are to judge from the never-ending racial wrangles over promotions, class-action bias law suits, reverse discrimination cases, acrimony over quotas and affirmative action, and the proliferation of racially exclusive professional organizations. Every good-sized police department in the country has a black officers' association devoted to explicit, racially competitive objectives. In large cities, there are associations for Asian, Hispanic, and even white officers.

Many government agencies and private companies hire professional "diversity managers" to help handle mixed work forces. This is a new profession, which did not exist before the idea that diversity is a strength. Most of it boils down to trying to bridge the gaps between people who do not understand each other, but since it concerns subjects about which management is afraid to ask too many questions, some of it is pure snake oil.

Maria Riefler has trained Nestlé, Walt Disney, Chrysler and Chevron. She likes to divide employees into groups that represent the body and the "triune brain." This is supposed to help them understand how "stereotypes are hidden deep within the primitive part of ourselves."

It is a very peculiar "strength" that requires the constant attention of experts and other buncombe artists. Like hiring black police officers to patrol black neighborhoods, "diversity training" is an admission that a mixed work force is a liability.

This is the merest common sense; it is hard to get dissimilar people to work together. Indeed, a large-scale survey called the National Study of the Changing Work force found that more than half of all workers said they preferred to work with people who were not only the same race as themselves, but were the *same sex and had the same level of education*. Even more probably felt that way but were afraid to say so.

These days there is much chirping about how diversity is going to improve profits. American companies are hard-headed about profits. A great deal of research, much of it quantitative, goes into decisions about product lines, new markets, establishing joint ventures, issuing stock or moving the head office. If there has been any serious research showing that "diversity" improves profits it would have been first-page news long ago. Not even the most desperate data massage seems to have produced a study that can make such a claim.

Just how big a headache diversity actually is for companies is clear from the endless stream of news stories about corporate racial discrimination. In just one month—November 1996—"diversity" made quite a lot of news. Texaco agreed to spend $176 million on black victims of company "racism," and lawyers for the firm that sued Texaco were getting about ten calls a day from people asking how to file for discrimination settlements. Just a few days later, 22 former employees of the nation's largest printing company, R.R. Donnelley and Sons, sued over what they claimed was $500 million worth of racism.

In the same month, both the US State Department and the Bureau of Alcohol, Tobacco, and Firearms settled multi-million dollar class action discrimination suits brought by blacks. Likewise in November, three blacks brought a class action suit against an Avis Rent-A-Car franchise with outlets in North and South Carolina, claiming they had been turned away because of race. Within the month, the owner of Avis said it would break its contract with the franchisee, and hired a law firm to check up on other Avis operators. Every one of these cases, which are expensive, time-consuming, and emotionally damaging, is a consequence of racial diversity—and these were just the cases that made the news.

It would be edifying to count the number of public and private organizations that exist in the United States only because of its diverse population, and that are not needed in places like Japan or Norway. The US Civil Rights Commission, Equal Employment Opportunity Commission, Office of Federal Contract Compliance, the Justice Department's Civil Rights Division, and every state and local equivalents of these offices exist only because of racial diversity. Every government office, every university, every large corporation, and every military installation has employees working full-time on affirmative action, discrimination claims, and other "diversity" issues.

Countless outreach programs, reconciliation commissions, blue-ribbon panels, and mayoral commissions fret professionally about race every day. Not one of these would be necessary in a nation of a single race. There must be tens of thousands of Americans consuming hundreds of millions of dollars every year enforcing, adjusting, tuning, regulating, and talking pure nonsense about the racial diversity that is supposed to be our strength.

Indeed, Tom McClintock, a former candidate for controller of the state of California estimated that before the 1996 state ballot initiative was approved to abolish racial preferences, the annual cost *just to administer* California's affirmative action programs was from $343 million to $677 million. This figure did not include the cost of private preference programs or the cost of state and local anti-discrimination machinery, none of which was affected by the 1996 measure.

If diversity were a strength people would practice it spontaneously. It wouldn't require constant cheer-leading or expensive lawsuits. If diversity were enriching, people would seek it out. It is in private gatherings not governed by some kind of "civil-rights" law that Americans show just how much strength and enrichment they find in diversity. Such gatherings are usually the very opposite of diverse.

Other Races

Generally speaking, whatever timid opposition to diversity that ever arises is characterized as the whining of resentful, ignorant whites. Non-whites are thought to have a better appreciation of the importance of inclusiveness. This is just so much more nonsense. Now that immigration has added Hispanics and Asians to the traditional black-white racial mix, fault lines are forming in all directions.

Though we are told over and over that it is ignorance and lack of contact that cause antipathy, it is groups that have the *most* contact that *most* dislike each other. This is why "outreach" and "bridge building" do not work, as even the *New York Times* unintentionally revealed in a June 18, 1990 headline: "Ethnic Feuding Divides Parade for Harmony."

The idea that hostility is cured through contact is now enshrined as part of the diversity myth. George Orwell noted the opposite in his essay, *England Your England*:

"During the war of 1914-1918 the English working class were in contact with foreigners to an extent that is rarely possible. The sole result was that they brought back a hatred of all Europeans, except the Germans, whose courage they admired."

In America one need not go overseas to have contact with foreigners. What has been the result? In Chicago, Los Angeles, Detroit, and New York City, blacks have tried to drive Korean merchants out of their neighborhoods. They firebomb stores, assault shop keepers, and mount boycotts against "people who don't look like us." In Los Angeles, relations were so bad that in 1986 a Black-Korean Alliance was formed to reduce tensions. It staggered on uselessly until late 1992, when it was dissolved in mutual recrimination and accusations. The more blacks and Koreans talked to each other the angrier they got.

There are now schools and school districts completely dominated by blacks and Hispanics, which have race wars involving no whites at all. Some examples? Locke High School in Los Angeles is almost exactly half-black and half-Hispanic. In February 1996, 50 police officers had to be called in to break up a pitched battle involving hundreds of students. After order was finally restored and school dismissed, police in riot gear had to keep students from rejoining battle in the streets. What touched off the battle? Hispanics were annoyed—certainly not "enriched"—by the February observances of Black History Month.

A similar incident took place at Los Angeles' North Hollywood High School, when it took police in riot gear to calm a melee that started when an estimated 200 to 700 black and Hispanic students pitched into each other. The spark was reportedly a clash over what kind of music to play at the homecoming dance, neither side having felt particularly "inclusive."

Norman Thomas High School is located at Park Avenue and 33rd Street in Manhattan. In 1992, tension between blacks and Hispanics erupted into a free-for-all involving both boys and girls. "The only thing people cared about was skin color," explained one 16-year-old. The New York City Board of Education has "rapid mobilization guards" for just such emergencies.

Farragut High School in Chicago is two-thirds Hispanic and one-third black. Recently, racial tension built up to what the principal called "total polarization," and it became dangerous to let students mix without police supervision. At the height of the tension, extracurricular activities were canceled for 30 days and the school's homecoming football game had to be played without a single student in the stands, for fear they would attack each other.

In Huntsville, Texas, Hispanic students say they need to arm themselves against violent blacks. In Dallas, Hispanic parents say their children are afraid to go to school for fear of attacks by blacks. Tensions of this kind are usually reported only in local newspapers, and are probably quite widespread.

There is the same racial animosity in jails. Guards keep some cell blocks in a near-constant state of lock-down because blacks and Hispanics kill each other if they are allowed to mingle. Life in prison is more intensely integrated than anywhere else in the country. If diversity is such a good thing why is racial segregation always one of the top demands when prisoners list their grievances?

Of course, high-school fistfights and jailhouse brawls are nothing compared to what can happen when diversity really goes wrong. In the summer of 1967, 83 people were killed and nearly 2,000 injured when blacks rioted all across the country. The National Guard had to be called out to stop violence in Tampa, Cincinnati, Atlanta, Newark, northern New Jersey, and Detroit.

Nor are race riots a relic from the 1960s. The single worst outbreak in the nation's history was in Los Angeles in 1992, when rioters killed 58 people and injured more than 2,300. They also burned 5,300 buildings, causing nearly a billion dollars in damage. There was smaller-scale violence—all of it directed at whites—in Atlanta, Las Vegas, New York City, and Richmond and San Jose, California.

The Los Angeles riots showed that Hispanics can behave as badly as blacks. Although the grievance was ostensibly about a miscarriage of justice for the black criminal, Rodney King, more than half of the 15,000 people arrested for looting were Hispanic.

"Diversity" can pit one set of Hispanics against another. Puerto Ricans in Miami have rioted, claiming to have been excluded by the city's Cuban power structure. "Cubans get everything; we get nothing," explained one rioter. The greater the diversity, the more varied the possibilities for disaffection and violence.

There has been a Sahara of hot air about why blacks riot, with the official pronouncement on reasons dating back to the Kerner Commission Report of 1968: "[T]he most fundamental is the racial attitude and behavior of white Americans toward black Americans." Whatever one may think of this finding, there is one conclusion no one can deny: Race riots cannot happen without racial diversity.

An occasional glance at a newspaper is all it takes to learn that diversity of the kind that is supposed to benefit the United States is a problem wherever it is found. Every large-scale and intractable blood-letting, be it in the Middle East, Ireland, Burundi, or the former Yugoslavia is due to "diversity," that is to say, people who differ from each other trying to live in the same territory.

Most of the time, the reasons for discord are not even as salient as race. They can be religion, language, or ethnicity. From time to time, Americans have fought each other for these reasons, but race is the deepest, most constant source of antipathy. Unlike language or religion, race cannot change. Differences between men that are written into their bodies will always be a source of friction.

The Diversity Double Standard

Diversity, of course, is only for whites. Wherever only whites gather charges of "racism" cannot be long in coming. On the other hand, it would be tedious to list the racially exclusive non-white gatherings the country takes for granted. Shule Mandela Academy in East Palo Alto, California, is only a little more outspoken than most when its students meet every morning and pledge to "think black, act black, speak black, buy black, pray black, love black, and live black."

The same racial double standard is found in national policies. It is only white nations—Canada, the United States, and Australia—that permit large-scale immigration. Non-white nations are careful to maintain racial and cultural homogeneity and most permit essentially no immigration at all.

Some nations, of course, could attract no immigrants even if they wanted to; there is not much pressure on the borders of Bolivia or Uganda. However, as soon as Third World countries become even only a little bit more prosperous than their neighbors they quickly become keen to keep strangers out. Malaysia, for example, recently announced that in the case of repeat offenders, it will flog illegal aliens, their employers, and anyone who smuggles them into the country. The Ivory Coast, which is better-run and more successful than its West African neighbors, has launched an *Ivoirite* (Ivorianness) campaign to expel all residents who cannot prove that their grandparents were born within the national territory.

Even nations that are unattractive to immigrants sometimes display their feelings about diversity by expelling the few aliens who arrived in the past. Idi Amin became ruler of Uganda in 1971. The very next year, his government expelled the 70,000 to 80,000 Indians and Pakistanis whom the British had brought in to be merchants. Black Ugandans, who did not like dealing with people unlike themselves, were delighted.

Hundreds of thousands of poor Mexicans sneak into the United States every year, but even Mexico is attractive to some Central Americans, whose countries are poorer still. Mexico guards its southern border with military troops, and is ruthless about expelling illegals. Not even United States citizens have an easy time moving to Mexico, which has no intention of diluting its national culture in the name of diversity.

Only whites talk about the advantages of diversity at their own expense. One of the alleged advantages is so nutty, it is hard to believe it can be proposed by people capable of human speech, but since we are shooting fish in a barrel why not fire a final round? We are told that since whites are a minority of the world population (they are about 15 percent of the total), they should happily reconcile themselves to minority status in America, that such a status will be good training for life on an ever-shrinking planet.

Of course, in a world-wide context, every human group is a minority. There are many more of everyone else than there are Hispanics or Africans, for example. Does this mean that Mexicans and Nigerians, too, should strive to become minorities in Mexico and Nigeria? Like so much that is said about race or immigration, this idea falls to pieces as soon as it is applied to anyone but whites.

It is only whites who have ever attempted to believe that race is a trivial matter, so it is only whites who think it may be "racist" to preserve their people and culture. Having decided to deny the findings of biology, the traditions of their ancestors, and the evidence of their senses, they have denied to themselves any moral basis for keeping out aliens. They have set in motion forces that will eventually destroy them.

E. Raymond Hall, professor of biology at the University of Kansas, is the author of the definitive work on American wildlife, *Mammals of North America*. He states as a biological law that, *"two subspecies of the same species do not occur in the same geographic area."* (emphasis in the original) Human races are biological subspecies, and Prof. Hall writes specifically that this law applies to humans just as it does to other mammals: "To imagine one subspecies of man living together on equal terms for long with another subspecies is but wishful thinking and leads only to disaster and oblivion for one or the other."

Human nature is part of animal nature. Racial diversity, which is promoted only at the expense of whites, is nothing more than unilateral disarmament in a dangerous world. If current population movements continue, and if the thinking of whites remains unchanged, there will be little doubt as to which group's fate will be the "disaster and oblivion" Prof. Hall so confidently predicts.

This article appeared in the July-August 1997 issue.

◆━◆━◈━◆━◆

Life Along the Fault Line

Elijah Anderson, *Street Wise: Race, Class, and Change in an Urban Community*, University of Chicago Press, 1990, 279 pp. (paperback), $11.95

reviewed by Thomas Jackson

Despite the official lip service Americans pay to racial integration, most whites live far away from underclass blacks and are glad they do. However, in a multiracial society, some whites will, inevitably live along the racial fault lines. Even middle-class whites sometimes live close to the ghetto and share parks and sidewalks with underclass blacks. How does this change the texture of life?

Street Wise, a fascinating account of just how powerfully race affects city life, is the result of more than ten years of careful observation of how the races deal with each other. The author of this remarkable study, Professor Elijah Anderson of the University of Pennsylvania, is black. He moves freely among whites but can also study an underclass world that is off limits to whites. He holds a conventional, liberal view of American race relations, but he faithfully reports what he finds, even when it contradicts that view.

Prof. Anderson never mentions the name of the city he studied, but it is probably Philadelphia. He writes mainly about a part of town, which he calls the Village, which was rediscovered by whites in the 1960s and is slowly becoming gentrified. Along with the attractions of its gracious old houses and convenience to the city center, the Village has a serious drawback that keeps gentrification in check: It borders on a black slum, which Prof. Anderson calls Northton.

In the 1950s, Northton was a well-kept, black working-class neighborhood, in which illegitimacy and welfare were thought to be deeply shameful. However, when housing in the suburbs became available to successful blacks they fled Northton and it is now home to all the underclass failings of crime, poverty, illegitimacy, welfare, and drugs. The working-class blacks who still live in Northton despise the underclass, though they do not use that term; instead, they talk about "street niggers," "lowlifes," and "pipers" (people who smoke crack pipes).

Welfare and Illegitimacy

The underclass thrives amidst welfare and illegitimacy. As Prof. Anderson explains, the young men of Northton take pride in fathering babies by different mothers and in doing nothing to support them. Sexual conquest and the deceit it requires are central to their lives, and the more blatantly they can exploit women the higher their status among other men. Marriage is the ultimate defeat. As Prof. Anderson writes, "If he [a young black] admits paternity and 'does right' by the girl, his peer group likely will label him a chump, a square, or a fool."

The young women long for marriage but console themselves with babies, and there is much rejoicing over a new-born child no matter how desperate the mother's circumstances. Teenage girls treat their babies like dolls, to be clothed as expensively as possible and paraded around the community. Mothers gain status if they have good-looking, light-skinned babies that other girls admire.

However, once a child is no longer a cute toddler, the mother is likely to lose interest in it and have another doll-baby to clothe and exhibit. Consequently, as soon as they are old enough to run, many children in Northton grow up with virtually no adult supervision.

Occasionally, if a woman can prove paternity she will sue the father for support. This is called "getting papers" on a man, or "going downtown on him," and makes sense only if the man has a real job. A man may therefore avoid work because he knows how many women would "go downtown" on him and how little would be left of his pay check.

For both men and women in Northton, a baby and the welfare income it brings are economic staples. On "mother's day," when the checks arrive, fathers appear and try to share the temporary wealth. As Prof. Anderson explains, "In cold economic terms a baby can be an asset . . . . [W]omen receive money from welfare for having babies, and men sometimes act as prostitutes to pry the money from them." Welfare is what fuels this vicious cycle of reckless procreation, but Prof. Anderson refrains from criticizing it.

Crack cocaine has had an appalling effect on Northton. People lie about in filth on the floors of crack houses smoking pipes and jabbing themselves with needles. Neighbors line up with television sets, stereos, food stamps, and anything else drug dealers accept in exchange for drugs. Women may wear no underwear so they can have quick sex in exchange for money or crack. These emaciated, glassy-eyed "crack whores," are universal objects of contempt, and drug dealers take pride in having dragged them down. They joke about stuck-up girls who refused them sex in high school but who are "now doing everything in the book."

The Color of Crime

Along with the drugs has come a huge crime wave and crime has a distinctive face. Everyone in Northton and in the Village—black and white, young and old—is afraid of young black men. They are a hostile, unpredictable element and their presence in a public place always means potential danger. Even young blacks recognize the menace. This is how one describes how he acts in the street:

"I watch my back. I observe everything, look in the bushes. . . . I never cross the street when I see dudes [other black men] coming . . . . When you cross the street, that means you're scared or you can't fight. . . . If someone bump into me on purpose, I keep on rollin'."

Just as Arabs did in uninhabited deserts and Medieval men-at-arms did in periods of lawlessness, young blacks have developed a set of greetings that are used to gauge hostile intent. At night, there is something like the military's "rules of engagement" that governs chance encounters with unknown blacks. It is important not to approach too quickly or come too close, or appear to be following someone, etc. Even the author, much as he decries "racial stereotyping," describes the elaborate avoidance procedure he used when he found himself alone in the street at 3:00 a.m. with an unknown black.

Black women in Northton structure their lives around fear of crime. If they buy a new appliance, they do it in secret. They may then cut up the cardboard box it came in and put it out with the garbage piece by piece. This way no one will see the box and think there is something in the house worth stealing.

Other women deliberately ingratiate themselves with teen-age neighbors by baking cakes for them or giving them candy. They wear their purses under their coats and wear no jewelry. If they are approached by a group of young blacks they will pretend to know some of them, and greet them with shouts of "Have you seen your sister?" or "How's Bea?"

Ploys like this do not work for white women, who are helpless prey. Young blacks know very well how much fear they inspire and sometimes feign an assault only to laugh uproariously when whites cower in terror. Some whites carry "mugger's money" so they will have at least a few dollars to give up; thugs who find no money on their victims have been known to thrash them.

When it comes to street encounters between whites and blacks, explains Prof. Anderson, "blacks have the upper hand." They know whites will run rather than fight. Blacks have the reputation of being willing to kill a man if provoked, so they can always make a white back down. As a result, says Prof. Anderson, "the white male is not taken seriously on the streets...."

Since whites are weak and despised, many young blacks taunt and insult then when they meet whites in public. One generalized insult to all whites is to walk down the sidewalk with a boom box blaring loud rap music. It is a way for blacks to claim the entire area within earshot as their turf. In the Village, impotent whites submit to this humiliation whereas if anyone walks though Northton making a noise, locals are likely to beat him up and break his radio.

Whites are the best targets for robbery, since a black runs little risk of resistance or injury if he assaults one. Interestingly, the only thing that changes the balance of power between black and white is a dog. Almost all blacks are reportedly afraid of dogs and give a white with a dog the right-of-way. As Prof. Anderson says:

"In the working-class black subculture, 'dogs' does not mean 'dogs in the house,' but usually connotes dogs tied up outside, guarding the backyard, biting trespassers bent on trouble. . . . When they [working-class blacks] see a white adult on his knees kissing a dog, the sight may turn their stomachs—

one more piece of evidence attesting to the peculiarities of their white neighbors."

In both the Village and in Northton, it is taken for granted that danger and hostility are one-way streets. As a black explains to Prof. Anderson, he could take an apartment in the Village and no white would trouble him, but a white who strays into Northton on a Saturday night is clearly in danger.

Prof. Anderson points out that many Northton blacks are ashamed of the reputation they have earned among whites. Some young men who understand why whites fear them, may go out of their ways to be polite to whites during chance encounters, and even explain that they are "not like that."

"Blaming the Victim"

Working blacks, who still believe in honesty and diligence, are more openly contemptuous and unforgiving of underclass blacks than whites are. To Prof. Anderson's chagrin, they are perfectly willing to "blame the victim": "[T]here are a lot o' guys out there who just don't wanta work . . ." says one man; "There's a different kind of black man today." A retired black tells him, "I'm getting like some of the white folks do. I don't want to be bothered with some of us neither."

Whites in the Village struggle against "racism" and recount their own muggings in earnestly race-neutral terms. Nevertheless, they learn to stay off the streets not just at night but also in the afternoon when the high school lets out. They learn elaborate evasion routines to avoid walking past young blacks. They put bars on their windows and buy expensive burglar alarms. Prof. Anderson finds that the new generation of yuppies is less forgiving, less "sensitive" about race, but older whites still talk about the benefits of diversity and wonder why they do not have more black friends.

Prof. Anderson concludes his book with a homily on how crime and racial hostility will get worse unless the government spends more money, but his heart does not seem to be in it. Elsewhere, he sums up the problem in the following house-that-Jack-built manner:

"The yuppie who is mugged and the [black] kid who does it; the old head [hard-working, older black man] who loses the respect of the kid, who impregnates the teenage girl, who goes on welfare, which raises taxes, which drives out local companies, which causes unemployment, which causes homelessness, which causes crime, which depresses property values and drives out middle-class residents . . . ."

The whole dismal cycle begins with the young black who mugs the yuppie and makes the teenager pregnant. Government wrote the welfare check that helped bring the young black into the world in the first place. Government spending will not reform him.

This article appeared in the February 1993 issue.

✦◇✦

White Might, Black Fright

Patricia Turner, *I Heard it Through the Grapevine: Rumor in African-American Culture*, University of California Press 1993, 260 pp., $25.00

reviewed by Thomas Jackson

Few whites are aware of the nonsense that circulates about them among blacks. Ever since the days of the slave trade, when Africans were convinced that whites planned to eat them, to the present, when more than half of all blacks think that illegal drugs may be part of a genocidal plot, blacks have believed all manner of things about whites.

Patricia Turner, a black associate professor at the University of California at Davis, has looked into today's anti-white rumors and tries to explain why blacks—even successful, college-educated blacks—believe them. She says they naturally expect the worst from whites because American society is so hopelessly racist that virtually any sort of white wickedness is plausible. Her book is therefore not just a study of credulity but also an exercise in it.

The Almighty Klan

One of the most persistent themes in the world of black rumors is the fearsome powers of the Ku Klux Klan. For example, during the 1980s and even up to the present, many blacks firmly believed that the Church's Fried Chicken fast food chain was owned by the Klan and that its food was doctored to sterilize black men. In 1984, a congressman actually had the FDA conduct mass spectrometry and gas chromatography tests on Church's chicken to see what was in it. Naturally, the FDA found nothing suspicious, but these results did not satisfy "the folk," as Prof. Turner often calls blacks. Some of her informants explained that the Klan would have had no trouble persuading the FDA to lie about the tests.

Another recent Klan enterprise is said to have been the Troop Sport clothing company, which was founded in 1985 and sold 95 percent of its clothes to blacks and Hispanics. The Troop name reportedly stood for "To Rule Over Oppressed People," and the linings of shoes and jackets were supposed to contain messages like "Thank you, nigger, for making us rich." Some young blacks who wore Troop clothes despite the rumor and subsequent boycott were attacked as traitors by other blacks.

Troop spent hundreds of thousands of dollars trying to fight the rumor. It hired the black singing group Gladys Night and the Pips to improve its image and posted anti-Klan posters in stores. The campaign failed and Troop went bankrupt, though the company denied that the boycott was the cause.

Prof. Turner tells us that the most recent alleged Klan front has been the Brooklyn Bottling Company, which sells a soda called Tropical Fantasy.

Like Church's chicken, the soda was said to be laced with a drug that would sterilize black men. There is no odorless, tasteless substance that sterilizes anyone, much less only black men, but the FDA duly trotted out its mass spectrometers and cleared Tropical Fantasy. The rumor was unaffected and caused serious losses for Brooklyn Bottling. It also provoked violence; blacks attacked delivery trucks and roughed up storekeepers who stocked Tropical Fantasy.

"The folk" credit the Klan with other achievements. It is said to have killed John Kennedy and to be deeply involved in the tobacco business. The eponymous founders of Philip Morris and R.J. Reynolds are both said to have been important Klan members (despite the fact that Philip Morris was British), and Kool menthol cigarettes are suspect because of the brand's ominous spelling.

The Klan is likewise thought to have killed Martin Luther King, though the government may have helped. As one informant said, "I heard it was the FBI or the KKK—one of those groups." Prof. Turner notes that for many of "the folk," there is no real difference between the two.

Genocidal Government

If the Klan has fearsome powers, those of the United States government are more fearsome still. As noted earlier, more than half of all blacks are either convinced that the government supplies illegal drugs to blacks or that it might well be doing so. Many blacks think it was Ronald Reagan who started spreading guns and crack cocaine in black neighborhoods out of a deep-seated hatred for blacks.

One reason many of Prof. Turner's informants give for believing the government is spreading illegal drugs is their complete confidence in its ability to keep them out of the country. Since there are drugs in America it must mean that the government lets them in so that blacks will take them and kill each other.

The Centers for Disease Control (CDC), was said to be behind the Atlanta child murders of the late 1970s and early 1980s. During that period 28 young blacks were killed before a black was finally convicted of the crimes. Even today, the conviction is commonly thought to have been a frame-up. The CDC employed the FBI to do the killings, because an essential ingredient for the manufacture of wonder drugs could be obtained only by extracting it from the sex organs of young blacks. The comedian Dick Gregory helped promote this rumor.

Many blacks, including the actor Bill Cosby, also believe that AIDS was invented by the government in order to kill blacks. Prof. Turner herself isn't quite sure what to believe. She finds it ominous that when government agencies deny that they invented the virus they argue that bio-engineering is too primitive for that. She hints darkly that this may mean that the government might just spread deadly diseases among blacks if only it knew how.

Suspicions about drugs and AIDS are so widespread and so ridiculous that they have broken into the news but there are always other rumors on the go among "the folk" that whites rarely hear.

The Reebok shoe company funnels its profits to South Africa to prop up apartheid. Whites adopt Latin American babies to kill them and harvest their organs for transplants. George Bush started the Gulf War because there are so many blacks in the military. Colonel Sanders stole his Kentucky Fried Chicken recipe from a black cook who worked for his parents. The offices of Planned Parenthood are located in black neighborhoods to keep blacks from reproducing. The police deliberately let the Los Angeles riots get out of hand so that blacks and Hispanics would look bad on television. Clothing designer Liz Claiborne said on the Oprah Winfrey television program that she didn't like to see black people wearing her clothes. Miss Claiborne has never been on that program, but many blacks threw out their Liz Claiborne dresses. Whites are always up to some kind of mischief.

Explanations

Why do blacks believe this nonsense? Whites usually look for a rational explanation. When a company is said to be trying to sterilize blacks, its officers suspect that a competitor is trying to do them down. When the government is accused of wanting to kill blacks, the CIA and the United States Information Agency go looking for Communist propaganda.

Prof. Turner is probably right to argue that this sort of thinking is a waste of time. "The folk" are sufficiently credulous and sufficiently ill-disposed towards whites to cook up and swallow rumors without much outside help. Prof. Turner does not quite put it this way. She says that whites have been and continue to be so implacably racist that any kind of anti-black evil is plausible even if scientifically impossible.

The first part of her book is therefore full of ancient Klan atrocities that are supposed to justify today's delusions, and the rest is sprinkled with the usual assumptions about contemporary white wickedness: random blacks are often beaten up while the police look the other way, television promotes anti-black stereotypes, the government is hostile to blacks, whites won't hire blacks, the police persecute blacks, etc. In Prof. Turner's world, affirmative action does not exist and it is always necessary to assume whites are racists.

Her assumptions about sex take us deeper still into the world of black delusion. For example, we learn that the early Ku Klux Klan was primarily motivated by a sense of sexual inferiority coupled with latent homosexual desires for black men. Southern whites called blacks "boy" in unconscious acknowledgment of their Ganymede attractions, and lynched them because of this unbearable, suppressed homosexual lust. We also learn that Ku Kluxers stuffed wads of paper down their pants before they went calling on blacks so as not to appear insufficiently endowed.

Current anti-white rumors, Prof. Turner repeatedly points out, are filled with sexual elements: the KKK is trying to sterilize blacks, AIDS will exterminate blacks because it is sexually transmitted, white doctors need to extract something from black sex organs, etc. She stops just short of saying that all this is evidence of sexual obsessiveness *on the part of whites*.

Prof. Turner cannot bring herself to admit that black beliefs are aberrant or deplorable. Though she concedes that they may be tough on innocent companies that are smeared, she thinks goofy rumors are good for blacks. For her, rumors are "tools of resistance" because the catharsis of naming oppressors—such as the Klan and the FBI—gives blacks "a sense of power" and "contributes to an atmosphere of communal problem-solving." "Sharing the rumor and joining the boycott," says Prof. Turner, "enables individuals to perceive themselves as powerful." What must Prof. Turner think of blacks if she really believes that swallowing preposterous nonsense "contributes to an atmosphere of communal problem-solving"?

The truth about these rumors is more stark and unpleasant than Prof. Turner seems to think. If today's blacks think their government is trying to kill them or that the KKK can tell the FDA what to put into a report, they will believe anything. Of course, foreign correspondents in Africa stagger back to civilization with reports more amazing than these: sorcerers who can steal a man's genitals with a handshake, religious fanatics who believe they can walk on water—and then drown en masse, witches who call down lightning and must therefore be burned to death. Africans are champions of credulity, ripe for rumor, superstition, and nonsense.

Another element in these rumors that escapes Prof. Turner's notice is the implied omnipotence of the white man. Whites *could* stop illegal drugs if they wanted, or invent viruses, or sterilize black men, or prevent riots, or just about anything else. "The folk," on the other hand, are dolts who, with a little coaxing, can be made to buy shoes, eat fried chicken, take drugs, shoot each other, and get AIDS. This is powerful commentary on how blacks see themselves.

Finally, a message that whites ignore at their peril is the implication of what *blacks* would want to do to a minority in their midst. Do not their delusions of genocide reflect their own desires and fantasies? Whether it be Idi Amin's massacres or South African necklacings or corpses by the truckload in Burundi, Africans often make short and bloody work of their tribal enemies.

Much as she tries to blame "the folk's" fantastic beliefs on white racism, Prof. Turner unwittingly points to the depths from which they flow.

This article appeared in the February 1994 issue.

Pushing Out Whitey
by Joseph E. Fallon

Hispanics, as we are so frequently reminded, are the fastest-growing minority group in America. At just under 12 percent of the population, they are poised to overtake blacks, and massive immigration of Hispanics is the main reason whites are projected to become a minority sometime in the middle of the new century. There are now some 32 million Hispanics in the country, and the figure could more than triple to 98 million and 24 percent of the population in 50 years. Who are these people, what do they want, and who speaks in their name?

The four main Hispanic-interests pressure groups are the League of United Latin American Citizens (LULAC), the Mexican American Legal Defense and Education Fund (MALDEF), the National Council of La Raza (La Raza), and the Movimiento Estudiantil Chicano de Aztlan (MEChA). They have different histories and go about their work in different ways, but they are essentially united in their objectives. They promote the agenda of a racially- and ethnically-conscious group, largely composed of immigrants, whose interests frequently conflict with those of the majority. Indeed, these groups exist precisely because of these conflicts, and it is at those points on which Hispanic and American interests are *most* at odds that the groups are most active.

There are several general issues on which all Hispanic organizations agree. They want more immigration of their own people to the United States. They want as many government benefits as possible for non-citizens, whether in the country legally or not. They want to stop deportation of illegal aliens as a prelude to full amnesty. They want to spread the rights of American citizenship—some would include even the right to vote—to non-citizens. They want official recognition of their own culture, language, and national holidays, and as much public money as possible to promote them. To this end they want public school instruction and all government services in Spanish. They want place and street names, public monuments, and official observances to commemorate their history and their culture. They want recognition of Spanish as at least co-equal with English, and they support Spanish as the official language in areas in which Hispanics predominate. They want to expand all racial preference programs, and gear as many as possible to the direct benefit of Hispanics.

In short, Hispanics want the very things they would achieve if they were able to invade and conquer the United States. Many activists do not hesitate to describe their goal as *reconquista*.

The League of United Latin American Citizens (LULAC), which is the oldest and largest of the groups, was established in 1929 in Corpus Christi, Texas, by the merger of three rival, and often feuding, Mexican-Texan organizations: The Order Sons of American [*sic*], the Knights of America, and the League of Latin American Citizens.

Until the 1950s, LULAC was a middle-class, patriotic citizens' organization with an agenda of traditional "Americanism"—Mexican-Americans must learn English and assimilate to "Anglo" culture. It stressed an American rather than Mexican identity, and an integral part of its work was promotion of US citizenship and loyalty to the United States. LULAC rejected the idea that the American Southwest should be returned to Mexico, and opposed establishment of Spanish-language enclaves. Because illegal aliens from Mexico were violating US laws and lowering wages for Mexican-Americans, LULAC endorsed immigration control and supported President Eisenhower's "Operation Wetback," which sent one million illegals back to Mexico.

By the 1950s, LULAC had discovered litigation, and in 1954 it took to the US Supreme Court *Hernandez v. Texas*, the first "Hispanic" civil rights case. The Court overturned the murder conviction of a Mexican-American in Jackson County, Texas, on grounds that the composition of the jury was unconstitutional. Although Mexicans were 14 percent of the county, none had served on a jury for 25 years. LULAC argued that the absence of Mexicans on the jury violated the convicted murderer's 14th Amendment rights. Chief Justice Earl Warren wrote that "persons of Mexican descent were a distinct class"—neither black nor white—and had to be an explicit part of the judicial process.

This victory spelled the beginning of the end for the original LULAC. No longer were Mexicans trying to be like Anglos; they were a separate class with separate goals to be achieved by separate interest groups. The old shell remains: The official colors of LULAC are still red, white, and blue; the official logo is still a shield emblazoned with the stars and stripes bearing the name "LULAC;" "Washington's prayer" is still the official league prayer; "America" is still the official hymn, and members still recite the Pledge of Allegiance before meetings. But the LULAC that so vigorously championed traditional "Americanism" is gone. Today, it is an ethnic pressure group that opposes everything its founders stood for.

While the original LULAC asserted that Mexican-Americans had no interests other than those of other Americans, today its goal is the group entitlements clearly spelled out in its Legislative Platform displayed on its website (www.lulac.org).

Among its objectives: preferences for Hispanic small businesses; affirmative action hiring policies "to ensure diversity in all workplaces;" establishment of "Hispanic Serving Institutions" that would have "many of the same benefits provided to Historically Black Colleges and Universities;" more Hispanics at all levels of the federal government, especially in "key positions in the State Department, the Foreign Service and the United Nations;" appointment of 60 Hispanic judges; appointment of a Hispanic as the next Supreme Court justice; more "Hispanic-oriented programming in TV and print" as well as more Hispanics in "creative positions" in major media companies.

US citizenship is no longer important to LULAC. "Residents of the United States" are now eligible for membership, and they don't have to be legal residents. US citizenship is no longer a qualification for league positions, whether elected or appointed.

In 1954, LULAC supported immigration control and mass deportation of illegal aliens. Today, it opposes both. José Velez, head of LULAC from 1990 to 1994, has said that the US Border Patrol is "the enemy of my people and always will be." Needless to say, LULAC opposes having the military defend US borders—not even to stop drug smugglers—because "military personnel are not trained for border patrolling and might easily violate the civil rights of those they intervene with."

In the 1950s, LULAC recognized English as the official language of the United States. Today, it vigorously opposes any official recognition of English. In 1996, when the US House of Representatives passed the "English Language Empowerment Act" declaring English the official language, the league responded with an "Action Alert" claiming that "English-only is incredibly divisive because it sends the message that the culture of language minorities is inferior and illegal. With a dramatic increase in hate crimes and right wing terrorist attacks in the United States, the last thing we need is a frivolous bill to fuel the fires of racism."

Compared to the multi-million-dollar Hispanic organizations funded by the Ford Foundation, LULAC is a financial piker. In 1997, for example, it had revenues of only $250,000, of which $67,000 was donations. It received $150,000 in membership fees, which does not exactly square with its claims to have a membership of "approximately 115,000." That would mean dues of $1.30 a year, whereas annual membership is $25.00. At that rate, its $150,000 take works out to 6,000 members. At the end of 1997, LULAC had $322,000 in assets, mostly cash. In its IRS filing it listed only two directors—a president and treasurer—both unpaid. At the same time and somewhat mysteriously, it managed to spend $150,000 on salaries and $62,000 on travel.

Every summer LULAC holds a National Convention & Exposition, which can be a big money-maker. In 1996 it appears to have turned a profit of more than $1 million. According to its IRS report for the year, it spent more than $390,000 on conferences and conventions, which must have been flossy affairs.

Ford Steps In

Ironically, one of the reasons LULAC dropped middle-class patriotism for the ethnic hustle was that it had to compete with the more radical Mexican American Legal Defense and Education Fund (MALDEF) and National Council of La Raza (La Raza)—which were not popular Hispanic organizations but creatures of the Ford Foundation.

Perhaps the best book about MALDEF is *Importing Revolution: Open Borders and The Radical Agenda* by William R. Hawkins, on which this account draws heavily. MALDEF's founder, Peter Tijerina, was a disaffected LULAC chapter chairman who didn't think the league had followed up on *Hernandez v. Texas* with enough legal activism. He wanted LULAC to copy the NAACP Legal Defense Fund (NAACP-LDF), and in 1966, he sent a league member to the NAACP-LDF's Chicago convention. On the strength of contacts made at the convention, Jack Greenberg, president of the NAACP-LDF, arranged for Mr. Tijerina to meet Bill Pincus, head of the Ford Foundation. Mr. Pincus agreed to fund a new organization to push Mexican interests exactly the way the NAACP-LDF pushed black interests. Mr. Tijerina was MALDEF's first executive director, and, in 1970, Mario Obledo, former Texas Attorney General, became General Counsel. The Foundation then awarded the organization a five-year grant of more than $2 million.

Ford handled more than just the money. It appointed the executive director, decided where the headquarters should be, and the type of legal cases to pursue. At first, MALDEF brought cases about education, school desegregation, voting rights, job discrimination, composition of draft boards, and the status of anti-Vietnam war protesters. Ford thought this wasn't radical enough. It wanted precedent-setting cases to go all the way to the Supreme Court for rulings that would change the country. MALDEF duly redirected much of its efforts towards bilingual education and immigration.

In one of its most famous cases, MALDEF supported the plaintiffs in *Lau v. Nichols*, in which the Supreme Court required that non-English speaking students be taught in English or "other adequate instructional procedures." MALDEF brilliantly misinterpreted this to mean education in languages *other than English*. The fund also sued for free public education for the children of illegal aliens, and got what it wanted in the 1982 ruling, *Plyer v. Doe*. These are perfect examples—just like *Brown v. Board of Education*—of clever, foundation-sponsored lawyers getting the courts to do things no democratically-elected legislative body would do.

MALDEF cases are exactly the kind one would expect. It fought California's Proposition 187 that denied social services to illegals, and once it was voted in, filed a class-action suit challenging every provision. It filed suit in 1997 to abolish the requirement that Texas high school students pass the Texas Assessment of Academic Skills (TASS), claiming that the "test contributes to the high drop out rates among Mexican Americans and African Americans." The fund sued in California, claiming school textbooks were biased against minorities. A number of figures associated with MALDEF have demanded that US citizenship be eliminated as a requirement for voting. The fund successfully lobbied for the "motor-voter" bill of 1993 that allows voter registration at welfare offices or when applying for a drivers license, and discourages states from verifying an applicant's eligibility or citizenship. Needless to say, it is now defending racial preferences at the University of Michigan at Ann Arbor.

MALDEF opposes securing the Mexican border even to stop the flow of illegal drugs. When the federal government launched "Joint Task Force Six" to combat drug smuggling along the border, MALDEF filed suit to halt the project, arguing that "it would cause irreparable damage to the human and physical environment in the area." What does MALDEF want? According to Mario Obledo, who rose to become head of the fund, "California is going to be a Hispanic state. Anyone who does not like it should leave." In 1998, President Clinton awarded Mr. Obledo the Presidential Medal of Freedom.

MALDEF gets funding from corporations—AT&T and IBM in particular—and foundations. For the period 1991-1995, the total amount of "gifts, grants and contributions" to MALDEF was over $17 million. Between 1996 and 1998, MALDEF received over nine million dollars from just three foundations: the vast majority—over six million dollars—from the Ford Foundation; $1,200,000 from the Carnegie Corporation, and another $1,525,000 from the Rockefeller Foundation. The fund does not even pretend to be a membership organization. Other than gifts, its main source of income is settlements and awards of attorneys' fees in court cases. In 1995, for example, it collected over $1.1 million spread over a number of different cases. The largest award was $299,000 in something called *Lopez v. Del Valle*.

Another important source of income for MALDEF is fund-raising dinners, which it holds in places like San Antonio, San Francisco, Los Angeles, and Chicago. In 1996, the Los Angeles dinner brought in gross revenues of $306,000 but cheapskates in Chicago came through with only $135,000.

At the end of 1996, MALDEF had total assets of over $7 million, most of which was money in the bank. It reported $2.7 million in securities and another $2.7 million in short-term cash accounts. This was after it had splashed out $120,000 in salary and benefits to its president, Antonia Hernandez, and $93,900 to vice president Teresa Fay-Bustillos. Three other vice presidents—all Hispanics—got just over $50,000 each. A hired gringo, Al Kauffman, was the Senior Litigator who ran the legal work. He got $85,000, and his four best-paid staff lawyers got $50 to $60,000.

MALDEF spends some of its money training Hispanic law students to take over Al's job. In 1996, Ruth Flores at Columbia Law School got the Valerie Kantor Memorial Scholarship and Christina Mireles at Northwestern School of Law got the Helena Rubenstein Scholarship. Thirteen other Hispanic law students got lesser scholarships; two thirds of the recipients were women, as are the top two officials at the fund.

MALDEF also wants more Hispanics in the media. As it explains, because of "the powerful position the media maintains in shaping and molding the beliefs and attitudes of the general public," this important work cannot be left in the hands of gringos. The fund therefore dishes out $3,000 and $4,000 scholarships to promising young propagandists who fit the right ethnic profile. In 1996, the fund granted a total of 25 scholarships, all to Hispanics. It is probably safe to assume that citizenship or even legal residency are not requirements for MALDEF grants. If there were a similar organization that boasted about giving scholarships only to whites, MALDEF would file a discrimination suit.

MALDEF is an aggressive, well-funded group designed to advance explicit racial-ethnic interests at the expense of the white majority. Ironically, its support comes almost entirely from "Anglo" sources, without which it would collapse. Ford Foundation and IBM would be indignant at the idea of an organization that promoted white interests.

Ford's other raven-haired child is the National Council of La Raza ("the Race"), which was established originally in 1968 as the Southwest Council of La Raza. According to its IRS filings La Raza's purpose is to "improve life opportunities for Hispanic Americans." In 1996, its biggest single expenditure for this purpose was to throw fancy parties. Every year it has a Congressional Awards Dinner, a national conference, and an American Latino Media Arts (ALMA) program at which it gives "Alma" awards. In 1996, these soirées cost no less than $3.9 million, or more than a quarter of the budget. La Raza says the hoopla is "designed to communicate the needs and concerns of the Hispanic community."

Its other most expensive program is distribution of money to "Hispanic community-based organizations." In 1996 it handed out cash to dozens of groups no one has heard of: $126,000 to El Hogar del Niño, $9,000 for Chicanos por la Causa, $30,000 to Cabrillo Economic Development, etc., etc. The boodle added up to $1.3 million, but La Raza appears to have spent another $2 million just administering the distribution. La Raza also spent more than $1 million "to improve education by placing academic concepts and skills in a context familiar to Hispanics, and forming a network of interactive community-based Hispanic healthcare providers." It was no doubt in this latter context that it carried on its books a $81,000 ten-year loan to a dentist by the name of Carlos de la Peña.

La Raza operates a Policy Analysis Center, which claims to be "the preeminent Hispanic 'think tank'," and uses its findings to lobby for the usual: affirmative action, bilingual education, mass immigration, more hate crime laws. In 1996, the pre-eminent Hispanic think tank had a budget of about $700,000, or less than one fifth the party budget.

On policy, La Raza sings the same Hispanic song. It says increased immigration control violates civil rights, and that Congress' 1996 cutback on handouts to immigrants was "a disgrace to American values." It wants another amnesty for illegals and is willing to make threats to get it: "Our elected officials should not be surprised if their failure to act on reforms of these terribly unjust [immigration] laws is met with a firm response at the ballot box."

In 1999, La Raza made a big noise about anti-Hispanic hate crimes, warning about "a growing pattern of harassment, hate violence, and law enforcement abuse against Hispanics." In a report called *The Mainstreaming of*

Hate, it fussed about such people as Samuel Francis, "member of a number of hate groups," and Jared Taylor, who argues that "the existence of civil rights organizations [like La Raza] require Whites to organize in self-defense." The glossy, 50-page report never mentioned that the FBI lists Hispanics as a hate crime victim category but not as a perpetrator category; any Hispanic who commits a hate crime is officially "white."

La Raza is the richest of the Hispanic organizations, with total revenue in 1996 of no less than $14 million, of which $8.5 million was private contributions, $3.2 million was government grants, and $2 million was largely government fees and contracts. In other words, the US government gives millions of dollars every year to an ethnic advocacy group that criticizes immigration legislation as "a disgrace to American values." The organization makes no pretense of grass-roots or even Hispanic support, and like MALDEF would disappear if its gringo patrons came to their senses.

From 1992-1996, La Raza got a total of $38 million in "gifts, grants and contributions," and this doesn't even include millions in government fees and contracts. Over three years, 1996-1998, La Raza received over $5 million from just three foundations: the majority—nearly $4 million—from the Ford Foundation, $850,000 from the Carnegie Corporation, and another $850,000 from the Rockefeller Foundation. In 1996, the president of La Raza, Raul Yzaguirre, got over $180,000 in pay and benefits, and his two senior vice presidents got $115,000 and $85,000. Four other employees made more than $50,000.

La Raza literally has more money than it knows what to do with. At the end of 1996 it reported $2.6 million sitting in non-interest-bearing cash accounts and only $114,000 in securities. It listed total assets of $7.8 million, of which $3.8 million were grants receivable.

At La Raza, the ethnic hustle is not as tightly focused or subversive as it is at MALDEF. La Raza likes to throw parties and give money to Hispanic tenants' organizations. However, any organization that can raise $14 million in a single year has the means for serious work.

Movimiento Estudiantil Chicano de Aztlan (MEChA) is the youngest, most incendiary, and unabashedly anti-white of the four Hispanic organizations. It is mainly a student group, and its first chapter was established at UC Santa Barbara in 1969. It now has chapters of varying size and effectiveness at a number of universities and high schools. It is not possible to confirm numbers like this but according to Miguel Carillo, a Chula Vista High School teacher, there are MEChA chapters at over 90 percent of the high schools in San Diego and Los Angeles.

In English, the group's name would be Chicano Student Movement for Aztlan. "Chicanos" are Mexicans living in America, and "Aztlan" is the pseudo-Aztec name radicals want to give to the Southwestern part of the United States after they kick out all the white people and make it an independent country.

MEChistas, as they call themselves, combine very militant talk with old-fashioned Communism. Ernesto "Che" Guevara, of all people, is still one of their big heroes. Miguel Perez of MEChA at Cal State Northridge has explained that Aztlan would have a government that would be closer to Communism than anything else and adds, "Non-Chicanos would have to be expelled . . . opposition groups would be quashed because you have to keep the power."

Rodolfo Acuña is a MEChA advisor and a California State University professor. He has said that "the [demise] of the Soviet Union was a tragedy for us" and that "Chicanos have to get a lot more militant about defending our rights." At a 1996 MEChA conference held to condemn California's Propositions 187 (ending benefits for illegals) and 209 (ending affirmative action), he said "anyone who's supporting 209 is a racist and anybody who supports 187 is a racist. . . . You are living in Nazi US We can't let them take us to those intellectual ovens."

In 1997, a MEChA representative declared during a rally in front of Los Angeles City Hall: "When the people in this building don't listen to the demands of our community, it's time to burn it down!" This was not an empty threat. In 1993, to underscore its demand for full departmental status for Chicano Studies at UCLA, MEChA started a riot that destroyed half a million dollars worth of campus property.

MEChA spreads the word in campus newspapers such as *El Popo*, *Aztlan News*, *Chispas*, *Gente de Aztlan* (UCLA), *Voz Fronteriza* (UC San Diego), *La Voz Mestiza* (UC Irvine), and *La Voz Berkeley*. These choleric broadsides are generally paid for out of school student-activity funds. While an independent Aztlan is a distant goal, MEChA's shorter-term objectives are essentially the same as the Hispanic groups for grown-ups; it is just nastier about them. For example, the May 1995, issue of *Voz Fronteriza* gave the following headline to a front-page article about a Hispanic INS agent who died in the line of duty: "Luis A. Santiago: Death Of A Migra Pig." "Migra" is a derisive term for the INS.

Voz Fronteriza ("Voice of the Frontier") is located in San Diego, "Califaztlan," and celebrated 25 years in print with a photo spread of Pancho Villa-type revolutionaries on the front page and more recent shots of Central American female revolutionaries on the back. It also printed a photo of Lolita Lebrón, a Puerto Rican lady who helped shoot up the US Congress in 1954. Inside was a huge, center-fold of Guevara. The lead editorial sets the tone. Titled, "If You Can't Take the Heat Get the Fuck Out the Kitchen," its first sentence is "God damn, the shit has really been flying at UCSD." Writers like to use "Raza," capitalized, to mean Hispanic, as in "Three Raza students confronted the power structure last weekend at...."

News stories included information about how the US government plants drugs in Hispanic neighborhoods and warnings like: "The gringo colonial establishment will hunt down and frame anyone who refuses to denounce the principles of Raza self-determination." One article ends with *"Que viva Mao!"* [Long live Mao!]

La Voz Mestiza is a sister publication printed at UC Irvine. In a typical issue we learn that "the materialism in the everyday lives of North Amerikkkans makes them blind and incapable of free thought." One editorial addressed to capitalist whites ends with: "You've spilled enough of our blood, now it's your turn to bleed you fucken [*sic*] subhuman beasts." We also learn that "in the US as well as in other countries the US government only protects the civil rights of its white racist citizens. . . . Thus we are caught in the middle between those who want to enslave us and those who call for our extermination." The back cover is a photo spread of people like Newt Gingrich, Pat Buchanan, Bob Dole, and Jesse Helms with swastikas printed on their foreheads. "ILLEGAL ALIENS," screams the headline, with the further explanation that they are "demonic, vicious, barbaric, rapist, bestial amerikkkan[s]."

Voz Mestiza lurches occasionally into spiteful feminism, which is a little surprising in a Hispanic publication. One article about respect for women begins: "Ramming his dick up, penetrating, with full force of a 3 inch penis that pretends to be a work-horse of pleasure. She: a hole in the wall for his two minute pleasure." Yet another fine campus publication supported by the taxpayer.

MEChA has a rather spotty web presence that pushes the same general line. The home page for the University of Oregon chapter boasts that the "site is maintained in the USA by illegal Mecha aliens."

MEChA does not appear to have a formal, corporate existence and does not have a national headquarters. From an organizational standpoint, it is essentially a network of school-funded student clubs. Since it is not a nonprofit organization it cannot accept grants from Ford or Carnegie, but would probably only have to tone down its language a little to get them.

It is impossible to know how many Mexican-Americans feel as the MEChistas do. Probably very few hate America with such intensity. MEChistas probably get scholarships from MALDEF and become professors of Chicano studies, get jobs at CBS or the *Los Angeles Times*, or go to work for the innumerable little Hispanic groups La Raza supports. Whatever they do, they probably never completely lose their dream of throwing all the white people out of California and moving into a Beverly Hills mansion.

In the long term, what the more moderate-sounding Hispanics are pushing amounts to the same thing: more Hispanics, more preferences, more "multiculturalism" (which is just another way of saying more Hispanics), which can only lead to eventual domination, cultural and demographic, of the United States. Hispanics have a strong, entirely natural sense of peoplehood, of *la raza,* and want to refashion America in their own image. They are different from other groups only in that they have stumbled onto an incredibly rich country full of people who not only accede to their ethnic demands but actually help pay for them. These are heady times for the *re-*

conquista crowd, and will continue to be until the majority comes out of its trance.

This article appeared in the March 2000 issue. Joseph Fallon is a writer living in Rye, New York.

THE PAST

Race, Nation and the Soldier
by Steven Schwamenfeld

What accounts for the extraordinary expansion of British power in the 18th and 19th centuries? Most "respectable" academics offer economic reasons for British success against European powers, and take the view that Western technological superiority accounts for colonial expansion. My study of the British army of the Napoleonic era suggests a different explanation: the moral power of the British soldier, as manifested in his devotion to his regiment, to his nation and—when he was fighting colonial wars—to his race. Patriotic conviction together with contempt for foreigners made the average British soldier the best in the world.

The Invincible Duke

The British army under the command of the Duke of Wellington won 15 general engagements between 1808 and 1815 without suffering a single defeat. Its victories shattered the myth of French invincibility and inspired the resistance of the other European nations.

The most sincere assessment of British arms came from the enemy. The French marshal Nicolas Soult described the victors after his defeat at Albuera in 1811 with rueful sarcasm: "[T]here is no beating these troops in spite of their generals. I always thought they were bad soldiers; now I am sure of it. I had turned their right, pierced their center and everywhere victory was mine, but they did not know how to run." Another French observer, General Chambray, praised the British infantry for its "orderliness, impetus and resolution to fight with the bayonet."

A Prussian observer left this description of Wellington's army:

"For a battle, there is not perhaps in Europe an army equal to the British, that is to say none whose tuition, discipline, and whole military tendency, is so purely and exclusively calculated to giving battle. The British soldier is vigorous, well-fed, by nature highly brave and intrepid, trained to the most rigorous discipline and admirably well-armed. The infantry resist the attack of cavalry with great confidence, and when taken in the flank or rear, British troops are less disconcerted than any other European Army."

Although it is the Duke of Wellington's forces that are of particular interest to us here, the British infantry had long been redoubtable, and maintained its prowess well after the Iron Duke's day. A Spanish chronicler, writing in 1486, left us this description of a force of English bowmen:

"This cavalier was from the island of England and brought with him a train of his vassals, men who had been hardened in certain civil wars which had raged in their country. . . . They were withal of great pride, but it was not like our own inflammable Spanish pride. . . . [T]heir pride was silent and contumelious. Though from a remote and somewhat barbarous island, they yet believed themselves the most perfect men on earth. . . .With all this, it must be said of them that they were marvelous good men in the field, dexterous archers and powerful with the battleaxe. In their great pride and self-will, they always sought to press in their advantage and take the post of danger. . . . They did not rush forward fiercely, or make a brilliant onset, like the Moorish and Spanish troops, but went into the fight deliberately and persisted obstinately and were slow to find out when they were beaten."

Likewise, in 1854, two years after Wellington's death, the armies he had commanded were still an astonishing force. The battle of Alma, during the Crimean War, gave rise to this first-hand account:

". . . the Grenadiers and Coldstreamers [and Scots Guards], though under a deadly fire, formed into line with as much precision and lack of hurry as if they had been on the parade ground, and began deliberately to advance up the glacis toward the Great Redoubt.

"It was an unforgettable sight. The men marched as if they were taking part in a review. Storm after storm of bullets, grape, shrapnel, and round shot tore through them, man after man fell, but the pace never altered, the line closed in and continued, 'ceremoniously and with dignity,' as an eyewitness wrote, on its way. . . . The Guards marched into the Great Redoubt, and there was a shout of triumph so loud that William Howard Russell [correspondent for *The Times*] heard it on the opposite bank—the battle of the Alma had been won.

"A French officer turned to [British Colonel] Evelyn Wood . . . . 'Our men could not have done it,' he said."

How were the British capable of such feats of arms? It was partially the result of intense training. The great French military theorist Baron de Jomini believed only British troops were adequately trained to fight in a thin, two-deep battle line. It required a maximum of discipline to maneuver in this unwieldy formation; less trained troops required a deeper formation to maintain cohesion.

In addition, British troops displayed a tremendous corporate loyalty, not only to their regiments but to their nation. Almost alone among the armies of the 17th and 18th centuries, the British army possessed no permanent mercenary units. It was always a national force. As the historian of 18th century warfare, Christopher Duffy, writes: "the most pronounced moral traits of the English were violence and patriotism. . . . All classes were united in their contempt for foreigners." It was this ferocious patriotism that helped breed, in Samuel Johnson's words, "a peasantry of heroes."

The uniquely nationalist sentiment of the English soldier dates back long into the past. To quote historian Linda Colley: "a popular sense of Englishness . . . considerably predates the French Revolution." An Italian visitor to England in 1548 described his hosts thus: "the English are commonly destitute of good breeding, and are despisers of foreigners, since they esteem him a wretched being and but half a man who may be born elsewhere than in Britain." This was true not only of the aristocracy but of the common people as well. It was especially true of bowmen. They were of peasant stock but, in the words of the 15th century jurist, Sir John Fortescue, who fought at their side, they were the men whom "the might of the realm of England standyth upon."

The English archers of the Middle Ages left no memoirs about their contempt for foreigners, but their successors in Wellington's time did.

Here is Private William Wheeler of the 51st Light Infantry on Britain's allies during the Peninsular War (1808-1814):

"What an ignorant, superstitious, priest-ridden, dirty, lousy set of poor devils are the Portuguese. Without seeing them it is impossible to conceive there exists a people in Europe so debased. The filthiest pigsty is a palace to the filthy houses in this dirty stinking city [Lisbon], all the dirt made in the houses is thrown into the streets, where it remains baking until a storm of rain washes it away. The streets are crowded with half-starved dogs, fat Priests and lousy people. The dogs should all be destroyed, the able-bodied Priests drafted into the Army, half the remainder should be made to keep the city clean, and the remainder if they did not inculcate the necessity of personal cleanliness should be hanged."

Sgt. John Cooper of the 7th Fusiliers was no more complimentary about Spaniards: "The lower orders of this nation are dirty in their persons, filthy in their habits, obscene in their language, and vindictive in their tempers. Their houses are intolerably smoky and vermin abound."

Observations such as these are to be found throughout soldiers' memoirs. About the military prowess of their Iberian allies, Sgt. William Lawrence of the 40th wrote: "the smell of powder often seemed to cause them to be missing when wanted." Sgt. William Surtees of the 95th Rifles recalled the Duke of Wellington's jest about a Spanish division fleeing the field from the Battle of Toulouse in 1814; Wellington "wondered whether the Pyrenees would bring them up again, they seemed to have got such a fright." Surtees asserted that the Duke "did not indeed depend on their valour, or he would have made a bad winding up of his Peninsular campaign."

On first viewing a Spanish army, Sgt. Andrew Pearson of the 61st recalled: "Falstaff's ragged regiment would have done honour to any force compared to the men before us." Surtees wrote of the Spanish officer corps:

"In short, they had all the pride, arrogance, and self-sufficiency of the best officers in the world, with the very least of all pretensions to have an high opinion of themselves; it is true they were not all alike, but the majority of them were the most haughty, and at the same time most contemptible creatures in the shape of officers, that I ever beheld."

The British had an entirely different view of their own superiors. Rifleman John Harris of the 95th wrote this of his Brigadier, William Beresford:

"He was equal to his business, too, I would say; and he amongst others of our generals, often made me think that the French army had nothing to show in the shape of officers who could at all compare to ours. There was a noble bearing in our leaders, which they, on the French side (as far as I was capable of observing) had not; . . . They are a strange set, the English! and so determined and unconquerable, that they will have their way if they can.

Indeed, it requires one who has authority in his face, as well as at his back, to make them respect and obey him."

Harris frankly believed that the British aristocracy produced the finest leaders of men in the world.

Britain was very much a class society, but in battle the shared characteristics of courage, stoicism and perseverance united all. Thomas Howell, of the 71st Highlanders, was a man of some gentility, who joined the army as a private as a result of financial disaster. He had a difficult time adjusting to life among men of a lower class. However, he left this moving account of his rough-hewn comrades during his first battle with the French:

"In our first charge I felt my mind waver, a breathless sensation came over me. The silence was appalling. I looked alongst the line. It was enough to assure me. The steady, determined scowl of my companions assured my heart and gave me determination. How unlike the noisy advance of the French!"

During the Peninsular War, the British had a far higher regard for their enemy than for their allies. They regarded the French as brave, if erratic, soldiers and generally chivalrous. One of the few really negative descriptions comes from Sgt. Edward Costello of the 95th Rifles, and it is a condemnation of only a specific group of men rather than of the French nation. It casts light on those qualities that either impressed or revolted British soldiers.

After the capture of Ciudad Rodrigo in 1812, some French prisoners were present at the interment of British dead:

"One more careless than the rest viewed the occurrence with a kind of malicious sneer, which so enraged our men that one of them, taking the little tawny-looking Italian by the nape of his neck, kicked his hind-quarters soundly for it. I could not, at the time, help remarking the very under-sized appearance of the Frenchmen. They were the ugliest set I ever saw, and seemed to be the refuse of their army, and looked more like Italians than Frenchmen."

Wellington's men had a stoic pride that, in their minds, set them apart from men of any other nationality. A remarkable incident was recorded by Sgt. Edward Costello when he was recovering from a wound received at the Battle of Salamanca in July 1812. His hospital ward was under the charge of a fellow Irishman, Sgt. Michael Connelly:

"Mike was exceedingly attentive to the sick, and particularly anxious that the British soldier, when dying, should hold out a pattern of firmness to the Frenchmen who lay intermixed with us in the same wards. 'Hould your tongue, ye blathering devil,' he would say in a low tone, 'and don't be after disgracing your country in the teeth of these ere furriners, by dying hard. Ye'll have company at your burial, won't you? Ye'll have the drums beating and the guns firing over ye, won't ye? . . . For God's sake, die like a man before these 'ere Frenchers.' "

After Waterloo, Costello again found himself in hospital, this time in Brussels, and recorded something even more remarkable:

"I remained in Brussels three days, and had ample means here, as in several other places, such as Salamanca, &c., for witnessing the cutting off of legs and arms. The French I have ever found to be brave, yet I cannot say they will undergo a surgical operation with the cool, unflinching spirit of a British soldier. An incident which came under my notice may in some measure show the differences of the two nations. An English soldier belonging to, if I recollect rightly, the 1st Royal Dragoons, evidently an old weather-beaten warfarer, while undergoing the amputation of an arm below the elbow, held the injured limb in his other hand without betraying the slightest emotion, save occasionally helping out his pain by spirting forth the proceeds of a large plug of tobacco, which he chewed most unmercifully while under the operation. Near to him was a Frenchman, bellowing lustily, while a surgeon was probing for a ball near the shoulder. This seemed to annoy the Englishman more than anything else, and so much so, that as soon as his arm was amputated, he struck the Frenchman a smart blow across the breech with the severed limb, holding it at the wrist, saying, 'Here, take that, and stuff it down your throat, and stop your damn bellowing!' "

The Colonial Campaigns

Warfare against non-Europeans inspired a far greater sense of distance and alienness. John Shipp of the 87th, the only man of his era to win two commissions from the ranks, wrote of battle against the "Caffres" of South Africa:

"At every farmhouse in our line of march we found appalling scenes of murder and desolation. Whole families had been massacred by these wild people, whose devastations it was now our duty to check. So ignorant were they, that I am convinced they were unaware that murder is a crime. . . . The savage Caffre exults in these appalling sights. To his bestial mind the groans of the wounded, and the dying, are the greatest of pleasures. When the frenzy of the attack is on him he is wrought up to ecstasy, dancing and jumping about, and hauling spears at man or beast with reckless abandon. . . . I have seen them with [murdered] women's gowns, petticoats, shawls and things tied round their legs and between their toes, capering about the woods in a frenzy of delight."

Sgt. George Calladine of the 19th recalled his first encounter with Africans: "I certainly saw little naked children running about which, if I had seen nothing of them but their faces, I should have taken them for monkeys." Sgt. Pearson wrote of the "Caffres" with more sympathy, marveling at their physiques: "six feet six inches to seven feet, with most symmetrical figures."

William Richardson was a common seamen who served in the Royal Navy between 1793 and 1819. Before being impressed into the Navy he served on several merchant vessels, including a slaver. He recorded his impressions of the trade:

"Some people in England think that we hunt and catch the slaves ourselves, but this is a mistaken idea, for we get them by barter as follows: their petty kings and traders get them not so much by wars (as is imagined) as by trade and treachery, and when they get a number for sale bring them to the coast and sell them. . . . There was one of their petty kings who, when he came on board, would strut along the deck as if he had been one of the greatest men in the world: he was a little fat fellow dressed in a suit of coarse blue cloth edged with something like yellow worsted, but what spoiled all was that he had no shirt, shoes or stockings on, and his naked black feet and legs being dabbed over with mud and salt water, made him a laughingstock to the sailors; but did not put him out of conceit of himself."

Colonial wars were not confined to Africa. Thomas Howell of the 71st Highlanders recorded his none too flattering impressions of the Indians of Montevideo:

"The native women were the most uncomely I ever beheld. They have broad noses, thick lips, and are of very small stature. Their hair, which is long, black and hard to the feel, they wear frizzled up in front in the most hideous manner, while it hangs down their backs below the waist. When they dress they stick in it feathers and flowers, and walk about in all the pride of ugliness. The men . . . are brave, but indolent to excess. . . . As for their idleness, I have seen them lie stretched, for a whole day, gazing upon the river, and their wives bring them their victuals; and if they were not pleased with the quantity, they would beat them furiously. This is the only exertion they make willingly—venting their fury upon their wives."

These remarks concerning the physical characteristics of Africans and Indians (not to mention Latins) point to the British soldier's racial consciousness as part of his patriotism. This is not to say that the British soldier loathed non-European foes because of race; it was because of the latter's savagery. Sgt. James Thompson served with the 78th Highlanders at Quebec in 1759, during one of the North American campaigns of the Seven Years War. He witnessed the repulse of a British attack on the Ile d'Orleans: "When the French saw us far enough on the retreat, they sent their savages to scalp and tomahawk our poor fellows that lay wounded on the beach."

During the War of 1812, British troops this time found themselves allied to Indians. Historian Donald Graves describes an event that took place after the Battle of Lundy's Lane in 1814: "Sergeant Commins of the 8th and Private Byfield of the 41st watched with horror as an Indian 'busy in plundering came to an American that had been severely wounded and not being able to get the man's boots off threw him into the fire.' A nearby British regular 'filled with indignation for such barbarity shot the Indian and threw him onto the fire to suffer for his unprincipled villainy.' "

Sgt. William Lawrence of the 40th described a grisly encounter with Indians near Buenos Aires in 1807. A corporal and a private were killed while destroying native huts: "This was a great glory to the natives; they stuck the corporal's head on a pole and carried it in front of their little band on the march." Later: "As we marched along on our next day's journey, about two hundred Indians kept following us, the foremost of them wearing our dead corporal's jacket, and carrying his head—I do not know for what reason, but perhaps they thought a good deal more of a dead man's head than we should feel disposed to do."

Later the 200 Indians attacked Lawrence's party of 20 infantrymen and were easily repulsed, they "not liking the smell and much less the taste of our gunpowder." The Indian chief who carried the corporal's head was wounded and captured by the British. He was not killed out of hand but was treated according to civilized custom and left with friendly Indians to be nursed back to health.

It did not take long for non-Europeans to discover and profit from the differences between British and native warfare. Sir Evelyn Wood writes of interrogating Zulu prisoners in 1879 after the battle of Kambula:

"When I had obtained all the information I required I said, 'Before Isandwhlana [an 1879 battle in which a Zulu army of 20,000 routed and massacred 800 encamped British infantry] we treated all your wounded men in our hospital. But when you attacked our camp your brethren, our black patients, rose and helped to kill those who had been attending on them. Can any of you advance any reason why I should not kill you?' One of the younger men, with an intelligent face, asked, 'May I speak?' 'Yes.' 'There is a very good reason why you should not kill us. We kill you because it is the custom of the black men [to kill prisoners]. But it isn't the white man's custom.' "

The Englishman reportedly had no answer to this, and the blacks were later freed.

When it came to actual warfare against non-white armies, the popular conception is of an unfair contest with European colonial troops discharging advanced weaponry on natives armed with sticks and clubs. The truth was often quite different. In discussing Wellington's great victory over a Mahratta (Indian) army six times the size of his own at Assaye in 1803, historian Jeremy Black points out that "success owed much to a bayonet charge, scarcely conforming to the standard image of Western armies gunning down masses of non-European troops relying on cold steel." This contemporary historian refrains from analyzing how that small red-coated force achieved its moral triumph, and certainly does not discuss any patriotic or racialist motivations. The British commander knew better.

The Duke of Wellington is notorious for describing his infantry as the "scum of the earth." Yet this was most of all a description of their social class and their vices (drink above all). In battle, the British soldier was "the item upon which victory depends." On his return from India in 1804, Wellington wrote a memorandum in which he offered an explanation for the incredible achievements of the British, especially in India. It should be studied by all military "experts" who would deride the importance of national (and racial) feeling among soldiers:

"The English soldiers are the main foundation of the British power in Asia. They are a body with habits, manners and qualities peculiar to them in the East Indies. Bravery is the characteristic of the British army in all quarters of the world; but no other quarter has afforded such striking examples of the existence of this quality in the soldiers as the East Indies. An instance of their misbehavior in the field has never been known; and particularly those who have been for some time in that country cannot be ordered upon any service, however dangerous or arduous, that they will not effect, not only with bravery, but a degree of skill not often witnessed in persons of their description in other parts of the world. I attribute these qualities, which are peculiar to them in the East Indies, to the distinctness of their class in that country from all others existing in it. They feel they are a distinct and superior class to the rest of the world which surrounds them; and their actions correspond with their high notions of their own superiority. . . . Their weaknesses and vices, however repugnant to the feelings and prejudices of the Natives, are passed over in the contemplation of their excellent qualities as soldiers, of which no nation has hitherto given such extraordinary instances. These qualities are the foundation of the British strength in Asia, and of that opinion by which it is generally supposed that the British empire has been gained and upheld. These qualities show in what manner nations, consisting of millions, are governed by 30,000 strangers ...."

Thus it was through a sense of national superiority, of the white Briton as a being apart, that the British Empire was won and held. Years later, Wellington would state plainly (in a parliamentary debate on Asian Indian participation in the higher levels of the Civil Service): "That the white man has an influence [of a moral kind] which the black man has not." Wellington would scarcely have been able to credit the notion that one day British governments would discourage racial feelings among their soldiers. He praised the racial arrangements in the Southern United States, and considered them essential if America's liberal system of government was to survive.

An understanding of the role of race has not entirely died among the British. A ranker (a soldier holding a rank other than that of officer) of the Second World War has left us with an analysis of the motivations of his comrades in Burma. George MacDonald Fraser's bluntly honest account (put to paper in 1992) should ring as a battle cry for anyone interested in his own nation's defense:

"There is much talk today of guilt as an aftermath of wars—guilt over killing the enemy, and even guilt for surviving. Much depends on the circumstances, but I doubt if many of the Fourteenth Army lose much sleep over dead Japanese. For one thing they were a no-surrender enemy and if we hadn't killed them they would surely have killed us. But there was more to it than that. It may appall a generation who have been dragooned into considering racism the ultimate crime, but I believe there was a feeling (there was in me) that the Jap was farther down the human scale than the European. It is a feeling that I see reflected today in institutions and people who would deny hotly that they are subconscious racists—the presence of TV cameras ensured a superficial concern for the Kurdish refugees and Bangladeshi flood victims, but we all know that the Western reaction would have been immeasurably greater if a similar disaster had occurred in Australia or Canada or Europe; some people seem to count more than others, with liberals as well as reactionaries, and it is folly to feel that racial kinship and likeness are not at the bottom of it."

A measured statement such as this would not be tolerated in America, and this bodes ill for the future, especially the future of our armed forces. As long as the basic principle of racial kinship is denied by our leaders, America's very existence will be in peril. There can be no stability in a society which will not allow its members to favor their own brethren. An army that will deny its soldiers this right is an army on the road to defeat.

This article appeared in the April 1997 issue. Mr. Schwamenfeld is a writer living in Dundee, New York. He holds an MA in European history.

The War with Mexico
by Erik Peterson

April 25, 1996, marked the 150th anniversary of the outbreak of the Mexican War. Today, most Americans have been taught that it was an imperialistic war of aggression, and Mexicans cite the "illegal seizure" of their territories to justify the current colonization of the American Southwest. In fact, by contemporary and even by today's standards, the war was far from unjustified.

The conflict began with Texas. When the colony of New Spain broke free from its European namesake in 1821 and christened itself Mexico, it inherited vast lands north of the Rio Grande that had been only nominally under Spanish control. Texas was a remote wilderness, constantly terrorized by Commanches, with a Mexican population of only 3,500.

Mexico could have concentrated on subduing the Indians and settling its northern territories. Instead, almost from the first days of independence, the country was wracked by a series of political upheavals. The small, predominantly white, Spanish-speaking elite consumed all of its energies in fratricidal power struggles, while the Mestizo and Indian majority remained mired in poverty.

In order to legitimize its claim on Texas, Mexico needed to occupy it. Since it was unable to do this itself, the Mexican government enlisted the help of immigration agents or *empresarios* to recruit settlers from the United States. The *empresarios*, chief among them Steven F. Austin, acted as representatives of the Mexican government. They were authorized to offer immigrants cheap land in return for accepting Mexican citizenship and converting to Roman Catholicism. The Americans appear to have made a good faith effort to fulfill the first requirement but often sidestepped the second.

The new settlers created a frontier version of the plantation-based, slave-owning society of the neighboring Southern states. By the early 1830s, however, Mexico began to fear that the *empresarios* had been too successful: American immigrants outnumbered Mexicans four to one, and seemed likely to identify with the land of their birth.

General Antonio Lopez de Santa Anna became president of Mexico in 1833, and in 1835 abrogated the constitution and declared himself dictator. This act alone provoked rebellion in seven Mexican states, including Texas, but Texans had additional reasons for discontent. Determined to reverse the Americanization of the territory, Santa Anna had decreed an end to American immigration, abolished slavery, repealed the local political autonomy Texans had enjoyed, and announced he would forcibly settle the land with Mexican convicts.

It is hard to imagine policies better calculated to rouse the ire of free-spirited Texans. In 1836 they overthrew local Mexican garrisons and declared independence. Santa Anna promptly invaded Texas with an army of

3,000 men, but after several engagements was decisively beaten by Sam Houston's army at the battle of San Jacinto. Santa Anna was captured, and in order to gain freedom agreed to recognize Texan independence, with the Rio Grande as its border. He later disavowed this treaty, and Mexico waged a nine-year guerrilla war against its former territory.

The United States recognized Texas as an independent republic in 1837, and recognition soon followed from France, Great Britain, Holland, and Belgium. Despite strong Texan sentiment to join the Union, the American government demurred; Mexico threatened war if Texas were annexed, and the United States was unwilling to upset the delicate balance between slave and free states.

Western Destiny

The presidential election of 1844 brought into office a firm believer in what soon became known as "manifest destiny." James K. Polk was determined to complete the annexation of Texas, buy California from the Mexicans, and bluff the British into ceding the better part of Oregon. The Texans were impatient for a settlement, and Polk's predecessor, John Tyler, had welcomed the Lone Star State into the Union three days before he left office. If the United States had continued to hesitate because of Mexican sentiments, Texas might have remained independent or even accepted protectorate status from Britain or France.

As for California, Mexico's position was so weak it was bound to be supplanted soon, if not by the US then by Britain, Russia, or perhaps even the Mormons. Polk had reason to believe that Mexico would be willing to sell. In the meantime, if Oregon joined the Union the careful balance of free and slave states could be maintained.

When Texas joined the United States in March 1845, Mexico immediately broke off diplomatic relations and threatened war. Polk sent General Zachary Taylor with 2,000 men to protect the new state from Mexican depredation while annexation was accomplished. Nevertheless, Polk had every reason to seek a diplomatic solution with Mexico, partly because he was afraid war might break out with Britain over the Oregon question. He decided to send a special emissary, John Slidell, to Mexico with instructions to resolve all outstanding issues.

On the question that had caused the rupture—annexation of Texas— Slidell was not to compromise. Mexico had been unable to reconquer her wayward territory, whose independence had been recognized by the major powers. By refusing to accept the loss of Texas and by persisting in border skirmishes, Mexico had perpetuated a crisis on the American border that could have led to European intervention. Texas was now part of the United States.

Several other matters were open to negotiation. One was the settlement of $3.25 million in claims by Americans on the Mexican government. Mexico had recognized these claims under international arbitration, but had later refused to pay. Another issue was final determination of the Texas-Mexico border. As a Mexican territory, the Texas border had been at the Nueces River, but after their revolution the Texans claimed the Rio Grande as the border—without, however, establishing full authority in the disputed territory. Slidell was authorized to release Mexico from the $3.25 million obligation in return for recognition of the Rio Grande border. This was a reasonable offer, especially since Mexico had already, in effect, declared war, and unpaid international obligations were then considered grounds for belligerency. By accepting this offer, Mexico could easily have avoided war.

Besides these immediate questions, Slidell was to offer $15 million but, if necessary, propose considerably more for the Mexican lands stretching from Texas to the Pacific. If the entire tract was not for sale, he was to offer $5 million for New Mexico.

The Mexican government, threatened by a militant opposition and wracked by internal dissension, refused even to receive Slidell. This was a fatal mistake. The rebuff left Polk with no means to negotiate a peaceful settlement. He ordered Zachary Taylor into the disputed region between the Nueces River and the Rio Grande, but he warned Taylor not to seek engagement with any Mexican troops he might encounter. In the meantime, he made preparations to ask Congress to declare war, but Mexico forced the issue.

On April 23, 1846, sixteen hundred Mexican troops crossed the Rio Grande. Two days later they ambushed a US Army patrol, inflicting sixteen casualties and taking prisoners. Mexico "shed American blood upon American soil," and the war began.

The Mexicans, of course, saw the war as a just effort to retake what was rightfully theirs. Why, though, would they make war on the United States when they had been unable to subdue a breakaway territory? Astonishingly enough, Mexico fully expected to win. It had a standing army of 27,000 men versus an American army of only 7,200. French advisors to the Mexican army had an exaggerated estimate of its fighting prowess, which the Mexicans gladly believed. The generals intended not only to take back Texas but to annex parts of the United States. Indeed, the Mexican dictator of the moment, General Mariano Paredes, boasted that he would not negotiate *until the Mexican flag flew over the capitol dome in Washington*. The Mexicans were also counting on diplomatic and even military support from Britain, but the Oregon issue was resolved just before they attacked.

In his two-volume work, *The War With Mexico*, Pulitzer prize-winning historian Justin H. Smith described the war fever among the generals: "Mexico wanted [war]; Mexico threatened it, Mexico issued orders to wage it." By no stretch of the imagination was Mexico thrust into an unwanted war by Yankee aggressors.

American Arms

The military history of the Mexican War makes interesting reading and is a credit to the tradition of American arms. Throughout the two-year campaign, small but superbly led and highly motivated American units consistently outfought the Mexicans. The Mexican army, impressive enough in numbers and parade-ground panache, was utterly unable to fight a determined adversary.

The American war effort was not all glorious. Although the Regular Army behaved with proper discipline, some of the volunteer militia units conducted themselves so badly they created guerrilla resistance among previously noncombatant Mexican civilians. Also, the war was all-too-effective training for America's fratricidal tragedy just 13 years later. Among the junior officers sent to Mexico, 200 would go on to be generals in the Union and Confederate armies.

The Treaty of Guadaloupe Hidalgo ended the war in 1848 on terms advantageous to the United States. Mexico agreed to cede California, Arizona, Nevada, Utah, and the western parts of Wyoming, Colorado and New Mexico—in all, 525,000 square miles of land that contained virtually no Mexicans.

All but overlooked today is the fact that the United States forgave the $3.25 million debt, and paid Mexico $15 million for the ceded territories. According to the rules of 19th century warfare, after routing Mexico's armies and occupying its capital, the United States could have seized territory under whatever terms it liked. To have paid what it considered a reasonable amount *before* fighting an expensive war—estimated to have cost $100 million—was a magnanimous gesture.

The Mexican position today is that the United States stole Mexican territory. However, Mexico could have refused the money or promptly returned it. By accepting payment it ratified the transfer. Furthermore, only five years later, Mexico agreed to sell an additional parcel of land to the United States, which was to be used for the southern route of the transcontinental railway. The Gadsden Treaty of 1853 settled a number of disputes about the post-1848 US-Mexico border and secured 19 million additional acres of territory for the United States. In return, the United States paid Mexico $10 million. There was no threat of war or coercion. This freely negotiated settlement of the new border and additional transfer of land were further ratification by Mexico of the consequences of war with the United States.

In conclusion, the United States had ample to reason to pursue, in 1846, the course that it did. As a practical matter, the real issue decided by the war was whether Britain, France, Russia, Mexico or the United States would acquire the vast territories of the American Southwest.

President Polk resolved the question in favor of the United States in a refreshingly straightforward nineteenth-century manner.

This article appeared in the September 1995 issue. Eric Peterson lives in Oregon and writes about American history.

Forgotten Black Voices
by Gedahlia Braun

In the June and July 1993 cover story in AR on black claims for reparations because of slavery, there was a discussion about slaves and the conditions in which they lived. Your readers may be interested to know that during the Depression someone had the idea of sending people to the South to interview the last remaining blacks who had been slaves—all then in their 80s and 90s. Someone named George P. Rawick has compiled these narratives into a 19-volume collection called *The American Slave: A Composite Autobiography*, which is published by Greenwood Press.

Several books have been based on these interviews, and a few years ago I read one called *Before Freedom: 48 Oral Histories of Former North and South Carolina Slaves*. It was edited by Belinda Hurmence, and published by Mentor (Penguin) in 1990. I recall that of these 48 interviews only two could be called hostile to former masters, slavery, or whites. Some were more or less neutral, but certainly the largest number expressed a positive attitude toward former owners and to slavery. Here are some excerpts:

Patsy Mitchner, age 84 when interviewed on July 2, 1937: "Before two years had passed after the surrender, there was two out of every three slaves who wished they was back with their marsters. The marsters' kindness to the nigger after the war is the cause of the nigger having things today. There was a lot of love between marster and slave, and there is few of us that don't love the white folks today. . . .Slavery was better for us than things is now, in some cases. Niggers then didn't have no responsibility; just work, obey, and eat."

Betty Cofer, age 81: "The rest of the family was all fine folks and good to me, but I loved Miss Ella better'n anyone or anything else in the world. She was the best friend I ever had. If I ever wanted for anything, I just asked her and she give it to me or got it for me somehow. . . . I done lived to see three generations of my white folks come and go and they're the finest folks on earth."

Adeline Johnson, age 93: "That was a happy time, with happy days. . . . I'll be satisfied to see my Savior that my old marster worshiped and my husband preach about. I wants to be in heaven with all my white folks, just to wait on them and love them, and serve them, sorta like I did in slavery time. That will be enough heaven for Adeline."

Mary Anderson, age 86: "I think slavery was a mighty good thing for Mother, Father, me and the other members of the family, and I cannot say anything but good for my old marster and missus, but I can only speak for those whose conditions I have known during slavery and since. For myself and them, I will say again, slavery was a mighty good thing."

Simuel Riddick, age 95: "My white folks were fine people. . . . I haven't anything to say against slavery. My old folks put my clothes on me when I was a boy. They gave me shoes and stockings and put them on me when I was a little boy. I loved them, and I can't go against them in anything. There were things I did not like about slavery on some plantations, whupping and selling parents and children from each other, but I haven't much to say. I was treated good."

Sylvia Cannon, age 85: "Things sure better long time ago then they be now. I know it. Colored people never had no debt to pay in slavery time. Never hear tell about no colored people been put in jail before freedom. Had more to eat and more to wear then, and had good clothes all the time 'cause white folks furnish everything, everything. Had plenty peas, rice, hog meat, rabbit, fish, and such as that."

As I reflect on these interviews, they remind me of what I find now among non-Westernized Africans. They like and respect whites because, generally speaking, whites treat them better than their fellow blacks do.

In the introduction to this collection, the editor is at pains to explain all of these favorable statements about whites and slavery. The best she can do is to point out that these interviews were conducted in the midst of the Depression and people must have looked back nostalgically to the past when blacks had food, clothing, housing, etc.

Even if this could explain the fond memories of the condition of slavery, it does not explain fond memories of white owners. What is especially surprising is that after sifting through thousands of interviews, and with the clearly expressed liberal bias of the editor, there is still such a preponderance of positive expressions about whites and slavery. One is bound to conclude that this was at least a very common reaction if not perhaps even typical.

This article appeared in the September-October 1993 issue. Gedahlia Braun is the pen name of an American philosophy professor who taught for twelve years at universities in black Africa and Papua New Guinea. Since 1988, he has lived in Johannesburg.

The "Reparations" Hoax
by William Robertson Boggs

The latest attempt by blacks to extract race-based benefits from whites is the increasingly popular demand for "reparations" for the injustice of slavery. Although neither Congress nor any state legislature is likely to pass a reparations act any time soon, black activists are laying the groundwork for what they hope will be a massive transfer of wealth from whites to blacks.

The demand for reparations is based on a misguided understanding of the origin, nature, and consequences of slavery. Nevertheless, the climate of our times is one in which whites listen patiently to virtually any demand blacks make in the name of race. Preposterous as the idea can be shown to be, our country may yet be capable of handing over money to today's blacks in atonement for practices that came to an end 130 years ago.

The rationale for reparations is that today's blacks have a moral right to compensation for the unpaid labor of their ancestors. That right is not open to question; the only disagreement is over the amount of compensation and how it should be distributed. Activists' convictions are based in part on the idea that blacks "built America," that slavery was uniquely profitable and productive, and that today's Americans owe their material comfort to the past labor of slaves. The billions of dollars to be handed over to blacks would be only fair compensation for their ancestors' vital contributions.

Reparations activists were vastly encouraged by the 1988 Wartime Relocations Act, which provided for payments of $20,000 to each of the 120,000 surviving Japanese-Americans who were interned during the Second World War. Blacks also point to the billions of dollars Germany has paid over the years as compensation for its wartime Jewish policies. Payments have gone not just to individuals but to the state of Israel. Transfers of this kind set a precedent for punishing today's (and tomorrow's) taxpayers for acts their governments committed in the past.

Although many different groups around the country agitate for reparations, the largest and best-organized is the National Coalition of Blacks for Reparations in America, which has the African-sounding acronym of N'COBRA. The group is based in Washington, DC, and has chapters and affiliates in other states. Vince Goodwin, the group's co-chairman, describes slavery as the "the largest holocaust committed," and sees reparations as the only way America can "heal itself."

N'COBRA was delighted when Rep. John Conyers of Detroit introduced a bill in Congress to establish a presidential commission to study black reparations. Today, N'COBRA's main mission is to encourage the introduction of similar legislation both in Congress and in state legislatures.

Massachusetts state senator William Owens has actually held hearings on a reparations bill, and one has been introduced in Michigan. Cities with large black populations have passed resolutions calling for reparations. Detroit and Washington, DC, have both issued official demands, and the Detroit chapter of N'COBRA has taken to picketing the local federal office building.

The Urban League and the NAACP have gotten on the reparations bandwagon and Jesse Jackson has endorsed the idea. Former Harvard Law School professor, Derrick Bell, believes in reparations because "The struggle against racism requires action . . . . Anything and everything should be tried." Louis Farrakhan of the Nation of Islam has long preached a form of reparations that would involve turning over several American states to blacks, along with huge cash payments.

Even one prominent white, neo-conservative Charles Krauthammer, has publicly endorsed reparations. He says that payments to blacks would be better for them than "the warm glow of condescension that permeates affirmative action." Once the debt of slavery were paid off, America could abandon affirmative action with a good conscience and finally institute color-blind policies.

For the reparations activists, that would not be enough. Dorothy Lewis of the Black Reparations Committee explains that affirmative action and reparations are remedies for different wrongs. As she explains, "Affirmative action is needed to curtail racism that exists now."

Reparations movements are gaining ground in Brazil, Jamaica, and England. As Cindy Owens, wife of the Massachusetts state senator says, "The slaves built not just this country but Jamaica, the Bahamas, England and other places. Why shouldn't we all be paid for that labor?"

Even the dark continent has caught reparations fever. In 1991, President Ibrahim Babangida of Nigeria made a public demand that Africa be compensated for the people it lost in the slave trade, and he is planning an international conference this summer [1993] to flesh out details. Speakers will include Nelson Mandela of the African National Congress and President Robert Mugabe of Zimbabwe.

There is great fun to be had in calculating the damages to be awarded. Andrew Jenkins, a Detroit real estate agent who has been a reparations activist for 27 years, says every black in the country is entitled to $1 million. It does not seem to bother him that this would work out to about $30 trillion, or the equivalent of the entire federal budget for the past 20 or so years. State Sen. Owens of Massachusetts is more modest. He calculates the debt at only $3 trillion, with perhaps another trillion in back interest.

One favorite way to calculate the debt is to figure what 40 acres and a mule were worth in 1865, and then add the accumulated interest up to the present. A theorist in Washington state concludes that this works out to $98,191.35 per black person. Mr. Krauthammer's is the stingiest proposal of all: $100,000 for every black family of four.

Like so much of what our country says and does in the name of race, all this is pure lunacy. First, slave owners certainly did buy and sell slaves and forced them to work without wages. However, all slaves and slave owners are dead. There is no legal basis either for punishing distant descendants for the wrong-doing of their ancestors or for rewarding the distant descendants of those who were wronged.

The parallel between compensation for interned Japanese and today's blacks is tenuous. First, only those who were actually interned have been compensated. Surviving children get nothing. Furthermore, internment was a deliberate act of the United States government, so a case can be made for government redress. Slavery was a private practice regulated by states and localities. The federal government never owned a single slave. When it abolished slavery it ended a private practice that had begun more than a century before the federal government even existed.

Those who ignore these obvious arguments and nevertheless insist on government compensation do so because they believe two things: that slavery was a unique and unparalleled evil done by whites to blacks, and that it was so productive America would have remained poor without it. The first of these ideas has been so widely promoted it is almost an article of faith, and it is worth looking into slavery in some detail in order to refute both charges.

The Slave Trade

Slavery and the trade in human property were well established on the continent long before Europeans ever arrived. There is no record of whites ever venturing into the interior of Africa in search of slaves; they had no need to. The 800,000 or so blacks who were brought to the United States were first captured by Africans and delivered to the coast by professional African slave traders.

Slaves were usually captured in tribal wars, but Africans had learned that it was impractical to enslave people from neighboring tribes, since they could easily escape back to their own people. Captives were therefore sold to traders who resold them only after they had marched the slaves so far from home they could not return. This infrastructure was easily adapted to meet the needs of white slave merchants.

Nevertheless, the trans-Atlantic trade had some requirements different from those of the traditional inter-tribal trade. In African warfare, the usual practice was to enslave captured women and children but to kill all male prisoners. It was an agreeable surprise for Africans to discover a profitable export market for men. Many of the slaves who were marched in coffles to the sea would therefore have been slaughtered had there been no demand for them in the New World.

Some Africans formed raiding parties specifically to supply European slavers, but the primary source for the trans-Atlantic trade was the overflow of captives from tribal warfare. The most promising slaving sites therefore moved up and down the coast, depending on the fortunes of war. When there was peace along the Gambia river, operations shifted to the Sassandra or the Konkoure.

Whites certainly did not rob Africa of its manhood. Unlike the Africans who supplied them, whites paid for what they got. If today's Africans have a quarrel, it is with their own warfaring ancestors rather than with whites.

As for American blacks, the idea that they should be paid because of the injustices done to their ancestors crumbles when one compares their present state with that of Africans. There has never been a group of blacks anywhere in the history of the world that has enjoyed the material prosperity of American blacks. Even the poorest American black is vastly better off than the average African. Whatever one may say about the wrongs that were done to slaves, their descendants have every reason to be grateful their ancestors were shipped to America rather than killed or left in Africa.

The high standard of living blacks enjoy in America is due to the fact that they live among whites. For an example of the kind of society they would have built for themselves one need only visit Liberia. This West African nation, established by freed American slaves, has long been one of the most miserable nations on an unhappy continent, and is now in a state of barbarous anarchy.

Moreover, despite the lip service they give to Afro-centrism, very few American blacks emigrate to Africa. Those who think they would like to "go home" usually change their minds after a single visit. The power of attraction runs entirely the other way; hundreds of thousands of Africans would come to America if they could

It is silly to claim, as reparationists do, that the United States was made uniquely prosperous by the labors of blacks. Blacks contributed to the development of America by laboring under the direction of whites. Moreover, it was those parts of the country where slaves were most common that have always been poorest and remain poor to this day.

Eugene Genovese, a Marxist historian of slavery who certainly has little sympathy for slaveholders, writes that the slave system retarded the development of the South. He argues that since slaves could not be taught to handle livestock carefully, the South did not develop a cattle industry. Modern agricultural equipment could not be introduced on plantations because slaves were sure to break it. The only farm implements that survived were simple, crude, and heavy. The "nigger hoe," for example, weighed three times as much as the more effective "English hoe," which slaves habitually broke. Slave labor in factories was virtually out of the question because slaves could not be trusted with machinery.

The slave was said to be the laziest, most untrustworthy servant on earth and had constantly to be watched. A common reflection on his abilities was that "It takes two slaves to help one to do nothing." Nor was it always possible to wring more work out of a slave by threat of punishment. "Every attempt to force a slave beyond the limit that he fixes himself . . ." wrote one owner, "only tends to make him unprofitable, unmanageable, a vexation and a curse."

Other than in the cotton fields, there is some doubt as to whether slavery was even profitable. Frederick Law Olmstead (1822-1903), the landscape architect who designed Central Park in New York City, made a study of slavery when he toured the antebellum South. He estimated that on many plantations slaves worked one third as much as a hired hand on a New England farm. He was convinced free blacks could be hired for considerably less than the cost of keeping slaves.

Although some slaves were driven for long hours, Northern anti-slavery tracts abounded with accounts of how the excessive leisure of slavery would be ended under strict, Northern employment practices. They promised that abolition would produce a decisive rise in the nation's productivity.

Northern working men were well aware of these arguments. Slaves were provided for as children and maintained in sickness and in old age. Northern wage earners, who had no sick leave, children's allowances, or retirement benefits, often wondered if they were not worse off than slaves.

A workingman's newspaper, *The Fall River Mechanic*, lashed out at "men who stand and dole out pity for the southern slave but would crush with an iron hand the white laborer of the north." Another paper, *The Man*, mocked the upper-class women who supported abolition:

> Their tender hearts were sighing
> As the negro's wrongs were told
> While the white slave was dying
> Who gained their father's gold.

Many Southerners firmly believed they treated slaves better than Yankee capitalists treated workers. James Hammond, a Southern senator once rebuked his colleague from New York on the Senate floor with the following words: "Our slaves are hired for life and well compensated. . . . Yours are hired by the day, not cared for, and scantily compensated."

One indication of the value placed on the lives of slaves was a practice Olmstead noted in his travels: Irish navvies were invariably hired to drain swamps and dig irrigation ditches. Malaria and intestinal disease made this some of the most dangerous work in the South. When Olmstead asked why the Irish were hired for it, he was told, "It's dangerous work and a negro's life is too valuable to be risked at it. If a negro dies it is a considerable loss you know."

The black man's value as a slave protected him in other ways. From 1840 to 1860, of the more than 300 people lynched by mobs in the South, fewer than ten percent were blacks. So long as the black man had tangible property value he was safer from lynch mobs than a white man.

As Olmstead noted, when the black man was definitely a slave, it seemed to break down the "natural" revulsion of whites for blacks, and lead to affection and intimacy of a kind that sickened Northerners. It was after Reconstruction, when free blacks were goaded on by carpetbaggers to mistreat and humiliate their former masters, that lower-class whites began to hate blacks and take pleasure in lynching them.

Reign of Terror

Today, as part of the reparations campaign, slavery must be described as a psychopathic reign of terror, the blackest blot on the record of the white man. There certainly were cases of barbarous mistreatment, but they were exceptions.

In *The Mind of the South*, W.J. Cash writes that the standard that "no one but a cur beat, starved, or overdrove his slaves became a living rule of daily conduct; a standard so binding as to generate contempt for whoever violated it." Many owners took pride in the kindness they showed "their people," and even among Northern abolitionists there was grudging acknowledgement of a certain *noblesse oblige* among the better element in the South. It is worth noting that even in that great abolitionist tract, *Uncle Tom's Cabin*, the sadistic villain was not a Southern slave owner but a Yankee overseer.

Slaves were valuable property, which only one Southern household in five could afford. The rougher classes who might have been abusive masters were generally too poor to own slaves.

Although it is unfashionable to acknowledge it today, the bonds of master and slave were often affectionate. A contemporary ditty illustrates why some slaveholders resisted the idea of "colonizing" blacks by sending them back to Africa:

> What! Colonize old coachman Dick!
> My foster brother Nat!
> My more than mother when I'm sick,
> Come, Hal, no more of that!

That slaves were commonly addressed as "Auntie," "Uncle," or "Mammie," showed the affection their masters felt for them. There certainly were acts of cruelty against slaves, but to dwell on them is to paint a false picture of the South. When Jefferson Davis took leave of the slaves on his Mississippi plantation to assume the presidency of the Confederate government in Montgomery, he wept and his slaves wept. Of course, the "happy darkies" picture of slavery is not the whole story either. Wherever Union armies marched through the South, all but the house servants usually escaped to join them.

Reparations activists commonly maintain that the government "promised" freed slaves 40 acres and a mule, and that this gives today's blacks a legal claim. It is true that Thaddeus Stevens, who wanted to punish the South, proposed legislation to seize all Southern land holdings worth $5,000 or more, break them up into 40 acre plots and give them to blacks. His intention was not so much to benefit blacks as to humiliate the Southern aristocracy, which he hated, and his bill never became law.

Reparations agitators also ignore the fact that some slaveholders were black. In 1830, more than 3,600 free blacks owned slaves, and a few were prosperous enough to own as many as a hundred. How would a reparations program treat the descendants of blacks who owned slaves—or who were owned by blacks?

Although it is specifically slavery over which the white man is supposed to beat his breast, by some measures slaves fared better than free blacks. According to one contemporary study, the slave infant mortality rate was 153 per thousand. As late as 1915, the infant mortality rate among blacks in Massachusetts was 163 per thousand, while in Pennsylvania it was 185 and in New York, 192.

The Final Tally

The reparations argument is based in part on the view that even if there are no longer any slaves who can be paid for their forced labor, the country as a whole has benefited so much from slavery that it should pay for that benefit. In fact, the final tally on the presence in America of blacks, whether slave or free, is overwhelmingly negative.

Far from contributing to the nation's progress, slavery was probably an obstacle to the South's development. Moreover, as Abraham Lincoln once pointed out to a delegation of blacks, the presence of their race was the cause of the nation's greatest frenzy of self destruction: "See our present condition—the country engaged in war!—our white men cutting one another's throats . . . . But for your race among us there could not be war, although many engaged on either side do not care for you one way or another."

Ever since abolition, those parts of the country with large black populations have been afflicted with crime and poverty, which have only worsened in recent decades. It is through only the most heroic "celebration of diversity" that the presence of blacks in the United States can be seen as anything short of a burden, and it is one for which whites continue to pay a high price.

Prisons, welfare, and crime prevention are disproportionately paid for by whites. Underclass blacks have made many of our cities so squalid and dangerous that whites rarely venture into them. School integration has so lowered the standards of public instruction that many whites now pay for two systems: public schools for blacks and private schools for their own children. As Southerners now sometimes observe, "If we had known then what we know now, we would have picked the cotton ourselves." They feel they have already suffered more than enough for the sins of their ancestors.

Slavery was practiced by a fraction of the people in just one section of the country. Only a tiny minority of the current white population counts slaveholders among its ancestors. Slavery came to an end nearly 130 years ago and it is because of slavery that today's black Americans enjoy a higher standard of living than blacks anywhere on earth. The call for "reparations" is therefore just one more attempt to blame whites for the failures of blacks and to use this as a pretext for more race-based spoils.

This two-part article appeared in the June and July 1993 issues. William Robertson Boggs is a pen name.

Madison Grant and the Racialist Movement
by George McDaniel

Perhaps more than any other man, Madison Grant created what we might call the "racialist moment" in American history. This was the period beginning approximately with the administration of Theodore Roosevelt (who wrote that the Negro was a member of "a perfectly stupid race") and continuing through the administration of Warren Harding, during which the country discarded its remaining, melting-pot sentimentalism about blacks and foreign immigration. The period also saw the emergence of a new science—eugenics—which promised to banish inherited evils. This era of explicit, intellectual racialism lasted until approximately the Great Depression, then withered under Franklin Roosevelt's massive shift to the Left, and finally collapsed during the war with Nazi Germany.

Madison Grant (1865-1937) worked tirelessly for the racialist movement for almost this entire period. He joined, chaired, and often founded its organizations. He counted among his closest associates US Presidents, top industrialists, best-selling writers, and some of the greatest scientists of the time. And he wrote two of the seminal works of American racial thought: *The Passing of the Great Race* (1916) and *The Conquest of a Continent* (1933).

Grant was born in New York in 1865, just as the first of the modern white-against-white conflicts was closing. He was descended from Jacobites who came to the colonies from Scotland after the defeat of "Bonnie Prince Charlie" in the Forty-Five uprising (1745), and throughout his life retained the Jacobite brand of conservative fire. He was graduated from Yale in 1887 and received a law degree from Columbia in 1890.

The Passing of the Great Race was published in 1916 to immediate popular success. It established Grant as an authority in anthropology, and laid the groundwork for his research in the emerging science of eugenics. It was read by presidents, dictators, scientists, and common people alike, and even today—excoriated as it is—it has much to teach. The impact of the book can be understood only in the cultural milieu in which it appeared.

Immigration just after the War Between the States proceeded at great speed. The decade of the 1880s saw the arrival of 5,246,613 immigrants; 788,992 were admitted in 1882 alone. Two hundred twenty thousand Chinese came from 1854 to 1882. Subsiding a bit in the nineties, the influx rose again after the turn of the century, averaging over 800,000 arrivals each year between 1900 and 1914. Most of these were immigrants from parts of the world unfamiliar to Americans: Russia, Poland, Austria-Hungary, Italy, the Balkans, and Turkey. Many newcomers brought Marxist and anarchist ideas alien to the old American stock.

Just as it does today, the American identity faced a double threat: a large influx of aliens and the presence of a large Negro element. Negro migration to the Northern industrial cities brought a slow awakening to the entire country of the true nature of the race problem, and Thomas Dixon's 1905 novel, *The Clansman*, was one of the first works in the new century to focus on it. The book's sympathetic account of the first Ku Klux Klan encouraged a reappraisal of often-sentimental notions about blacks.

In a sense, this reappraisal came to a head in August 1908, in Lincoln's own Springfield, Illinois. A black habitual criminal attacked a white girl in her bedroom and, killed her father with a razor when he defended her. At least one other attack on a white woman was also reported, and the white people responded by killing two blacks and burning down a crime-ridden black neighborhood called the "Badlands." Thousands of local blacks fled Springfield. It was this event that inspired the creation of the National Association for the Advancement of Colored People (NAACP) in Springfield in 1909.

In 1915, a new entertainment medium widened the audience for the racialist message when D. W. Griffith debuted his film masterpiece, *Birth of a Nation*. Based upon *The Clansman*, and, to some degree, on Dixon's 1902 novel, *The Leopard's Spots*, this movie was hailed as a technical triumph even by its harshest critics. Nevertheless, the NAACP, along with other black and some Jewish organizations, picketed the movie and threatened violence in the cities where it opened.

The success of the film was in some doubt when Dixon contacted his old Johns Hopkins classmate, President Woodrow Wilson, and arranged a special showing at the White House. Wilson is said to have leapt to his feet, exclaiming, "It is like writing history with lightning. And my only regret is that it is all so terribly true."

With the news that the President loved it, audiences flocked to see *Birth of a Nation*. During its opening in Atlanta, William J. Simmons announced the founding of the second Ku Klux Klan, in nearby Stone Mountain, Georgia. This Klan organization went on to sweep the country, becoming especially strong in the midwest.

The Passing of the Great Race was published the next year, in 1916. Grant intended it as a call to American whites to counter the dangers both from blacks and non-traditional immigration. Adopting the then-popular racial taxonomy of William Z. Ripley in *The Races of Europe*, Grant describes the three European subraces of Nordic, Alpine, and Mediterranean. As was common in his day, he unabashedly favored the Nordic and went to great pains to contrast Nordic civilization and traits with those of other races and subraces. For example, he faulted Nordic, altruistic devotion to blacks and other unsuccessful groups, a devotion that he warned was always self-destructive.

Grant concluded that America should abandon a largely open-door immigration policy. He favored a eugenics program that would promote the Nordic race and discourage the expansion of the colored races in the white world. In particular, he condemned miscegenation.

It is worth noting that one of the reasons Grant and other racial thinkers opposed the new immigration was that it brought alien ideologies. The First World War had seen the triumph of Bolshevism, and continuing immigration from Eastern Europe brought Marxists. Like most racialists, Grant saw socialism as unfit for Nordics. When he was helping found the Galton Society in 1918, he wrote to the other organizers: "My proposal is the organization of an anthropological society . . . confined to native Americans, who are anthropologically, socially, and politically sound; no Bolsheviki need apply."

The Passing of the Great Race became an immediate best-seller, with new editions in 1918, 1920, and 1921, multiple printings, and translations into German, French, and Norwegian.

It was reviewed favorably by *Science*, the journal of the American Association for the Advancement of Science, and by periodicals as diverse as the *Journal of Heredity* and *The Saturday Evening Post*. The editor of the *Post* commissioned a series of articles on immigration in a similar vein, and in an editorial in the May 7, 1921, issue wrote: "Two books in particular that every American should read if he wishes to understand the full gravity of our present immigration problem: Mr. Madison Grant's *The Passing of the Great Race* and Dr. Lothrop Stoddard's *The Rising Tide of Color*. . . . These books should do a vast amount of good if they fall into the hands of readers who can face without wincing the impact of new and disturbing ideas."

The Passing of the Great Race did indeed fall into the hands of such readers, turning up in the personal libraries of some of the most important figures of the day. It was typical, for example, that Dr. Rupert Blue, Surgeon General of the United States, gave a copy personally to Sir Henry Wellcome the British pharmaceutical manufacturer.

Grant was not alone in sounding the alarm. Some of the other books published during this period include: *Mankind at the Crossroads* by E.G. Conklin (1914), *America's Greatest Problem: The Negro* by Major R. W. Shufeldt (1915), *The Rising Tide of Color Against White World Supremacy* by Lothrop Stoddard (1920, Introduction by Grant); *Race and National Solidarity* by Charles Josey (1923) (reviewed in AR, Aug. 1992), *Applied Eugenics* by Paul Popenoe and Roswell Johnson (1923); and *The Fruit of the Family Tree* by Alfred E. Wiggam (1924). These were all intended for a mass audience, but academic textbooks soon joined them, including *Genetics and Eugenics* by W.E. Castle (1916) and *Evolution, Genetics, and Eugenics* by H.H. Newman (1921).

The effect was felt at both the state and federal level. Twenty-four states passed laws encouraging sterilization of those who were retarded, insane, or had criminal records. At the federal level, in 1921, Albert Johnson, head of the House Committee on Immigration and Naturalization, began a series of hearings on immigration. He appointed Harry Laughlin, who in 1922 would be one of Grant's co-founders of the American Eugenics Society, as an expert witness on eugenics. In 1922, Laughlin reported extensively on racial differences in IQ as measured by the new army intelligence test.

In 1923, Grant's close friend Henry Fairfield Osborn, the famous pale-ontologist who named "Tyrannosaurus Rex," spoke enthusiastically about intelligence testing: "We have learned once and for all that the Negro is not like us."

This was precisely the kind of thing Grant and others had been saying for years. These ideas helped pass the Johnson Act of 1924, which established national origin immigration quotas of 2 percent of the number of foreign-born already in America as determined by the census of 1890. This greatly reduced the flow of immigrants from non-traditional sources, a policy that remained essentially unchanged until 1965.

Grant called the act a "new Declaration of Independence," and his entry in *The Dictionary of American Biography* credits him with helping it pass. In its 1937 obituary, the *New York Times* said of Grant's book: "Besides being a recognized book on anthropology, it has often been called to Congressional attention in the passage of restrictive immigration laws. . . . Mr. Grant . . . helped frame the Johnson Restriction Act of 1924."

Eugenics

Grant was active throughout the 1920s, serving as president of both the Immigration Restriction League and the Eugenics Research Association. He was also treasurer of one of the most important events in the history of eugenics, the Second Eugenics Congress of 1921. This event continued the pattern of the First Eugenics Congress, which had been held in London in 1912, with Winston Churchill as one of the sponsors and at which Prime Minister Arthur Balfour delivered the inaugural address. The second con-gress was hosted by the American Museum of Natural History in New York. More than 300 delegates came from Europe, Latin America, Asia, Australia and New Zealand. No German scientists were invited because of the policy of ostracism that continued after the First World War.

Among the notables in attendance were future president Herbert Hoover, Alexander Graham Bell (the Congress's honorary president), conservationist and future governor of Pennsylvania, Gifford Pinchot, and Leonard Darwin, son of Charles Darwin. Henry Fairfield Osborn, director of the museum, was president. Harry Laughlin was in charge of exhibits, and Lothrop Stoddard handled publicity. One hundred eight papers were presented on topics rang-ing from plant and animal genetics to anthropology and political science. The conference signaled the vitality of a young science that was nevertheless destined to die an early death.

Madison Grant continued to lobby for immigration control even after the passage of the Johnson Act. In 1927, he and other eugenicists signed a "Memorial on Immigration Quotas," urging the President and Congress to extend "the quota system to all countries of North and South America . . . . in which the population is not predominantly of the white race."

Grant continued to write. In 1930, along with Lothrop Stoddard, Harry Laughlin, Charles Davenport, Paul Popenoe, and Henry Fairfield Osborn, and others, he contributed to *The Alien in Our Midst*, subtitled *Selling Our Birthright for a Mess of Pottage*.

The book was Grant's idea and—like *Conquest* a few years later—was written to defend the 1924 immigration act. It included essays on race and immigration from both contemporary writers and from great Americans of the past like Thomas Jefferson, Patrick Henry, James Madison, and George Washington. The book was widely distributed to legislators and editors by the American Coalition of Patriotic Societies.

In 1933, Grant's second major work, *The Conquest of a Continent*, appeared. In it, he explained why he wrote the book:

"A controversy immediately arose over this new basis [the national origins immigration quotas], as it was to the interest of every national and religious group of aliens now here to exaggerate the importance and size of its contribution to the population of the country, especially in Colonial times.... The purpose of this opposition was to warp public opinion in regard to the merits of various national groups and to exaggerate the non-Anglo-Saxon elements in the old Colonial population. This book is an effort to make an estimate of the various elements, national and racial, existing in the present population of the United States and to trace their arrival and subsequent spread."

He then embarks on what Henry Fairfield Osborn in the introduction calls the "first racial history of . . . any nation." Especially interesting today is Grant's analysis of the Negro problem. He writes: "Among the various outland elements now in the United States which threaten in various degrees our national unity, the most important is the Negro." He discusses several proposed solutions.

First, "slow amalgamation with the Whites," he rejects immediately, arguing that this would "produce a racial chaos such as ruined the Roman Empire." He considers repatriation at somewhat greater length, but rejects this as well, for reasons no longer applicable in our time: "Today, [repatriation to Africa] is not possible, because Africa, with the exception of Liberia, is under the control of white states, which certainly would not welcome such an enormous addition to their own color problem . . . ."

The third solution Grant considers is the establishment of a separate black nation within the territory of the United States. This he tends to reject because it would involve the abandonment of large sections of the South, but he admits that something similar had already occurred in some areas, both in America and, especially, in the West Indies:

"This has actually happened in some places along the lower Mississippi River, where the numbers of the Negroes have become so overwhelming that the few remaining Whites have simply moved out and abandoned the district to them. It has happened and is happening in the West Indies. Haiti and Santo Domingo have been entirely turned over to Negroes and other examples of West Indian Islands almost abandoned to Negroes can be found."

In the final analysis, Grant has no easy answers to the problem. He urges states to adopt laws prohibiting intermarriage and he castigates Christian churches in the North for "trying to break down the social barriers between Negro and White." Social separation is paramount, he says, and to that end public opinion "might well stop exalting the Mulatto and thereby putting its stamp of approval on miscegenation. Negroes should be encouraged to respect their own racial integrity." And, finally, contraception should be made "universally available to them."

Perhaps because *Passing of the Great Race* had been so influential, *Conquest of a Continent* provoked an immediate storm of opposition. On December 13, 1933, the director of the Anti-Defamation League, Richard E. Gutstadt, sent the following letter to the publishers of a number of Jewish-owned periodicals:

> "Gentlemen:
>
> "Scribner & Sons have just published a book by Madison Grant entitled 'The Conquest of a Continent.' It is extremely antagonistic to Jewish interests. Emphasized throughout is the 'Nordic superiority' theory, and the utter negation of any 'melting pot' philosophy with regard to America.
>
> "We are interested in stifling the sale of this book. We believe that this can be best accomplished by refusing to be stampeded into giving it publicity. Every review or public criticism of the book of this character brings it to the attention of many who would otherwise know nothing of it. This results in added sales. The less discussion there is concerning it, the more sales resistance will be created.
>
> "We therefore appeal to you to refrain from comment on this book, which will undoubtedly be brought to your attention sooner or later. It is our conviction that a general compliance with this request will sound the warning to other publishing houses against engaging in this type of venture."

In fact, Grant wrote very little about Jews, noting only his view that they were of Central European, Khazar origin: "It is doubtful whether there is a single drop of the old Palestinian, Semitic-speaking Hebrew blood among these East European Jews."

Nevertheless, by this time, Hitler had begun consolidating power in Germany and his excesses were undermining eugenics and scientific racial theory. The *New York Times*, in its review of *Conquest*, was quick to make the connection: "Substitute Aryan for Nordic and a good deal of Mr. Grant's argument would lend itself without much difficulty to the support of some recent pronouncements in Germany."

Grant actually had occasion to caution others about the National Socialist government. In 1934, he wrote to Laughlin warning that American eugenicists should be careful in their relations with Germany and should "proceed cautiously in endorsing" the actions being taken by the German government.

Conservationism

Another aspect of Grant's career that he considered intimately related to his work in racial science was conservationism, and his involvement with nature and wildlife was long and varied. Just as with the racialist movement, he was always a leader. In 1895, along with Theodore Roosevelt and a handful of others, he co-founded the New York Zoological Society (now the Wildlife Conservation Society), and served as its secretary until 1924. He helped found the American Bison Society in 1905; was president of the Bronx Zoo for many years; was co-founder and president of the Bronx Parkway Commission (which built the road to the Zoo); co-founder of the Save the Redwoods League; and a founding member of the Boone and Crockett Club, which helped establish Yellowstone National Park.

In an excellent essay in the April 1995 issue of *The Mankind Quarterly*, Roger Pearson writes about the link between conservation and racial thinking:

"The success of the conservationist movement in the United States at this vital period in the nation's history was facilitated by the sympathy of President Theodore Roosevelt, who was deeply concerned about the threat to the quality of both the natural and human stock of America. . . .

"With Madison Grant serving as secretary and later as president, the Boone and Crockett Club was largely comprised of eugenicists and eugenics sympathizers. Renowned as one of the more active members of the eugenics movement, and especially for his efforts to preserve the 'Old American' component of the American population, Grant worked just as ardently to preserve the natural heritage for future generations of Americans and should be remembered always with honor as one of the nation's greatest benefactors."

Despite disavowals by American eugenicists, Nazism had already begun to erode support for the eugenics movement by the 1930s. German policies played into the hands of people like the anti-eugenicist, Franz Boas of Columbia, a socialist who launched a one-man crusade to destroy eugenics and "undermine the belief in race as a primary factor in cultural behavior." Through his many books and students (including Margaret Mead and Ashley Montagu), Boas' views began to prevail.

Even so, Grant's efforts never flagged. In 1932, he again served as treasurer of the third and final Eugenics Congress. This Congress was also held at the Museum of Natural History, and included as sponsors Mrs. E. H. Harriman, Mrs. H. B. Dupont, Dr. J. Harvey Kellogg (of Kellogg's cereals), and Leonard Darwin.

Conquest was published in 1933, after which Grant served on the advisory board of *Eugenical News*. He continued to write, to plan, to lobby. But the old days were ending. A schism had developed among eugenicists between those who favored "negative eugenics" and those in the "mainstream" who promoted "positive eugenics." Moreover, Nazism was rapidly discrediting the science. By mid-decade, Osborn had died, and Grant himself died on May 30, 1937. The man who had devoted so much of his life to preserving his race left no children.

Two years later, Hitler invaded Poland. From then on, eugenics would be equated with concentration camps, Nazi doctors, Holocaust, and war crimes. As a science it was dead. Ironically, Grant's views on nature and wildlife have been largely adopted, and conservation is at the forefront of mainstream thought. Of course, Grant receives little credit for this. His dreams of racial preservation, which he saw as part and parcel of nature conservation, are reviled today by all but a few. They owe it to the memory of this early activist to carry on his work, to ensure that the ideals of Madison Grant do not perish.

This article appeared in the December 1997 issue. George McDaniel is the editor of this book and is the webmaster for the American Renaissance *website.*

Multiculturalism and Marxism
by Frank Ellis

"For the purposes of everyday life it was no doubt necessary, or sometimes necessary, to reflect before speaking, but a Party member called upon to make a political or ethical judgment should be able to spray forth the correct opinions as automatically as a machine gun spraying out bullets."
—George Orwell, 1984

No successful society shows a spontaneous tendency towards multiculturalism or multiracialism. Successful and enduring societies show a high degree of homogeneity. Those who support multiculturalism either do not know this or, what is more likely, realize that if they are to transform Western societies into strictly regulated, racial-feminist bureaucracies they must first undermine those societies.

This transformation is as radical and revolutionary as the project to establish Communism in the Soviet Union. Just as every aspect of life had to be brought under political control in order for the commissars to impose their vision of society, the multiculturalists hope to control and dominate every aspect of our lives. Unlike the hard tyranny of the Soviets, theirs is a softer, gentler tyranny but one with which they hope to bind us as tightly as a prisoner in the Gulag. Today's "political correctness" is the direct descendent of Communist terror and brainwashing.

Unlike the obviously alien implantation that was Communism, what makes multiculturalism particularly insidious and difficult to combat is that it usurps the moral and intellectual infrastructure of the West. Although it claims to champion the deepest held beliefs of the West, it is in fact a perversion and systematic undermining of the very idea of the West.

What we call "political correctness" actually dates back to the Soviet Union of the 1920s (*politicheskaya pravil'nost'* in Russian), and was the extension of political control to education, psychiatry, ethics, and behavior. It was an essential component of the attempt to make sure all aspects of life were consistent with ideological orthodoxy—which is the distinctive feature of all totalitarianisms. In the post-Stalin period, political correctness even meant that dissent was seen as a symptom of mental illness, for which the only treatment was incarceration.

As Mao Tse-Tung, the Great Helmsman, put it, "Not to have a correct political orientation is like not having a soul." Mao's little red book is full of exhortations to follow the correct path of Communist thought, and by the late 1960s Maoist political correctness was well established in American universities. The final stage of development, which we are witnessing now, is the result of cross-fertilization with all the latest "isms:" anti-racism, feminism, structuralism, and post-modernism, which now dominate university curricula. The result is a new and virulent strain of totalitarianism, whose parallels to the Communist era are obvious. Today's dogmas have led to rigid requirements of language, thought, and behavior, and violators are treated as if they were mentally unbalanced, just as Soviet dissidents were.

Some have argued that it is unfair to describe Stalin's regime as "totalitarian," pointing out that one man, no matter how ruthlessly he exercised power, could not control all the functions of the state. But, in fact, he didn't have to. Totalitarianism was much more than state terror, censorship, and concentration camps; it was a state of mind in which the very idea of a private opinion or point of view had been destroyed. The totalitarian propagandist forces people to believe that slavery is freedom, squalor is bounty, ignorance is knowledge, and that a rigidly closed society is the most open in the world. And once enough people are made to think this way, it is functionally totalitarian even if a single dictator does not personally control everything.

Today, of course, we are made to believe that diversity is strength, perversity is virtue, success is oppression, and that relentlessly repeating these ideas over and over is "tolerance and diversity." Indeed, the multicultural revolution works subversion everywhere, just as Communist revolutions did: judicial activism undermines the rule of law; "tolerance" weakens the conditions that make real tolerance possible; universities, which should be havens of free inquiry, practice censorship that rivals that of the Soviets. At the same time, we find a relentless drive for equality: the Bible, Shakespeare, and rap "music" are just texts with "equally valid perspectives;" deviant and criminal behavior is an "alternative life-style." Today, Dostoevsky's *Crime and Punishment* would have to be repackaged as *Crime and Counseling*.

In the Communist era, the totalitarian state was built on violence. The purges of the 1930s and the Great Terror (which was Mao's model for the Cultural Revolution) used violence against "class enemies" to compel loyalty. Party members signed death warrants for "enemies of the people" knowing that the accused were innocent, but believing in the correctness of the charges. In the 1930s, *collective* guilt justified murdering millions of Russian peasants. As cited by Robert Conquest in *The Harvest of Sorrow* (p. 143), the state's view of this class was, "not one of them was guilty of anything; but they belonged to a class that was guilty of everything." Stigmatizing entire institutions and groups makes it much easier to carry out wholesale change.

This, of course, is the beauty of "racism" and "sexism" for today's culture attackers—sin can be extended far beyond individuals to include institutions, literature, language, history, laws, customs, entire civilizations. The charge of "institutional racism" is no different from declaring an entire economic class an enemy of the people. "Racism" and "sexism" are multiculturalism's assault weapons, its Big Ideas, just as class warfare was for Communists, and the effects are the same. If a crime can be collectivized all can be guilty because they belong to the wrong group. When young whites are victims of racial preferences they are today's version of the Russian peasants.

Even if they themselves have never oppressed anyone they "belong to the race that is guilty of everything."

The purpose of these multicultural campaigns is to destroy the self. The mouth moves, the right gestures follow, but they are the mouth and gestures of a zombie, the new Soviet man or, today, PC-man. And once enough people have been conditioned this way, *violence is no longer necessary*. We reach steady-state totalitarianism, in which the vast majority know what is expected of them and play their allotted roles.

The Russian experiment with revolution and totalitarian social engineering has been fully chronicled by two of that country's greatest writers, Dostoevsky and Solzhenitsyn. They brilliantly dissect the methods and psychology of totalitarian control. Dostoevsky's *The Devils* has no equal as a penetrating and disturbing analysis of the revolutionary and utopian mind. The "devils" are radical students of the middle and upper classes flirting with something they do not understand. The ruling class tries to ingratiate itself with them. The universities have essentially declared war on society at large. The great cry of the student radicals is freedom: freedom from the established norms of society, freedom from manners, freedom from inequality, freedom from the past.

Russia's descent into vice and insanity is a powerful warning of what happens when a nation declares war on the past in the hope of building a terrestrial paradise. Dostoevsky did not live to see the abominations he predicted but Solzhenitsyn experienced them first hand. *The Gulag Archipelago* and *August 1914* can be seen as histories of ideas, as attempts to account for the dreadful fate that befell Russia after 1917.

Solzhenitsyn identifies education and the way teachers saw their duty as instilling hostility to all forms of traditional authority as the major factors that explain why Russia's youth was seduced by revolutionary ideas. In the West, during the 1960s and 1970s—which can collectively be called "the 60s"—we hear a powerful echo of the collective mental capitulation of Russia that took place in the 1870s and continued through the revolution.

One of the echoes of Marxism that continues to reverberate today is the idea that truth resides in class (or sex or race or erotic orientation). Truth is not something to be established by rational inquiry, but depends on the perspective of the speaker. In the multicultural universe, a person's perspective is "valued" (a favorite word) according to class. Feminists, blacks, environmentalists and homosexuals have a greater claim to truth because they are "oppressed." In the misery of "oppression" they see truth more clearly than the white heterosexual men who "oppress" them. This is a perfect mirror image of the Marxist proletariat's moral and intellectual superiority over the bourgeoisie. Today, "oppression" confers a "privileged perspective" that is essentially infallible. To borrow an expression from Robert Bork's *Slouching Towards Gomorrah*, black and feminist activists are "case-hardened against logical argument"—just as Communist true believers were.

Indeed, feminist and anti-racist activists openly reject objective truth. Confident that they have intimidated their opposition, feminists are able to make all kinds of demands on the assumption that men and women are equal in every way. When outcomes do not match that belief, this is only more evidence of white-male deviltry.

One of the most depressing sights in the West today, particularly in the universities and in the media, is the readiness to treat feminism as a major contribution to knowledge and to submit to its absurdities. Remarkably, this requires no physical violence. It is the desire to be accepted that makes people truckle to these middle-class, would-be revolutionaries. Peter Verkhovensky, who orchestrates murder and mayhem in *The Devils*, expresses it with admirable contempt: "All I have to do is to raise my voice and tell them that they are not sufficiently liberal." The race hustlers, of course, play the same game: Accuse a late-20th century liberal of "racism" or "sexism" and watch him fall apart in an orgy of self-flagellation and Maoist self-criticism. Even "conservatives" wilt at the sound of those words.

Ancient liberties and assumptions of innocence mean nothing when it comes to "racism:" You are guilty until proven innocent, which is nearly impossible, and even then you are forever suspect. An accusation of "racism" has much the same effect as an accusation of witchcraft did in 17th century Salem.

It is the power of the charge of "racism" that stifles the derision that would otherwise meet the idea that we should "value diversity." If "diversity" had real benefits whites would want more of it, and would ask that yet more cities in the US and Europe be handed over to immigrants. Of course, they are not rushing to embrace diversity and multiculturalism; they are in headlong flight in the opposite direction. Valuing diversity is a hobby for people who do not have to endure its benefits.

A multicultural society is one that is inherently prone to conflict, not harmony. This is why we see a huge growth in government bureaucracies dedicated to resolving disputes along racial and cultural lines. These disputes can never be resolved permanently because the bureaucrats deny one of the major causes: race. This is why there is so much talk of the "multicultural" rather than the more precise "multiracial." Ever more changes and legislation are introduced to make the host society ever more congenial to racial minorities. This only creates more demands, and encourages the non-shooting war against whites, their civilization, and even the idea of the West.

How is such a radical program carried forward? The Soviet Union had a massive system of censorship—the Communists even censored street maps—and it is worth noting there were two kinds of censorship: the blatant censorship of state agencies and the more subtle self-censorship that the inhabitants of "peoples' democracies" soon learned.

The situation in the West is not so straightforward. There is nothing remotely comparable to Soviet-style government censorship and yet we have deliberate suppression of dissent. Arthur Jensen, Hans Eysenck, J. Philippe

Rushton, Chris Brand, Michael Levin, and Glayde Whitney have all been vilified for their racial views. The case of Prof. Rushton is particularly troubling because his academic work was investigated by the police. The attempt to silence him was based on provisions of Canadian hate speech laws. This is just the sort of intellectual terror one expected in the old Soviet Union. To find it in a country that prides itself on being a pillar of Western liberal democracy is one of the most disturbing consequences of multiculturalism.

A mode of opinion control softer than outright censorship is the current obsession with fictional role models. Today, the feminist and anti-racist theme is constantly worked into movies and television as examples of Bartold Brecht's principle that the Marxist artist must show the world not as it is but as it ought to be. This is why we have so many screen portrayals of wise black judges; street-wise, straight-shooting lady policemen; minority computer geniuses; and, of course, degenerate white men. This is almost a direct borrowing from Soviet-style socialist realism, with its idealized depictions of sturdy proletarians routing capitalist vermin.

Multiculturalism has the same ambitions as Soviet Communism. It is absolutist in the pursuit of its various agendas, yet it relativizes all other perspectives in its attack on its enemies. Multiculturalism is an ideology to end all other ideologies, and these totalitarian aspirations permit us to draw two conclusions: First, multiculturalism must eliminate all opposition *everywhere*. There can be no safe havens for counter-revolutionaries. Second, once it is established the multicultural paradise must be defended at all costs. Orthodoxy must be maintained with all the resources of the state.

Such a society would be well on its way to becoming totalitarian. It might not have concentration camps, but it would have re-education centers and sensitivity training for those sad creatures who still engaged in "white-male hegemonic discourse." Rather than the hard totalitarianism of the Soviet state we would have a softer version in which our minds would be wards of the state. We would be liberated from the burden of thought and therefore unable to fall into the heresy of political incorrectness.

If we think of multiculturalism as yet another manifestation of 20th century totalitarianism, can we take solace in the fact that the Soviet Union eventually collapsed? Is multiculturalism a phase, a periodic crisis through which the West is passing, or does it represent something fundamental and perhaps irreversible?

Despite the efforts of pro-Soviet elements, the West recognized the Soviet empire as a threat. It does not recognize multiculturalism as a threat in the same way. For this reason, many of its assumptions and objectives remain unchallenged. Still, there are some grounds for optimism, for example, the speed with which the term "political correctness" caught on. It took the tenured radicals completely by surprise, but it is only a small gain.

In the long term, the most important battleground in the war against multiculturalism is the United States. The struggle is likely to be a slow, frustrating war of attrition. If it fails, the insanity of multiculturalism is something white Americans will have to live with. Of course, at some point whites may demand an end to being punished because of black failure. As Prof. Michael Hart argues in *The Real American Dilemma*[1] there could be racial partition of the United States. We may find that what happened in the Balkans is not peculiar to that part of the world. Race war is not something the affluent radicals deliberately seek but their policies are pushing us in that direction.

I have argued so far that the immediate context for understanding political correctness and multiculturalism is the Soviet Union and its catastrophic utopian experiment. And yet the PC/multicultural mentality is much older. In *Reflections on the Revolution in France*, Edmund Burke offers a portrait of the French radicals that is still relevant 200 years after he wrote it:

"They have no respect for the wisdom of others; but they pay it off by a very full measure of confidence in their own. With them it is sufficient motive to destroy an old scheme of things, because it is an old one. As to the new, they are in no sort of fear with regard to the duration of a building run up in haste; because duration is no object to those who think little or nothing has been done before their time, and who place all their hopes in discovery."

Of course, multiculturalism is far from being a solution to racial or cultural conflict. Quite the contrary. Multiculturalism is the road to a special kind of hell that we have already seen in this gruesome 20th century, a hell that man, having abandoned reason and in revolt against God's order, builds for himself and others.

This article appeared in the November 1999 issue. Frank Ellis is professor of Russian at the University of Leeds in England.

---

[1] Published in 1998 by New Century Foundation.

The Decline of National Review
by James P. Lubinskas

The October 11, 1999, cover story of *National Review* was a piece by Senior Editor Ramesh Ponnuru called "A Conservative No More," which argued that Patrick Buchanan has abandoned conservative principles. The article complained about Mr. Buchanan's isolationism, opposition to free trade, and support for certain government programs, but the most serious charge appeared in the subtitle: "The tribal politics of Pat Buchanan." According to Mr. Ponnuru, "Buchananism is a form of identity politics for white people—and becomes more worrisome as it is married to collectivism." Any expression of white identity is now apparently a betrayal of conservatism. It was not always so.

National Review is considered the flagship publication of post-World War II conservatism. William F. Buckley founded it in 1955, declaring that it "stands athwart history yelling Stop, at a time when no one is inclined to do so, or to have much patience with those who so urge it." Mr. Buckley was yelling "stop" to the spread of communism abroad and liberalism at home. That *National Review* should now attack Mr. Buchanan for supporting protectionism and market intervention is consistent with founding principles and no surprise. But few would have thought that after 44 years of publication, a senior editor with an Indian surname would condemn a popular white conservative for speaking up for whites.

In fact, the *National Review* of the 1950s, 60s and even 70s spoke up for white people far more vigorously than Pat Buchanan would ever dare to today. The early *National Review* heaped criticism on the civil rights movement, *Brown v. Board of Education*, and people like Adam Clayton Powell and Martin Luther King, whom it considered race hustlers. Some of the greatest names in American conservatism—Russell Kirk, Willmore Kendall, James Kilpatrick, Richard Weaver, and a young Bill Buckley—wrote articles defending the white South and white South Africans in the days of segregation and apartheid. NR attacked the 1965 immigration bill that opened America to Third-World immigration, and wrote frankly about racial differences in IQ. There were always hints of compromise, but passages from some back issues could have been lifted right out of *American Renaissance*. No longer. NR still supports immigration reform and is not afraid of the IQ debate, but Mr. Ponnuru's article is just one example of its complete abandonment of the interests of whites as a group. What used to be a central part of the NR message it now dismissed as illegitimate "white identity politics."

"Why the South Must Prevail"

A famous example of the early NR stance on race was an August 24, 1957 unsigned editorial titled "Why the South Must Prevail." It was almost certainly written by Mr. Buckley, since he uses similar language in his book

Up From Liberalism. The editorial argued against giving blacks the vote because it would undermine civilization in the South:

"The central question that emerges . . . is whether the White community in the South is entitled to take such measures as are necessary to prevail, politically and culturally, in areas in which it does not prevail numerically? The sobering answer is *Yes*—the White community is so entitled because, for the time being, it is the advanced race. It is not easy, and it is unpleasant, to adduce statistics evidencing the cultural superiority of White over Negro: but it is a fact that obtrudes, one that cannot be hidden by ever-so-busy egalitarians and anthropologists."

"*National Review* believes that the South's premises are correct. . . . It is more important for a community, anywhere in the world, to affirm and live by civilized standards, than to bow to the demands of the numerical majority."

"The South confronts one grave moral challenge. It must not exploit the fact of Negro backwardness to preserve the Negro as a servile class. . . . Let the South never permit itself to do this. So long as it is merely asserting the right to impose superior mores for whatever period it takes to effect a genuine cultural equality between the races, and so long as it does so by humane and charitable means, the South is in step with civilization, as is the Congress that permits it to function."

The final passage about "genuine cultural equality between the races" can be read either as a last-minute loss of will *or* as a description of a criterion for the black franchise that *could never be met.* In any case, the editorial recognizes a principle NR would never articulate today: the right of a civilized minority—racial or otherwise—to impose its will upon an uncivilized majority. NR Contributing Editor L. Brent Bozell dissented from the editorial on constitutional grounds but still admitted, "It is understandable that White Southerners should try to have it both ways—they can't *know* what would happen should Negroes begin to vote, and they naturally want to cover their bet."

Needless to say, even in the 1950s, when the interests of whites were more openly recognized, the editorial called down the wrath of the liberals. Prof. William Muehl of the Yale Divinity School wrote: [I]n that vicious and wholly amoral thesis you exposed again the basic savagery of the reactionary mentality at bay." Would anything NR publishes today evoke such fury from established liberals?

But Mr. Buckley's magazine stood firm. A book review from the July 13th issue of the same year—1957—by Richard Weaver was called, "Integration is Communization." Mr. Weaver found Carl Rowan's *Go South to Sorrow* "a sorry specimen of Negro intellectual leadership," and went on to express deep suspicion about the whole integrationist enterprise:

" 'Integration' and 'Communization' are, after all, pretty closely synonymous. In light of what is happening today, the first may be little more than a euphemism for the second. It does not take many steps to get from the 'integrating' of facilities to the 'communizing' of facilities, if the impulse is there."

He concluded with a restatement of the principles of voluntary association. "In a free society, associations for educational, cultural, social, and business purposes have a right to protect their integrity against political fanaticism. The alternative to this is the destruction of free society and the replacement of its functions by government, which is the Marxist dream." Government's current "civil rights" powers to limit freedom of association have, indeed, brought virtually every corner of our lives under bureaucratic control, but would NR dare say so today?

Likewise in 1957, Sam M. Jones interviewed segregationist Senator Richard Russell of Georgia. In a Q&A format, Mr. Jones asked, "Do the people of the South fear political domination by the Negro or miscegenation or both?"

Senator Russell replied, "Both. As you know, Mr. Jones, there are some communities and some states where the Negro's voting potential is very great. We wish at all costs to avoid a repetition of the Reconstruction period when newly freed slaves made the laws and undertook their enforcement. We feel even more strongly about miscegenation or racial amalgamation.

"The experience of other countries and civilizations has demonstrated that the separation of the races biologically is highly preferable to amalgamation.

"I know of nothing in human history that would lead us to conclude that miscegenation is desirable."

Sam M. Jones wrote another article that year criticizing integration in the Washington, D.C., public schools. Titled "Caution: Integration at Work," the article accurately predicted that "the problem of school integration in the nation's capital may be eventually solved by the steady migration of the white population out of the District of Columbia." Jones criticized school integration on the grounds of IQ differences, citing "a white average ranging from 105 to 111 and a Negro average of 87 to 89. (An intelligent quotient of 85 is generally considered the minimum for receiving education.)" He went on to note:

"Data on juvenile delinquency . . . revealed a marked increase in truancy, theft, vandalism and sex-offenses in integrated schools. Dances and dramatic presentations have been quietly given up by most high schools. Senior and junior class plays have been discontinued. Inter-racial fights are frequent and constant vigilance is required to prevent molestation or attempted molestation of white girls by Negro boys or girls. In contrast, the schools outside the integrated neighborhoods have no more such problems than they had four years ago." Mr. Jones concluded that "the record shows . . . that the problems of integration are extremely serious and that no solution is in sight."

The September 28, 1957, issue contained a piece by James Kilpatrick called "Right and Power in Arkansas," in which he endorsed Arkansas Governor Orval Faubus' call-up of the National Guard to prevent forced integration at Little Rock's Central High School. Defending a community's right to keep the peace, he wrote that "the State of Arkansas and Orval Faubus are wholly in the right; they have acted lawfully; they are entitled to those great presumptions of the law which underlie the whole of our judicial tradition." Predicting a "storm" of white resistance he wrote, "Conceding, for the sake of discussion, that the Negro pupil has these new rights, what of the white community? *Has it none?*"

Cartoon from the issue of June 13, 1957
Would we see its like today?

An unsigned editorial in the September 21, 1957, issue put the blame for the whole incident squarely on the Supreme Court:

"Under the disintegrating effects of *Brown v. Board of Education*, the units of our society are forced into absolute dilemmas for which there is literally no solution within the traditional American structure.

"Violence and the threat of violence; base emotions; the cynical exploitation of members of both races by ruthless ideologues; the shameful spectacle of heavily armed troops patrolling the lawns and schoolyards of once tranquil towns and villages; the turgid dregs of hatred, envy, resentment, and sorrow—all these are part of the swelling harvest of *Brown v. Board of Education*."

On the tenth anniversary of *Brown*, NR offered this June 2, 1964, editorial:

"But whatever the exact net result in the restricted field of school desegregation, what a price we are paying for *Brown*! It would be ridiculous to hold the Supreme Court solely to blame for the ludicrously named 'civil rights movement'—that is, the Negro revolt . . . . But the Court carries its share of the blame. Its decrees, beginning with *Brown*, have on the one hand encouraged the least responsible of the Negro leaders in the course of extralegal and illegal struggle that we now witness around us. . . .

"*Brown*, as *National Review* declared many years ago, was bad law and bad sociology. We are now tasting its bitter fruits. Race relations in the country are ten times *worse* than in 1954."

In the 1960s NR continued to oppose the civil rights movement and the assumption that race could somehow be reduced to irrelevance. A July 2, 1963, editorial declared: "The Negro people have been encouraged to ask for, and to believe they can get, nothing less than the evanescence of color, and they are doomed to founder on the shoals of existing human attitudes—their own included." Race, as AR continues to point out, cannot be made not to matter, and NR once understood that.

An article by James Kilpatrick in the September 24, 1963, issue argued that the Civil Rights Bill (eventually passed in 1964) should be voted down. He wrote, "I believe this bill is a very bad bill. In my view, the means here proposed are the wrong means. . . . In the name of achieving certain 'rights' for one group of citizens this bill would impose some fateful compulsions on another group of citizens." After it passed, an editorial declared: "The Civil Rights Act has been law for only a little over two months, yet it already promises to be the source of much legalistic confusion, civic chaos and bureaucratic malpractice."

Mr. Kilpatrick also took aim at the 1965 Voting Rights Act in the April 20, 1965, issue. "Must We Repeal the Constitution to Give the Negro the Vote?" he asked, accusing the bill's supporters of "perverting the Constitution." He thought certain blacks should be given the right to vote but notes, "Over most of this century, the great bulk of Southern Negroes have been genuinely unqualified for the franchise." He also defended segregation as rational for Southerners. "Segregation is a fact, and more than a fact; it is a state of mind. It lies in the Southern subconscious next to man's most elementary instincts, for self-preservation, for survival, for the untroubled continuation of a not intolerable way of life."

Mr. Buckley softened his position on civil rights in the 1960s but to a point that would still be intolerable for conservatives today. In a column written five months before the passage of the 1965 Voting Rights Act and called "The Issue at Selma," he called for giving blacks the vote but perhaps restricting the franchise to high school graduates. He sympathized with the Southern position writing, "In much of the South, what is so greatly feared is irresponsible, mobocratic rule, and it is a fear not easily dissipated, because it is well-grounded that if the entire Negro population in the South were suddenly given the vote, and were to use it as a bloc, and pursuant to directives handed down by some of the more demagogic leaders, chaos would ensue." He also warned of "a suddenly enfranchised, violently embittered Negro population which will take the vote and wield it as an instrument of vengeance, shaking down the walls of Jericho even to their foundations, and reawakening the terrible genocidal antagonisms that scarred the Southern psyche during the days of Reconstruction."

Mr. Buckley expressed similar doubts about multiracial democracy in his 1959 *Up From Liberalism*: "Democracy's finest bloom is seen only in its natural habitat, the culturally homogenous community. There, democracy induces harmony. Harmony (not freedom) is democracy's finest flower. Even a politically unstable society of limited personal freedom can be harmonious if governed democratically, if only because the majority understand themselves to be living in the house that they themselves built."

NR loathed the "Black Power" movement, which it described in a July 19, 1966, editorial as a natural outgrowth of the civil rights movement:

"It isn't surprising when you come to think of it, that the militants in the civil rights movement should move to a new concept—they call it Black Power—at this stage, the movement having come into doldrums. What made it inevitable was the ravenous rhetoric of the past few years, whose motto 'Freedom Now' called for nothing less, when analyzed, than the evanescence of color. Since no such thing could be brought about, can be brought about, there is a sense of disappointment among those civil rights workers who somehow permitted themselves to believe that the passage of a few bits and pieces of legislation would transform the life of the American Negro. . . . It never followed that Negroes would suddenly cease to be poor, that whites would cease to prefer the company of whites, that the overwhelming majority of the American population would not continue to concentrate on individual and family concerns."

The February 12, 1963, issue attacked another element of the movement: "the Black Muslims—who have no connection with real Mohammedanism—are ferociously anti-white and anti-Christian . . . believe in violence, and train actively for the War of Armageddon, in which the blacks will kill all the whites."

An October 8, 1968, article called "Black Power and the Campus" by David Brudnoy observes: "Black power today means a total striving by embittered groups of Negroes for everything their fancies demand. In its path lie the crumpled remains of the Constitution, the tattered sleeves of law, the punctured corpse of Reason, and literally the bodies of those Negroes and whites who oppose it."

In the July 15, 1969, issue we find an editorial about the Black Panthers: "Under a portrait of Che Guevara they installed in a church auditorium, they distribute free food and comic books to kids at breakfasts. The food is contributed by local merchants, who risk having their stores burned down (one case so far—enough to make the point) if they refuse. The comics are crude, nasty affairs depicting heroic black kids killing and intimidating pigs in police uniforms."

NR used to be forthright about dressing down prominent blacks. A June 7, 1958, editorial on Adam Clayton Powell, Jr. stated, "That Powell is a racist has been clear for years. Last June, in *National Review*, Miss Maureen Buckley covered the subject neatly: 'Adam Clayton Powell's championing of the Negro cause has led him to a strange racist extremism. . . . In 1946 he pronounced in the *Congressional Record* his fixed conclusion that, 'the best thing that could happen would be the passing of the white man's world [which] has stood for nationalism, oppression, and barbarism.' "

In the same manner, a September 7, 1965, article by Will Herberg blames Martin Luther King and the civil rights movement for the 1965 Los Angeles riots:

"For years now, the Rev. Dr. Martin Luther King and his associates have been deliberately undermining the foundations of internal order in this country. With their rabble-rousing demagoguery, they have been cracking the 'cake of custom' that holds us together. With their doctrine of 'civil disobedience' they have been teaching hundreds of thousands of Negroes . . . that it is perfectly all right to break the law and defy constituted authority if you are a Negro-with-a-grievance. . . . And they have done more than talk. They have on occasion after occasion, in almost every part of the country, called out their mobs on the streets, promoted 'school strikes,' sit-ins, lie-ins, in explicit violation of the law and in explicit violation of the public authority. They have taught anarchy and chaos by word and deed . . . ."

In 1979 Mr. Buckley was still criticizing Martin Luther King saying, "When it was black men persecuting white or black men—in the Congo, for instance—he was strangely silent on the issue of human rights. The human rights of Chinese, or of Caucasians living behind the Iron Curtain never appeared to move him." This is pretty mild criticism but it would not appear in today's NR, which fawns over King as much as the liberals do.

A Reliable Voice

Criticism of the American Civil Rights movement was not the only way in which NR used to promote "identity politics for white people." It wrote articles about South Africa clearly endorsing apartheid as the only workable system for the country. In the March 9, 1965, issue Russell Kirk decried court-enforced black voting rights as "theoretical folly" that the US would nevertheless survive, but declared prophetically that the same dogma in South Africa, "if applied, would bring anarchy and the collapse of civilization." For Kirk, civilization required apartheid: "In a time of virulent 'African nationalism,' . . . how is South Africa's 'European' population . . . to keep the peace and preserve a prosperity unique in the Dark Continent?" White rule, he answered, is a prudent way, "to govern tolerably a society composed of several races, among which only a minority is civilized." He called for humane treatment of South African blacks but dismissed their leaders as "witch doctors" and "reckless demagogues." He wrote frankly about the " 'European' element which makes South Africa the only modern and prosperous African country."

NR also used to understand immigration. A September 21, 1965, article by Ernest van den Haag called "More Immigration?" took on the impending reform [signed into law on October 3, 1965, by Lyndon Johnson] that would open up America to the Third World. Mr. van den Haag, who is still listed as a contributing editor to NR, argued that our then-sound immigration laws should be made even stricter, not looser. Rejecting the charge that the laws were "racist," he wrote: "one need not believe that one's own ethnic group, or any ethnic group, is superior to others . . . in order to wish one's country to continue to be made up of the same ethnic strains in the same proportions as before. And, conversely, the wish not to see one's country overrun by groups one regards as alien need not be based on feelings of superiority or 'racism'." He goes on to say, "the wish to preserve one's identity and the identity of one's nation requires no justification . . . any more than the wish to have one's own children, and to continue one's family through them need be justified or rationalized by a belief that they are superior to the children of others."

A September 26, 1975, review of Jean Raspail's *The Camp of the Saints* makes much the same point.[1] Prof. Jeffrey Hart, who is currently listed as a senior editor, called the book a "sensation" that rocked liberal sensibilities. He wrote: "Most people . . . are able to perceive that the 'other group' looks rather different and lives rather differently from their own. Such 'racist' or 'ethnocentric' feelings are undoubtedly healthy, and involve merely a preference for one's own kind. Indeed—and Raspail hammers away at this point throughout his novel—no group can long survive unless it does 'prefer itself.' . . . The liberal rote anathema on 'racism' is in effect a poisonous assault upon Western self-preference."

Mr. van den Haag took a thoroughly sound position on IQ differences. In the December 1, 1964, issue—a full thirty years before *The Bell Curve* and five years before Arthur Jensen's celebrated article in the *Harvard Educational Review*—he interviewed an unnamed "eminent sociologist" (who happened to be himself). Under the title "Intelligence or Prejudice?" and the subtitle, "An eminent sociologist discusses Negro intelligence and accuses certain of his colleagues of prejudice against logic and discrimination against facts," the article took on the ever-trendy nonsense that intelligence cannot be tested and that the concept of IQ is meaningless. The "eminent sociologist" defended IQ testing by citing the work of Hans Eysenck, and research on identical twins. He claimed intelligence is largely heritable and that environmental factors cannot improve it by much. Mr. van den Haag wrote that integrated education impairs whites and "demoralizes" blacks, and advocated separation: "I am all in favor of improving the quality of education for all.

---

[1] The AR review of this book appears on page 291.

But this can be done only if pupils are separated according to ability (whatever determines it). And this means very largely according to race."

In an April 8, 1969 column, called "On Negro Inferiority" Mr. Buckley wrote about the furor caused by Arthur Jensen's research about race and IQ, calling it "massive, apparently authoritative." Mr. Buckley even bragged that "Professor Ernest van den Haag, writing in *National Review* (Dec. 1, 1964) . . . brilliantly anticipated the findings of Dr. Jensen and brilliantly coped with their implications."

The late Revilo Oliver, classicist and outspoken racialist, made regular appearances in the early NR. Mr. Buckley thought so highly of him he put his name on the masthead and invited him to his wedding. Oliver, who refused to compromise and was eventually banished from the magazine, also knew something about race and IQ before Arthur Jensen did. This is from his November 2, 1957, review of Ashley Montagu's *Man: His First Million Years*:

"Dr. Montagu, who composed the UNESCO Statement on Race, has again skillfully trimmed the facts of anthropology to fit the Liberal propaganda line. Every anthropologist knows, for example, that aborigines in Australia propagated their species for a hundred thousand years without ever suspecting that pregnancy might be a consequence of sexual intercourse. Equally striking evidence of intellectual capacity is provided by the many peoples that never discovered how to kindle a fire or plant a seed. But Dr. Montagu, after making a great show of cautious objectivity, proclaims that 'anthropologists are unable to find any evidence' of 'significant differences in mental capacity' between 'ethnic groups.' If you can tell such whoppers with a straight face, you too can ask the 'United Nations' to recognize your right to largesse from the pockets of American taxpayers."

No Longer Yelling "Stop"

Clearly, the early *National Review* was often a voice for white Americans. It not only defended their culture, it defended their race. White Southerners had a right—both constitutionally and morally—to protect themselves from black rule and black incivility. White South Africans had the same right. The nation as a whole had a right to defend its European heritage and racial identity by closing its borders to non-whites. As Mr. van den Haag wrote, this policy needed no justification. And if low black intelligence and high crime rates hindered white students from learning, that was sufficient reason for separate education.

Today's NR has not yet abandoned every subject of interest to whites *qua* whites. It is solidly against affirmative action and multicultural education. It defended *The Bell Curve* and has published reviews of J. Philippe Rushton's work. It still advocates immigration reform, though its position now is that a pause in immigration will make it easier for the non-whites who are already here to assimilate. Even that stance could crumble. In 1998 Mr. Buckley demoted the two men most responsible for the magazine's anti-immigration tone, editor John O'Sullivan and senior editor Peter Brimelow. Filling their places are people like Mr. Ponnuru and John Miller, who like immigration and are afraid of "identity politics for white people." Today's NR is no longer the brave journal that fought integration and tried to keep America European. It is not yelling "stop" to multiracialism and the displacement of the country's founding stock by aliens. That, as Mr. Ponnuru explains, would be to play "tribal politics."

This article appeared in the September 2000 issue. James Lubinskas is a former assistant editor of American Renaissance.

Mr. Buckley is Silent

After reading James Lubinskas' article about the firm positions NR used to take on racial matters, I was curious to know how Mr. Buckley would explain the change, and inquired about the possibility of an interview. His secretary asked that I fax her an outline of the subjects I wanted to cover, so I sent several past and present quotations from NR, explaining that I wanted to know why the magazine had shifted its ground. A few days later, I telephoned her again to ask about the interview, and she told me Mr. Buckley is writing a book and giving no interviews. I asked why I had been told to summarize what I wanted to talk about if he is giving no interviews, and she told me to fax the same material again.

The next day, August 5, 2000, Mr. Buckley's syndicated newspaper column was about the very subjects I had raised in my faxed message. It was a meandering piece about the Republican convention's celebration of diversity, but added that Jared Taylor, "a white separatist of sorts," had wondered whether whites are allowed to have racial interests as a group. Mr. Buckley then quoted several sentences from the passage from Ernest van den Haag's 1965 article that Mr. Lubinskas cited, and which I had included as part of my letter to Mr. Buckley. The column managed to avoid reaching a conclusion about the legitimacy of white racial consciousness.

I telephoned Mr. Buckley's secretary again, pointed out that Mr. Buckley had used my letter as material for a column, and asked once again for an interview. No, she said, Mr. Buckley is writing a book and must not be disturbed. — *Jared Taylor*

Undue Process

Arnold Krammer, *The Untold Story of America's German Alien Internees*, Rowan & Littlefield, 1997, 209 pp., $27.95

reviewed by Joseph E. Fallon

Since 1948, the internment and re-location policies implemented by the Roosevelt Administration during World War II have been presented by Congress, the news media, some historians, and the Japanese-American lobby as an expression of racist war hysteria against Japanese living in the United States.

This distortion of history has been used to justify financial compensation to "victims" of those policies on nine separate occasions between 1948 and 1992. It has now become part of the ideology of "white racism" and a precedent for demands by blacks for reparations because of slavery and by Hispanics because of the Mexican-American War.

In *Undue Process: The Untold Story of America's German Alien Internees*, Arnold Krammer, professor of history at Texas A&M University, describes the extensive wartime policy of interning *Europeans*—a policy that has disappeared from history books and that gives the lie to the now orthodox view that Japanese relocation was a race-based policy. Using government documents, newspaper accounts, and interviews with former internees, Prof. Krammer has documented the officially-forgotten history of the internment of Germans and German-Americans.

It is important at the outset to distinguish between *internment* and *relocation*. Internment was literal incarceration, and was reserved primarily for enemy aliens. Relocation was the requirement that people considered to be threats to American security—some of whom were US citizens—move out of the Western part of the United States. It is the relocation of Japanese, both citizens and aliens, that is now represented as a shameful example of "racism," but Prof. Krammer's book puts this policy in proper perspective.

Internment of Enemy Aliens

According to a 1798 law still on the books, an enemy alien is any citizen of a country at war with the United States. He need not show hostility towards the US to be included in this category. While not all enemy aliens are interned, by law *only* enemy aliens can be interned, and internment often leads to deportation. US citizens may "voluntarily" join their enemy alien spouses or parents in internment.

Prof. Krammer points out that President Roosevelt's internment policy followed a precedent set by Woodrow Wilson, who interned approximately 6,300 enemy aliens during the First World War. This number included crewmen from German and Austro-Hungarian ships visiting US ports at the time war was declared, and nationals of Germany and Austria-Hungary living in the United States. Approximately one third of the World War I internees were repatriated to Europe, and the last internees were not released until April 1920—seventeen months after the war ended. German nationals not interned were required to register at post offices and carry a government registration card at all times. They were also forbidden to, among other things, "own guns, radios, or explosives" or "live within a half-mile of munitions factories, aircraft stations, forts, arsenals, or naval vessels."

President Roosevelt's internment policy during World War II was vastly greater in scope. As early as 1939—well before America entered the war in December 1941—Roosevelt authorized FBI Director J. Edgar Hoover to collect information on people to be interned if war broke out. Much, if not all, of the information was unsubstantiated allegations from unnamed sources, but once a person's name was on the FBI list only death could remove it.

The United States started to intern German and Italian merchant seamen in US ports in April 1941 while the country was officially neutral—a clear violation of law. By October 1941, it had formal plans for interning Germans and Italians living in the United States, and began implementing them on December 8, 1941—three days before the US was officially at war with Germany and Italy. Some Germans who were naturalized citizens were stripped of US citizenship so they could be interned "legally."

The total number of enemy aliens interned by the Roosevelt Administration was 31,275. This included 10,905 Germans, 16,849 Japanese, and 3,278 Italians. The rest consisted of Hungarians, Romanians, Bulgarians, and others, with Europeans constituting 46 percent of the total. Among the internees were more than 6,600 Latin Americans—approximately 4,100 Germans, 2,300 Japanese, and 300 Italians—who were rounded up by Latin American governments at the request of the Roosevelt administration and sent to the United States. All Japanese enemy aliens were released from internment by June 1946, but some Germans and other Europeans were kept until August 1948.

The Roosevelt Administration also deported enemy aliens, and continued shipping German and German-Latin American internees to Germany even after the war in Europe had ended. It took Congressional legislation in 1947 finally to end deportation of Germans.

Prof. Krammer tells the stories of a number of German internees, many of whose careers and reputations were ruined by internment. Alfred Heitmann, for example, was an engineer for Standard Oil. He was interned in 1942 and released on parole in 1945, on condition that he not return to his old job at Standard Oil. For the rest of his life, this professionally-trained engineer could get work only as a grave digger, a foundryman, and a maintenance man.

Robert Minner had been a journalist. After his release in 1946, the only job he could get was shoveling coal. Albert Krause was a physics teacher.

He was also released in 1946, but never again worked as a physics teacher. His family survived on his wife's income and the part-time and summer earnings of their three daughters.

Arthur D. Jacobs was 11 years old when, on three separate occasions, the FBI ransacked his family's home looking for contraband or Nazi propaganda. Although the FBI found nothing, his father was interned in 1944 on the basis of unsubstantiated accusations from unnamed sources. Left without an income, the family "voluntarily" joined the father in internment. In 1946, the Jacobses were repatriated to Germany. Twenty-two months later, Arthur and Lambert, US citizens by birth, managed to return, but they came alone. Their father could not forgive the US government for the way it treated him, and their mother stayed with their father.

Relocation

Relocation of Japanese-Americans is largely outside the scope of Prof. Krammer's study, but this is the policy that is so frequently described as "racist." It was not at all the same as internment. Internment was national in scope and involved incarcerating specific individuals for the purpose of deportation, whereas relocation did not begin until February 1942, and was limited to the West Coast. It authorized the Secretary of War or the appropriate military commander temporarily to exclude any or all persons—US citizens, resident aliens, and enemy aliens, Germans and Italians, as well as Japanese—from all of California, the western halves of Washington and Oregon, and the southern third of Arizona. The government encouraged anyone who was excluded to resettle in the eastern halves of Washington and Oregon or in any of the other unaffected 44 states.

It is widely assumed that people excluded from the West coast were forcibly kept in "concentration camps." This is not true. Exclusion prohibited residence in certain areas—nothing more—and anyone excluded could move anywhere else in the country. The relocation centers, which provided free housing, food, medical care, and education for children, were made available to anyone who would rather live at government expense than find another place on his own. As the US Supreme Court wrote in the 1944 case of *Korematsu v. United States* that found exclusion constitutional, no Japanese citizen or enemy alien was compelled "either in fact or by law" to go to a relocation center. The Court added, "We deem it unjustifiable to call them concentration camps with all the ugly connotations that term implies." Anyone living in a relocation center was free to leave at any time so long as he did not return to the exclusion zone, and during the war, some 30,000 Japanese moved out of the centers.

It is not well known that Germans and Italians were excluded from the West Coast along with the Japanese. The relocation centers, however, were open only to Japanese. Originally only Japanese excluded from the West Coast could live in them but later, Japanese from other parts of the country were allowed in after petitioning the government.

It is true that far more Japanese than Europeans were forced out of their homes on the West coast—112,000 as opposed to just a few hundred. It is this difference that was presumably "racist," but in *Korematsu*, the Court explained that "there were disloyal members of that population [the Japanese] whose number and strength could not be precisely and quickly ascertained." The Court also evoked the fear of a Japanese invasion.

Both reasons were legitimate. To begin with, there was a real question about the loyalty of Japanese-Americans even before the war. According to a Japanese government census, 78 percent of Japanese-Americans held dual Japanese citizenship, which indicated a less-than-total attachment to America. Once the war began, unlike German- and Italian-Americans, many Japanese-Americans were openly disloyal. For example, approximately 14,000 filed to renounce US citizenship. The demand for renunciation was so great that in 1944 Congress amended the Nationality Act of 1940 to allow US citizens to renounce citizenship during wartime. Of these 14,000 petitioners, 5,620 followed the process through to full renunciation, and gave up citizenship. They were then interned as enemy aliens, a consequence that probably kept many other disloyal Japanese-Americans from renouncing citizenship. Without this group of 5,620 Japanese—officially known as "renunciants" and, in effect, self-selected internees—the number of European internees would have been greater than the number of Japanese. Researchers are unaware of any case of a US citizen of European origin renouncing citizenship during the war.

What other indications do we have of the Japanese attitude towards the United States? Just five weeks after the West Coast exclusion order, the government offered Japanese resident aliens naturalized US citizenship if they would serve in the American war effort. This was a remarkably generous offer at a time when Japanese were otherwise barred from naturalization. Virtually no one accepted.

Japanese-Americans living in relocation centers were free to join the armed forces but only six percent of those of military age did so. In most cases this was because they would not side with the United States. In fact, many wanted to go back to Japan. By 1945, more than 20,000 US citizens and enemy aliens in relocation centers had filed papers with Washington to return to Japan. Eventually, over 8,000 Japanese, including Japanese-Latin Americans, were repatriated.

Another indication of the state of mind of Japanese-Americans was the refusal of hundreds of young men to register for the draft—at a time when draft evasion was virtually unheard of. Eventually 85 citizens of Japanese descent were tried and sentenced to prison in the largest mass trial of draft resisters in US history. Also, approximately 20,000 Japanese-Americans who were living in Japan at the time of the Pearl Harbor attack remained in Japan and supported the war effort against the United States.

Finally, by means of MAGIC, the project that broke Japan's diplomatic codes, the government learned of espionage rings organized by and operating out of Japan's West Coast consulates. Both enemy aliens and US citizens were among the spies.

What about the fear of Japanese attack? Unlike Germany and Italy, Japan invaded and occupied American territory: the Philippines, Guam, Wake Island, and Attu and Kiska just off Alaska. On a number of occasions, particularly during the early part of the war, Japan shelled or bombed the West Coast, or sunk US ships off the coast. Near the end of the war, Japan launched over 9,000 transoceanic balloon bombs against the West Coast.

Given these circumstances—open disloyalty by many Japanese-Americans and what appeared to be direct Japanese military threats against the West Coast—the exclusion order appears entirely reasonable. If there had been parallel circumstances with Germans and Italians in the eastern part of the United States, there can be little doubt there would have been an East Coast exclusion order as well. Both in its internment and exclusion policies, the American government appears to have been making strictly military decisions, which did not take race into account.

Perhaps it should have considered race. The record shows that Japanese-Americans were far more likely than German-Americans to favor their homeland over the United States—and quite naturally so. Loyalty to the US required that German-Americans turn their backs on an ethnic and cultural identity; Japanese-Americans were renouncing not just their culture but their race.

Compensation

Ironically, it is now on racial grounds that Japanese claim *they* were wronged. Activists succeeded in winning financial compensation from Congress on seven separate occasions—in 1948, 1951, 1952, 1956, 1960, 1972, and 1978—before their most recent success.

In 1988, Congress issued an official apology, and awarded $20,000 to each former internee and relocated person of Japanese descent. Four years later, Congress extended eligibility for the $20,000 to non-Japanese spouses of Japanese internees who voluntarily joined their families in internment. In June 1998, the Clinton Administration announced it would pay financial compensation to Japanese-Latin Americans interned in the United States during the war.

Note that for Japanese, internment and relocation were treated the same, but that only Japanese and no Europeans have received money or an apology. Japanese who were relocated but then returned to Japan out of loyalty to their country of origin were eligible for the $20,000 just as were Japanese who were relocated, enlisted in the US Army, and served the United States. The government has never awarded financial compensation, or offered an apology of any kind to the thousands of Europeans it interned, relocated, or deported during and after the war.

As Prof. Krammer concludes, America's German and Italian internees have suffered a double tragedy. During the war, many were locked up on suspect grounds, and today, virtually no one even knows about it. It has now become virtually impossible to acknowledge the truth because this would knock an important prop out from under the now-essential ideology of "white racism."

This article appeared in the January 1999 issue.

Sowing the Seeds of Destruction

Gunnar Myrdal, *An American Dilemma: The Negro Problem and Modern Democracy*, Harper and Row 1962, 1,483 pp., $16.50

reviewed by Jared Taylor

An American Dilemma, written by the Swedish economist, Gunnar Myrdal, is unquestionably the most influential book ever written about race relations in America. Published in 1944, this 1,400-page treatment of "the Negro problem" went through 25 printings—an astonishing record for a heavily academic work—before it went into a second, "twentieth anniversary" edition in 1962. It influenced presidential commissions and Supreme Court decisions, and established rules for public discussion about race that endure to this day. More than any other book, it laid the groundwork for integration, affirmative action, and multiracialism, and destroyed the legitimacy of white racial consciousness.

Although the title is as famous as ever, virtually no one now reads *An American Dilemma*. Partly this is because its exhaustive statistics are out of date, and the legal segregation it set out to eradicate has been gone for 30 years. Another reason is that by today's standards the book is grossly "insensitive," not only to Southern whites whom Myrdal obviously despised, but even to blacks whose cause he championed.

Yet another reason may be that for anyone with an interest in the ideas that have paved the way for an increasingly Third-World America, this book is a gold mine. Every anti-white cliché is here, as is every excuse for black failure. What is more, Myrdal pronounces them in the starkest, most unsubtle terms. Liberal race policies had not yet been tried. Myrdal had not witnessed their failure and therefore did not temper his language as liberals do today. The result is the clearest possible statement of the calamitous ideas that have shaped the last 40 years.

For Myrdal, "the Negro problem" has only one cause. Today he would have called it "racism" or "bigotry" but those words were not yet part of the liberal vocabulary. He writes instead of "prejudice" and "discrimination," and this is perhaps his key passage:

"White prejudice and discrimination keep the Negro low in standards of living, health, education, manners and morals. This, in its turn, gives support to white prejudice. White prejudice and Negro standards thus mutually 'cause' each other."

In other words, whites degrade blacks and then point to their degradation as justification for degrading them. Myrdal saw several ways out of this vicious cycle. If whites could be cured of prejudice, they would not oppress blacks so much, blacks would improve themselves, and their example would further cure whites of prejudice. Alternatively, the government could take measures to improve the circumstances of blacks, which would reduce white prejudice, which would permit blacks to improve themselves still further. Myrdal devotes an entire appendix to this "principle of cumulation," whereby even the smallest improvement will constantly magnify itself.

For this to work, though, blacks must be, aside from their oppression, no different from whites. Although anthropologists had been promoting this egalitarian view since the 1930s, Myrdal was the first *economist* to write that discrimination rather than low intelligence caused black poverty. Myrdal knew this claim was central to his argument and repeated it throughout the book.

"Social research," he says, is "constantly disproving inherent differences and explaining apparent ones in cultural and social terms." He cites the assertions of Franz Boas and his disciples (but offers no data) to discredit conventional views about racial differences in intelligence and temperament: "[T]he popular race dogma is being victoriously pursued into every corner and effectively exposed as fallacious or at least unsubstantiated." As a result, "the undermining of the basis of certitude for popular beliefs has been accomplished." Myrdal is sure science is on his side, and voices a complaint that is, ironically, echoed in the pages of AR—that there is a "wide gap between scientific thought and popular belief."

The difficulty, he says, is that unlike biological differences, the cultural explanation is just too much for rubes: "It requires difficult and complicated thinking about a multitude of mutually dependent variables, thinking which does not easily break into the lazy formalism of unintellectual people." We can be optimistic, though, because "white prejudice can change . . . as a result of an increased general knowledge about biology, eradicating some of the false beliefs among whites concerning Negro racial inferiority."

Already in 1944, Myrdal sensed the demise of theories about racial differences: "Most of them never reach the printing press or the microphone any more, as they are no longer intellectually respectable. The educated classes of whites are gradually coming to regard those who believe in the Negro's biological inferiority as narrow-minded and backward."

The better class of whites now understood that "the Negro problem in America represents a moral lag in the development of the nation," and this was, in fact, the American dilemma. Blacks were in every respects the equals of whites, yet were treated as inferiors. This injustice was particularly jarring in the United States because it violated what Myrdal calls "the American creed" of equality.

Why did Americans persist in violating the creed? In the South, Myrdal discovered elaborate mechanisms of racial separation that he called the "caste system." He notes that although caste rules govern virtually all contact between blacks and whites they serve one central function: to keep blacks from marrying or having sex with whites. In both the North and the South Myrdal found a universal revulsion among whites for miscegenation and the "amalgamation of the races" that this would bring. In virtually all the states, this revulsion was reflected in laws that forbade interracial marriage.

Myrdal scoffs at this. He even "jestingly argues" that amalgamation "might create a race of unsurpassed excellence: a people with just a little sunburn without extra trouble and even through the winter; with some curl in the hair without the cost of a permanent wave; with, perhaps, a little more emotional warmth in their souls; and a little more religion, music, laughter, and carefreeness in their lives."

Myrdal never even accepted white opposition to amalgamation as *genuine*. With no data to support his view, he insisted that opposition was nothing more than a pretext for keeping blacks out of economic competition. He went on to call it "an irrational escape on the part of the whites from voicing an open demand for difference in social status between the two groups for its own sake." Whites, he said, have a purely tyrannical desire for supremacy, but claim that they are trying to prevent miscegenation.

What, then, underlies the desire for supremacy? Myrdal claimed to understand white Americans better than they understood themselves: "Without any doubt there is also in the white man's concept of the Negro 'race' an irrational element which cannot be grasped in terms of either biological or cultural differences. . . . In this magical sphere of the white man's mind, the Negro is inferior, totally independent of rational proofs or disproofs. And he is inferior in a deep and mystical sense."

The Vicious South

This form of mysticism was particularly prevalent in the South; some of Myrdal's comments about Southerners beggar the imagination:

"[It would be correct to say that] the white South is virtually obsessed by the Negro problem, that the South has allowed the Negro problem to rule its politics and its business, fetter its intelligence and human liberties, and hamper its progress in all directions . . . ."

"The issue of 'white supremacy vs. Negro domination,' as it is called in the South, has for more than a hundred years stifled freedom of thought and speech and affected all other civic rights and liberties of both Negroes and whites in the South. It has retarded its economic, social and cultural advance. On this point there is virtual agreement among all competent observers."

"White Southerners are prepared to abstain from many liberties and to sacrifice many advantages for the purpose of withholding them from the Negroes."

These charges—that Southerners are obsessed with blacks, that obsession retards progress, that whites deny themselves liberties in order to withhold them from blacks—are tossed off without elaboration or substantiation.

Although Myrdal conceded that by the time he studied race relations lynchings were unusual and widely condemned, he finds great significance in them:

"The South has an obsession with sex which helps to make this region quite irrational in dealing with Negroes generally. . . . The sadistic elements in most lynchings also point to a close relation between lynching and thwarted sexual urges."

Oddly, he thought that Southern Christianity was partly to blame for lynching:

"[Another factor is] the prevalence of a narrow-minded and intolerant, 'fundamentalist' type of Protestant evangelical religion. Occasional violently emotional revival services, and regular appeals in ordinary preaching to fear and passion rather than to calm reasoning, on the one hand, and denunciations of modern thought, scientific progress, and all kinds of nonconformism, on the other hand, help to create a state of mind which makes a lynching less extraordinary."

Of course, lynching was part of the "amazing disrespect for law and order which even today characterizes the Southern states in America and constitutes such a large part of the Negro problem." Thanks to this lawlessness, "a white man can steal from or maltreat a Negro in almost any way without fear of reprisal . . . ." This is part of a long tradition: "[A] main way to get and remain rich in the South has been to exploit the Negroes and other weaker people, rather than to work diligently, make oneself indispensable and have brilliant ideas." Exploiting blacks is apparently known as "mattressing the niggers."

Myrdal writes that although Southerners claim to understand blacks, this is "one of the most pathetic stereotypes in the South." On the contrary, the Southern white is willfully ignorant: "The ignorance about the Negro is not, it must be stressed, just a random lack of interest and knowledge. It is a tense and highstrung restriction and distortion of knowledge, and it indicates much deeper dislocations within the minds of Southern whites."

Mental dislocations characterize Southern politics: "[F]ear of the Negro shadows every political discussion and prevents the whites from doing anything to improve themselves." This, says Myrdal, results in "an amazing avoidance of issues in Southern politics." Debate is one-sided: "Even at present the South does not have a full spectrum of political opinions . . . . There are relatively few liberals in the South and practically no radicals." He describes Southerners as the only true reactionaries in the developed world; their goal is "to accept the static state as ideal and to denounce progress."

What little hope there may be is found in Southern liberalism, which he finds "beautiful and dignified." As for its proponents, "they are the intellectuals of the region and are responsible for a large part of the entire high-grade literary, journalistic and scientific output of the region. . . . They are, indeed, the cultural facade of the South." This "gives to liberalism in the South a flavor of intellectual superiority . . . ."

Victims of Discrimination

As these passages suggest, when *An American Dilemma* turns to analysis, its subject is whites rather than blacks. This is consistent with Myrdal's view that "the Negro problem" begins and ends in the minds of whites. Without discrimination, blacks would be perfectly ordinary Americans, so it is only whites who must be dissected and denounced.

The descriptive passages, on the other hand, are largely of the circumstances of blacks, with detailed accounts of agriculture, education, the professions, social life, criminal justice, government employment, black churches, protest movements, and much more. Myrdal finds a great deal that is unpleasant, even "pathological," but he always has explanations: slavery, Jim Crow, and discrimination.

If blacks riot it is because their just resentments have boiled over. Blacks have been given a place in popular music but "have been greatly hampered in more serious music." Violent crime is a reaction to Southern lawlessness. Slavery broke up the black family. Discrimination causes poverty—and prostitution, drug addiction, even bad manners and anti-white crime.

What is striking about these arguments is not that Myrdal made them—in the pre-civil rights 1940s they were powerful and persuasive—but that people make them today. This habit of trotting out white wickedness to explain every form of black failure is one of the most persistent and destructive elements of liberal thinking. Myrdal was its most influential progenitor.

On the other hand, it may have been Myrdal's confidence in his explanations for black deviance that allowed him to write about it with candor that would today be called "racist."

"[M]any Negroes, particularly in the South, are poor, uneducated, and deficient in health, morals, and manners; and thus not very agreeable as social companions," he writes. Any given black is "more indolent, less punctual, less careful, and generally less efficient as a functioning member of society." He notes that blacks are more likely to be repeat criminals, and that "Negro criminals have become more addicted to crime and less corrigible."

Myrdal finds black thought narrow and sloppy: "Negro thinking in social and political terms is thus exclusively a thinking about the Negro problem . . . . Particularly in the lower classes, and in the Southern rural districts, the ideological structure of Negro thinking—even in its own narrow, caste-restricted realm—is loose, chaotic and rambling."

He also notes the hypocrisy of middle-class blacks who denounce segregation but profit from the monopoly business of serving black customers. He also writes that much as blacks may claim to be proud of their race, they often describe themselves as lighter-skinned—and never darker than they actually are. He observes that successful black men invariably marry light-skinned women.

Although many authors praise the black church, Myrdal was repelled by black worship services and writes disapprovingly of "rolling in a sawdust pit in [a] state of ecstasy, tambourine playing, reading of the future, healing of the sick, use of images of saints, footwashing, use of drums and jazz music, etc." "These 'rousements,' " he goes on to say, "bring most of the congregation into some degree of 'possession.' " "There is a tendency to emotionalize the collection so as to elicit more money."

Preachers are worse than congregations: "The chief prerequisite for becoming a minister in most of the denominations to which Negroes belong is traditionally not education, but a 'call' which is more often the manifestation of temporary hysteria or opportunistic self-inspiration than of a deep soul-searching."

Myrdal doesn't see much use for church at all: "The small upper class of Negroes tends to belong to the Episcopalian, Congregational, and Presbyterian churches, since for them a main function of church membership is to give prestige." Furthermore, "Negro preachers condemn extra-marital sex relations, but they seldom take any specific steps to stop them because usually so many of their congregation engage in the condemned behavior."

Even when he is complimenting blacks, Myrdal can adopt a contemptuous tone:

"Negroes have acquired the art of enjoying life more than have whites. Because they have no direct background in puritanism, they have taken sex more as it comes, without all the encumbrances and inhibitions. . . . The habit of spending a good deal of leisure time out-of-doors, due in part to the over-crowdedness of the Negro home, has contributed to the social pleasantness of Negro life, since being outside involves meeting friends and having no worries about destroying furniture." Destroying furniture?

Myrdal professes to admire the "wholesome" way blacks entertain themselves while working: "Singing, for example, accompanies all work, even on the chain gang; gambling while working is another example." Gambling while working?

Myrdal can't seem to decide whether black illegitimacy is good or bad. He notes that the black rate is eight times higher than the white rate but adds that "the Negro community also has the healthy social custom of attaching no stigma to the illegitimate child . . . ." This means that "the Negro lower classes, especially in the rural South, have built up a type of family organization conducive to social health, even though the practices are outside the American tradition."

On the other hand: "The over-crowdedness of the homes and the consequent lack of privacy prevent the growth of ideals of chastity and are one element in encouraging girls to become prostitutes." Myrdal sometimes seems as sex-obsessed as he claims Southerners to be. Indeed, he spends several pages in fascinated speculation about the illicit couplings that gave blacks so many white genes.

Social Engineering

Today, one of the most striking aspects of *An American Dilemma* is its touching faith in social science. Myrdal writes with much satisfaction about his "scientific" methods and solutions. Rather more ominous is his infatuation with "social engineering." The following passage is one of the clearest statements imaginable of the goals and tactics of liberalism:

"Many things that for a long period have been predominantly a matter of individual adjustment will become more and more determined by political decision and public regulation. . . . [T]he social engineering of the coming epoch will be nothing but the drawing of practical conclusions from the teaching of social science that 'human nature' is changeable and that human deficiencies and unhappiness are, in large degree, preventable."

This passage, which could have been written by Karl Marx, is worth re-reading for its breathless arrogance. Society will make all sorts of decisions for people that they used to make for themselves. Social engineering will then prevent unhappiness by changing human nature. It was, of course, enlightened liberals like Myrdal who would boss us around for our own good. The first project for Americans was to stamp out their pathological attitudes towards blacks and their false opposition to racial amalgamation.

Myrdal's arrogance leads to contempt for American institutions, especially if they stand in the way of "social engineering." He writes of the "nearly fetishistic cult of the Constitution" and goes on to complain that "the 150-year-old Constitution is in many respects impractical and ill-suited for modern conditions and . . . drafters of the document made it technically difficult to change . . . ." Once again he sounds like Marx when he writes, "the Constitutional Convention was nearly a plot against the common people."

Given that he seems to make no attempt to conceal his politics—he even refers to Eleanor Roosevelt as the President's "gallant lady"—it is baffling to find an appendix in *An American Dilemma* on how to avoid bias in social science. Mere description, Myrdal writes, is actually bias because it implies that society cannot or should not be changed. His approach—vastly superior—is to analyze rather than describe, and to do so with the clear intent of transforming society. Unlike many who followed him, he was at least honest about his goals, yet he makes the astonishing claim that his analysis was *unbiased*:

"In a particular problem where public opinion in the dominant white group is traditionally as heavily prejudiced in the conservative direction as in the Negro problem, even a radical tendency might fail to reach an unprejudiced judgment . . . ."

Just as remarkable is another appendix called "A Parallel to the Negro Problem." He argues that men oppress women just as whites oppress blacks, and predicts massive social transformation. Myrdal concludes that the Soviet Union is perhaps the only country in the world to get sex roles right.

Without Opposition

Why, though, was the Myrdal vision of race able not only to sweep everything before it but prepare the ground for all the other "liberation" movements? One reason, undoubtedly, was selective reporting, combined with repeated assertions of moral superiority. But there is another reason that Myrdal himself unwittingly suggests. He notes that even the most conservative whites rarely defend segregation personally, but say that "community feeling" or "tradition" requires it. He says this about the intellectual bases for white solidarity and an understanding of racial differences:

"They live a surreptitious life in thoughts and private remarks. There we have had to hunt them . . . . When they were thus drawn out into the open they looked shabby and ashamed of themselves. Everybody who has acquired a higher education knows that they are wrong."

He then adds the very interesting observation that the white man "does not have the moral stamina" to codify and defend a system based on explicit racial differences.

Those who would promote white consciousness today face the same obstacles. The Myrdal vision triumphed because there was no thoughtful, moral argument to oppose it. Many conservatives were ashamed of their views and afraid to voice them. Compared to maintaining segregation, the goal of preserving a people and a way of life should, by anyone's terms, be morally irreproachable. And yet hesitancy, shame, and fear of opprobrium are still the greatest obstacles to the pursuit of legitimate white interests.

It is for this reason that the expression of group interests, which for others is simply a matter of stamina is, for whites, a matter of *moral* stamina. The Myrdal vision succeeded because it harnessed, in a dangerously deluded way, the moral energy of whites. Only by directing that energy toward their own survival will whites break the shackles that Myrdal and his followers forged for them.

Although Gunnar Myrdal is best known in the United States for his work on race, he was primarily an economist and politician. From his student days in Sweden he had dreamed of a "party of the intelligent" that would manipulate the masses and guide the nation. He was radicalized in 1929 when he first visited the United States. The depression-era contrast between millionaires and paupers convinced him that "market forces work to perpetuate inequality."

Myrdal had already served in the Swedish Riksdag and had established himself as an architect of the Swedish welfare state by the time the Carnegie Foundation asked him, in 1936, to do a study of American blacks. Myrdal writes that he was chosen for the job because the foundation wanted a foreigner's untainted perspective. A Swede was the perfect choice because the foundation thought blacks would trust an author who was not from a nation with an overseas empire. The foundation gave Myrdal $300,000—a huge sum at the time—and free rein to hire staff and commission research. One reason the book was so well received is that Myrdal deliberately involved as many prominent liberals as possible in the project. They became co-authors, in a sense, and promoted the book in universities and the press. Myrdal called *An American Dilemma* his "war work," because he considered its message an attack on Nazism.

After the war, Myrdal returned to Sweden and was Minister of Commerce from 1945 to 1947. He continued to spread a socialist, redistributionist message, and even argued that once enough welfare states had been established in the advanced countries, they could inaugurate a global "welfare world." Not everyone approved of Myrdal. The FBI compiled a list of 41 people acknowledged in the preface of *An American Dilemma*, noting that many were Communist Party members, sympathizers, or members of front groups. Myrdal's wife and son, Alva and Jan, were investigated by the FBI for pro-Communist activity. Alva Myrdal was eventually denied entry to the United States and Jan Myrdal went on to organize a communist "festival" in Bucharest.

Meanwhile *An American Dilemma* was helping change the United States. Myrdal was a personal friend of Supreme Court Justice Felix Frankfurter, and his book was cited in the *Brown v. Board of Education* decision. When President Truman established a presidential commission on civil rights, its members used *An American Dilemma* as their central text. In 1947 the commission issued a report, "To Secure These Rights," which followed Myrdal's recommendations. Truman implemented the report in his 1948 civil rights program that abolished segregation in the armed forces, set up a civil rights division in the Justice Department, and promoted national legislation to combat racism. During the first sit-in demonstration, in Greensboro, North Carolina, blacks cited Myrdal as an important influence. In the 1960s, *Saturday Review* asked American intellectuals which book of the previous 40 years had been most influential. Only John Maynard Keynes' *General Theory* got more votes than *An American Dilemma*.

Myrdal went on to win the Nobel Prize in economics in 1974, and cultivated a role as international elder statesman. In his later years he lost faith in "social engineering" and began to see that it led inevitably to tyranny. At the time of his death in 1987, he was working on *An American Dilemma Revisited*. The black sociologist Kenneth Clark was to be co-author but withdrew because of Myrdal's "egocentricity and desire to dominate the project."

Not surprisingly, blacks still cite *An American Dilemma*. Last year, the W.E.B. Du Bois Institute for Afro-American Research held a three-day conference to mark the book's 50th anniversary. Black academics from two dozen universities gathered at Harvard for the occasion. As a spokesman for the Du Bois Institute explained, "Myrdal was not only on the mark 50 years ago but continues to provide a scathing analysis of the contemporary scene." Wilbur Rich of Wellesley College no doubt summed up the thinking of many blacks when he said that, compared to 50 years ago, "blacks are more complicated and whites are less enlightened." The spirit of Myrdal lives on.

This article appeared in the April 1999 issue.

Integration . . . Disintegration

Raymond Wolters, *The Burden of Brown*, University of
Tennessee Press, 1984 (paperback edition 1992)
346 pp., $14.95

reviewed by Thomas Jackson

The most unjustifiable excesses of "civil rights"—affirmative action, busing, racially gerrymandered voting districts—have invariably been the work of the US Supreme Court. Nine unelected justices have repeatedly endorsed ruinous policies that flouted the Constitution, the Congress, and the will of the American people. In *The Burden of Brown*, Professor Raymond Wolters of the University of Delaware chronicles the formulation of one of those ruinous policies: the mandatory racial mixing that transformed the American public school system.

The United States has a written Constitution that is supposed to be the basis for all laws. There is a procedure for amending it. However, in Professor Wolters' view, Supreme Court justices have essentially appointed themselves as a standing constitutional convention. On matters of race and education, they have ignored the framers' intent and simply draped their own liberal values in constitutional language.

The mischief began in 1954 with the Court's famous decision in *Brown v. Topeka Board of Education* which Professor Wolters calls one of the most important events in recent American history. As is well known, this ruling repudiated the 1896 decision of *Plessy v. Ferguson*, which established that the races could be separated if they were treated equally.

The Supreme Court ruled that separate schools were inherently unequal, but this is not necessarily so. In fact, the NAACP had successfully sued many districts and forced them to give black schools equal facilities. Professor Wolters notes that in many segregated districts, black schools were better appointed and black teachers were better paid than their white counterparts. Whites were willing to pay higher school taxes in order to maintain separate instruction.

The Court's assumption about the inequality of separateness was based largely on the work of Kenneth Clark, a black sociologist. In a famous experiment, Dr. Clark had shown black children a white doll and a black doll, and asked them to pick the one they liked. Most picked the white doll, and Dr. Clark argued that segregated schools made blacks feel inferior.

What Dr. Clark did not publicize was the fact that when black children attending integrated schools in Massachusetts were given the same test, they chose the white doll more often than did Southern blacks attending segregated schools! The Supreme Court was persuaded by Dr. Clark's data and searched the Constitution for a way to order school integration. The justices found it in the 14th Amendment, which requires that states give all citizens equal protection under the law.

However, to read this amendment as forbidding segregated schools was an act of pure imagination. The same 1866 Congress that passed the amendment established racially segregated schools in the District of Columbia. Twenty-three of the 37 states then in the Union also had legally segregated schools and did not desegregate them after ratifying the amendment. Neither Congress nor the states saw any contradiction between equal protection and racial separation. The *Brown* decision forced upon the 14th Amendment concepts alien to the men who had written and ratified it.

Massive Resistance

One of the great strengths of *The Burden of Brown* is that in explaining the machinations of the Court, Professor Wolters describes in fascinating detail what the ruling meant to real people in real schools. By the time *Brown* was decided, it was a consolidation of suits filed in five different districts. Professor Wolters recounts the depredations of 30 years of integration in each of them. It is startling to realize what has changed since the 1950s—and what has not.

One thing that has certainly changed is the extent to which whites are willing to mobilize to defend their own racial interests. One of the districts to which Brown immediately applied was Prince Edward County in Virginia, a state that briefly mounted what was called "massive resistance" to integration.

The governor, Lindsay Almond, insisted states have the right to resist unlawful federal tyranny. Under his guidance, the state legislature voted to withhold funds from any school that integrated and to issue tuition vouchers for students to use in private schools.

In 1958, when federal judges ordered integration, the state cut off funds and the schools closed. Many students found places in private schools, but others were left in the lurch. The next year, the Virginia supreme court ruled that the state constitution required the operation of public schools, and pronounced the closures illegal. Governor Almond, realizing that the only way to forestall integration was to defy the court and keep all schools closed, gave up and agreed to integrate.

However, as Professor Wolters points out, massive resistance collapsed only because whites broke ranks. Whites who lived in areas with few blacks were the first to capitulate. They assumed that a trickle of blacks would not ruin their schools, and they were not willing to hold out for the benefit of districts in which whites would be swamped. Also, it is important to remember that in the late 1950s, no one had heard of busing. Everyone thought desegregation simply meant the removal of racial barriers so that blacks who wanted to cross them could. If the Virginians in their safe suburbs had known that blacks would one day be bused into their midst from the slums, they might have fought on against the federal government.

The whites of Prince Edward County, 65 miles southwest of Richmond, did fight on. There were more black than white students in the county, and whites had good reason to fear integration. Blacks were not only far behind whites in academic subjects, they were 14 times more likely to have venereal diseases and ten times more likely to have illegitimate children. Whites also feared that racial mixing could lead to miscegenation.

The county therefore closed its public schools and reduced property taxes to offset the difference. With a tremendous outpouring of unity, whites built private schools—first in temporary quarters and then in sturdy, permanent buildings. Contractors donated materials, parents volunteered time, and a private, all-white school system known as Prince Edward Academy was born.

Whites offered to set up similar schools for blacks, where students could spend their vouchers just as whites did. On the advice of the NAACP, the blacks refused. It made much better copy for liberal newspapers if blacks were left with no schools at all; idle children made whites look like cruel bigots.

Prince Edward County was free to act as it did because counties were not under a state constitutional obligation to provide public instruction. As it happened, the public schools stood empty from 1959 to 1964—longer than anyone had anticipated. When President John Kennedy took office he urged foundations and big corporations to donate money and materials for public schools. The Free Schools, as they were called, opened with great fanfare in 1963, with per pupil expenditures twice as high as those at the Academy.

Finally, in 1964, the US Supreme Court ruled that since Prince Edward County had closed its public schools solely to evade an integration order, it must reopen them. Of course, there is nothing in the Constitution that forbids doing something legal for the sole purpose of avoiding something illegal—people do it all the time—but legalities scarcely mattered since segregationists had to be taught a lesson. Even some liberals worried that the Court was exercising tyrannical powers by ordering a county to raise taxes and spend money against its will.

Prince Edward County obeyed the Court. Per pupil spending at the re-opened public schools was slightly more than at Prince Edward Academy, but blacks still complained that it was less than at the Free Schools.

The county has continued with its two school systems. The voucher system was, of course, struck down by the courts and whites had to reach into their own pockets for tuition. Most were glad to. During the 1970s, while the national average SAT scores dropped by nine percent, scores at the Academy rose by five percent. As graffiti, vandalism, and violence spread through integrated schools, they were practically unknown at Prince Edward Academy. Unlike students elsewhere who locked up their belongings for fear of theft, academy students left things wherever they liked. As the rest of the country plunged into the blackboard jungle of the 1970s and 1980s, the academy retained the civility and demeanor of the 1950s.

Across the Country

Professor Wolters' accounts of what happened in the other districts directly affected by Brown are equally illuminating and well told. In Washington, DC, there was little resistance to integration; whites simply vanished.

During the brief, initial collision whites were astonished at the language of blacks. One school principal said that he "heard colored girls at the school use language that was far worse than I have ever heard, even in the Marine Corps." At Theodore Roosevelt High School, blacks shouted so many obscenities at cheerleaders during the 1954-5 school year that the school switched to boy cheerleaders. Blacks were notorious for pawing white girls in the halls. Noting that black high school students were 23 times more likely to have venereal disease than whites, some principals stopped having school dances.

Some things never seem to change. The *Washington Post* used to sponsor an annual football game between the champions of the public schools and the parochial schools. By 1962, the public league was almost all black and the parochial league was almost all white. That year, when the black team lost, thousands of blacks poured onto the field, brandishing sticks and shouting "Get the whites." In the two-hour brawl that followed, all but 30 of the 346 injured were white. Newspapers solemnly reported that race had nothing to do with the melee.

As the DC school district turned black, standards plummeted. In 1976, the valedictorian at one high school was in the 39th national percentile in verbal ability and in the 16th percentile in math. Schools saw the inevitable increase in shootings, muggings, knifings, rapes, etc.

Another Brown district was in South Carolina. Here, whites mounted a full-blown court case against integration based on the view that blacks were intellectually inferior to whites and that the gap in inherent ability was wide enough to justify separate education. No matter how good their case, the South Carolinians were in the awkward position of asking a district court to overturn the Supreme Court's ruling in Brown. This the lower court refused to do, and the state became the last to integrate its schools. As happened all across the country, whites promptly left the public schools which, when left to blacks, descended into chaos.

During this time, it was common for Southerners to argue that if Northerners only had blacks in their midst they would understand the folly of school integration. Senator Richard Russell of Georgia even advocated a plan to pay black families $1,500 each if they would move to the North and show Yankees just what a scourge they were. Robert Patterson, founder of the anti-integration Citizens' Councils, used to argue that a sure cure for integration was a stiff dose of Negroes.

The Burden of Green

Of course, Northerners got their comeuppance when the Supreme Court decided that schools must not merely be open to all races but that students had to be forced to mingle whether they wanted to or not. This resulted in the nightmare of busing, which wracked Boston and Louisville as much as it did any city in the South.

As Professor Wolters explains, until 1968, when the Supreme Court once again decided to amend the Constitution, virtually everyone thought the Brown decision required only the dismantling of legal segregation. Black students who had been denied admission to white schools now had the right to attend them. All that the NAACP asked in 1954 was that race be disregarded when students were assigned to schools. No one dreamed that race could be made the primary criterion for assigning students to schools in order to mix the races.

That, however, was the result of *Green v. New Kent County*. After the failure of "massive resistance" this Virginia county had duly ended legal segregation. It allowed all students to attend the schools of their choice and provided free transportation to make this possible. However, no whites transferred to black schools and only a few blacks transferred to white schools. Though the system was no longer legally segregated, most children of both races still had classmates of the same race.

The Court held the then-fashionable view that unless the races were thoroughly mixed they could not be properly educated. As Judge J. Skelly Wright had written in a 1967 lower court decision, "Racially and socially homogeneous schools damage the minds and spirits of all students who attend them." He wrote that schools should "produce attitudes of tolerance and mutual sharing," and had visions of "Negro and white children playing innocently together in the schoolyard."

By no stretch of the imagination can the Constitution be read to allow the federal government to force black students to go to school with whites if blacks are free to do so but choose not to. And yet, in its wisdom and its bliss, the Supreme Court decreed that Americans could not be left with free choice if they did not exercise it in a way that brought the races together in promiscuous contact. The Court decided that the children of New Kent County must once again be assigned to schools on the basis of race, but this time in order to mix them rather than separate them.

Professor Wolters notes that on the day after the Court heard the oral arguments in *Green v. New Kent County*, Martin Luther King was assassinated. A wave of race riots swept the country as the Court deliberated. No doubt the justices thought their ruling benefited the country, but Professor Wolters quotes Daniel Webster: "It is hardly too strong to say that the Constitution was made to guard the people against the dangers of good intentions." The folly of busing had begun.

One of the school districts that bore the full brunt of busing was New Castle County, Del., another Brown district that Professor Wolters describes in detail. This case was yet another striking triumph of rule by the judiciary.

New Castle County contains the city of Wilmington, whose schools had become black, dangerous, and ineffective, as well as a number of surrounding white suburbs that had good schools. There were 11 different school districts in the area, none of which practiced segregation but all of which reflected the essential racial homogeneity of their neighborhoods.

Professor Wolters explains that those who first brought the suit to disperse Wilmington's black students throughout the county had two motives they did not reveal to the courts. First, they wanted whites to share the burden of dealing with troublesome blacks. Second, they thought that if the suburbs lost the advantage of having all-white schools, there would be less incentive for whites to shun Wilmington. Some might return to the city and property prices might recover. The argument they made to the Court, however, was the usual one about how racial separation was bad for education.

The Court's 1978 ruling was a breathtaking intrusion on local autonomy. It dissolved the 11 separate districts and appointed a single school board for the entire 250 square-mile area. It also ordered that students, both black and white, be bused so that every school would reflect the 80:20 white-to-black ratio of the total student population.

In the suburbs, property taxes were raised 20 percent to pay for the costs of busing and to establish a new, uniform curriculum. White teachers attended dewy-eyed seminars on how to see themselves as "facilitators" rather than lecturers, who would teach "cooperation" as much as the three Rs and thereby raise the "self-esteem" of ghetto blacks. An "interfaith taskforce" was set up to prepare teachers for "empathetic listening" and "values clarification." Big companies like DuPont, whose executives already sent their children to private schools, churned out propaganda in favor of the new plan.

Of course, shipping underclass thugs to the suburbs where "facilitators" greeted them with "empathetic listening" was no cure for delinquency. Along with the blacks came graffiti, false fire alarms, broken windows, theft, extortion, fights, and assaults on teachers. Gangs of thieves would clear out suburban lockers by the score and bring the booty home to Wilmington in school buses. Although blacks were only 20 percent of the student population, they accounted for 66 percent of all racial assaults.

Whites responded as they always do. In just the first four years, 35 of the 103 public schools in the area closed as whites cleared out. The number of private schools went from 44 to 78, and most had waiting lists and were bursting at the seams. Before busing, the suburban schools had a rich array of options for gifted students. After busing, these programs shriveled to nearly nothing, with all the old effort devoted to remedial education.

Judge Murray Schwartz had personally overseen the execution of the Supreme Court ruling. Three years after busing—to the hoots and jeers of angry whites—he took his own children out of public schools and sent them to private academies. Even Joseph Biden, the relentlessly liberal Democratic senator from Delaware, had to admit that the New Castle County plan was a failure.

New Castle County is a symbol for virtually every school district in which blacks were sent in large numbers to white schools. The schools deteriorated. Whites fled. Whites who cared about education had to pay for two school systems: a taxpayer-financed one for blacks and a privately financed one for themselves.

Did this upheaval accomplish anything? If racial mixing was the goal, it was a modest success in some areas. In others, the transition from free choice of schools to forced busing left schools more segregated than ever. Whites welcomed the motivated blacks who came to white schools for better educations, but civility and learning could not survive court-ordered bus loads of underclass truants.

What about the racial gap in test scores? As Professor Wolters explains, the media trumpeted the cheerful prediction that integration would help blacks and not harm whites. For a brief period this seemed true. Studies in the early 1960s showed that blacks in majority-white schools had slightly better test scores than blacks in all-black schools. Few people realized that this was because of free choice. It was smart, ambitious blacks who went to majority-white schools. They would have done better work than other blacks no matter where they studied.

Thirty years after Brown, which ravaged the public schools, emptied the cities of whites, and sowed chaos in the lives of millions of Americans, the brute facts remained unchanged: average black test scores were at the 15th percentile for whites. Black first-graders were still one year behind whites, and black high school students were still three years behind. Just as before integration, household income could not explain these gaps. Whites from the poorest families got higher test scores than blacks from the richest families.

The hopes of school integration foundered, as egalitarian hopes always do, on the unyielding facts of biology. The Supreme Court trampled the Constitution in the name of liberal pieties about the dominance of environment over genetics. Willful ignorance has a price and, as always, it was whites who paid it.

This article appeared in the July 1993 issue.

Selma to Montgomery, 30 Years Later
by Marian Evans

March 1995 marked the 30th anniversary of the Selma-to-Montgomery voting-rights march. The surviving leaders of the demonstration recently met to commemorate what was one of the most effective efforts of the civil rights era. The atmosphere was one of amity and self-congratulation, in which it was taken for granted that the marchers and their purposes were noble and their opponents were despicable racists. In an act of contrition, Joe Smitherman, who was mayor of Selma 30 years ago, presented the keys to the city to a group of aging civil rights leaders.

Rituals like this firmly establish today's view of who was right and who was wrong. And yet, does Mr. Smitherman, who saw the now-sanctified event as it really unfolded, not harbor even fleeting reservations about the new America that the civil rights movement created? Perhaps not. George Wallace, former governor of Alabama, recently gave a framed photograph of himself to Rosa Parks, who started the Montgomery bus boycott in 1955. He inscribed it "To a great lady."

The 1965 demonstrations in Selma and Montgomery were part of a massive campaign to secure voting rights for blacks. In the states of the former Confederacy, it had been only during Reconstruction that blacks had had more or less uncontested voting rights. In Alabama, blacks were first given the vote under a state constitution written in 1867 by Northerners and forced upon the state by the US Congress.

A new constitution, written in 1901, eliminated most blacks from politics, by limiting suffrage to people who could read and understand the US Constitution, and who had been employed during the previous year or who had paid property taxes. The new constitution also required separate schools for black and white children. Since that time, as in most of the South, the vigor with which suffrage restrictions were applied to blacks varied from region to region.

In 1965, black civil rights leaders seemed to be winning every battle they fought. The Supreme Court outlawed school segregation in 1954, and the "sit-in" movement, begun in 1960, successfully integrated many Southern lunch counters, restaurants, hotels and churches. President Eisenhower used federal troops forcibly to integrate public schools in Little Rock, Arkansas, and in 1962 President Kennedy used them to overwhelm resistance to integration at the University of Mississippi. The movement's greatest success, however, had been the passage of the Civil Rights Act of 1964, which prohibited discrimination in employment and public accommodation.

The national press was warmly sympathetic to black demonstrators and their white supporters. The movement basked in an aura of great moral superiority, and the obvious next step for what seemed to be an unstoppable juggernaut was to secure unrestricted voting rights for Southern blacks.

Martin Luther King, who led this stage of the movement, was by then world famous. Having come to prominence only ten years earlier during the Montgomery bus boycott, he was now a winner of the Nobel Peace Prize and a frequent guest at the White House. He chose Dallas County, Alabama, as the target for demonstrations because it had been particularly inhospitable to black voters. Although there were more blacks than whites of voting age in the county, 28 white voters were registered for every black. Selma, 50 miles from Montgomery, was the county seat.

A Board of Registrars examined prospective voters, black and white. It had a small office in the Selma courthouse and could handle no more than 50 applicants per day. On January 18, 1965, King and his close assistant, Ralph Abernathy, led six or seven hundred people to the courthouse and demanded that they be registered. There was already a line of ordinary applicants, and the demonstrators were turned away. They marched back to their headquarters at Brown's Chapel Church, and held a press conference, claiming—correctly—that blacks had been denied registration. Overlooked were the facts that blacks had been among those waiting to be tested and that in the days before the demonstration a number of blacks had been duly registered.

Similar nationally-reported exercises took place throughout the months of January and February. King was constantly in and out of town, flying around the country raising money and holding press conferences. He returned to give speeches and lead marches. Meanwhile, more and more Northern whites trickled into town.

At the time, Selma had a population of 29,000 people, of whom 15,000 were black. It took only a small crowd to paralyze the town, and at the height of the demonstrations approximately 11,000 outsiders were swarming the streets. Selma's mayor, Joe Smitherman, complained that for three months he spent three quarters of his time dealing with out-of-town demonstrators. Selma police were swamped with complaints of thievery, and townspeople were soon heartily sick of the visitors, many of whom were drunk and left garbage wherever they went.

Some Northerners came just to have a good time. Many were "beatniks," who drifted across the country from one demonstration to another. They had no money for hotels which were, in any case, commandeered by the hundreds of journalists covering the demonstrations. Many whites of both sexes found accommodation in black churches and in the George Washington Carver Homes, the black housing project.

Intimate mixing of the races in this fashion was unheard of in the rural South, but even more shocking to the people of Selma was the public sexual behavior of the demonstrators. If the accounts of what can only be described as public debauchery were not given in sworn affidavits by citizens, state troopers, and national guardsmen, they would be difficult to believe. Residents of Selma could be forgiven for beginning to wonder whether the demonstrations were as much about public interracial copulation as they were about voting rights. Many of the journalists were disgusted by what they saw, and complained that candid accounts of the demonstrators' behavior were edited out of the stories they filed.

Language as well as behavior was edited. On one occasion, James Forman, secretary of the Student Non-Violent Coordinating Committee (SNCC), spoke at the Beulah Baptist Church in Montgomery. Addressing a mixed-race group that included many ministers, nuns, and church women, he said: "If the Negro isn't given his place at the table of democracy . . . it's time for us to knock the f***ing legs off the table." Some of the ministers expressed surprise at this language, but Forman offered no apology.

A few minutes later, Ralph Abernathy tried to smooth things over by saying, "I'm sure that God will forgive him, that the television crews will delete it from their films, and newspapermen will not print it." A beatnik came to Forman's defense: "What's wrong with 'f**k'?" he asked; "It's a good old American word, and expressive."

There were demonstrations in Montgomery during this period as well. On March 10, at about 8:00 p.m., approximately 100 people were being harangued on a well-lit street a short distance from the state capitol. One of the black leaders of the group then said in a loud voice, "Everyone stand and relieve yourselves." Practically the entire crowd, male and female, young and old, black and white, did as they were told, as rivulets ran almost to the next block. Two blacks were arrested for, according to a bystander, particularly lewd and offensive exposure of their private parts.

Adding to public revulsion for the demonstrators was the sight of men and women in religious garb drunk in public and fondling each other. The civil rights movement had always draped itself in religion, and King made a point of giving ministers and priests very visible roles. The presence of clerics was so useful that some of the demonstrators dressed as priests or nuns appear to have been impostors.

This may have been the case during a small demonstration in Montgomery on March 16. A group of 34 men, most dressed as priests, arrived at the capitol late in the evening and insisted on praying on the capitol steps. Finally, at 3:00 a.m. the police let them say the Lord's Prayer on the bottom step. As they broke up to leave, two photographers came running across the street. One of the men dressed as a priest said to one, "You stupid son-of-a-bitch, after all this time here, you didn't get a picture of us saying a prayer on the bottom step." An Alabama state policeman said that many of the "priests" swore like sailors and that he doubted more than half were authentic.

It may have been the disgraceful behavior of false clerics that prompted one of the three killings associated with the Selma demonstrations. On March 8, a white Unitarian minister from Boston, James Reeb, was brutally clubbed to the ground as he left a restaurant, and died two days later. The night before Reeb died, the demonstration leaders held an all-night, out-door vigil to pray for his recovery. Disgusted journalists noted that a number of young couples at the rear of the crowd fornicated during the services.

About this time, Jimmie Lee Jackson, a black civil rights leader, was shot and wounded in an altercation with police. Activists swept him away, medical treatment was delayed, and the man died. The Chief Deputy Sheriff of Dallas County thought the delay was deliberate. "I believe they wanted him to die," he said; "They wanted to make a martyr out of him . . . ."

The day after Rev. Reeb was clubbed, Selma demonstrators defied a court order and set out to march the 50 miles to Montgomery. As they crossed the Edmund Pettus Bridge leading out of town, they were met by a line of state troopers standing shoulder to shoulder. "This march will not continue . . . ." boomed the public address system, but there was deadlock for 15 to 20 minutes, while King and his associates knelt to pray, and police pleaded with the demonstrators to go home. When officers finally moved forward with night sticks held horizontally and tried to push the demonstrators back, the resulting mayhem ended in clouds of tear gas. Eighteen officers were injured by flying rocks and bottles.

According to press accounts, the police had "whipped and clubbed" unoffending demonstrators, and television pictures showed crowds of fleeing blacks choking on tear gas. Reeb died the day after the confrontation at the bridge. These two events were a tremendous propaganda advantage for King, and they brought thousands more demonstrators to Selma from the North.

A few days later, President Lyndon Johnson went before Congress and evoked Reeb's name in a strong call for legislation to ensure voting rights for blacks. He also ordered mobilization of the Alabama National Guard to protect a second attempt at a Selma-to-Montgomery march, this one newly sanctioned by a federal judge.

Thus began, on March 21, 1965, the now-famous march. King, Abernathy, and U.N. Undersecretary Ralph Bunche—also a Nobel Peace Prize winner—took the lead down Selma's Sylvan Street. On the way to the Pettus Bridge, the crowd marched past a record store, where an outside speaker alternately blared "Dixie" and "Bye, Bye, Blackbird." At the head of the procession a mixed group of young men carried the US flag upside down— the sign of distress. Many demonstrators wore "GROW" buttons, which stood for "Get rid of Wallace." Nearly two thousand Alabama National Guardsmen, 100 FBI agents, 75 federal marshals, and dozens of state and county police officers guarded the marchers.

Just outside Selma, the Citizens' Council of America, an anti-integration group, had set up posters showing King sitting next to known Communist leaders at the Highlander Folk School in Tennessee. The caption read, "Martin Luther King at Communist Training School."

History books call this a "massive" demonstration and, indeed, some 11,000 people set off on the first leg of the journey. However, the highway to Montgomery narrowed to two lanes shortly after leaving Selma, and permission was granted for only 300 marchers on all but a few miles of roadway. Most of the crowd therefore streamed back to Selma.

Although it is impossible to know even their approximate numbers, some of the demonstrators were shills. A few openly boasted that they were in Selma because they had been offered food, money and sex. Dora Brown's unusual financial arrangements came to light when the checks stopped coming. In a sworn affidavit she testified as follows:

"I was at Brown's Chapel Church with the movement along with a blind man and a one-legged man who were both white people. I am one-armed and we were told at the time that we were the ones they needed worst, since we were handicapped it would help the movement. We were told that if we would make the march from Selma to Montgomery we would be paid $100.00 per month plus food and clothes. . . . James Gildersleeve would pay us."

"I have received three checks from Gildersleeve for $100.00 each but now he has quit paying me."

Gildersleeve was not to blame. Rev. Frederick Reese, president of the Dallas County Voters League, was arrested after other blacks accused him of stealing thousands of dollars in movement funds.

Miss Brown's unhappy testimony continues: "Gildersleeve told me that he couldn't pay me since Frederick Reese had gotten all the money. Gildersleeve gave me one pound of lard, some greens, a watermelon and $1.00 in money. He said that is all he could give."

It is not recorded whether Miss Brown or the one-legged white man were among the select 300 who spent four nights on the road to Montgomery. It is known that the evenings were characterized by the now-usual drunkenness and fornication. On at least one occasion, police officers prevented newspapermen from photographing the revelry. And even among this inner circle, there were frequent complaints about stolen clothes and missing bed rolls.

Most of the marchers slept in the open except for King, who set up housekeeping in a trailer that was moved from camp to camp. There are no reports on how he spent his evenings, but his inclinations are now well known. His companion, Ralph Abernathy, was not a model cleric, either. In 1958, a Mr. Davis was arrested for threatening Abernathy with a hatchet because Abernathy kept trying to have sex with Mrs. Davis. She testified in her husband's defense that Abernathy had first seduced her when she was a 15-year-old member of his congregation.

As the march went on, the press continued its adulatory, front-page coverage. All around the country, supporters held sympathy marches and worship services.

The night before the last leg of the trek, more than 30,000 people gathered in a field a few miles outside of Montgomery for a free concert. Harry Belafonte, Nina Simone, Sammy Davis, Jr., Billy Eckstein, Mahalia Jackson, the Chad Mitchell Trio, and Frankie Laine serenaded the crowd until nearly one in the morning.

On March 25, the 30,000 were joined by another 5,000 as King and Abernathy led the march into Montgomery, up to the steps of the state capitol. The city was festooned with Confederate flags, one of which fluttered along with the state flag over the capitol building. It was widely—and falsely—reported that not a single United States flag flew in Montgomery that day. The Stars and Stripes waved, as it always did, from a tall flag pole on the capitol grounds.

The leaders of the march asked to see Governor George Wallace, so they could present him with a list of grievances. He refused to meet them. The rest of the day was filled with speeches by Hosea Williams, Roy Wilkins, James Forman, Ralph Bunche and other black leaders. Joan Baez and Peter Paul and Mary were among those who entertained the crowd, which finally broke up around 4:00 p.m. The march was over. It took until midnight for sanitation crews to clean up the mountains of trash demonstrators had left behind.

Late that evening, a third killing took place when a white civil rights worker name Viola Liuzzo was shot to death as she was driving between Selma and Montgomery. Both the press and President Johnson were outraged, although accounts of the killing were often incomplete.

Given the sanitized view of the demonstrations that had been broadcast to the world, Alabama congressman William L. Dickinson undoubtedly met much skepticism on March 30 when he tried to convey a different picture to his colleagues on the floor of Congress:

"Drunkenness and sex orgies were the order of the day in Selma, on the road to Montgomery. There were many—not just a few—instances of sexual intercourse in public between Negro and white. News reporters saw this— law enforcement officials saw this . . . .

"Has anyone stopped to ask what sort of people can leave home, family and job—if they have one—and live indefinitely in a foreign place demonstrating? This is no religious group of sympathizers trying to help the Negro out of a sense of right and morality—this is a bunch of godless riffraff out for kicks and self-gratification that have left every campsite between Selma and Montgomery littered with whiskey bottles, beer cans, and used contraceptives."

The nation was profoundly uninterested. In fact, the Selma-to-Montgomery march was probably one of the most effective events in the entire civil rights movement. Unlike the "March on Washington" in 1963, in which 200,000 people took part and where King gave his "I Have a Dream" speech, the agitation in Selma and Montgomery led directly to national legislation. The nation was riveted by the march, and President Johnson constantly referred to it in his push for a voting rights bill. The killings of James Reeb and Viola Liuzzo were also a great stimulus to lawmakers.

The legislation passed and was signed into law in August 1965. In what would appear to be a direct abrogation of the reserved powers specified in the Tenth Amendment, it prohibited all state tests of voter literacy and education. It even authorized federal elections examiners to register voters who had been rejected by state authorities, and to patrol the polls to see that such people voted. The law affected states outside the South, notably New York, which had required that voters be literate in English. New York promptly sued on Tenth Amendment grounds, but the Supreme Court ruled in 1966 against the literacy provisions—to great rejoicing among the state's Puerto Ricans.

With a total of three deaths, the march was one of the most sanguinary episodes in the civil rights period. However, very few demonstrators were harrassed or assaulted. In retrospect, it is surprising that there was not more violence.

As invariably happens in racial matters, a group of whites with little experience of blacks saw fit to give instruction on race relations to people with a great deal of experience. Northerners invaded the South, a deeply conservative society, demanding that Southerners change their way of life. To add insult to arrogance, Northerners then proceeded publicly to violate some of the most deeply felt norms of privacy and decency. The self-control—even passivity—of the citizens of Selma and Montgomery is as astonishing as the degeneracy of the demonstrators. Perhaps even Mayor Smitherman, desperately trying to run a city overrun with disorderly demonstrators, harbored thoughts of homicide.

Now, 30 years later, Selma is a sacred name, one of the stations of the cross on the road to integration and racial equality.

The following excerpts are from sworn affidavits made by witnesses to the events in Selma and Montgomery in March 1965.

V.B. Bates, Deputy Sheriff of Dallas County: "To begin with, I saw white females in from other counties, other states I believe, building up their sexual desires with Negro males. After a few minutes of necking and kissing, the Negro male would lead them off into the Negro housing project. I watched this procedure many times."

Black man, name withheld: "[M]en and women used this room [in the Student Non-Violent Coordinating Committee headquarters] for sex freely and openly and without interference. On one occasion I saw James Forman, executive director of SNCC, and a red-haired white girl whose name is Rachel, on one of the cots together. They engaged in sexual intercourse, as well as an abnormal sex act . . . . Forman and the girl, Rachel, made no effort to hide their actions."

"During this same period, March 8, 9 and 10, a large number of young demonstrators of both races and sexes occupied the Jackson Street Baptist Church for approximately forty-eight hours. . . . On one occasion, I saw a Negro boy and a white girl engaged in sexual intercourse on the floor of the church. At this time, the church was packed and the couple did nothing to hide their actions. While they were engaged in this act of sexual intercourse, other boys and girls stood around and watched, laughing and joking."

Corporal H.M. Brown, Alabama State Trooper: "I observed on many occasions the so-called men of the cloth, who were white, fondling the breasts and buttocks of black female demonstrators. On numerous occasions, I saw couples of the opposite sex and color leaving the crowd, fondling each other and going into the houses and alleys along Sylvan Street.

"Since 1961, I have observed mobs and demonstrations, but the crowd of demonstrators in Selma, Alabama, was the lowest scum of the earth. This gathering of demonstrators in Selma included the largest crowd of sex degenerates that I have ever observed in one place in my life. They had no morals or scruples and did not appear to care who saw them during their orgies."

Captain Lionel Freeman, Alabama State Troopers: "One Negro who was standing beside a priest and both standing about three feet from a line of troopers, made several attempts to provoke a trooper into hitting him. The Negro waved three dollar bills in the trooper's face and then dropped them, saying 'Why don't you pick them up, I know you need it.' . . . . The Negro then said, 'I'll sleep with a white woman tonight.' The priest seemed to think this was real funny."

"[S]everal newspapermen who were allowed to go to the rear of the demonstration came back up to the front and told us they observed white and Negro couples in the act of sexual relations. They told us that they had sent the story and pictures home to their papers. One told me that the only thing he recognized about his story when it was printed was his name."

Lieutenant J.L. Fuqua, Alabama State Trooper: "I also saw Negro men feel the breasts and butts of white girls, making no attempt to hide this, but rather appearing like they wanted everyone to see them."

Charles R. McMillan, Selma policeman: "Both Negroes and white demonstrators were bedding down side by side. A young teenage Negro boy and girl were engaged in a sexual intercourse [sic] that was interrupted by a newsman who attempted to take a picture of the act."

Selma citizen: "I, Marion J. Bass, did, on the night of the 23rd of March, 1965, see at the camp site of the Selma-to-Montgomery march, a young white girl and a colored man having sex relations. They were on the ground out in the open and did not try in any way to hide as I walked within six or eight feet of them.

"There were many colored girls and white boys laying in the same sleeping bags. I also saw a white girl about 17-years-old and four colored boys get into the back of a truck and close the doors. . . . They were in the truck about 45 minutes and when they opened the door to get out, the girl was dressing."

Lieutenant R.E. Etheridge, Alabama State Trooper: "The action and movement of the two wrapped in the quilt left no doubt whatever that they were having sexual intercourse. They were within 30 feet of the main body of demonstrators, and in plain view of them. They remained on the ground for about 20 minutes, got up and went toward Brown's Chapel Church."

"On the morning of March 14th, at about 11:00 a.m. I saw a white preacher with a Negro girl in the back seat of an automobile. He had her breasts out of her blouse and was handling them."

"I observed white ministers on at least three occasions who were in what appeared to be a very intoxicated condition."

First Lieutenant Samuel Carr, Alabama National Guard: "I hereby further swear and attest that during such time of duty with my National Guard unit, I personally saw one case of sexual intercourse between a young white boy and Negro girl. I further swear and attest that I saw occasions of public urination . . . ."

Cecil Atkinson, resident of Prattville, Alabama: "Between Selma and the first stop, I observed both men and women relieving themselves in public, all together and making no attempt to conceal themselves at all."

"At one point I observed a young beatnik-type man with his collar turned around to resemble a priest. He told me that it was 'the way to get along.' Another told me that he had been offered $15 a day, three meals a day, and all the sex he could handle if he would come down and join in the demonstration from up North."

Mrs. Nettie Adams, resident of Montgomery: "There were white and Negro people all over the Ripley Street side of St. Margaret's Hospital [in Montgomery on March 15] . . . . They were all kissing and hugging. This one particular couple on St. Margaret's lawn was engaged in sexual relations—a white woman (skinny blond) and a Negro man. After they were through, she wiggled out from beneath him and over to the man lying to the left of them on the lawn and started kissing and caressing his face."

The Many Deaths of Viola Liuzzo

On March 25, 1965, a woman from Michigan named Viola Liuzzo was driving along Highway 80 from Selma towards Montgomery. Riding with her was Leroy Moton, a 19-year-old local black who had become her inseparable companion during her stay in Selma. She had just dropped off a carload of demonstrators in Selma, and was on her way to Montgomery to pick up more, when she was killed by a volley of bullets fired from a passing car. Moton was uninjured.

The *Birmingham News* of March 26, 1965 set the tone for the national coverage when it described her as "the red-haired, attractive Mrs. Liuzzo," and the press widely published a photograph of her that had been taken twenty years earlier. By contrast, the coroner's report noted that she was 39 years old and a "moderately obese white female" with needle marks in her arms and very dirty hands and feet. She was not wearing panties when she was shot, but the coroner did not examine her for recent sexual relations.

The *Birmingham News* also referred to Liuzzo as "a mother of five." This was correct, but the press left out a few other facts. She had been married three times, the first marriage having lasted only one day. One of her daughters had run away from home at age sixteen, and Liuzzo herself had been arrested and fined for failing to send her children to school. In 1964, her husband had reported her missing and she later turned up in Canada. At the time she went to Selma she was under psychiatric care.

Although she had registered to vote in her home state of Michigan, Liuzzo was dropped from the rolls after a few years because she never voted. She was demonstrating for a right for blacks that she, herself, had never exercised.

President Johnson took an intense interest in her murder and within 24 hours of Liuzzo's death went on television and radio, with FBI Director J. Edgar Hoover at his side, to announce the arrest of four members of the Ku Klux Klan. Due to a mix-up in timing, some of the men had not yet been arrested, and at least one listened in amazement as the President of the United States announced that he was in custody.

Johnson heaped praise on "the very fast and always efficient work of the special agents of the FBI who worked all night long, starting immediately after the tragic death of Mrs. Viola Liuzzo . . . ." He did not mention that the arrests were so quick because one of the arrested Klansmen, Gary Rowe, was a paid FBI informer who had been present at the killing. Nor did he mention that the FBI had advised against sending condolences to Viola Liuzzo's husband because, according to one bureau report, "the man himself doesn't have too good a background and the woman had indications of needle marks in her arms where she had been taking dope." Johnson also urged Congress to mount a full-scale investigation of the Klan, which was promptly undertaken by the House Un-American Activities Committee (HUAC).

The trials of Liuzzo's accused killers were a remarkable story in themselves—in part because of the speed with which they took place. The first trial of Collie Wilkins, the alleged trigger-man, was held in a segregated courtroom in Hayneville, Alabama, just two months after the killing. Wilkins was defended by Matt Murphy, "Imperial Klonsel" of the United Klans of America. Women were not then eligible for jury duty in Alabama, and the one black prospective juror excused himself, so Wilkins was tried by 12 white men. The case was covered by approximately 40 newsmen, and a direct telephone line to London, England, was set up in the courthouse for on-the-spot reports.

Imperial Klonsel Murphy, a third-generation Klansman, made much of the fact that the state's case depended almost entirely on the testimony of a paid informer who had broken his oath of loyalty to the Klan to betray his brothers. "What kind of man is this," he thundered, "who comes into a fraternal order by hook and crook, takes the sacred oath, and sells his soul for 30 pieces of silver?"

Throughout the trial, he wore a lapel button that said "Never," which was a popular anti-integration slogan. He also tried to turn the trial into a question of white supremacy and segregation rather than of guilt or innocence. "I'm proud of my heritage; I'm proud that I am a white man," he shouted in his closing argument; "I'm for white supremacy. The communists and the niggers have taken us over. . . . Racial integration breaks every moral law God ever wrote."

The jury's decision was complicated by its having to decide whether the informer, Rowe, was an accomplice, since under Alabama law a felony conviction could not depend on the uncorroborated testimony of an accomplice. In the end, the jury deadlocked, ten-to-two in favor of conviction on manslaughter charges. The two holdouts later explained that they could not rely on Rowe's testimony, since he "swore before God [in his Klan initiation] and broke his oath." Several jurors also said they were insulted by the defense's attempts to make white supremacy an issue in the case.

Wilkins was retried in October 1965. Interest in the case was heightened, if that could be possible, by the HUAC Klan hearings, which started on almost the same day. Kleagles, Kludds and Kligrapps testified before a Klan-happy Washington press corps while the out-of-town correspondents descended once again upon Hayneville.

This time, the prosecutor tried to show that some prospective jurors were racist by asking them, "Do you believe a white person is superior to a Negro?" and if they believed in the inferiority of whites, like Liuzzo, "who come down here and try to help Negroes integrate our churches and schools." Eleven of 30 prospective jurors answered that they did, but they also claimed that they could fairly consider the evidence and impose the death penalty on a man who killed an "inferior" civil rights worker. The judge ruled that the men could be fit jurors.

The total jury pool was composed of 49 whites and six blacks. Some of the blacks were disqualified because they did not believe in the death penalty or, in one man's case, because he was a police officer. The resulting panel was all white. Klan lawyer Murphy had died in a car crash shortly after the first trial, so Arthur Hanes, former mayor of Birmingham, conducted the defense.

Once again, Rowe swore that Wilkins fired the fatal shots, but he also admitted that he, too, held a gun out the car window and *pretended* to shoot. For the defense, Hanes called the informer a "Judas goat" and the alleged trigger man a "scape goat," and referred to the trial as the "Parable of Two Goats." Hanes also managed to find two alibi witnesses, who testified they had seen Wilkins drinking beer at a VFW Hall near Birmingham, 125 miles from the murder scene, an hour or less after Liuzzo was shot.

In his closing argument, Hanes gave no sermons about segregation or white supremacy, but the "Judas goat," he said, "sells information for money. If there is no information, he makes—he fabricates—information and then he goes and peddles it." Wilkins was acquitted.

Martin Luther King's reaction to the verdict was not Gandhian. He said the civil rights movement would "possibly institute economic sanctions against communities which perpetrate such a mockery of justice. It is either this or the risk of the beginning of vigilante justice."

The federal government then put the three Klansmen on trial in late November, 1965, in the District Court at Montgomery. This was Wilkins' third trial in eight months. The charge, based on a Reconstruction-era civil rights law, was complicated: "conspiracy to injure, oppress, threaten, and intimidate citizens . . . in the free exercise and enjoyment of rights and privileges secured them by the Constitution of the United States." The expected arguments about double jeopardy were quashed. Once again, an all-white jury was empaneled, but the court room was integrated.

By now, lawyers and witnesses could practically recite each other's lines, but the results were dramatically different: The jurors, mostly from small Alabama towns, found all three men guilty. The judge imposed the maximum sentence of ten years. One Klansman died of a heart attack not long afterwards, but Collie Wilkins and Eugene Thomas served full terms in federal prison.

The legal drama was not yet over; in 1966, Thomas—now a prisoner—was tried by the state of Alabama on murder charges. In the same Hayneville courthouse that had already seen two Liuzzo trials, he now faced a jury of eight blacks and only four whites. The prosecution decided *not* to use Rowe, their star witness in the three previous trials, because earlier jurors had disbelieved the testimony of an "oath-breaker." Instead, the state relied on an FBI expert who explained that the bullet that killed Liuzzo could have been fired only from Thomas' gun. Hanes once again used the alibi defense. It worked. "Jury With Negroes Acquits Klansman in Liuzzo Slaying," was the surprised headline in the *New York Times*.

The case lay dormant for more than ten years before it resurfaced during investigations of the FBI's covert Internal Security Counterintelligence Program, known as COINTELPRO. By now, J. Edgar Hoover was dead, and the program that had hired Rowe was under intense scrutiny—mainly for its infiltration of leftist organizations.

Much was revealed about Rowe. Although some press reports had referred to him as an FBI "agent," he was nothing of the kind. The FBI had found the former bartender and night club bouncer, thought he would make a good Klansman, and asked him to be a spy. Rowe was the agency's star informer for years—partly because he threw himself so enthusiastically into Klan work.

Investigations in 1978 implicated him as an *agent provocateur*, and he was accused of helping plant the bomb that killed four black girls in a Birmingham church in 1963. Wilkins and Thomas, now out of jail, scuttled their beer-drinking alibi and claimed they had seen Rowe kill Viola Liuzzo. Rowe himself said that the FBI had approved his participation in beating Freedom Riders in 1961, and had ordered him to make internal trouble for the Klan by all possible means, including the seduction of Klansmen's wives. Rowe even claimed to have shot a black to death during a Birmingham race riot in 1963—though police had no record of such a killing—and that the FBI covered up his violence.

The bureau claimed this was all nonsense, and that Rowe was simply drumming up publicity for the TV-movie version (starring former Dallas Cowboys quarterback Don Meredith as Rowe) of his 1976 autobiography, *My Undercover Years with the Ku Klux Klan*. The Alabama district attorney thought otherwise. In November, 1978 a grand jury indicted Rowe for first-degree murder in the killing of Viola Liuzzo. The state initiated extradition proceedings against Rowe, who was living in Savannah, Georgia, where the FBI had set him up with a new identity.

In 1980, still fighting extradition, things got worse for Rowe. An internal FBI file came to light, which acknowledged that Rowe had led the beating of freedom riders, whom he clubbed with a lead-weighted baseball bat. The FBI paid the medical bills for Rowe's own injuries and gave him a $125 bonus. One of his FBI handlers was found to have said, "If he happened to be with some Klansmen and they decided to do something [violent] he couldn't be an angel and [still] be a good informant."

Mrs. Liuzzo's children now waded in, convinced they were on to a good thing. With the help of the ACLU, they sued the FBI for $2 million, charging that the bureau's agent, Rowe, was at least partially responsible for the death of their mother.

Luckily for Rowe, in October 1980, a federal judge blocked extradition to Alabama, saying that a federal "agent" has rights that protect him when "placed in a compromising position because of his undercover work." This surprising ruling was sustained by the federal appeals court.

The Liuzzo children did manage to get Rowe into court in Ann Arbor, Michigan, for their 1982 trial against the FBI. Eugene Thomas duly identified Rowe as Liuzzo's killer but the trial judge disbelieved Thomas. He threw out the Liuzzo children's case, ordering them to pay the $80,000 the government had spent defending itself.

Viola Liuzzo has not since been in the news. The story about the woman whose death helped spur passage of the landmark Voting Rights Act may finally have come to an end.

This article appeared in the May 1995 issue. Marian Evans has written frequently for American Renaissance.

✦◆✦

The Doctor in Spite of Himself

Theodore Pappas (Ed.), *The Martin Luther King, Jr. Plagiarism Story*, The Rockford Institute, 1994, 107 pp., $10.00 (soft cover)

reviewed by Thomas Jackson

Late in 1987, a graduate student working on the project to publish the collected papers of Martin Luther King discovered that King had plagiarized huge parts of his doctoral dissertation. Clayborne Carson, the director of the project, decided to suppress this fact, thus setting in motion one of the most sordid tales of academic dishonesty and race-based special pleading in recent memory.

This book is an invaluable collection of several accounts of what King did and of the contemptible coverups and justifications that followed. Not surprisingly, its editor, Theodore Pappas, could not find a commercial publisher, so the book is unlikely to be in book stores or even in libraries. Only if enough people buy and read it will its story survive the whitewash.

Starting Early

It is now clear that King began plagiarizing as a young man and continued to do so throughout his career. At Crozier Theological Seminary in Chester, Pennsylvania, where he received a bachelor's degree in 1951, his papers were stuffed with unacknowledged material lifted verbatim from published sources. The King papers project has dutifully collected this juvenilia, and Mr. Pappas explains how it strikes the reader today:

"King's plagiarisms are easy to detect because their style rises above the level of his pedestrian student prose. In general, if the sentences are eloquent, witty, insightful, or pithy, or contain allusions, analogies, metaphors, or similes, it is safe to assume that the section has been purloined."

Mr. Pappas notes that in one paper King wrote at Crozier, 20 out of a total of 24 paragraphs show "verbatim theft." King also plagiarized himself, recycling old term papers as new ones. In their written comments on his papers, some of King's professors chided him for sloppy references, but they seem to have had no idea how extensively he was stealing material. By the time he was accepted into the PhD program at Boston University, King was a veteran and habitual plagiarist.

Some of the most devastating parts of Mr. Pappas' book are nothing more than side-by-side comparisons of material from King's PhD thesis and from the sources he copied without attribution. King was overwhelmingly dependent on just one source, a dissertation written on the same subject as his own—the German-born theologian, Paul Tillich—by another Boston University student named Jack Boozer.

Here is a typical passage from King's thesis that is lifted, word for word, from Boozer's:

"Correlation means correspondence of data in the sense of a correspondence between religious symbols and that which is symbolized by them. It is upon the assumption of this correspondence that all utterances about God's nature are made. This correspondence is actual in the logos nature of God and *logos* nature of man."

There is word-for-word copying throughout the thesis. Mr. Pappas notes that the entire twenty-third page is lifted straight out of Boozer, and that even when King was not stealing Boozer's words without attribution, he was stealing his ideas: "There is virtually no section of King's discussion of Tillich that cannot be found in Boozer's text."

Even when King is "quoting" Tillich, complete with footnotes, he may actually be quoting Boozer. Boozer occasionally typed the wrong page number in a Tillich footnote, or made an error transcribing Tillich's words. King copied the errors along with everything else.

King's plagiarism is even more breath-taking than it seems. Boozer was not just any BU graduate student. He had written his thesis in 1952, only three years before King wrote his, and *had submitted it to the same advisor.* Since the advisor is now dead, we will never know whether he failed even to notice the copying or was simply practicing early affirmative action. The second faculty reader of King's thesis now excuses himself by saying he read it early in his career, at a time when he was naive about plagiarism.

Even after he became famous, King continued to plagiarize. His "Letter From Birmingham City Jail," is now known to contain passages he had cribbed so often he knew them by heart. Some of the best-known passages from his "I Have a Dream" speech are taken from a 1952 address by a black preacher named Archibald Carey. His Nobel Prize Lecture and his books, *Strength to Love* and *Stride Toward Freedom*, are also extensively plagiarized.

Moreover, it is clear that King did not take from others because he thought ideas and words were common property. He copyrighted the "I Have a Dream" speech, pilferings and all, and vigorously defended it against unauthorized use. King's estate continues to enforce the copyright. Only last year, in a paroxysm of adulation, *USA Today* printed the full text of the speech, beginning on the front page. The estate sued.

Shielding the Saint

Like his penchant for adultery, King's intellectual dishonesty detracts from his reputation as Saint and Great Man. Perhaps it is because they reveal other failings that his FBI files are still sealed. King, alone of all Americans, is honored with a national holiday, and it is awkward for a saint to be caught stealing. The line of defense has therefore been predictable: He didn't do it, and even if he did, it doesn't matter.

A three-year cover-up began with Mr. Carson at the King papers project. He forbade anyone on the staff to use the word "plagiarism," and has since written of the "similarities" and "textual appropriations" that were part of King's "successful composition method." Mrs. Coretta Scott King also appears to have played a role in the cover-up by refusing to release King's handwritten dissertation notes. Mr. Carson deliberately misled reporters who had heard rumors of plagiarism, and came clean with the facts only when it became clear that the story would break anyway.

The project leader's disingenuousness has not affected funding for the King papers. They have probably swallowed up nearly a million dollars in tax money as well as support from the Ford and Rockefeller Foundations, IBM, Intel and many other donors. In eight years, the project has published only one volume of a projected fourteen.

To the profound discredit of the American press, it was a British paper, the *Sunday Telegraph*, that first published a story, in December 1989, about allegations of plagiarism. It was not until nearly a year later, in November 1990, that the *Wall Street Journal* reported the story to a large American audience. *Chronicles* had briefly mentioned the rumors a little earlier, and Mr. Pappas had prepared a thorough exposé but was beaten into print by the nimbler *Journal*. It is now established that the *New York Times*, *Washington Post*, *Atlanta Journal-Constitution*, and *New Republic* all had heard about the plagiarism but had decided not to investigate it.

Once the truth was out, official reactions were just as craven. The *Wall Street Journal* wrote a typically lickspittle editorial, arguing that King's plagiarisms do not reflect on his character but "tell something about the rest of us.[!?]"

Boston University formed a committee to look into the matter and concluded that since King had stolen only 45 percent of the first part and 21 percent of the second part of his dissertation, it was an "intelligent contribution to scholarship" and that "no thought should be given to revocation of Dr. King's doctoral degree." The second reader of the thesis actually defended the plagiarism by saying that King had accurately conveyed Boozer's thinking—something not hard to do, since King copied him verbatim.

Boozer, who lived just long enough to learn of the plagiarism, was perhaps the greatest groveler of all. As his wife later explained, "He told me he'd be so honored and so glad if there were anything that Martin Luther King could have used from his work."

Keith Miller of Arizona State University has already written a full-length exculpation of King called *Voice of Deliverance: The Language of Martin Luther King, Jr.* Mr. Pappas notes that Prof. Miller has come up with an astonishing variety of ways to say "plagiarism" without using the word: voice merging, intertextualization, incorporation, borrowing, consulting, absorbing, alchemizing, overlapping, quarrying, yoking, adopting, synthesizing, replaying, echoing, resonance, and reverberation.

Prof. Miller says that non-whites, who have strong oral traditions, should not be held to stuffy, Western standards of bibliography, and that King could not be expected to understand the demands of an alien white culture. "How could such a compelling leader commit what most people define as a writer's worst sin?" he asks; "The contradiction should prompt us to rethink our definition of plagiarism." Since Martin Luther King did it, it must be all right.

Even those who condemn plagiarism claim to have no idea why King should have done it. Mr. Pappas drops us a hint when he writes, "[W]e know from his scores on the Graduate Record Exam that King scored in the second lowest quartile in English and vocabulary, in the lowest ten percent in quantitative analysis, and in the lowest third on his advanced test in philosophy—the very subject he would concentrate in at BU." People steal ideas when they are too lazy or unoriginal to come up with their own.

Blacks and Whites

Of course, the story that Mr. Pappas tells says far, far more about white America than about Martin Luther King. King was a dishonest scholar and got away with it—a small-time con-man whose degree would be revoked if Boston University had any integrity.

There is no doubt about what would have happened had King been white. Mr. Pappas reminds us that Joseph Biden's bid for the Presidency ended when he was shown to have copied from a speech by Neil Kinnock, the British Labor Party leader. Boston University itself recently stripped a dean of his position when it was learned he had cribbed from a *Wall Street Journal* article for a commencement address.

There is not a single white person, dead or alive, whose reputation academics and journalists would go to degrading lengths to preserve, but blacks are different. It is now well established that Alex Haley, the author of *Roots*, did not merely fake his African family tree but stole parts of it from a novel by a white man. His reputation remains unsullied, his Pulitzer Prize unrevoked. The black poet Maya Angelou's "Inauguration Poem" likewise appears to have been an unattributed adaptation, but her reputation and academic sinecure are unshaken.

To criticize Maya Angelou or Alex Haley is merely in bad taste but to question the sanctity of Martin Luther King is *lèse majesté*. Why?

In his forward to this book, Jacob Neusner writes that the impulse to defend a shameless plagiarist "stems from insufficient faith in the authentic achievements of Martin Luther King . . . ." In other words, anyone who does not find room in King's spacious personality for a few personal failings does not grasp the man's true greatness. Nonsense.

People toady to King's memory because he is a symbol of white racial atonement. To evoke his name is to confess white sinfulness and to ask forgiveness. Any attitude towards him other than worshipfulness suggests insufficient yearning for atonement or, to call it by its every-day name, "racism."

To go further and actually criticize King is to risk more than the taint of bigotry; it is to insult the contemporary idea of America itself. King's birthday is a holiday because he symbolizes what is thought to be America's finest triumph—the triumph over white wickedness. King stands for integration and racial egalitarianism, from which flow quotas, multiculturalism and non-white immigration. Policies that will weaken the country and dispossess the white majority must have nothing less than a saint as their symbol.

This article appeared originally in the April 1994 issue.

SCIENCE

The Descent of Man

Richard Lynn, *Dysgenics: Genetic Deterioration in Modern Populations*, Praeger Publishers, 1996, 237 pp., $59.95

reviewed by Thomas Jackson

Human traits are heritable. Children resemble their parents. Does it therefore make any difference who has children and who doesn't?

Farmers have understood selective breeding for thousands of years, and common sense suggests that the same principles apply to man. Indeed, from the mid-19th century until part way through the 20th, it was understood that if people of low ability outbred their betters it posed a threat to society. Only in the 1950s and 1960s did dogmatic egalitarianism force eugenic thinking underground (see AR, Feb. 1997).

The publication of *Dysgenics*, by Professor Richard Lynn of the University of Ulster in Northern Ireland, marks a very significant and promising beginning to the rehabilitation of eugenics. Some recent books, such as *The Bell Curve* (reviewed in AR, Feb. 1995) and *The Decline of Intelligence in America* (reviewed in AR, Feb. 1996) have pointed in this direction, but *Dysgenics* is the first book in decades to make a comprehensive case for protecting the human gene pool.

Benedict Morel

As Professor Lynn points out, it was a now-forgotten Frenchman, Benedict Morel, who first argued for eugenics. Writing in 1857, even before Charles Darwin's *Origin of Species*, Morel noted that the upper classes were having fewer children than the lower classes. He thought this could not help but drag down the population, since the upper classes were healthier, more intelligent, and of better character than the lower. The eugenicists of Victorian England took the same view, but it was not until 1974 that William Shockley gave the name dysgenics to society-wide genetic decline.

Professor Lynn explains that from the dawn of human existence up until only a century or so ago, people with the best qualities had the most children, thus spreading superior characteristics through populations. This is still happening in primitive societies, where able men achieve high status and have the most children. For example, a 1979 study of the Kung San tribe (Bushmen) of the Kalahari desert found that 62 percent of the men—the least successful hunters—had no children, whereas the most successful men had multiple wives and many children.

In most non-Christian societies polygamy has been one of the rewards of high status, and to the extent that status reflects ability, polygamy is eugenic. It allows huge differences in the numbers of children men can produce;

Moulay Ismail the Bloodthirsty (1672-1727), a Moroccan emperor, is said to have fathered 888 children.

In Europe as well, up until about 1800, the wealthy had considerably more children than the poor. There was no pubic assistance for single mothers, so there were strict sanctions against illegitimacy. Women generally did not marry men who could not support them, and many people in the serving classes therefore did not marry or have children. Prof. Lynn notes that when the lower classes had illegitimate or unwanted children they often exposed them; dead babies were a common sight in gutters or on rubbish heaps.

The 20th century has eased many of the forces that once culled the lower classes, but a few remain. Infant mortality is still higher among the poor than among the middle and upper classes, and this is true without regard to access to medicine. Prof. Lynn writes that this is because poor parents are less disciplined and health-conscious.

The poor show other signs of what Prof. Lynn calls a lack of conscientiousness. They are more likely to die from drowning, fire, traffic accidents, and suffocation. They are also more likely to smoke cigarettes and drink to excess. Sexually transmitted diseases are also far more common among the lower classes; venereal diseases can render women infertile and AIDS is lethal. Until cures are found, reckless sexual behavior will have a reproductive price.

How then do the less able manage to outbreed the more able? As Prof. Lynn explains, the main reason is birth control, which the provident use more successfully than the improvident. Until its invention there was no "dysgenic fertility," to use the specialist term.

The first book on contraception to have a real influence on the English-speaking world was *Every Woman's Book*, published in London in 1826. It explained the withdrawal method and how to use sheep-gut condoms. This was followed by an even more successful American book, somewhat opaquely entitled *The Fruits of Philosophy*. Later in the 19th century, contraception got an enormous unintended boost from the obscenity trials of several Englishmen who had published books on birth control. With the invention of the rubber condom in the 1870s, people who wanted to limit their families had a reliable way to do so.

Of course, not all social strata had the foresight, discipline, and means to use condoms. The intelligent and far-sighted were most likely to use them. As Prof. Lynn writes: "Once contraception became widely available, dysgenic fertility became inevitable."

Proof by Numbers

Although the eugenicists of the 19th century had a common-sense understanding of the dysgenic threat, it was not until the 20th century that its effects could actually be measured. One of the great strengths of Prof. Lynn's book is his careful presentation of the data that have been gathered over several generations of research.

Once IQ tests became available in the 1920s, researchers found a clear trend: children with high IQs tended to have few brothers and sisters. This was later shown conclusively to be an effect of dysgenic fertility rather than any kind of IQ-depressing effect of large families. The correlation between IQ and number of siblings is on the order of -.18.

Later population studies have taken a different approach, measuring the IQs of parents and counting their children. On the basis of all available data, Prof. Lynn concludes that the overall genetic IQ decline in the developed world is something like one point per generation. In Britain, for example, he estimates genetic IQ to have declined 6.2 points from 1890 to 1980. All studies seem to show that the decline was greatest in the first half of the 20th century, when contraception use was even more concentrated in the upper classes than it is today.

Recent, fine-grained studies of fertility have confirmed other important findings. In the United States, multiracialism itself is dysgenic since blacks and Hispanics have more babies than whites. Also, dysgenic trends are more pronounced among blacks than among whites, since the black underclass is outbreeding high-IQ blacks at a greater rate than the equivalent populations among whites. The IQ of white Americans is probably declining at a rate of just under one point per generation, whereas the decline for blacks is estimated at just over two points.

Another interesting finding is that dysgenic trends are sharper among women than men. The most intelligent women often spend many years in school and at work. Once they are in their mid-30s they may not find husbands, and they have also cut short their child-bearing years. Intelligent, successful men who delay marriage have less trouble finding suitable wives.

As Prof. Lynn explains, the sex difference is exacerbated by behavior at the low end of the intelligence curve as well:

"Low-IQ women tend to have higher fertility because they are inefficient users of contraception and there are always plenty of men willing to have sex with them. Low IQ men, on the other hand, tend not to have such high fertility because many of them are unattractive to females and lack the social and cognitive skills required to secure sexual partners."

Greater dysgenic fertility among women than men is particularly pronounced among blacks. College-educated black women have a notoriously small number of children whereas the underclass is fertile.

Although Prof. Lynn considers contraception to be the primary dysgenic force, he also notes the baleful effects of welfare. This has been the medium in which the underclass grows, and it has fueled illegitimacy rates among blacks that now approach 70 percent. Prof. Lynn notes that this cannot but be dysgenic:

"It is easy to understand why single mothers tend to have low intelligence and weak character. They are less able to foresee, and they care less about, the adverse consequences of having an illegitimate child."

In fact, in the United States, over half of the single women on welfare are in the bottom 20 percent for IQ.

Interestingly, much of the developing world is going through the same, steep dysgenic decline that Europe and the United States suffered earlier in the century. In much of Latin America, for example, contraception is used almost exclusively by the upper classes while peasants still show "natural fertility." Black Africa is the one great exception. Prof. Lynn reports that almost no one practices birth control there, so the genetic stock is not deteriorating.

Professor Lynn devotes a chapter to the so-called Flynn effect, the finding that performance on IQ tests has actually been *rising* during the 20th century despite dysgenic fertility. This trend is confirmed when IQ tests are routinely renormed to give an average score of 100. Today's test-takers score better on tests normed for the 1940s and 1950s than they do on tests normed for the 1990s.

How can this be? Prof. Lynn accepts that the approximate three-point-per-decade rise in IQ since the 1930s is real, and not an artifact of better education or greater literacy. Since the rise has been the same for small children as for adults, experience with test-taking appears not to be the cause. Prof. Lynn believes that better nutrition and the control of most childhood diseases explain performance gains that have masked the decline in underlying genetic intelligence.

Prof. Lynn likens this to using progressively poorer seed on increasingly fertile land. Crops may improve in the short-run but even the best land will some day be unable to make up for degraded seed. Figures for IQ decline are therefore calculations of what must be happening at the genetic level despite higher measured intelligence.

The Flynn effect—named for the New Zealander, J.R. Flynn, who publicized it—is one of the most perplexing findings in current IQ research. Prof. Lynn's treatment of it is as convincing as any in the literature.

Other Consequences

Intelligence is not the only important trait now shaped by modern techniques. Medicine has a dysgenic effect on health, since weak children who would ordinarily have died young now survive to have children of their own. In the case of some heritable diseases that can now be treated, there will be a sharp increase in defective genes. In the next 30 years, hemophilia is likely to become 25 percent more common, and cystic fibrosis and phenylketonuria (PKU) will increase by 120 percent and 300 percent.

Prof. Lynn also notes that criminal propensities, which he considers separately from intelligence, are also spreading through the population. Although this is a field that has been almost completely ignored, Prof. Lynn's own findings are that, at least in Britain, criminals and psychopaths are 77 percent more fertile than other people. Given heritability estimates for criminality derived from twin and adoption studies, Prof. Lynn finds that the excessive fertility of criminals alone probably accounted for a 52 percent crime increase in Britain in a single generation. He considers the spread of criminality a potentially greater problem than the decline of intelligence.

Perhaps the book's most dismal assertion is that the current reproductive habits of Western populations not only ensure decline, they rule out even the theoretical possibility of genetic improvement. In an era when the most able members of society limit themselves to two or three children, even the most dramatically favorable mutation would have no way to spread through a population. Improvement requires *eugenic* fertility, which is no longer found in Western populations. They have reached a genetic dead end.

What can be done? Prof. Lynn is silent on the subject of policy, but not from shyness. *Dysgenics* is to be followed by a second volume, which will outline the steps that can and must be taken to stop genetic deterioration. This volume could be even more important than the first.

This article appeared in the April 1997 issue.

A New Theory of Racial Differences

J. Philippe Rushton, *Race, Evolution, and Behavior*,
Transaction Publishers, 1995, 334 pp., $34.95

reviewed by Jared Taylor

*R*ace, Evolution, and Behavior is one of the most important books about race to be written in many years. Not only does it describe the myriad ways in which the races differ, it advances a persuasive and original explanation for what these differences mean and how they came about. Prof. J. Philippe Rushton of the University of Western Ontario has written a rigorously scholarly book that is not always easy to understand, but it could well become a classic in its field, like *Race* by John Baker and *Bias in Mental Testing* by Arthur Jensen.

Just how different are the races? Most experts now take differences in intelligence for granted. Prof. Rushton has gone much farther and marshaled a wealth of data on other important differences. Some of these are summarized in the chart below. The most striking finding is not just that Asians, whites, and blacks are different, but that the differences fit a pattern, with Asians and blacks at opposite ends of a spectrum, and whites in the middle.

A large part of the book—and a good portion of this article—are devoted to reviewing these data, but Prof. Rushton's most provocative and original contribution is his application of what is called *r-K* theory to this pattern of Asians-whites-blacks. The central element of *r-K* theory is represented graphically in the drawing below.

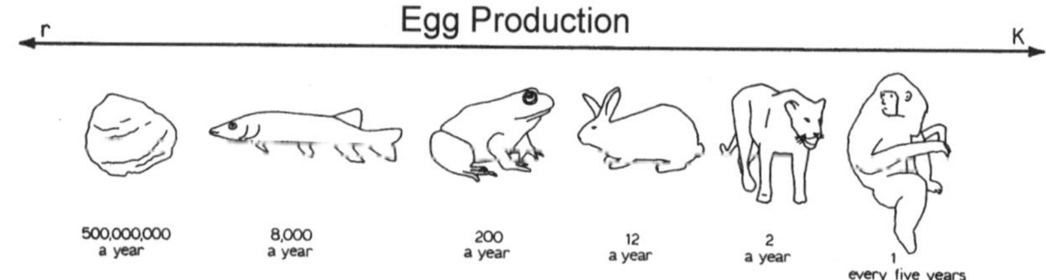

Different species have evolved different approaches to propagation. At one extreme is the *r*-strategy, by which an organism produces a very large number of offspring, but gives them little or no care. The oyster is a good example. Every year it releases millions of eggs into the ocean and leaves them to the mercies of weather and predators. Almost all of them die, but a few survive.

r organisms must mature quickly because they get no help from their parents. The ones that survive repeat the cycle by producing huge numbers of eggs, only a few of which will live. The symbol *r* stands for the maximum rate of increase in a population, and when the conditions for reproduction are good, an *r*-strategist can increase its numbers at a terrific rate.

At the other extreme is the *K*-strategy, which is used by more advanced animals, including man. The number of offspring is much smaller, but great effort is taken to give each one a good chance of survival. *K*- and *r*-strategists consequently are very different both in biology and in what Prof. Rushton calls life histories.

K-strategists live longer, have larger brains, and take longer to reach sexual maturity. Unlike the simpler *r*-strategists, they tend to have some kind of social organization. Besides the care they give their young, adults may share food, cooperate in the hunt, and fight predators together. The *K*-symbol stands for the carrying capacity of the breeding area, and represents the production of small numbers of offspring that are carefully nurtured for a particular environment.

All humans follow an extreme *K*-strategy. They have few young, who take years to mature and require a great deal of care. They have large brains and complex societies based on cooperation. However, human races are not identical. The chart on the next page (Table 1) shows that Asians consistently show more *K* behavior than whites, who in turn show more than blacks. There is virtually no departure from this pattern.

Maturation and Reproduction

In almost every respect, racial differences in the physiology of reproduction show an *r-K* pattern that runs from blacks to whites to Asians. Fraternal twinning, for example, which happens when a mother releases more than one egg during ovulation, is clearly an *r*-strategy of producing more and smaller young, who are more likely to be miscarried, be born underweight, die in infancy, and receive less parental care.

Fraternal twinning is twice as common among blacks as among whites, and twice as common among whites as among Asians. Triplets are ten times more common among whites than among Asians and 17 times more common among Africans than among whites. In some African populations, multiple births account for 60 out of every 1000. In Japan, where twins are very rare, they are viewed suspiciously as the products of a "litter," more akin to dogs than to humans.

Offspring of the different races gestate and mature according to different *r-K* strategies. Blacks are born earlier and smaller than whites, are stronger and better coordinated. They can sit up and roll over sooner than whites, who can do so sooner than Asians. On average, blacks walk at age 11 months, whites at 12 months, and Asians at 13 months.

Race and r-K Variables			
Variable	Asians	Whites	Blacks
Brain size	Large	Intermediate	Small
IQ	105	100	85
Decision Times	Fast	Intermediate	Slow
Cultural Achievements	High	High	Low
Gestation Times	?	Intermediate	Short
Development	Late	Intermediate	Early
Age of first intercourse	Late	Intermediate	Early
Life Span	Long	Intermediate	Short
Twinning per 100,000	4	8	16
Hormone Levels	Low	Intermediate	High
Genitalia	Small	Intermediate	Large
Intercourse Frequency	Low	Intermediate	High
AIDS/Syphillis	Low	Intermediate	High
Aggressiveness	Low	Intermediate	High
Cautiousness	High	Intermediate	Low
Dominance	Low	Intermediate	High
Self-Concept	Low	Intermediate	High
Marital Stability	High	Intermediate	Low
Criminality	Low	Intermediate	High
Administrative Ability	High	High	Low

Table 1

Although it is a specialized measure of development, permanent tooth eruption occurs sooner in Africans than in Europeans, and later in Asians. Among primates in general, there is near-perfect correlation between lateness of permanent tooth eruption and such things as length of life, brain size, years to maturity, and complexity of social organization.

Blacks reach sexual maturity sooner than whites, who reach it sooner than Asians. By age twelve, 19 percent of American black girls have fully developed breasts and pubic hair whereas only five percent of white girls do. Blacks, on average, have earlier first menstruation than whites, and Asians menstruate later than whites. In the United States, the average white woman is two full years older than the average black woman when she first has sexual intercourse, and Asians start having intercourse even later than whites.

Professor Rushton has bravely taken on the delicate subject of genital size, which has received reluctant but official attention because of AIDS. International organizations that try to provide condoms to people all over the world have discovered that one size does not fit all. Blacks have larger penises than whites, who have larger penises than Asians. The length of the vagina also differs proportionately in each race. Black men produce more sperm than do whites, and Asian men produce the least.

In the United States, black married couples report the greatest frequency of sexual intercourse, and Asian married couples report the lowest frequency. AIDS, like other sexually transmitted disease, is most common among blacks, rarest among Asians.

In Africa, compared to Europe or Asia, it is common to have sexual relations with many partners and to expend less effort on child-rearing. Older brothers and sisters often look after smaller children. There are also huge racial and regional differences in the number of offspring produced. In the United States, the average woman produces 14 children, grandchildren and great-grandchildren; in Africa the figure is 258. This prodigious African reproductive effort takes place over a shorter life-span. Blacks do not live as long as whites who, in turn, do not live as long as Asians.

Here, clearly, are patterns of maturational and reproductive behavior that show a consistent r-K pattern. Quick maturity, early reproduction, numerous offspring, and shorter lives put blacks closer to the oyster end of the scale than whites, who are closer to it than Asians.

Differences in sexual activity, life-span, and number of children are usually attributed to "culture" or "environment," but there is every reason to believe that they are at least partly genetic, just as size of sex organs or age of sexual maturity are almost entirely genetic. Life-span, for example, is clearly hereditary in part. The age at which an adopted child will die is more easily predicted from the life-spans of the biological parents than from those of the adoptive parents. Likewise, identical twins die, on average, only 37 months apart whereas fraternal twins die 78 months apart.

What about the other components of the human K-strategy, such as altruism, law-abidingness, and the other characteristics that make up distinctly human social organizations? To what extent are what we think of as personality—and the cultural institutions that reflect a population's group personality—the products of heredity, and thus properly included in an analysis of r-K strategy? Prof. Rushton has exhaustively surveyed recent studies of heredity, which suggest a powerful genetic influence on virtually all aspects of human behavior.

Some of the most startling and convincing data on the relative influences of genes vs. environment come from studies of identical twins who were separated at birth and reared apart. Identical twins come from a single egg that splits in two; the twins are genetically identical. Fraternal twins are produced by a double ovulation and are no more genetically alike than ordinary siblings. (Unlike fraternal twinning rates, there are no racial differences in the frequencies of identical twinning.)

The crucial finding is that identical twins reared apart are more like each other in virtually every way than are fraternal twins who were reared in the same household. From these similarities it is possible to estimate how much of the variation in personality traits is caused by genes and how much by environment.

Table 2 shows twin-study estimates of the genetic contribution to various attitudes. These estimates almost certainly undervalue heritability because the method used to calculate it assumes that all aspects of environment are arbitrary. In fact, to a very large degree, people influence their own environments according to traits that are at least partly genetic. Thus, *even within the same family*, an aggressive child elicits different responses from parents and playmates—and thus has a different environment—from a child who is placid and cooperative. Once they are independent of their parents, young people follow their genetic propensities even more freely by choosing entirely different environments.

Estimated Heritabilities of Attitudes Toward:	
Death Penalty	.51
Royalty	.44
Apartheid	.43
White superiority	.40
Divorce	.40
Sabbath Observance	.35
White Lies	.35
Mixed Marriage	.33
Legalized Abortion	.32
Nudist Camps	.28
Socialism	.26
Learning Latin	.26
Computer Music	.26
Bible Truth	.25
Pajama Parties	.08
Coeducation	.07

Table 2

The methodology of heritability estimates ignores this. Thus, much of the influence on personality traits that is due to "environment" undoubtedly reflects personal surroundings that differ primarily because people shape their surroundings to match their genetic predilections.

Intelligence, which is one of the most important, stable and most frequently measured traits, is also one of the most heritable. Variations in intelligence within a population appear to be 60 to 80 percent governed by heredity.

It is important to note that heritability estimates are for *variations* in IQ, not total IQ. Thus, for two brothers with IQs of 100 and 120, a genetic component of 60 percent (and an environmental component of 40 percent) does not imply that 40 IQ points of the 100-IQ brother's intelligence are theoretically attributable to environment. It means only that 40 percent of the 20-point *difference* between the brothers—8 IQ points—is theoretically governed by non-genetic factors.

Furthermore, no one is really sure how environment influences the 40 to 20 percent that is presumably non-genetic. Non-genetic factors may well be grossly biological events like malnutrition, childhood diseases, and mishaps in the womb, rather than the household or educational differences that most people think of as environment. Such things as Head Start or special education appear to have very little lasting effect on IQ differences either between individuals or races.

For the different racial groups, Prof. Rushton has aggregated the results of a great many IQ studies to arrive at the following averages: Whites - 100, Asians - 105, American blacks (who are about 25 percent white) - 85, African blacks - 70 to 75, Amerindians (including Central and Latin Americans with little or no European blood) - 89, Polynesians, Micronesians, Melanesians, and Maoris - 80 to 95.

Although Asians have a higher general intelligence than whites, the difference is mainly in visuo-spatial performance rather than verbal ability. This makes Asians good engineers and mathematicians, but they do not have a pronounced advantage in careers like law or language teaching. Not surprisingly, a 1980s survey of professions in the United States found that Chinese-Americans were over-represented in the sciences at a rate six times their proportion in the population. However, there were only one fourth as many Chinese-American lawyers as their numbers would suggest. Blacks were minimally represented in both fields.

Although it is common to criticize IQ tests precisely because they give disparate results by race, there are other, more obviously biological indicators of intelligence that cannot be accused of "cultural bias." One that Prof. Rushton himself has studied in depth is brain size.

Larger heads (containing larger brains) are positively correlated with intelligence. This is true within families, with the sibling with the largest head likely to be the most intelligent. It is also true within races, with large-brained blacks or Asians likely to be more intelligent than their small-brained co-racialists.

As groups, whites and Asians have larger brains than blacks. At age seven, for example, black children are 16 percentile points taller than white children, but their head perimeter is eight percentile points smaller. Asians are likely to have larger brains than whites, though some indications of larger size appear only after correcting upward for the fact that Asians are smaller than whites. A small person with the same sized brain as a big person can be thought of as having a "larger" brain, because smaller bodies require less brain to maintain basal functions.

Whites probably have about 100 million fewer cerebral neurons, on average, than Asians and blacks have about 480 million fewer than whites. The black/Asian difference is especially significant because of differences in body size. Blacks with small brains in large bodies are at a serious intellectual disadvantage compared to Asians because a larger proportion of their already-smaller brains is probably occupied with basal functions and not available for conscious thought.

Yet another directly physiological assessment of intelligence is the type of reaction-time test pioneered by Prof. Arthur Jensen of Berkeley. These tests require people to make simple choices when a light goes on. Intelligence is correlated with both speed and consistency of reaction time, and Asians perform better than whites, who perform better than blacks.

Prof. Rushton cites several additional reasons to suspect that racial differences in intelligence are due to genetics rather than environment. One is something called regression towards the mean. Individuals who are at extreme points in a normal distribution of any trait are likely to have children not so extreme as themselves. Very tall people, for example, are likely to have taller-than-average children, but their children's heights tend towards the average for the population. With respect to IQ, studies have repeatedly shown that black Americans regress towards a mean of 85 while whites regress towards a mean of 100.

Inbreeding depression scores are another persuasive indicator that racial differences are genetic. Children that result from unions of very close relatives often have unusually low scores on certain kinds of intelligence tests, indicating that the abilities measured by those tests are highly susceptible to genetic influence. As it happens, these measures of intelligence are the very ones that show the *greatest* black-white differences, which suggests that the intelligence gap is also genetic.

Other Personality Differences

High intelligence is not the only hallmark of *K*-strategy. Professor Rushton explains that the races with more *K* traits have more complex and cooperative social organizations, are more sexually restrained and law abiding, and show more altruism. In terms of *r-K* strategy, altruism and social cooperation permit individuals to rear their young under more dependable and peaceful circumstances—which is a precondition for groups that have staked their survival on producing small numbers of large-brained but slow-maturing offspring.

For traits like altruism and aggression to be properly included in an *r-K* pattern, they must be shown to be, like intelligence, at least partly controlled by heredity and to differ from race to race. Research suggests that these traits are greatly influenced by heredity, and that they appear early in life. In one study, children who were rated as "aggressive" by their peers at age eight were rated the same way by a different set of peers 10 years later. By the time they were 19 years old, those in the "aggressive" group were three times more likely to have a police record than those who were not considered "aggressive."

Identical twins are about twice as much alike in terms of altruism and aggression as fraternal twins. Studies in both Europe and Japan have confirmed that when a twin has been convicted of a crime, an *identical* co-twin is two to three times more likely also to have been convicted than is a *fraternal* co-twin.

Shyness and sociability also appear very early in children and endure through adulthood. Studies of identical twins reared apart have shown astonishing similarities not only in personality, but in careers, marriage patterns, style of dress, and individual mannerisms.

Research also shows that predictions about criminal behavior in adopted children can be made more accurately from the behavior of biological parents rather than adoptive parents. Some time between the ages of 21 and 30, the adult personality is "set like plaster," and environment seems to have little effect on it.

Prof. Rushton points out that most people marry and make friends with people who are genetically like themselves. They seek others who not only look but think like they do. Durability of marriage has been shown to be linked to genetic similarity of the partners—in intelligence, appearance, and in other personality traits that are to some extent under genetic control.

It is therefore not surprising that biological siblings have more similar friends than do adopted siblings. Likewise, young criminals—who appear to have a genetic propensity for crime—commonly make friends with other young people with the same propensity.

This clearly demonstrated human preference for associating with others who are similar has important implications for race relations. Even very young children are conscious of race and show racial preferences. Prof.

Rushton writes that ethnocentrism and "racism" are probably natural mechanisms built into the human genotype.

Expressions of altruism also have important implications for race relations. In virtually all species, the closer two individuals are, genetically, the more likely they are to help each other. This makes evolutionary sense if genes are thought of as the basic units of evolution. Genes for altruism are likely to leave more copies of themselves in future generations if they produce a trait that causes individuals to help their close kin survive.

Ants and bees are especially altruistic—frequently dying in great numbers to protect the colony—because they have an unusual reproductive pattern that causes workers to share 75 percent of their genes. Squirrels and monkeys can detect genetic distance between themselves and others, and are more cooperative towards close relatives.

Male Rhesus monkeys are promiscuous and cannot be sure that the child of a mate is their own. However, they have some unknown way of recognizing their offspring, and are kinder to them than they are to unrelated youngsters. (Actual kinship has been confirmed through blood tests.)

Belding's ground squirrels mate with multiple partners, and females have litters that contain both sisters and half sisters. Despite the fact that they share the same womb and the same nest, full sisters fight less often and help each other more often than half sisters.

Among humans, preschool children are 40 times more likely to be assaulted by a step-parent—that is to say, a genetic stranger—than by a biological parent. In promiscuous societies in which fathers are not sure which children are their own, they put more effort into caring for their sisters' children than for those of their wives. A sister's child is always close kin, whereas a promiscuous wife's child may not be kin at all.

Experiments in altruism confirm the obvious: People are more willing to help people like themselves. Similar appearance is a good indicator of genetic similarity, and Prof. Rushton observes that racial solidarity can be viewed as a kind of extended nepotism. He also argues that it is often fruitless to look for sociological or economic reasons for the racial conflicts found all around the world. Genetic similarity and the desire to preserve a common set of genes are more likely explanations.

Racial Differences

The races differ consistently in the personality traits that can be classified according to r-K theory, just as they do in intelligence. Asians are more restrained, cooperative, and less aggressive than whites; whites are more restrained and less aggressive than blacks. These rankings are the same, whether subjects are assessed by personality tests or by their peers. From an early age, blacks are more impulsive and dominant than whites. Asians are least dominant and impulsive.

Differences in crime rates by race are too well established to bear repeating. (See "Race, Crime, and Violence," page 28.) These differences are consistent across multi- and mono-racial societies. Nevertheless, stiff resistance to genetic explanations leads to environmental theories that are unintentionally funny. As Prof. Rushton notes, earlier in this century, all forms of deviance were so low in American Chinatowns—despite their poverty—that the ghetto was thought to *protect* people from crime. For blacks, isolation is routinely said to *cause* crime.

Although trendy talk of "self-esteem" suggests otherwise, blacks have higher opinions of themselves than whites, who have higher opinions of themselves than Asians. Asians are the most introverted and anxious; blacks are the least. Suicide figures reflect this: Whites kill themselves twice as frequently as blacks, and Asians kill themselves more often than whites. Self-consciousness and introspection seem to rise along with K characteristics.

Rates of mental instability show the opposite trend. Two hundred and forty out of every 100,000 blacks are in mental institutions whereas only 162 of every 100,000 whites are. Nor is this a function of poverty or wealth; blacks suffer from mental disorders, drug addiction, and alcoholism at higher rates than whites in all social classes. Asians, despite their introversion and anxiety, have the fewest mental problems.

Differences Within Races

Prof. Rushton points out that r-K theory can account for differences between individuals *of the same race*. That is to say, people of the same race tend to vary according to the same pattern that distinguishes the races. In both Europe and Africa, the following traits tend to go together: large families, short life-span, criminality, high levels of sexuality, loose family ties, frequency of twinning.

Mothers of fraternal twins are more likely than other mothers to have had early first periods, larger families, lower birth-weight children (even when they are singletons), more infant mortality, to have been promiscuous, and to have shorter lives. Prof. Rushton has found that in all societies, fraternal twins are more likely to be born into the lower than the upper classes.

A Swedish study determined that girls who have early first periods are more likely to cheat, be truant, and try marijuana than girls who have late first periods. In the United States, early maturation is correlated with promiscuity, illegitimate births, leaving school, crime, and other social problems. Early sexual maturity seems to be heritable, with daughters resembling their mothers.

If altruism is an important K trait, crime would be an extreme r trait. Across broad populations, crime is associated with behavior that almost perfectly describes how blacks differ from whites and whites differ from Asians: large families, illegitimacy, low intelligence, early sexual maturity, promiscuity, weak family ties, little investment in children, and a short life.

Prof. Rushton suggests that the entire complex of r-K trait differences is therefore largely under genetic control, and that it characterizes different social classes just as it does races. There is little question that the most physiological *r-K* traits are heavily influenced by heredity. Prof. Rushton makes the additional point that physiology is closely correlated with many other forms of behavior previously thought to be independent of heredity but now found to be greatly influenced by it. The result is a strong case for believing that the patterns of behavior that distinguish races as well as individuals are largely inherent, reflect a consistent *r-K* pattern, and are impervious to social "programs."

Prof. Rushton takes the argument one provocative step further. In the current era of social mobility, in which most hereditary social privileges have disappeared, people succeed or fail in life very much according to their native abilities. The children of the rich are usually smart and talented because they inherit the qualities that made their parents rich.

As Prof. Rushton points out, a child's IQ is a better predictor of his adult social status than is the social status of his parents. And, when the unintelligent children of the rich start descending the social scale, they take on the habits and values of their new class rather than keep the ones of the class into which they were born. Even the most *K*-oriented parents can have an *r* child, whose life increasingly reflects his genetic inclinations.

Prof. Rushton's findings are a serious blow to contemporary egalitarian dogma. Unfortunately, the usual reaction to his work is simply to make wild accusations about his motives. In an article called "Professors of Hate," the October 20, 1994, issue of *Rolling Stone* claims to have unmasked him as a vicious racist.

Of course, it is the haters of science and free inquiry who build societies that cannot but degenerate as ours has. Anyone who wants to understand the world as it, and to base policy on facts rather than on fantasies, cannot ignore this very important book.

This article appeared in the December 1994 issue.

Race and Psychopathic Personality
by Richard Lynn

For as long as official statistics have been kept, blacks in white societies have been overrepresented in all indices of social pathology: crime, illegitimacy, poverty, school failure, and long-term unemployment. The conventional liberal explanation for this is white "racism," past and present, which has forced blacks into self-destructive choices. More clear-headed observers, however, have sought a partial explanation in the low average IQ of blacks.

Low IQ can lead to crime because less intelligent children do poorly at school and fail to learn the skills needed to get well-paid jobs, or even any job. Unemployment is therefore two to three times higher among blacks than whites. People without jobs need money, and have relatively little to lose by robbery or burglary, and may therefore commit property crimes. The association between low intelligence and crime holds for whites as well, among whom the average IQ of criminals is about 84.

Nevertheless, as Charles Murray and the late Richard Herrnstein showed in their book *The Bell Curve*, low IQ cannot entirely explain a black crime rate that is six-and-a-half times the white rate. When blacks and whites are matched for IQ, blacks still commit crimes at two-and-a-half times the white rate. This shows that blacks must have some other characteristic, besides low intelligence, that explains their high levels of criminality.

Prof. Herrnstein and Dr. Murray found the same race and IQ relationship for social problems other than crime: unemployment, illegitimacy, poverty, and living on welfare. All of these are more frequent among blacks and are related to low IQ, and low IQ goes some way towards explaining them, but these social problems remain greater among blacks than among whites with the same IQs. Low intelligence is therefore not the whole explanation. Prof. Herrnstein and Dr. Murray did not offer any suggestions as to what the additional factors responsible for the greater prevalence of these social problems among blacks might be. They concluded only that "some ethnic differences are not washed away by controlling for either intelligence or for any other variables that we examined. We leave those remaining differences unexplained and look forward to learning from our colleagues where the explanations lie" (*Bell Curve*, p. 340).

Psychopathic Personality

I propose that the variable that explains these differences is that blacks are more psychopathic than whites. Just as racial groups differ in average IQ, they can also differ in average levels of other psychological traits, and racial differences in the tendency towards psychopathic personality would explain virtually all the differences in black and white behavior left unexplained by differences in IQ.

Psychopathic personality is a personality disorder of which the central feature is lack of a moral sense. The condition was first identified in the early nineteenth century by the British physician John Pritchard, who proposed the term "moral imbecility" for those deficient in moral sense but of normal intelligence. The term psychopathic personality was first used in 1915 by the German psychiatrist Emile Kraepelin and has been employed as a diagnostic label throughout the twentieth century. In 1941 the condition was described by Hervey Cleckley in what has become a classic book, *The Mask of Sanity*. He described the condition as general poverty of emotional feelings, lack of remorse or shame, superficial charm, pathological lying, egocentricity, a lack of insight, absence of nervousness, an inability to love, impulsive antisocial acts, failure to learn from experience, reckless behavior under the influence of alcohol, and a lack of long-term goals.

In 1984 the American Psychiatric Association dropped the term psychopathic personality and replaced it with "anti-social personality disorder." This is an expression of the increasing sentimentality of the second half of the twentieth century, in which terms that had acquired negative associations were replaced by euphemisms. There are other examples. Mentally retarded children are now called "slow learners" or even "exceptional children;" aggressive children now have "externalizing behaviors;" prostitutes are "sex workers;" tramps are now "the homeless," as if their houses were destroyed by earthquake; and people on welfare are "clients" of social workers. However, the term psychopathic personality remains useful.

While psychopathic personality is a psychiatric disorder, it has long been regarded as the extreme expression of a personality trait that is continuously distributed throughout the population. In this respect it is like other psychiatric disorders. For instance, severe depression is a psychiatric disorder, but everyone feels depressed sometimes, and some normal people are depressed more often and more severely than others. It is the same with psychopathic personality. There are degrees of moral sense throughout the population, and psychopaths are the extreme group.

There is a difference between blacks and whites—analogous to the difference in intelligence—in psychopathic personality considered as a personality trait. Both psychopathic personality and intelligence are bell curves with different means and distributions among blacks and whites. For intelligence, the mean and distribution are both lower among blacks. For psychopathic personality, the mean and distribution are higher among blacks. The effect of this is that there are more black psychopaths and more psychopathic behavior among blacks.

In 1994 the American Psychiatric Association issued a revised Diagnostic Manual listing 11 features of anti-social personality disorder: (1) inability to sustain consistent work behavior; (2) failure to conform to social norms with respect to lawful behavior [this is a euphemism for being a criminal]; (3) irritability and aggressivity, as indicated by frequent physical fights and assaults; (4) repeated failure to honor financial obligations; (5) failure to plan ahead or impulsivity; (6) no regard for truth, as indicated by repeated lying, use of aliases, or "conning" others; (7) recklessness regarding one's own or others' personal safety, as indicated by driving while intoxicated or recurrent speeding; (8) inability to function as a responsible parent; (9) failure to sustain a monogamous relationship for more than one year; (10) lacking remorse; (11) the presence of conduct disorder in childhood.

This is a useful list. Curiously, however, it fails to include the deficiency of moral sense that is the core of the condition, although this is implicit in virtually every feature of the disorder. All of these behaviors are more prevalent among blacks than among whites, and suggest that blacks have a higher average tendency towards psychopathic personality.

Questionnaires can be used to measure psychopathic personality in normal populations. The first to be constructed was the Minnesota Multiphasic Personality Inventory (MMPI), which was devised in the 1930s. This instrument consists of a series of scales for the measurement of a variety of psychiatric conditions regarded as continuously distributed in the population, such as hysteria, mania and depression, and includes the Psychopathic Deviate Scale for the measurement of psychopathic personality.

During the 65 or so years following its publication, the MMPI has been administered to a great many groups. Mean scores have been published by different investigators for a number of samples of blacks, whites, Asian-Americans, Hispanics and American Indians. All of these studies show a consistent pattern: Blacks and Indians have the highest psychopathic scores. Hispanics come next followed by whites. Ethnic Japanese and Chinese have the lowest scores. The same rank order of racial groups is found for all the expressions of psychopathic personality listed by the American Psychiatric Association, and these differences are found in both children and adults.

Conduct Disorder

The terms psychopathic personality and anti-social personality disorder, however, are not used for children or young adolescents up to the age of 15 years. They are instead said to have conduct disorders. The principal criteria set out by the American Psychiatric Association (1994) for a diagnosis of conduct disorder are persistent stealing, lying, truancy, running away from home, fighting, arson, burglary, vandalism, sexual precocity and cruelty. Childhood conduct disorder is therefore an analogue of psychopathic personality in older adolescents and adults. A number of studies have shown that conduct disorder in children is a frequent precursor of psychopathic behavior.

Studies have found that the prevalence of conduct disorders is about twice as high among blacks as among whites. This is the case not only in the United States but also in Britain and the Netherlands. Other racial groups also differ in the prevalence of conduct disorders among children. As with all the other expressions of psychopathic personality, conduct disorders are frequent among American Indians.

Children with conduct disorders are sometimes suspended or expelled from school because of constant misbehavior, particularly aggression. In both the United States and Britain, black children are disciplined in this way three or four times as frequently as white children, while East Asians have low discipline rates. In misbehavior in schools, as in so much else, East Asians are the "model minority." In the United States, Indians have a high discipline rate.

Lack of honesty is one of the core features of the psychopathic personality, and one measure of this characteristic is the default rates on student loans. About half of American college students take out loans but not all graduates repay them. The 1987 National Postsecondary Student Aid Study consisting of 6,338 cases reports default rates as follows: whites—5 percent, Hispanics—20 percent, American Indians—45 percent, blacks—55 percent.

Bad credit ratings also reflect a failure to honor financial obligations. A report by Freddie Mac of 12,000 households in 1999 found the highest percentage of poor credit ratings was among blacks (48 percent). The next highest was among Hispanics (34 percent), while whites had the lowest at 27 percent.

A prominent feature of psychopathic personality is a high level of aggression, which is expressed in a number of ways including homicide, robbery, assault, and rape. All of these are crimes, so racial and ethnic differences appear in crime rates. High black crime rates have been documented by Jared Taylor and the late Glayde Whitney in *The Color of Crime*. For homicide, rates for black males are about six times the white rate, and for black females they are about four times higher. The homicide rate for East Asians is about half that of whites. The high homicide rate of blacks is also found in South Africa, and homicide is generally higher in black countries than in white and East Asian countries.

As regards other crimes, the robbery rate for blacks is about twelve times the white rate, while the assault rate is about five times higher. The high black rates for these crimes are followed in descending order by Hispanics, American Indians, whites and East Asians. The rate for rape is about five-and-a-half times greater for blacks than whites, and two to three times greater among Hispanics and Indians as compared to whites, while East Asians commit rape at about half the white rate.

Domestic violence shows the same race differences. Severe violence by husbands against wives is about four times more common among blacks as whites. Black wives assault their husbands at about twice the white rate. American Indians assault their spouses even more often than blacks do. High crime rates among blacks have been found not only in the United States but also in Britain, France, Canada and Sweden.

A prominent feature of psychopathic personality is an inability to form stable, long-term loving relationships. David Lykken, a leading expert on psychopathic personalities, writes of the psychopath's "undeveloped ability to love or affiliate with others," and Robert Hare, another leading expert, writes that "psychopaths view people as little more than objects to be used for their own gratification" and "equate love with sexual arousal."

Marriage is the most explicit expression of long-term love, and a number of studies have shown that blacks attach less value to marriage than whites. Questionnaire surveys have found that blacks are less likely than whites to agree that "marriage is for life." Two American sociologists, R. Staples and L. B. Johnson, write that "Blacks do not rank marriage as highly as whites" and that "Black Americans' acceptance of this form of relationship is inconsistent with their African heritage."

In a study of an American sample of 2,059 married people, C. L. Broman found that "blacks are significantly less likely to feel that their marriages are harmonious and are significantly less likely to be satisfied with their marriages." Other studies of racial and ethnic differences in attitudes have found that whites think about marriage more often than blacks, and have a stronger desire than blacks to find the right marriage partner. There are also racial differences in rates of cohabitation, which also reflects a commitment to a long-term relationship. A survey of 24- to 29-year-olds in Britain found that 68 percent of whites had cohabited but only 38 percent of blacks.

Blacks in the United States, Britain, France and the Caribbean are less likely than whites to marry or enter into stable relationships. In an American survey of 18- to 64-year-olds carried out from 1990 to 1996, 61 percent of whites were married but only 35 percent of blacks. The most likely to be married were East Asians (66 percent). Fifty-five percent of Hispanics and 48 percent of American Indians were married. The same race differences are found in Britain. In a survey carried out in 1991, among 30- to 34-year-olds 68 percent of whites were married but only 34 percent of blacks. Studies of marriage rates for France in the 1990s have also found that blacks are less likely to be married than whites. These differences are also found for cohabitation, with fewer blacks living in unmarried cohabitation relationships than whites.

Differences in marriage rates are reflected in differences in illegitimacy rates. In the United States, black illegitimacy rates are down slightly from their high in 1994, when 70.4 percent of black women who gave birth were unmarried. The 2000 figure of 68.7 is still the highest for any racial group, and is followed by American Indians at 58.4 percent, Hispanics 42.7 percent, whites 22.1 percent, and Asians 14.8 percent. The Asian figure includes populations with greatly differing illegitimacy rates, with native Hawaiians, for example, at 50 percent, Japanese at 9.5 percent, and Chinese at 7.6 percent.

Low rates of stable relationships are found among blacks in the Caribbean islands. In a review of the literature the sociologists B. Ram and G. E. Ebanks write that "In the Caribbean in general . . . there is a substantial amount of movement from one sex partner to another and also a very high percentage of reproduction outside marriage."

When they do marry, blacks are less tolerant than whites of monogamous constraints. An extreme form of intolerance is murder of one's spouse. In Detroit in 1982-3, 63 percent of the population was black but 90.5 percent of those who killed their spouses were black. Less extreme forms of aversion to monogamy are adultery and divorce. The Kinsey data on college graduates, collected in the 1940s and 1950s, found that 51 percent of blacks were unfaithful to their spouses during the first two years of marriage compared with 23 percent of whites. Several other studies have confirmed that the incidence of marital infidelity is greater among blacks than among whites. Blacks cite infidelity more frequently than whites as a cause of divorce.

Blacks also have more sexual partners than whites. The Kinsey survey found that about twice as many black college graduates had had six or more partners before marriage than whites. Many later studies have confirmed this. A survey of 2,026 15-to-18-year-olds in Los Angeles in the mid-1990s found that 38 percent of blacks had had five or more sexual partners, 26 percent of whites, 21 percent of Hispanics and eight percent of East Asians.

The same differences are found in Britain. In a study of a nationally representative sample of approximately 20,000 16- to 59-year-olds carried out in 1990, 36 percent of blacks had had two or more sexual partners during the previous five years, compared with 29 percent of whites and 18 percent of Asians.

Delay of Gratification

The impulsiveness component of psychopathic personality includes an inability or unwillingness to delay immediate gratification in the expectation of long-term advantage. The first study to demonstrate differences between blacks and whites in the delay of gratification was carried out by W. Mischel in Trinidad in the late 1950s. He offered black and white children the choice between a small candy bar now or a larger one in a week. He found black children were much more likely to ask for the small candy bar now, and this difference has been confirmed in three subsequent American studies. This racial difference has been noted but given different names by different writers. In *The Unheavenly City Revisited*, Edward Banfield writes of the "extreme present-orientation" of blacks, and Michael Levin writes of "high time preference," an economist's term for preferring cash now rather than a greater sum in the future.

The APA Diagnostic Manual refers to the psychopathic personality's "inability to sustain consistent work behavior," and a number of studies have shown that blacks are less motivated to work than whites and Asians, while Hispanics are intermediate. For example, black students do fewer hours of homework than whites and Asians. Among college students with the same Scholastic Aptitude Test scores, blacks get poorer grades than whites, probably because they don't work as hard.

This helps explain black unemployment. Several American ethnographic studies of inner city blacks have concluded that many are unwilling to work.

Thus, E. Anderson writes that "there are many unemployed black youth who are unmotivated and uninterested in working for a living, particularly in the dead-end jobs they are likely to get." The sociologist S. M. Petterson writes that "it is commonly contended that young black men experience more joblessness than their white counterparts because they are less willing to seek out low paying jobs." American Asians are the opposite of blacks in this respect. They have low rates of unemployment and it has been shown by James Flynn that they achieve higher educational qualifications and earnings than would be predicted from their intelligence, suggesting they have strong work motivation.

In the United States, unemployment rates are highest among Indians followed in descending order by blacks, Hispanics, whites and ethnic Chinese and Japanese. These differences are frequently attributed to white racism but it is difficult to reconcile this explanation with the lower rate of unemployment among East Asians as compared with whites, and also with the higher rate of unemployment among Indians as compared to blacks.

Blacks in Britain, Canada and France are frequently unemployed. In Britain, the 1991 census found that 26 percent of black men were unemployed, compared with 11 percent of whites and ethnic Chinese. In Canada in 1991, 13 percent of black men were unemployed compared with seven percent of whites. In France in 1994, 11 percent of black men were unemployed compared with eight percent of whites.

Recklessness

Psychopaths appear to enjoy taking risks because it stimulates them, and there are several ways in which blacks show greater recklessness and risk taking than whites or Asians. In the 1989-93 American Teenage Attitudes and Practices Survey, 9,135 youths aged 12 to 18 were asked to consider the question: "I get a kick out of doing things every now and then that are a little risky or dangerous." Fifty-six point nine percent of blacks agreed, as compared with 38.6 percent of whites. Driving habits are an index of risk taking and recklessness. A number of studies have shown that blacks run red lights more often than whites, and have more frequent accidents. Five studies have shown that blacks do not use seat belts as often as whites. Hispanics and Native Americans likewise have more accidents caused by recklessness and risk-taking than whites and East Asians.

Sexual behavior can be reckless. Among those who do not wish to have children, blacks are less likely to use contraception than whites, and this has been found in both the United States and Britain. One result is that black women have more unplanned babies than whites. In the United States in the 1990s blacks had about twice the proportion of unplanned babies as whites and Asians. In Britain, a survey of teenage births carried out in 1994 found that these were three-and-a-half times more common among blacks than among whites and Asians.

The behavior of reckless men also causes unplanned pregnancies. Surveys have asked adolescent males if they would feel "very pleased" or whether they would care if they were responsible for an unplanned pregnancy. Twice as many blacks as whites say they would be very pleased or that they would not care. To be very pleased or not care about saddling a teenage girl with an unplanned pregnancy expresses a great degree of recklessness regarding the well-being of others. In the United States, the percentage of teenage blacks who have fathered an illegitimate child is approximately three times greater than that of whites, with Hispanics intermediate.

Another consequence of reckless avoidance of contraceptives is that blacks are more likely to get sexually transmitted diseases—including HIV and AIDS—all of which are more prevalent among blacks than among whites and Asians. At the present time, about 80 percent of the word's HIV carriers are blacks in sub-Saharan Africa.

A common expression of conduct disorder in children and young adolescents is sexual precocity. Many studies have shown that blacks are more sexually precocious than whites and Asians. Surveys in the United States in the 1990s have found that about a third of black 13-year-olds have had sexual intercourse compared with 14 percent of whites and Hispanics, and four percent of East Asians. Similarly, a survey in Britain in 1990 found that by the age of 16, 18 percent of blacks had had intercourse compared with 13 percent of whites and five percent of Asians.

We consider finally the psychopathic characteristic described by the American Psychiatric Association as "inability to function as a responsible parent." One of the most straightforward measures of this is abuse and neglect. The American Association for Protecting Children has found that black children constitute approximately 15 percent of the child population and about 22 percent of cases of child abuse and neglect. The First (1975) and Second (1985) National Family Violence Surveys carried out in America examined the use of violence towards children, defined as hitting them with the fist or with some object, and kicking, biting and beating them up. It does not include slapping or spanking. It found that 1.2 percent of white parents and 2.1 percent of blacks inflict this kind of severe violence on their children.

Data published by the United States Department of Health and Human Services for 1996 showed that maltreatment was about three times more common among blacks and about one-and-a-half times more common among Hispanics, than among whites.

The most extreme expression of the inability to function as a responsible parent consists of killing a child. Racial differences in the homicide of infants in their first year of life were examined for approximately 35 million babies born in the United States between 1983-91. This study found that 2,776 of these had been murdered, the great majority by mothers or the mothers' husbands or partners. The rate of infant homicides for blacks and Native Americans was 2 per 10,000, compared with 0.6 per 10,000 for whites and 0.4 per 10,000 for East Asians. In the early 1990s the racial differences became even greater, with blacks having four-and-a-half times the infant homicide rate of whites.

Complete Consistency

There is almost complete consistency in the racial differences in outcomes that can be considered measures of psychopathic personality. In everything from child behavior to sexual precocity to adult crime rates we find Asians at one extreme, blacks at the other, and whites, Hispanics and American Indians in between. These differences are not only consistent through time but are found in countries such as France, Britain, Canada, and the United States, which have very different histories of what could be called "racism." Indices of high psychopathic personality in blacks are likewise found in the virtually all-black societies of Africa and the Caribbean.

Racial differences in psychopathic behavior persist even when IQ is held constant, and the same racial differences are found in essentially every kind of measurable behavior that reflects psychopathic personality. The most plausible explanation for these differences is that just as there are racial differences in average IQ, there are racial differences in what could be called "average personality," with blacks showing greater psychopathic tendencies. The argument that white "racism" is responsible for black social pathology is increasingly unconvincing.

Richard Lynn is professor emeritus of psychology of the University of Ulster. This article originally appeared in the July 2002 issue, and is based on a longer paper published in Personality and Individual Differences, *2002, Vol. 32.*

The Definitive Word on Intelligence

Arthur Jensen, *The* g *Factor*, Praeger Publishers, 1998
648 pp., $39.95

reviewed by Jared Taylor

Arthur Jensen of U.C. Berkeley is one of the greatest social scientists of our time. He virtually single-handedly resurrected the scientific study of intelligence, and he has been at the center of many breakthroughs in this field. Needless to say, he is a courageous man, who has never let hysterical opposition or even death threats keep him from studying some of the most important and contentious issues we face.

The g *Factor* is only the latest of the many publications that resulted from what can now be seen as a watershed event: the 1969 appearance in the *Harvard Educational Review* of Prof. Jensen's famous article on the heritability of IQ and how difficult it is to raise. This article not only reestablished the connection between genetics and intelligence but set the direction of Prof. Jensen's career. He has since written countless articles in this field and three major books: *Educability and Group Differences* (1973), *Bias in Mental Testing* (1980), and now, *The* g *Factor*.

These books chart the recent remarkable progress in the study of intelligence. If Prof. Jensen had so dominated any less controversial field he would certainly be a candidate for the Nobel Prize. Unfortunately, his real stature is recognized only by a small number of specialists and professional colleagues, but the implications of his work continue to reverberate through the larger society. Whatever recognition he may ultimately receive, his work has gone far to set the study of mental ability once more on a firmly scientific basis.

The *g* Factor

This book is an investigation of the nature of intelligence, the extent to which it is under genetic control, and its uneven distribution between individuals and groups. The first part is a complete and sometimes technical treatment of "*the* g *factor*" itself, which appears to be a unitary mental ability underlying all activities we think of as requiring intelligence. "Factors" are the end result of a mathematical procedure called factor analysis, and the g factor is the "general" factor of intelligence, first hypothesized by the British psychologist, Charles Spearman (1863-1945). Spearman thought of g as a direct analogy to the "G" of physics, that is Newton's gravitational constant. Spearman's view, substantiated by almost a century of research, was that g is of central importance to psychology just as G was to Newtonian physics.

g can be thought of as the undifferentiated raw cognitive power of the brain. It cannot be directly measured, but it manifests itself in all types of cognitive activity, and people who are good at one kind of mental test tend to be good at all of them. To use the statistical term, a person's different abilities are *correlated*, and similar abilities tend to correlate most closely with each other. For example, someone who is exceptionally good at *any* mathematical test is likely to be very good at *all* mathematical tests—but he is likely to perform well on verbal tests, too. As we will see, *g* is at work when even the smallest demands are made on the mind.

If people take enough different kinds of mental tests, their scores can be analyzed for factors, or the tendency of the correlations between similar abilities to cluster in groups. There will be factors for such things as verbal, musical, mathematical, and spatial manipulation abilities. Further analysis of these factors reveals a fundamental factor common to them all, which is the *g* factor.

We can therefore imagine a series of different factories in the brain, all powered by the same energy source. One of the factories manufactures solutions to mathematical problems, while another produces correct understandings of words and sentences. Other factories produce solutions to other kinds of mental problems, but all of them can be thought of as running off a common power source, which is *g*.

People differ in the efficiency of their individual factories, which is why smart people have different strengths in different areas despite being smart in a general sort of way. But people differ most significantly in the level of the general power source, or *g*. Someone with an IQ of 100 may have a math factory that is relatively more efficient than his verbal or music factory, but even in math he is likely to fall well behind someone with an IQ of 130 whose math factory is relatively *less* efficient than his verbal factory. It is the difference in levels of power available to *all* of a person's factories that produce the marked differences in ability that characterize our species.

Many kinds of mental performance can be taught and people can show improvement, but what is improving is an ability that is not *g*. As Prof. Jensen explains, "At the level of psychometrics [mental testing], ideally, *g* may be thought of as a distillate of the common source of individual differences in all mental tests, completely stripped of their distinctive features, of information content, skill, strategy, and the like."

Interestingly, Prof. Jensen reports that it is at the highest levels of *g* that people show the most variation in abilities that are independent of *g*. Thus, very intelligent people may have markedly different mental ability profiles despite similar levels of *g*. If all the factories are getting lots of power from their common source, some of the factories are likely to be unusually efficient so that the pattern of different levels of efficiency can differ considerably from one smart person to another.

Some critics have complained that *g* is not real because it cannot be measured directly and must be derived by a complex statistical process. Prof. Jensen shows that it is not, for this reason, artificial. If there were no *g* factor, sophisticated mathematics could not coax it into existence. Moreover, the same g factor is found in all human populations, and can be derived from the results of mental tests prepared by people who have never heard of g or who have even doubted there was such a factor. g can be calculated only because it exists, and in that sense is purely objective. Prof. Jensen believes that it reflects one of the basic functions of the brain, and that although all normal people share the same biological structures they differ greatly in the efficiency of certain neurological processes.

ECTs

Direct assessment of brain functions gives strong evidence that g is a real, physiological phenomenon, and Prof. Jensen has been a pioneer in using what are called elementary cognitive tasks (ECTs) to study intelligence. The simplest sort of ECT involves a test device with two push-buttons (see below). The subject holds down the black button while he waits for a light to go on inside the smaller, white button. He then presses the illuminated button as quickly as possible. This measures two things. The first is reaction time: the time between the light going on and the subject taking his finger off the black button. The second is movement time: the time it takes the subject to move his finger from the black button to the illuminated button.

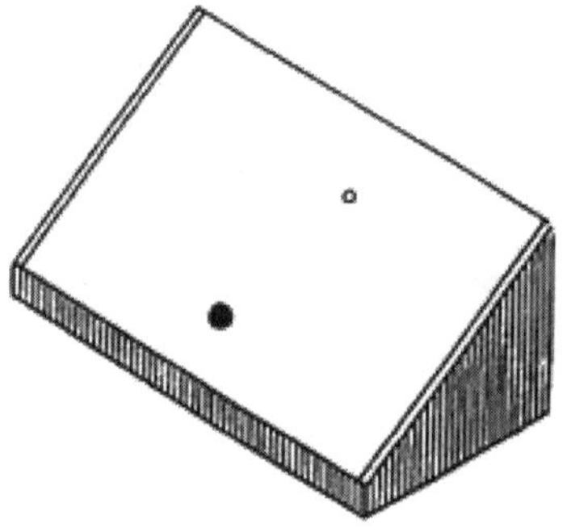

ECT Device

Obviously, this is a very simple (indeed, elementary) task, though tests of this kind can be made more complicated. For example, there can be a number of smaller buttons that can light up in different patterns, requiring the subject to make slightly more complicated decisions before moving his finger. We do not think of this sort of thing as mentally demanding—no one ever *fails* these tests—but the neurological processing that goes into these very simple tasks is closely related to intelligence.

Prof. Jensen has found that reaction speed is strongly correlated with g level, but that the highest correlation is between g and *consistency* of reaction time. With a set of scores from various different ECTs, it is possible to achieve a 0.7 correlation with g as calculated from conventional IQ tests.

This approaches the *g* correlation (0.8) of Ravens Progressive Matrices, the IQ test that comes the closest to measuring *g* itself. Surprising as it may seem, careful monitoring of the processes that underlie ECTs can give results that are so reliable they rival pencil-and-paper tests.

ECT performance matches group differences in intelligence. It is worse in children than in adults, and better in gifted children than in normal children. Blacks have quicker movement times than whites while whites have quicker and more consistent reaction times. Asians do slightly better than whites, and performance for no group improves with practice; ECTs appear to measure something basic to the brain.

Another direct assessment of mental processing is the inspection time test. This uses an instrument called a tachistoscope to throw an image on a screen for a very brief period. Starting at the millisecond level, which is too quick for anyone to see the image, the exposure is gradually increased until a subject can just make it out. There is a correlation of .54 between speed of inspection time and IQ—remarkably high for a task that is so different from an IQ test. Once again, the test seems to be measuring a neurological process closely associated with mental processing.

Yet another direct assessment is the study of brain waves. Prof. Jensen explains that a wave pattern called average evoked potential can be analyzed in specialized ways that show a surprisingly high correlation with IQ.

Finally, researchers have devised something that is essentially a direct test of brain efficiency. The brain's fuel is glucose, or simple sugar. When a radioactive isotope of glucose is injected into a subject's blood stream it is possible to measure the rate at which the brain takes it up and metabolizes it. When rate of metabolism is measured while subjects are taking an IQ test, the high scorers use *less* sugar than the low scorers, with a remarkable correlation with IQ of around .7 or .8. The less powerful brains get wrong answers despite burning more fuel. If we return to the analogy of the brain as composed of factories, the common power supply simply appears to be less efficient.

If advances continue to be made in direct assessment of the brain, conventional IQ testing may be superseded. This would certainly silence any complaints about "test bias."

Heritability

Because the issue of whether education or environment can influence IQ levels is central to so much policy-making, *The* g *Factor* thoroughly covers the question of heritability. Kinship and adoption studies have provided some of the most illuminating data on this question, and Prof. Jensen reports them in detail.

Some of the most significant findings are the correlations of IQs of identical twins reared in the same family (.86), identical twins separated at birth and reared in different families (.75) and fraternal twins reared in the same family (.60). That identical twins separated at birth should have more similar

IQs than fraternal twins reared by the same parents is perhaps the single most powerful argument for the view that genes have a greater effect on IQ than environment. As Prof. Jensen points out, "similarities in the MZA's [monozygotic (identical) twins reared apart] environments cannot possibly account for more than a minute fraction of the IQ correlation of +.75 between MZAs."

Studies of siblings and adopted children likewise confirm the power of heredity in determining differences in IQ, and it is now generally agreed among specialists that 60 to 80 percent of human IQ variation is due to genes. This does not mean, however, that the remaining environmental influences are well understood or can be used to raise IQ. As Prof. Jensen explains, "a large part of the specific environmental variance appears to be due to the additive effects of a large number of more or less random and largely physical events—developmental 'noise'—with small, but variable positive and negative influences on the neurophysiological substrate of mental growth."

What is this developmental "noise"? "[S]uch effects as childhood diseases, traumas, and the like, as well as prenatal effects such as mother-fetus incompatibility of blood antigens, maternal health, and perinatal effects of anoxia and other complications in the birth process, could each have a small adverse effect on mental development." These appear to be the kind of non-genetic factors that influence IQ, and they are not the sort of thing that can be easily manipulated.

As Prof. Jensen makes emphatically clear, the non-genetic influence comes only slightly, if at all, from what are called between-family differences: education of parents, social status, family income, school quality, etc. Liberals believe that these are the crucial factors that make people different from each other, but liberals are wrong. IQ (like other personality traits) is astonishingly impervious to any but the most degraded and unfavorable environments.

Prof. Jensen calls the environmentalist view "the sociologist's fallacy." It is true that children from wealthy homes tend to be smarter than children from poor homes, but wealth does not make them smart. They get genes for intelligence from their smart parents, and their parents are likely to be well off (and have homes full of books and speak in complete sentences) because they are smart. Of course, children do differ from their parents in intelligence, and these differences explain how families rise and fall. A person's IQ has a correlation of .7 with his own adult socio-economic status but only about .4 with that of his parents.

Error though it be, the sociologist's fallacy has driven not only an enormous number of government uplift programs but several well-publicized private efforts to raise the IQs of poor black children. Prof. Jensen reviews the results of the Milwaukee Project, Head Start, and the Abecedarian Project, some of which made extraordinary attempts to improve environments.

In some cases, the early results were very encouraging: gains of 20 or even 30 points compared to control groups. But as Prof. Jensen convincingly argues, what the children learned at intensive "infant stimulation centers" and the like was information and strategies that helped them take the tests. *g* very probably did not change. In most cases, administrators did not give a battery of tests and attempt to calculate *g*. Instead, they gave the same test at different ages and rejoiced to find improvement.

Professor Jensen gives a striking example of how training can improve test results without raising *g*. He notes many children's IQ tests have a memory component: How long a string of letters or numbers can the child repeat back to the tester? Most adults can't remember more than about seven numbers, but with lots of practice and training, people can remember as many as 70 or even 100 digits. They can do this because they develop a specific strategy or skill, not because their memory or *g* level has improved. The tricks a person uses to remember 70 digits are so specialized, in fact, that they do not even help the same person remember more than an average number of letters (rather than digits)!

Children who took part in these widely-acclaimed IQ-raising programs probably learned specific skills of this kind during the thousands of hours of instruction they received. But even the most intensive enrichment programs had virtually no permanent effect on school performance or IQ, which suggests that *g* itself was unchanged. Prof. Jensen concludes that IQ cannot be appreciably increased by specialized education.

It is true that the IQ test scores of children are affected to some degree by the environment their parents make for them. This is almost certainly because they learn more facts and absorb test-taking strategies and not because the love and care of good parents improves *g*. In fact, as children grow older they create environments that suit their own genetic endowments, and Prof. Jensen is categorical about what then happens: "By adulthood, all of the IQ correlation between biologically related persons is genetic. . . . [T]he environmental contribution to the familial correlations is nil." Surprising as it may seem, once a child grows up, his IQ score is similar to that of family members *only* because he is genetically related to them, not because they spent many years in the same household.

Racial Differences

Prof. Jensen is equally forthright in explaining that genes account for the well-established IQ differences between the races. First, he points out that approximately half—or 50,000—of the genes that vary in human beings play a role in brain functions, and that 30,000 affect the brain exclusively. It would be astonishing if genes did not play a central role in intelligence and if the races, which differ physically in so many ways, did not differ in brain function.

He also offers an arresting refutation of the fashionable view that race is purely a social construct and is not biological. Prof. Jensen likens race to the visible colors. A rainbow forms when the wave-length of light changes continuously and uniformly, but we do not perceive a continuous change. Instead, we see distinct bands of color. Though there may be some blurring of race at the edges because of cross mating, races are as distinct as the bands of visible color. Prof. Jensen also cites the increasingly persuasive genetic evidence for the biological distinctness of different populations (genetic distance between populations is graphically illustrated below).

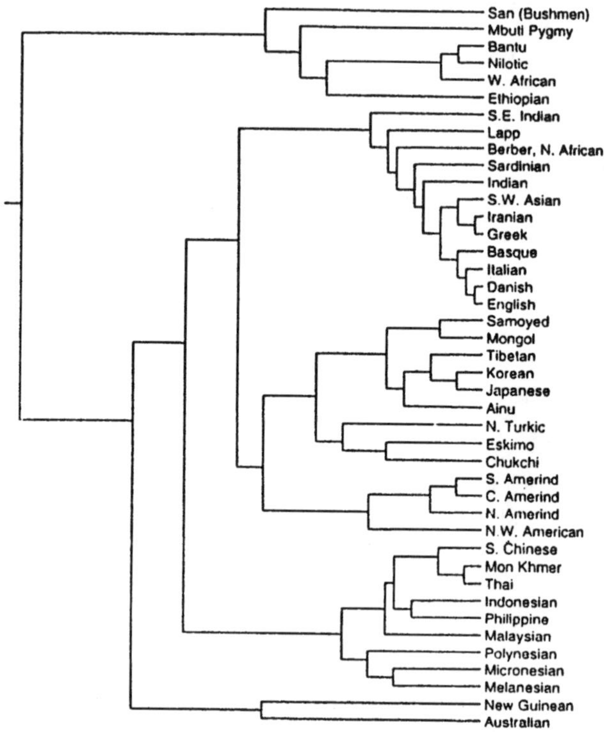

A number of elegant demonstrations based on the principle of regression toward the mean strongly suggest a genetic origin for group differences. This principle is a biological law according to which parents who are at the extremes of any trait are likely to have children who are less extreme. Two very tall parents are likely to have children who are not quite so tall, and two very short parents are likely to have children who are not quite so short. In the children, these traits revert toward the average, or the mean. The same effect is found in intelligence, but the mean toward which the black IQ regresses is a full 15 points lower than the white mean.

Therefore, when black couples and white couples are matched for IQ, the black/white IQ difference in their children *increases* as parental IQ increases. In other words, high IQ is an anomaly in all races, but more of an anomaly for blacks than for whites, and the children of high-IQ blacks regress further because they are regressing toward a lower mean.

Prof. Jensen reports a study of high-IQ children in one school district that provides more evidence for the difference in means. When white and black students were perfectly matched for IQs of 120, the average IQs of the siblings of the whites was 113 whereas the average IQs for the siblings of the blacks was 99. Among blacks, an IQ of 120 is simply a much greater deviation from the norm than it is for whites, and this is reflected in the IQs of their more ordinary siblings.

Regression toward the mean explains something that has always baffled the "sociologists:" children of low-income whites (and Asians) get better SAT scores than the children of high-income blacks. If environment controls IQ, the children of wealthy blacks should be enjoying the benefits of good environment. They are, but those benefits are meager and do not make up for the effects of heredity and the lower mean toward which black children regress.

There is no non-genetic explanation for group differences that can account for phenomena of this kind, but they are perfectly consistent with widely accepted principles of genetics. Specialists understand the force of arguments of this kind, which is why the view that "racism" and other environmental factors cause the black/white IQ gap persists mostly among the ignorant—who are the great majority.

More strong evidence for a substantially different biological mean for IQ is found in studies of the low end of the IQ distribution curve as well. Mental retardation—IQs below 70—is generally of two types, familial and organic. Familial retardation occurs in children who are otherwise normal but were simply dealt a very poor hand of the genes that affect intelligence. Given a normal distribution of intelligence, a few people are inevitably going to have very low IQs, just as a few will have very high ones. Organic retardation, on the other hand, is caused by clear biological defects, like Down's syndrome (Mongolism) and children who suffer from it are obviously abnormal.

An important racial difference lies in the fact that half of whites with IQs below 70 are organic retardates but only 12.5 percent of the blacks are. The source of this difference is the racial disparity in naturally occurring distributions of intelligence. Given that the distribution curve for black intelligence is shifted approximately 15 points toward the left, a substantially larger proportion of otherwise normal blacks will fall below an IQ of 70.

The opposite is true at the high end of the curve. The percentage of whites with IQs higher than 130 is 20 times that of blacks. Because there are approximately six times as many whites as blacks in America, in real terms there are perhaps 120 times more whites than blacks with IQs at this level. This is why, without racial preferences, it is impossible to admit large numbers of blacks to competitive universities or to promote them to challenging positions.

Brain and head size studies likewise confirm the biological origins of group differences. It is now well established that brain size correlates with intelligence, and Prof. Jensen reports that the heads of black newborns are a full .4 standard deviation smaller than those of whites. Black and white children matched for IQ have similar head sizes, but matching for head size alone does not produce populations with the same intelligence levels. Similar head size appears to be a necessary but not sufficient condition for racial parity in IQ.

It has long been known that near-sightedness, or myopia, is correlated with intelligence; children with IQs over 130 are three to five times more likely to be nearsighted than children with normal IQs. There seems to be no functional, cause-and-effect connection between myopia and intelligence, but a *pleiotropic* relationship exists in that some of the same genes affect both traits. Intelligence and myopia are somehow "side effects" of each other to some degree. Prof. Jensen finds that myopia is most common in Jews, next in Asians, then in whites, and least common in blacks—precisely the distribution one would expect. Moreover, reading does not cause myopia. An oculist can examine the eyes of children who are too young to read and who are not yet near-sighted, and accurately predict whether they will need glasses later in life.

It is well known that the test score gap between blacks and whites varies from one IQ test to another, and that the gap narrows on the least abstract, most information-laden tests. Prof. Jensen explains that the meaningful difference lies in the extent to which a test measures g; the more g-"loaded" a test is and the fewer specific non-g abilities it measures, the greater the black/white gap.

Like many others who have studied the question, Prof. Jensen finds that the racial gap in IQ is increasing because of dysgenic birth patterns. In both races, less intelligent mothers are having more children than more intelligent mothers, but the disproportions are higher among blacks than whites. Also, since blacks have children, on average, two years earlier than whites, the generation time for blacks is shorter and dysgenic effects spread more rapidly.

One of Prof. Jensen's most interesting racial findings is that the average IQ difference for blacks and whites *in the same social class* is 12 points—almost as great as the average difference between the two races (there is an average 17-point difference between any two people in the population picked at random). This is explained not only by preferential policies but also by racial differences in IQ distribution. If, for example, a demanding profession requires a minimum IQ of 125, blacks in that profession will tend to have IQs that cluster at the minimum, whereas whites will show greater variety. Because of this effect, the IQ gap between blacks and whites in the same social class narrows as one moves down the social scale.

Prof. Jensen finds that the geographic distribution of IQ is also uneven. For both blacks *and* whites, there is a continuous gradient that rises from the south towards the north and west. The gradient is sharper for blacks than whites, and both gradients are apparent in pre-school children, so regional differences in education do not explain it.

It has been widely reported that from infancy black children develop motor skills more rapidly than whites. Interestingly, Prof. Jensen finds that lower-class children (both white and black) develop more quickly than upper-class children, which suggests that slow maturation and high intelligence are correlated not just between races but within races.

For the most part, Prof. Jensen does not make policy recommendations; the facts alone are persuasive enough. He does point out, though, that life itself is a kind of continuous intelligence test, and that high g is one of the most important ingredients of success. He explains that scores on a highly g-loaded test are the best indicators of performance on any but the most specialized jobs. IQ is an excellent predictor for performance even on jobs that require manual dexterity and coordination. To a remarkable degree, g is the central mental characteristic of humans. Of course, intelligence is not everything. It takes more than brains to become a doctor—it takes persistence and discipline too, but persistence is not enough. For many things, a certain level of g is indispensable, and low g cuts off desirable options at every stage of life. Low g is therefore a more accurate predictor of achievement than high g, since a lack of intelligence cannot usually be made up for by other qualities whereas high intelligence can be wasted.

When people with low g are scattered through otherwise normal communities it affects only individuals. Friends and relatives step in to help them. However, as Prof. Jensen points out, when people of low intelligence gather in large numbers, as they do in welfare housing, society falls apart. Prof. Jensen notes that in America there are now entire apartment blocks in which, even with welfare, the residents cannot get by without help from social workers. Dysgenic trends and increased immigration of low-g stock mean areas like this will only expand.

In this connection, Prof. Jensen makes some interesting observations about adult illiteracy. Most people assume that the cause is poor schooling, but he argues that the problem is usually not the process of decoding written language but understanding it. Most illiterates do no better on reading comprehension tests when the selections are read to them than when they try to do the reading themselves! Illiteracy, in Prof. Jensen's view, is much more a problem of low g than of somehow not learning how to read.

There are a few points on which Prof. Jensen's data differ from results AR has reported elsewhere. Some researchers have found that although the average IQs of men and women are the same, a greater standard deviation for men means that more of them are bunched at both high and low IQs. Prof. Jensen does not find sufficient evidence to draw this conclusion. He does confirm the standard sex differences in verbal and spatial abilities and even reports that some higher mammals show the typical male superiority in spatial ability. He also writes that in addition to their well-known advantage in verbal ability, one of the largest sex differences favoring women is in something called "speed and accuracy," which is similar to clerical checking.

Prof. Jensen also takes up the question of why black women are so much more successful than black men. They are more likely to graduate from high school and college, pass high-level civil service tests, and enter skilled professions. This difference is not found among whites, and some researchers have wondered if black women may have a higher average IQ than black men. Once again, Prof. Jensen finds no such difference—but he offers no other explanation.

Prof. Jensen also differs from researchers who explain part of the black/white crime rate difference in terms of high black testosterone levels and an inability to defer gratification. He argues that population differences in *g* alone explain differences in crime rates. He notes that criminals of all races have IQs that are some 10 points below those of their siblings, and finds that within the same ranges of IQ, blacks and whites have essentially the same crime rates.

More than Generous

Needless to say, Prof. Jensen has spent his career disagreeing with others, and from time to time in *The g Factor* he must explain why his critics are wrong—and he is always a gentleman. Even with those who have disagreed with him in strong terms, he is more than generous in pointing out the parts of their theories that may be correct, and couches his own criticism in the gentlest terms. He treats his wildest, least scientific critics to nothing more than dignified silence: The names of Leon Kamin and Stephen Jay Gould do not even appear in an otherwise exhaustively researched and footnoted work.

The g Factor is not an easy book to read. Prof. Jensen writes clearly and repeats explanations when it would be unreasonable to expect perfect recall in his readers, but he writes for an informed, even specialist audience. He has already begun collaboration with a journalist on a more popular version of *The g Factor*. But those who are willing to invest the effort this book requires, will find that it is the monumental work of an extraordinary mind. A review can only begin to touch on its breadth and detail. This book is likely to become one of the landmark works in psychology, and it is the great good fortune of our society that a man of Prof. Jensen's stature has made his career in this crucially important but thankless field

This review appeared in the September 1998 issue.

Why Race Matters

Michael Levin, *Why Race Matters: Race Differences and What They Mean*, Praeger Publishers, 1997, 415 pp.

reviewed by Jared Taylor

Michael Levin's long-awaited book on race has finally arrived, every bit as powerful and insightful as his admirers had hoped it would be. *Why Race Matters* does exactly what the title promises—it removes all illusions about the insignificance of race, and explains what racial differences mean for a multiracial society. It is a thorough, overwhelmingly convincing treatment of America's most serious and least understood problem. Like the work of Arthur Jensen and Philippe Rushton, it destroys the egalitarian myth, but Prof. Levin parts company with other academics in his willingness to tell us what biology means for policy. Facts imply conclusions, and this book draws them.

Basic Data

As Prof. Levin points out, a book like *Why Race Matters* should not have to be written. The only sensible conclusion to be drawn from simple observation is that races differ: "To put the matter bluntly, the question is not why anyone would believe the races are unequal in intelligence, but why anyone would believe them equal." For centuries, people as different as Arabs and Englishmen have judged Africans to be unintelligent, lascivious, jolly, and keen on rhythm. Today, in whatever corner of the globe one looks, blacks behave in certain consistent ways.

Nevertheless, every important racial policy in this country is based on the assumption that race differences in ability are *known* not to exist. Current beliefs are a remarkable victory of dogma over not only the evidence of our senses but the findings of science.

Prof. Levin begins by presenting the data. This has been done many times by others, and the basics need not be repeated here. Prof. Levin capably and thoroughly presents twin studies, adoption studies, test data, and heritability estimates, all while dismantling the desperate attempts of egalitarians to dismiss them.

There is now not much informed opposition (though a great deal of *unin*-formed opposition) to the conclusion that IQ tests test intelligence, that intelligence is at least partly hereditary, and that the races differ in average IQ. The last-ditch battle of the egalitarians is to try to save the idea that race differences are caused by environment—primarily by malevolent white people, past and present.

To counter this view, Prof. Levin gives a thorough account of recent work on the strictly biological correlates of intelligence. When smart people think, their brains emit different electrophysiological signals from those of the less smart. Prof. Levin notes that advances in the study of brain waves could probably establish quite precise racial differences, but fear appears to have halted the research. Brain size also has a robust correlation with intelligence, and intelligent people's brains metabolize glucose relatively slowly.

Egalitarians claim that childhood nutrition accounts for this sort of thing, but the differences remain when nutrition is held constant (when only those blacks and whites who get the same diet are compared). Moreover, black children mature more rapidly than white children, are more athletic, and go on to dominate professional sports—not what one would expect from the malnourished. Likewise, diet does not explain metabolic or brain size differences in fraternal twins reared in the same family on the same food. If the anti-biology camp is not to be silenced completely it must argue that people unconsciously single out children with large heads for favorable treatment or give white children subtle training in how to retard glucose oxidation.

It is nevertheless *theoretically* possible that the most hotly-defended egalitarian position is correct: that the black-white IQ gap persists only because the two populations are reared in different environments. According to this view, blacks and whites should be thought of as identical twins reared apart, but with the black twin's environment so dismal it robbed him of 15 IQ points.

Such a view might be plausible if intelligence is easily molded, but it is not. Prof. Levin points out that since it is generally accepted that 70 percent of the variation in IQ is controlled by genes and only 30 percent by environment, "it is almost but not quite irrational to believe that the interracial IQ difference of +1 SD [standard deviation, or 15 points] can be completely explained by differences in black and white environments." Blacks and whites would have to live in fantastically different worlds (Prof. Levin calculates them as 1.85 SD apart) to account for this IQ difference, yet the difference has been unchanged by integration, huge transfers of wealth, and the very considerable *reduction* in the gap between black and white environments.

There have, of course, been many attempts to raise black IQ by "enriching" the environment. As Prof. Levin explains, the most ambitious such efforts, including Head Start, the Perry Preschool Program, and the Milwaukee Project all failed to produce lasting gains in IQ. Recent ingenious testing methods for young children have shown that the one SD difference between blacks and whites is present by age three. It is hard to imagine white society managing to damage black children permanently during the very years when most blacks have virtually no contact with whites.

The tenacity with which egalitarians hold to social rather than biological explanations for group differences probably bespeaks a fear that biology is immutable in its power to determine our lives. And yet, if blacks are so vulnerable to environment that they have been collectively beaten out of 15 points of IQ, environment must be just as ruthless and deterministic as biology. The difference is that so long as there is a *chance* that white people are to blame for black failure, there is joy in denouncing and persecuting "racists." All the fun goes out of the game if nature and not bigots is to blame. Thus, as Prof. Levin explains, so long as there is even the flimsiest, *post facto* environmental explanation for differences, there will be zealots to defend it.

In the end, however, unless the data are somehow suppressed, Prof. Levin expects the Human Genome Project to identify intelligence-related genes and to show that they are not distributed with the same frequency in all races. He expects the distributions to match the social science data, which is indirect but relentlessly consistent. He tips his hat to W.E.B. Du Bois who, he says, will stand vindicated by science. When Du Bois spoke of "the talented tenth"—the minority of blacks on whom racial progress depends—he was very close to the truth. Approximately 12 percent of blacks are born at or above the white average in intelligence.

Mental Acrobatics

The modern debate about IQ has been quietly raging ever since Arthur Jensen relaunched it in 1969.[1] Since many of the data are now unassailable, debate centers on how they should be interpreted. Much of Prof. Levin's book is therefore devoted to taking the stuffing out of the sometimes comical arguments of people like Steven Jay Gould and Andrew Hacker. As his book shows, egalitarians are always shifting their ground, ignoring data, and creating mysteries where none exists.

Examples of the latter are the currently fashionable views that race is a purely social artifact that should be junked, and that intelligence is undefined and unknowable. Prof. Levin notes that acrobatics of this kind are pure tendentiousness. Those who would discard the idea of race in any discussion of IQ find it *essential* for affirmative action. As for the pose that intelligence is unknowable:

"People who make a point in argument of not understanding 'intelligence' invariably do understand it in all other contexts. They know an 'intelligent' child is one who learns quickly, and that, of the two, Nobel laureates tend to be more 'intelligent' than manual laborers. . . . People pretend not to understand 'intelligence,' I suspect, to avoid embarrassment over race."

There is also much ignorant shrieking about the "bias" of IQ tests designed by white men, but it is an odd bias that permits Asians to outscore whites. As Prof. Levin explains, a real example of bias would be a test of hand-eye coordination that involved only the right hand. Lefties could prove the bias of such a test by demonstrating their ability with their left hands. "If the races are equally intelligent," he writes, "it should be possible to find a task intuitively requiring intelligence that blacks perform as well as whites." No such task has ever been found.

---

[1] See "The Definitive Word on Intelligence," page 212.

This is what leads otherwise reasonable people to insist that musical and athletic abilities are forms of intelligence in which blacks may surpass whites. As Prof. Levin points out, it tortures the language to claim that Babe Ruth was a genius, but egalitarians must either take fantastic positions or cease to be egalitarian.

Even scientists lose their bearings when it comes to race. It is now fashionable to point out—correctly—that there is more genetic variation among African populations than in all other groups combined and then to suggest—stupidly or deceitfully—that this means genetic racial differences do not matter. Prof. Levin patiently explains that there is vastly more genetic variation among dogs than in giraffes, but that does not prevent people from noticing that giraffes are taller than dogs. The egalitarian literature is full of "science" of this kind, and one of this book's great strengths is its relentless pursuit and exposure of claims that may well be deliberately deceptive.[2]

Egalitarians may be best at deceiving themselves, as Prof. Levin shows in his neat analysis of the trendy view that blacks *cannot* be racists. When people say this, they are probably thinking of "racism" as the claim that one's race is superior to others. In some dark recess of their minds, liberals cannot imagine *anyone* really believing that blacks are superior to whites, so blacks cannot be "racist." Since this reasoning is taboo, they instead claim that only members of "the dominant culture" or the group with "power" can be racist.

Morality

Prof. Levin is at his most original and provocative when he moves beyond well-established data on intelligence, and takes up the even more controversial question of morality. Other researchers have suggested that blacks differ from whites in ways other than IQ, but have not followed this argument very far.

For example, the widely used Minnesota Multiphasic Personality Inventory (MMPI), which subdivides personality into a number of categories, shows consistent differences in how blacks and whites evaluate themselves. Blacks, for example, hold themselves in higher regard than whites (or, in today's jargon, have "higher self-esteem"). They are consistently more likely to agree with statements like:

- I am an important person.
- I am entirely self-confident.
- If given the chance I could make a good leader of people.
- I have often had to take orders from someone who did not know as much as I did.

---

[2] For a comprehensive debunking of the view that race does not exist, see Glayde Whitney, "Diversity in the Human Genome," in *The* Real *American Dilemma*, also published by New Century Books.

The common assumption that blacks are "taught to hate themselves" is wrong; blacks are quite pleased with themselves. At the same time, they consistently score higher than whites on the MMPI scales for such things as Hypomania, Psychopathy, Schizophrenia, and Masculinity, which are precisely the traits that distinguish incarcerated criminals from the rest of us. They tend to agree, for example, with statements like:

- Most people are honest chiefly through fear of being caught.
- Most people make friends because friends are likely to be useful to them.
- Most people will use somewhat unfair means to gain profit or an advantage rather than lose it.
- It is not hard for me to ask help from my friends even though I cannot return the favor.

Another finding is that blacks are more impulsive or present-oriented than whites. Given a choice between a small candy bar today and a big one tomorrow, black children are more likely than white children to want the small one today.

Finally, even within races, moral reasoning is closely associated with intelligence. Intelligence does not guarantee good behavior, but a certain level is necessary for self-knowledge and the comprehension of moral distinctions.

Prof. Levin does not flinch from drawing what may appear to be an unkind conclusion: Given the crime rates, social irresponsibility, lack of foresight, impulsiveness, and general self-centeredness of black behavior, blacks probably have a different inherent capacity and appreciation for morality.

He proposes that this difference can be explained by the environments in which blacks and whites (and Asians) evolved. In a warm climate in which food can be gathered year-round, people do not need to develop habits of cooperation and planning in order to get through the winter. In the north, it took mutual trust and cooperation for groups of men to bring down large game, so reciprocal morality evolved along with intelligence.

Climate and terrain could also have influenced sexual behavior. Since African women could gather food for themselves and their children even if a mate abandoned them, there was less pressure to insist that men support their children. For the same reason, there was less evolutionary pressure on fathers to stick around. In the north, a man who abandoned his children might well leave no descendants to behave in like manner. And in fact, the family habits of Africans and transplanted blacks are extremely loose by white standards.

What we think of as moral behavior, including sexual morality, is now known to be heavily influenced by genes. As Prof. Levin points out, there is no biological reason to expect different populations to have evolved exactly the same distribution of morality-influencing genes. Therefore it is likely that "the races have . . . evolved divergent *evaluations* of cooperativeness, aggression, rule-following, and concern with the future."

That blacks care less about others and worry less about the future is suggested in virtually every area of behavior. Crime is only the most obvious example, nor is it the expression of wretchedness and self-loathing that excuse-making whites pretend it to be. Prof. Levin notes that "the criminal behavior of young black males just does not look like an expression of despair. In account after account, these individuals come across as full of themselves and unrepentant." He might have added that if blacks were really reduced to hopelessness by white oppression, they would presumably have high suicide rates, whereas in every age group blacks kill themselves at only one half to one quarter the white rate.

The other prominent black deviation from white morality is reckless procreation, but other traits are just as striking: unwillingness to do volunteer work, support charities, donate organs, volunteer as medical test subjects, keep quiet in theaters, recycle trash, save money, exercise, or keep houses in good repair. Black mothers are twice as likely as white mothers to smoke, drink, and take drugs during pregnancy, even when doctors tell them not to. Blacks between ages 15 and 24 are ten times as likely to have fatal gun accidents as whites of the same age even when gun availability is controlled for. By white standards, black behavior is impulsive, shiftless, and inconsiderate.

People respond better to norms their ancestors evolved than to norms imposed on them by strangers. This may explain why black children get into trouble when held to standards of classroom decorum not "natural" to African societies. It may also explain current calls for "respecting the black learning style" or for Afrocentric curricula, but it is hardly fair of blacks to insist that the rules be changed to suit them after pushing their way unbidden into white institutions.

The personality differences Prof. Levin emphasizes explain why standardized tests "overpredict" black performance. Black students do not get grades as good as their SAT scores suggest they should, and even when IQ is held constant blacks are more likely than whites to be criminals. Why? It is likely that impulsiveness, a lack of concern for the future, and a lower regard for moral norms keeps blacks from performing at the levels IQ alone would predict.

Prof. Levin nevertheless warns whites against the mistake of thinking any human standard is absolute. Blacks can find whites moralistic, repressed, and incomprehensible: "A degree of helpfulness considered obligatory by hunters is considered foolish by gatherers, whereas hunters might regard gatherers as selfish. Each may think 'something is wrong' with—and dislike—the other." He goes on to say that for people who have evolved under different circumstances "a propensity to violate white norms need not be disordered or dysfunctional." Such differences are inherently no more value-laden than the fact that owls live in trees and moles live in holes. Blacks are simply different from whites and it may be foolish to expect them to behave like whites.

Of course, in a society built to white standards, it is difficult to refrain from ranking groups invidiously according to intelligence and morality. Prof. Levin argues that whites may therefore have valid reasons for wanting to avoid blacks. In this sense whites may well think whites (and Asians) "better" than blacks. Is this shocking? "The ranking of individuals and groups goes uncontested in nonracial contexts," he notes, and adds that "few egalitarians would have the effrontery to deny that the average minister has more qualities he admires than the average murderer."

At the same time, low intelligence and low self-control may mean blacks are simply less able to govern themselves. In Prof. Levin's view, "a person of limited mental ability, not given to worrying about the quality of his desires or the likely consequences of following them, is relatively less free. So are people who follow an impulse as soon as it enters their heads." This suggests that "the white advantage in intelligence and self-restraint implies that, on average, whites are more autonomous and responsible for their actions than are blacks . . ." and that blacks may be "less capable of scrutinizing the self and its choices."

Curiously, many liberals unintentionally speak of blacks in much the same way. They describe deviance as the understandable and even inevitable consequence of "oppression," thus implicitly accepting black helplessness. The literature on race is filled with the hunt for "root causes," which is another name for excuses. And yet if the environment excuses blacks why does it not excuse the whites who are said to oppress them? That liberals never speak sympathetically of the "root causes" of racism suggests they think whites are more autonomous and responsible than blacks.

Affirmative Action

Affirmative action is a somewhat less controversial subject but Prof. Levin tackles it with characteristic thoroughness and none of the mumbled apologies common even among "conservatives." He notes that justifications for preference keep shifting:

"As the compensation argument has tottered—mainly with growing awareness that the beneficiaries of affirmative action have never been discriminated against, and that its white victims have never discriminated—there has been a migration to new grounds, few of which were heard of in 1965." Nonsense about role models, self-esteem, fighting stereotypes, diversity, etc. is now spouted by "people who have forgotten, or never knew, why they supported racial preferences in the first place."

Prof. Levin explains that the only valid excuse for preferences is compensation for past wrongs, but far from deserving compensation, American blacks have benefited enormously from life in a white-dominated society. Since black limitations are overwhelmingly likely to be inherent, whites have no obligation to help them overcome them. If anything, whites deserve compensation for the continuing violence and larceny they suffer at the hands of blacks.

Prof. Levin also points out the contradictions in affirmative action thinking when preferences are justified on probabalistic grounds: Even if it cannot be proven than any given black has suffered from white wickedness or that any given white has benefited from it, the reasoning is that chances are high enough to justify rewarding the one group and punishing the other. However, preference advocates refuse to consider *any* probabalistic policies that might inconvenience blacks. Blacks are vastly more violent than whites but liberals would gasp at the idea of making it more difficult for blacks than whites to own guns. Preventing violence is a far more legitimate role of government than promoting "diversity," so why is probabalistic reasoning unwarranted in crime control?

Affirmative action also violates the liberals' cherished notion that "separate is inherently unequal." If separate employment or promotion standards are valid for blacks, why not separate schools—which would presumably be designed to meet their special needs? Incoherence on questions of this kind is mere cover for the conviction that the state may never allow race to be used against blacks but can *require* that it be used against whites.

Affirmative action is, of course, a policy that Prof. Levin would abolish today. While he is at it, he would legalize all private forms of discrimination. On libertarian grounds, people should be free to choose their associates or neighbors even for irrational reasons, and on empirical grounds it is often rational for whites to avoid blacks.

Prof. Levin would also abolish welfare. He argues that a social safety net may be a permissible luxury in a society of whites who will not abuse it but is, for blacks, too great a temptation to indolence. Likewise, the minimum wage is an unnecessary obstacle to blacks (and others) whose labor is simply not worth what government insists it should be.

Although blacks may be less able than whites to control behavior it does not mean wrongdoing should go unpunished, but that different punishments may be appropriate for different races. For blacks it should perhaps be swifter and include corporal punishment, especially for men who treat a jail term as a badge of honor and a rite of passage. It might also be sensible to try some black juveniles as adults, since blacks mature more rapidly than whites. Finally, since blacks have frequently shown themselves unable to transcend racial loyalty, they might be excluded from juries in trials that could inflame racial passion.

Interestingly, Prof. Levin's exhaustive study of racial differences leads to policies strikingly similar to those of the pre-civil rights era American South. It may be no coincidence that the latest scientific findings support the traditions of whites who lived for generations in the most intimate contact with blacks.

The only real objection to this excellent book is what some readers will consider its *excessive* thoroughness. As the author himself concedes, he sometimes appears to be "defending the obvious with complicated rejoinders." He explains that "where race is concerned, however, people seem capable of doubting what they elsewhere find self-evident, so argumentative overkill is difficult to avoid."

The symbolic logic is confined to footnotes, but some readers will still find the overkill heavy going, especially when Prof. Levin veers into his own field of philosophy. Nevertheless, this is an invaluable volume, packed with insight and information, and deserves the close attention of anyone with a serious interest in the American racial dilemma.

This review appeared in the October 1997 issue.

PHILOSOPHY

Why Race Matters
by Samuel Francis

There is an old saying—supposedly an ancient Chinese curse: "May you live in interesting times."

Today the curse has come true. The interesting times are here. What is most interesting about them is that for perhaps the first time in history, certainly for one of the few times in history, we are witnessing the more or less peaceful transfer of power from one civilization and from the race that created and bore that civilization, to different races.

In South Africa, the transfer has already been completed, at least in a formal political sense, with the apparent support of most of the white population. In the remainder of what was once the common imperium of the European people in Africa and Asia, the transfer has long since taken place, occurring when the imperial powers withdrew or were chased out of the territories they had conquered.

In Europe the transfer has probably not quite yet begun on any major scale, and it probably will not begin until the immigration of non-whites is considerably further along than it is now. But in North America and more especially in the United States the transfer is well under way. It is in our own nation that the times are most interesting and therefore most cursed.

Culture and its Symbols

We see the transfer of power in almost every dimension of public and private life. Thus far, the transfer is more cultural than political or economic; it is clear in the rise of multiculturalism, Afro-centrism, and the other anti-white cults and movements in university curricula, and in the penetration of even daily private life by the anti-white ethic and behavior these cults impose. It is clear in the ever-quickening war against the traditional symbols of the old civilization and the elevation of the symbols of the new peoples who aim at their displacement.

The Martin Luther King holiday in 1983 was the first and most important instance of the trend but by no means the last; indeed, it can be argued that the King holiday was merely the legitimizing agent of the attacks on other symbols that have occurred since. Attacks on the display of the Confederate battle flag and on other Confederate and Southern white symbols are now commonplace, but the Alamo in San Antonio is another traditional white symbol that is also under attack—by Hispanics. The Custer battlefield in Montana now celebrates the Indian victory, although what is historically memorable about the battle of the Little Big Horn is not the victory of several thousand Indians over a small American cavalry detachment but rather the defeat of whites at the hands of non-whites.

The holidays, public anniversaries, flags, songs, statues, museums, symbols, and heroes that a people shares are fundamental to its identity and its existence as a people. What we are witnessing on the official level of public culture in the attacks on these traditional symbols and their displacement by the symbols of other races is the effective abolition of one people and the gradual creation of another.

Of course, this process is not limited to official culture, which is often merely the plaything of politicians. It is also true even more clearly on the level of popular culture, by which is meant today not the culture created by the people but rather the culture created by elites for consumption by the people. Western movies now routinely define the whites as the villains and the Indians and Mexicans—or, even more fantastically, blacks—as the heroes or martyrs. Almost all TV and cinematic depictions of the Civil War now unequivocally portray the South and Confederates as the villains; perhaps at best misguided but nonetheless on the wrong side of history.

It is routine also to display almost all criminals—rapists, murderers, robbers—as whites, though the statistical truth, of course, is that violent crime in the United States is largely the work of non-whites. A few years ago, political scientist Robert Lichter showed in a study that while during the last 30 years, whites were arrested for 40 percent of the murders committed in the United States, on television whites committed 90 percent of the murders.

Non-whites are frequently shown as not only heroic but also dominant over whites. It is a staple feature of police movies to portray blacks as the administrative superiors of the white protagonists, Mel Gibson's "Lethal Weapon" series being perhaps the best-known. The second installment in the series even depicted white South Africans—today's Hollywood version of Nazis, no doubt—as masterminding drug smuggling into the United States.

While the explicit racial hatred of whites expressed in black-directed films is well known, an increasingly common theme in mainstream television and film is that of the dangers represented by hordes of violent and vicious white supremacists, skinheads, neo-Nazis, paleo-Nazis, and racist terrorists who seem to lurk in every city, behind every storefront, in every small town throughout the country, everywhere, all the time. Recently, in the ABC-TV production of the eight-hour film of Stephen King's "The Stand," a tale of the final struggle at the end of the world between supernatural forces of good and evil, the personification of goodness and of God was an elderly black woman, while the devil was portrayed as a blue-eyed, blond-haired white man, whose evil followers waved the Confederate flag. Even at the end of the world, it seems, Hollywood cannot rid us of white racism.

Most of these examples, to be sure, are trivial enough. Euro-American civilization and the people who created it can survive the artistic contributions of Stephen King and Mel Gibson—maybe. But these examples are of interest precisely because they *are* so trivial and because for the most part they do *not* represent the main, explicit subject matter of popular culture today. In the 1960s, a film like "Guess Who's Coming to Dinner" explicitly explored the subject of interracial marriage and brought it up for discussion, but today anti-white themes more typically provide the background and the context of popular entertainment. As such they either sneak into the public consciousness unexamined or in many cases are already there.

The erasure and displacement of official cultural symbols and the similar process in elite-produced, mass-consumed popular culture represents the expropriation of cultural norms, the standards by which public and private behavior is legitimized or condemned and a culture defined. While the traditional norms that are being attacked and discarded were almost never explicitly racial, the new norms that are being constructed and imposed are, and they are not only explicitly racial but also explicitly and vociferously anti-white.

This is a calculated tactic aimed at seizing cultural legitimacy and cultural hegemony and ultimately coercive political power on behalf of non-whites at the expense of whites. At the most extreme, the anti-white racialist movement resembles the ideology of German National Socialism. It offers a conspiratorial interpretation of history in which whites are systematically demonized as the enemies of the black race, and a myth of black racial solidarity and supremacy. "Afro-racism" is the ideological and political apparatus by which an explicit race war is prepared against the white race and its civilization, not as part of "rage" nor as a response to "injustice" and "neglect" but, like any war, as part of a concerted strategy to acquire power. It is not confined to blacks but extends also to other non-whites who care to sign up.

Digging Our Own Grave

Of course non-whites are by no means the only peddlers of anti-white racism. One of the most remarkable features of our interesting times is the degree to which whites themselves help dig their own racial and civilizational grave. I have in my hand here a relatively new magazine to which I am sure you will all want to subscribe at once, entitled *Race Traitor: A Journal of the New Abolitionism*, published in Cambridge, Massachusetts, whose motto is, "Treason to Whiteness is Loyalty to Humanity." The editors quote Julius Lester as writing that "White is not in the color of the skin. It is a condition of the mind, a condition that will be destroyed."

While *Race Traitor* does not seem to advocate physical genocide, it assumes that race is merely a social invention rather than a fact of nature and argues for the abolition of the concept of race as applied to whites. Racial identity is forbidden for whites but not for non-whites (or at least blacks). Of course the explicit goal is to destroy white civilization by doing away with the symbols and institutions of the collective consciousness that defines the race and is the foundation of the culture.

Yet the war against the white race and its civilization is not new. It is part of a world-historical movement that began in the late 19th century, perhaps not coincidentally, around the time of the battle of the Little Big Horn, and which the American racialist writer Lothrop Stoddard called, in the frank language of the 1920s, "The Rising Tide of Color Against White World Supremacy" and which Oswald Spengler a few years later called the "Coloured World Revolution."

It is easy to smile at such formulations today, but Martin Luther King himself explicitly and repeatedly linked the American civil rights movement with what in a 1960 address entitled "The Rising Tide of Racial Consciousness" he called a "worldwide struggle." In his *Playboy* interview in 1965, King remarked, in a frank endorsement of racialist sentiment, that the American Negro "feels a deepening sense of identification with his black African brothers, and with his brown and yellow brothers of Asia, South America and the Caribbean."

We recently witnessed just such a display of racial solidarity at the inauguration of Nelson Mandela in South Africa, when King's widow, Coretta Scott King, arrived to stand by his side. Mrs. King, of course, does not travel thousands of miles to celebrate the victories of democracy in Eastern Europe, but only to countries where her racial comrades are being empowered.

It is true that Martin Luther King, Mrs. King, Mr. Mandela, and many other spokesmen for the "rising tide of [non-white] racial consciousness" espouse a liberal rhetoric that ostensibly promises racial equality rather than domination. But whether these spokesmen really believe in such a liberal vision or whether they merely wield it as a weapon against whites, there is little question that most blacks in the United States do not share liberal views about equality, freedom, and tolerance.

A recent Harris poll conducted for the National Conference released in March 1994 showed that non-white minorities (Hispanic as well as black) "are more likely than whites to apply harsh stereotypes to other minorities but are united in the view that whites are 'bigoted, bossy and unwilling to share power,'" and the poll found that each minority believed it "is discriminated against by a white-controlled economy and educational system." Regardless of the liberalism espoused in public by many non-whites, these are hardly the attitudes from which a genuinely liberal policy can be expected to develop.

Some who support racial revolution may be sincere in invoking liberty, equality, and fraternity, but historical evidence suggests that it cannot be so. Historian William H. McNeill argues in a set of lectures delivered in 1985 at the University of Toronto that what he calls "ethnic hierarchy" is "on the rise, everywhere," and that it is indeed the normal condition of human civilizations. "Other civilized societies," writes McNeill, "have almost always accepted and enforced inequality among the diverse ethnic groups of which they were composed."

McNeill's term "ethnic hierarchy," of course, consists of words derived from Greek; if those words are loosely (but not too loosely) translated into their Latin equivalents, it is clear that McNeill is saying that racial domination, in one form or another, is the norm of human civilizations, that equality has little historical foundation, and that the illusion of such equality is about to be rudely dispelled.

The fraudulence of the liberalism espoused by the leaders of the racial revolution was clear to Spengler himself. "The hare," he wrote in his last book, *The Hour of Decision*, "may perhaps deceive the fox, but human beings can *not* deceive each other. The coloured man sees through the white man when he talks about 'humanity' and everlasting peace. He scents the other's unfitness and lack of will to defend himself. . . . The coloured races are *not* pacifists. They do *not* cling to a life whose length is its sole value. *They take up the sword when we lay it down.* Once they feared the white man; now they despise him."

What is happening in our interesting times, then, to summarize briefly, is this. A concerted and long-term attack against the civilization of white, European and North American man has been launched, and the attack is not confined to the political, social and cultural institutions that characterize the civilization but extends also to the race that created the civilization and continues to carry and transmit it today. The war against white civilization sometimes (indeed often) invokes liberal ideals as its justification and as its goal, but the likely reality is that the victory of the racial revolution will end merely in the domination or destruction of the white race and its civilization by the non-white peoples—if only for demographic reasons due to non-white immigration and the decline of white birth rates.

We know from the population projections by the US Census Bureau last year that by the middle of the next century the present white majority of the United States will have dwindled to a minority in its own country, and given that fact and the increasing legitimization of anti-white racism in the United States, the situation in this country for whites is not going to get any better, to say the least.

Of course, the revolution could not have succeeded or gone as far as it has without the active assistance of whites. Some have supported the racial revolution against their own race and civilization and even larger numbers have acquiesced passively, their allegiance to their own people steadily subverted by the infusion of hidden assumptions hostile to them.

Self-Generated Poisons

Stoddard and Spengler as well as the late James Burnham in his *Suicide of the West* analyzed these self-generated poisons by which the Western people prepare their own destruction. The ideological poison has assumed several different names: Marxism, liberalism, globalism, egalitarianism, and indeed much of the conservatism now espoused by people like Jack Kemp, Newt Gingrich, Bill Bennett, and William Buckley, as well as a good part of Christianity, especially in its "Social Gospel" forms. But behind all of these ideologies and slogans lies the pervasive venom of universalism, the vision of mankind with a capital M, which now often extends to include "animal rights" so as not to offend our brothers of field and stream.

In the universalist world-view, there is neither history nor race nor even species, neither specific cultures nor particular peoples nor meaningful boundaries. Therefore there are no concrete duties to race, nation, community, family, friend or neighbor and indeed no distinctions to be drawn between neighbor and stranger, friend and foe, mine and thine, us and them.

In the happyland of universalism, we owe as much to the children of Somalia—indeed, more—than we do to the hapless citizens of Los Angeles, and Marines who could not have been sent from Camp Pendleton to Los Angeles during the riots of 1992 and who are not ordered to prevent violation of the Mexican border adjacent to their own installation in southern California are speedily dispatched to Somalia. Even to invoke "our" identity, our interests, our aspirations is to invite accusations of all the "isms" and "phobias" that are deployed to prevent further discussions and to paralyze the formation or the retention of a common consciousness that might at some point swell up into actual resistance to our dispossession. The principal white response to the incipient race war thus far, manifested in neo-conservative critiques of "Political Correctness" and multiculturalism, is merely to regurgitate the formulas of universalism, to invoke the spirit of Martin Luther King, and to repeat the universalist ideals of equality, integration, and assimilation. The characteristic defense of Western civilization by most conservatives today is merely a variation of the liberal universalism that the enemies of the West and whites also invoke. It is to argue that non-whites and non-Westerners ought to value modern Western civilization as in their own best interests. It is to emphasize the liberal "progress" of the modern West through the abolition of slavery, the emancipation of non-whites, the retreat from imperialism, the achievement of higher living standards and political equality, etc.

Of course, if the liberalism espoused by non-whites is a thin veil for the assertion of their own racial solidarity against whites, then all such argumentation is vain. It accomplishes nothing to preach liberalism to those who despise liberalism along with everything else derived from the white West. The uselessness of doing so was pointed out by the 19th century French rightist Louis Veuillot in his ironic comment, "When I am the weaker, I ask you for my freedom, because that is your principle; but when I am the stronger, I take away your freedom, because that is my principle." Or, as Neitzsche put a similar thought even more succinctly, "The values of the weak prevail because the strong have taken them over as devices of leadership."

Instead of invoking a suicidal liberalism and regurgitating the very universalism that has subverted our identity and our sense of solidarity, what we as whites must do is reassert our identity and our solidarity, and we must do so in explicitly racial terms through the articulation of a racial consciousness as whites. The reassertion of our solidarity must be expressed in racial terms for two major reasons. In the first place, the attack upon us defines itself in racial terms and seeks through the delegitimization of race for whites and the legitimization of race for non-whites the dispersion and destruction of the foundations of our solidarity while at the same time consolidating non-white cohesiveness against whites.

Historian Isaiah Berlin noted in 1991 that "nationalism and racism are the most powerful movements in the world today," and at a time when the self-declared enemies of the white race define themselves in racial terms, only our own definition of ourselves in those terms can meet their challenge. If and when that challenge should triumph and those enemies come to kill us as the Tutsi people have been slaughtered in Rwanda, they will do so not because we are "Westerners" or "Americans" or "Christians" or "conservatives" or "liberals" but because we are white.

Secondly, we need to assert a specifically racial identity because race is real—biological forces, including those that determine race, are important for social, cultural, and historical events. I do not suggest that race as a biological reality is by itself *sufficient* to explain the civilization of European man—if race were sufficient, there would be no problem—but race is *necessary* for it, and it is likely that biological science in the near future will show even more clearly how necessary racial, biological, and genetic explanations are to understanding social and historical events more fully.

The civilization that we as whites created in Europe and America could not have developed apart from the genetic endowments of the creating people, nor is there any reason to believe that the civilization can be successfully transmitted to a different people. If the people or race who created and sustained the civilization of the West should die, then the civilization also will die. A merely cultural consciousness, then, that emphasizes only social and cultural factors as the roots of our civilization is not enough, because a merely cultural consciousness will not by itself conserve the race and people that were necessary for the creation of the culture and who remain necessary for its survival. We need not only to understand the role of race in creating our civilization but also to incorporate that understanding in our defense of our civilization. Until we do so, we can expect only to keep on losing the war we are in.

Unwitting Identification

The fundamental problem of the American white population was unwittingly identified by *Newsweek* in its March 29, 1993 cover story on "White Male Paranoia." In an effort to puncture any tendencies among white men to think of themselves as victims, endangered or exploited, *Newsweek* pointed out that "White males make up just 39.2 percent of the population, yet they account for 82.5 percent of the *Forbes* 400 (folks worth at least $265 million), 77 percent of Congress, 92 percent of daily-newspaper editors, 77 percent of TV news directors." From this avalanche of numbers, *Newsweek* infers that it's "still a statistical piece of cake being a white man, at least in comparison with being anything else." *Newsweek* may be right in its numbers, but the numbers miss the point.

What the numbers tell us is that whites do not act cohesively or think of themselves as a unit, that whites have no racial consciousness; if they did, they would be using their persisting political, economic, and cultural power in their own interests, and the very perceptible "white male paranoia" that *Newsweek* was talking about—the very real sense of an incipient slippage from a position of control—would not exist.

In the United States today, whites exist objectively but do not exist subjectively, and that is in my view the fundamental racial problem they face, the basic reason they (I should say "we") are losing the racial war against us, the very reason we are in a war at all. *Newsweek*'s numbers offer proof of the objective existence of whites and of white power as measured materially and quantitatively; the spineless abnegation of their own country and culture that is at the root of white male paranoia offers proof of the absence of a subjective existence. Whites do not exist subjectively because they do not think of themselves as whites, they do not act cohesively as whites, and they do not think being white is important or even meaningful.

As long as whites continue to avoid and deny their own racial identity, at a time when almost every other racial and ethnic category is rediscovering and asserting its own, whites will have no chance to resist their dispossession and their eventual possible physical destruction. Before we can seriously discuss any concrete proposals for preserving our culture and its biological and demographic foundations, we have to address and correct the problem we inflict on ourselves, our own lack of a racial consciousness and the absence of a common will to act in accordance with it.

What Benjamin Franklin told his colleagues at the birth of the American Republic remains true today as the Republic, and the race and civilization that gave birth to the Republic, approach their death: If we do not hang together—not only as members of a common nation but also as part of a common race, a common people—then most assuredly we will all hang separately.

Samuel Francis is a syndicated columnist and author of Beautiful Losers *and* Revolution from the Middle. *This is an abbreviated version of a lecture he gave at the 1994 AR conference in Atlanta. It appeared in the September 1994 issue. Dr. Francis was fired from his position as staff columnist at the* Washington Times *after the contents of this lecture become widely known.*

The Morality of Survival
by Michael W. Masters

"[The West] has not yet understood that whites, in a world become too small for its inhabitants, are now a minority and that the proliferation of other races dooms our race, my race, irretrievably to extinction in the century to come, if we hold fast to our present moral principles." [emphasis added]

—*Jean Raspail,* The Camp Of The Saints

The loss of racial identity in the Western world is symptomatic of a deeper crisis within the European peoples, whose culture and technology have provided the world with much of what we know today as modern civilization. At its core, the crisis is the inevitable consequence of a profound, and perhaps fatal, misunderstanding of the nature of morality. We have lost sight of ancient and eternal laws of Nature on which our civilization must be based if we are to survive. We no longer have the luxury of indulging in universalist altruistic principles that, no matter how noble they may appear, have driven us to the brink of ruin.

Demographic projections based on American and European immigration policies, as well as the evidence of one's own observations as one walks the streets of any large Western city, point to a bleak future. Within a century or two, perhaps less, the peoples of the West, those whose ancestry derives from the Nordic and Alpine subraces of Europe, will have ceased to exist as a cohesive entity. How quickly the end will come depends on immigration rates, differential birthrates among ethnic groups, and mixed-race childbearing rates. But the final outcome is fixed so long as we adhere to our present course.

And yet, frank discussion of the outcome, the submergence of the race that produced the world's first, and perhaps only technological civilization, is usually silenced with words like "racist," "bigot," and "xenophobe." Neither the flawed moral system that enforces this silence nor the people who support it will outlive the demise of the West. But when the West is gone, it will be of little consolation that those responsible will have expired as well. If we are to reverse course, it is vital that we take steps now, before it is too late.

If, today, the West's moral system is flawed, how can it be corrected? The first question we must ask is whether it is moral for ethnic groups as well as individuals to seek survival. And if so, what are the moral actions we may undertake to secure survival? What must be the moral basis of our civilization if it is not to be lost? In his book, *Destiny of Angels*, Richard McCulloch calls these questions a matter of "ultimate ethics."

The Moral Dilemma of the West

The dilemma of our people is the product of a deep misconception about nature and morality. It arises from the mistaken, sentimental belief that altruism can be extended beyond its evolutionary origin—kinship and within-group altruism—to all of humanity. It results from failure to accept the role of genetic factors in defining human temperament and potential.

The standards that govern public debate are reminiscent of the Dark Ages in that they have no basis in science or in human experience. Instead, they consist of moralistic assertions derived from a world view rooted in radical egalitarianism. The long term consequence of adherence to these principles is rarely examined, let alone subjected to scientific scrutiny.

Most Western people would agree that an innate sense of right and wrong plays a key role in the Western moral system, a system that values individual worth and reciprocal fairness. The tragedy of this moral view is that it has been extended to the world at large—seemingly the most noble behavior humanity has ever exhibited—and has become *the* threat to the survival of the West.

As biologist Garrett Hardin argued in his 1982 essay, "Discriminating Altruisms," universalism—a chimerical One World without borders or distinctions—is impossible. Groups that practice unlimited altruism, unfettered by thoughts of self-preservation, will be disadvantaged in life's competition and thus eliminated over time in favor of those that limit their altruistic behavior to smaller groups, usually their own genetic kin, from whom they receive reciprocal benefits.

Professor Hardin writes:

"*Universalism* is altruism practiced *without discrimination* of kinship, acquaintanceship, shared values, or propinquity in time or space . . . . To people who accept the idea of biological evolution from amoeba to man, the vision of social evolution from egoism to universalism may seem plausible. In fact, however, *the last step is impossible* . . . . Let us see why.

"In imagination, picture a world in which social evolution has gone no further than egoism or individualism. When familialism appears on the scene, what accounts for its persistence? It must be that the costs of the sacrifices individuals make for their relatives are more than paid for by the gains realized through family solidarity . . . .

"The argument that accounts for the step to familialism serves equally well for each succeeding step—except for the last. Why the difference? Because the One World created by universalism has—by definition—no competitive base to support it . . . [Universalism] cannot survive in competition with discrimination." [emphasis in original]

Professor Hardin adds:

"[W]e must not forget that for three billion years, biological evolution has been powered by discrimination. Even mere survival in the absence of evolutionary change depends on discrimination. If universalists now have their way, discrimination will be abandoned. Even the most modest impulse toward conservatism should cause us to question the wisdom of abandoning a principle that has worked so well for billions of years. It is a tragic irony that discrimination has produced a species (*homo sapiens*) that now proposes to abandon the principle responsible for its rise to greatness."

It is to the advantage of non-Europeans, virtually all of whom retain their cohesion as distinctive, discriminating groups, to exploit the economic wealth and social order of the West, benefits many demonstrably cannot create for themselves. When this cohesive drive is placed in competition with self-sacrificing Western altruism, there can be only one outcome. In the near term, Europeans will be displaced by groups acting in their own self-interest. In the long run, biological destruction awaits us. Since those who displace us do not, by definition, maintain our morals standards—for if they did, they would not be replacing us—our flawed moral system will vanish with us.

The fact that universal, self-sacrificing altruism destroys its practitioners is its most obvious flaw. Any survivable moral order must recognize this.

The Cosmic Race

The dream of a Utopia in which racial harmony prevails, has never come true. Today, racial encroachment is a threat to the very existence of Western peoples. Lawrence Auster, author of *The Path to National Suicide, An Essay on Immigration and Multiculturalism,* has elsewhere summarized the situation thus:

"Modern liberalism told us that racial differences don't matter, and on the basis of that belief, liberals then set about turning America into a multiracial, integrated, race-blind society. But now that very effort has created so much race consciousness, race conflict and race inequality, that the same liberals have concluded that the only way to overcome those problems is to merge all the races into one. The same people who have always denounced as an extremist lunatic anyone who warned about 'the racial dilution of white America,' are now proposing, not just the dilution of white America, but its complete elimination. Race-blind ideology has led directly to the most race-conscious—and indeed genocidal—proposal in the history of the world."

This change of strategy was signaled by the cover story of a fall 1993 special edition of *Time*. The story featured a computer synthesized image of a woman representing the intermixture of all of the ethnic population elements of the United States in their present proportions. The subliminal message conveyed by this computerized android, obviously still of predominantly European ancestry, was: "Don't worry, this is harmless." Or, in the current idiom of multiculturalism, "let us celebrate our diversity." Of course, this image represents the utter destruction of diversity, not its conservation.

This computer-generated android is a lie. The American population base is in a state of rapid change. Whites are now having fewer children, and there are thus fewer whites of child-bearing age than *Time* assumes. This is happening worldwide. The question is, what would be the result of this plan being carried forward on a larger scale, carried to its logical conclusion in a world *sans* borders? *Time*'s android is but a way station on the road to what some lovingly call the Cosmic Race.

People of European ancestry constitute something over ten percent of the world's population, but since 1980, white births amount to only a little more than five percent of the world's new children. The birth rate in the West has fallen to dangerously low levels, now about 1.8 children per woman. A level of 2.1 is required to balance deaths. Birth rates in the Third World remain very high, thanks in large measure to the infusion of Western food, medicine, and "peacekeeping."

Because people are not computer morphs but have discrete ancestors, let us assume that the fraction of people with European ancestry is now one-sixteenth of the child-bearing population. When the *Time* experiment is complete on a world-wide scale, the resulting human will have only one white great-great-grandparent. He will be visibly Asian since about 60 percent of the world's population is Asian. In round numbers, this amounts to ten of the sixteen great-great-grandparents, including four from China alone. Three would come from India and three more from Southeast Asia and the Middle East. Africa would supply three and non-white Latin America and the Caribbean basin the remaining two.

In this scenario, which is already unfolding on the North American continent and in Europe and Australia, the single European ancestor would leave no discernible residue in *homo cosmicus*. Europeans would be extinct, fulfilling the nightmare vision that Jean Raspail described in *The Camp Of The Saints*.[1] This is not a condemnation of any real human being with such an ancestry. Nevertheless, this process would eradicate the biological diversity that multiculturalists claim to cherish. In its place would be only uniformity, the irreversible submergence of all races.

The passing of any race is an event of great significance. The destruction of an entire population is, in fact, genocide by the definitions of the UN Genocide Convention, which defines genocide as ". . . the destruction, in whole or in part, of an ethnic, racial or national group. The acts so defined include. . . the destruction of the conditions of life necessary for the physical existence of the group . . . ."

The debate about race must be framed in these terms in order to convey its true importance. The battle cannot be won by allowing the other side to limit the terms of debate by declaring certain subjects beyond discussion. The consequences are too important.

The Dual Code of Morality

Why, though, does race matter? The answer lies in the biology of genes and in the impact of genetic kinship on altruism. For many decades, altruism was a paradox for theories of evolution. Darwin himself realized that altruism was difficult to explain in terms of individual "survival of the fittest." In

---

[1] See the review on page 291.

his book, *Race, Evolution and Behavior,* Philippe Rushton writes, "If the most altruistic members of a group sacrifice themselves for others, they run the risk of leaving fewer offspring to pass on the very genes that govern the altruistic behavior. Hence, altruism would be selected against, and selfishness would be selected for."

Prof. Rushton suggests that this paradox is resolved by genetic similarity theory, a field pioneered by biologist W. D. Hamilton and others. Prof. Rushton writes:

"By a process known as kin selection, individuals can maximize their inclusive fitness rather than only their individual fitness by increasing the production of successful offspring by both themselves and their genetic relatives . . . . Genes are what survive and are passed on, and some of the same genes will be found not only in direct offspring but in siblings, cousins, nephews/nieces, and grandchildren . . . . thus, from an evolutionary perspective, altruism is a means of helping genes to propagate."

Over time, kin selection has resulted in a dual code of morality, an altruistic code for one's genetic kin and a non-altruistic code for everyone else. Anthropologists have suggested that humans evolved through a process of migration and tribal warfare between groups composed of genetically related individuals. In *A New Theory of Human Evolution*, Sir Arthur Keith wrote, "The process which secures the evolution of an isolated group of humanity is a combination of two principles . . . namely, cooperation with competition . . . . I hold that from the very beginning of human evolution the conduct of every local group was regulated by two codes of morality, distinguished by Herbert Spencer as the 'code of amity' and the 'code of enmity.'"

Garrett Hardin writes, "The essential characteristic of a tribe is that it should follow a double standard of morality—one kind of behavior for in-group relations, another for out-group." In-group relations are characterized by cooperation while out-group relations are characterized by conflict. Liberals have tried to discredit the role of tribal conflict, claiming that such distinctions have been lost as groups reached nation size. But in so doing, they miss the vital message of genetic similarity theory. National ethnic groups represent the growth and consolidation of genetically related tribes over time.

Professor Hardin argues that, because of the nature of altruism and competition, the dual code of morality is inescapable and cannot be eliminated from human society:

"In the absence of competition between tribes the survival value of altruism in a crowded world approaches zero because what ego gives up necessarily . . . goes into the commons. What is in the commons cannot favor the survival of the sharing impulses that put it there—unless there are limits placed on sharing. To place limits on sharing is to create a tribe—which means a rejection of One World. . . . A state of One World, if achieved, would soon redissolve into an assemblage of tribes."

The in-group out-group distinction still operates today; it is only the battleground that has shifted. Tribal warfare has been replaced by territorial irredentism and competing birthrates.

The liberal campaign to eliminate feelings of national, cultural, or racial solidarity among Western peoples was undertaken largely in the hope that the abolition of "tribalism" would inaugurate an era of world peace. As Professor Hardin has shown, tribalism cannot be eliminated. Worse still, any idealistic group that unilaterally dismantles its own tribal sense will be swept away by groups that have retained theirs. Unless the current direction is changed, the West will be destroyed in this new form of biological competition.

The dual code of morality is therefore the cornerstone on which any enduring moral order must be based. It is also an answer to the question of ultimate ethics posed earlier: "Is it moral for ethnic groups to seek to survive?" Since it is impossible to eliminate "tribes" from the human race, the answer to this question must be yes. That which is built inextricably into the laws of the universe cannot be immoral.

Universalists might try to caricature the dual code of morality as an invidious double standard, but it is something we practice every day without even thinking about it. Without it, no group—be it a family, club, corporation, political party, nation, or race—would exist. It is how groups distinguish between members and non-members. Employees of the same company treat each other differently from the way they treat competitors. Members of the same political party cooperate with each other and run against opponents. Families draw sharp distinctions between members and strangers. It is easy to overlook the dual code of morality precisely because it is so fundamental a part of human nature.

The "code of amity, code of enmity" explains racial loyalties. It is an extension of the biologically necessary fact that parents love their children more than the children of strangers. Such feelings are normal and natural. Yet "racism" has become the curse-word that stops discussion. Those who use the word as a weapon say that racial loyalty is racism when exhibited by whites but is justifiable pride when exhibited by non-whites. The word is simply a means of gaining power over people who have exaggerated moral scruples.

The Biology of Diversity

Feelings of racial loyalty are grounded in biological differences. These are discussed authoritatively in J. Philippe Rushton's *Race, Evolution, and Behavior*, but they do not imply that one race has a right to rule over another. Frank discussion of real differences must not be considered morally repugnant. Scientific truth cannot be racism, at least not in the pejorative sense that the word is now used.

Most forms of behavior (by whites) that are characterized as racism do not involve unprovoked assault on people of other races, but are simply the natural loyalty of humans for their own group. They are necessary for survival. Unprovoked violence is a moral evil, but by all statistical measures, whites are overwhelmingly the victims of crimes of racial violence, not the perpetrators.

Blacks are twelve percent of the population but commit almost two-thirds of the violent crime in America, are over twelve times more likely to murder whites than the reverse, are more than *a thousand times* more likely to rape white women than the reverse, and choose whites as crime victims fifty percent of the time compared to whites choosing blacks as victims only two percent of the time.

Interracial crime is just one manifestation of a fundamental biological principle called Gause's Law of Exclusion. In his book, *The Mammals of North America*, University of Kansas biology professor Raymond Hall states the law as follows: *"Two subspecies of the same species do not occur in the same geographic area."* [emphasis in original] One will inevitably eliminate or displace the other. Prof. Hall specifically includes humans in this rule: "To imagine one subspecies of man living together on equal terms for long with another subspecies is but wishful thinking and leads only to disaster and oblivion for one or the other."

Oblivion need not come in the form of physical destruction. It may simply involve the loss of habitat. Harlem, Watts, East St. Louis, and many other black neighborhoods were once occupied by whites. The arrival of blacks (or other non-whites) in sufficient numbers makes it impossible for whites to survive, whereas the process does not work in reverse. Even without the carnage of inter-racial crime, whites could be eliminated through sheer loss of territory. Viewed in biological terms, ethnic diversity is prelude to destruction.

The great majority of people, of any age and origin, do not concern themselves with the rise and fall of civilizations. Like fish in water, they are conscious of their environment only when it changes rapidly and threateningly, a rarity in most people's lifetimes. Yet civilizations do fall, and the warning signs for ours have been present for more than a century. Rudyard Kipling's line, "East is East, and West is West, and never the twain shall meet," presaged the message of early twentieth century Americans, Madison Grant and Lothrop Stoddard, whose books, *The Passing of the Great Race* and *The Rising Tide of Color*, helped bring about the immigration restrictions of 1924.

The 1924 national origins quota system was dismantled in 1965 during the wave of self-recrimination that accompanied the Civil Rights era. Should Chinese historians of the twenty-second century be writing the final history of Western civilization, no doubt they will cite the 1965 Immigration Act as the blow that broke the back of Western man.

Elmer Pendell, in his book, *Why Civilizations Self-Destruct*, surveyed historians' theories as to why civilizations fall. They include Oswald

Spengler's analogy to individual aging and death, theories of moral decay, and theories based on ecological deterioration.

Pendell's own hypothesis seems closest to the mark. A civilization arises when natural selection produces a people of above-average intelligence. As the founders conquer natural culling forces, those who would have been removed from the population due to their lesser abilities survive and produce more children than the more intelligent founders. Francis Galton, Charles Darwin's cousin and author of *Hereditary Genius*, first noted that 'men of eminence' have fewer children than the average. Eventually the intelligence level of the population falls below that needed to sustain civilization.

Pendell suggests another factor in the collapse of civilizations, the gradual adulteration of ethnically homogeneous founding populations through losses in wars and, in ancient times, the taking of slaves. The modern analogue of slavery is immigration. Tenny Frank, in his book *History of Rome*, wrote, "The original peoples were wasted in wars and scattered in migrations and colonization and their places were filled chiefly with Eastern slaves." We cannot speak of the spirit of Rome or the culture of Rome, Frank said, "without defining whether the reference is to the Rome of 200 BC or 200 AD."

Theodor Mommsen wrote in *The History of Rome*, "The patrician body... had dwindled away more and more in the course of centuries and in the time of Caesar there were not more than fifteen or sixteen patrician gentes (clans) still in existence." In 9 AD laws were passed requiring each patrician family to have three children. Lead poisoning has been implicated in the failure to reverse the decline of Roman blood, but the reasons do not change the outcome. Even in ancient Rome, slaves did not stay slaves forever, and their gradual suffusion through the population by intermixture would have contributed to Rome's demise. The same situation, massive infusion of non-Western peoples and a birthrate below replacement level, threatens the West, and for reasons quite unrelated to lead poisoning.

After The Fall

Eric Fischer, writing in *The Passing of the European Age*, said that a new civilization never arises where an earlier civilization has died. If Pendell's theory is correct and if the hypothesis of Tenny Frank and others explains the loss of a hereditary capacity for civilization, then Fischer's observation has a genetic explanation. Civilization cannot arise on the site of an earlier civilization once the hereditary character of the people is permanently altered. This process is happening in the Western world today through immigration, welfare, and liberal policies that promote the submergence of ethnic groups into a global "melting pot."

Should the West suffer the fate of Rome, there will be no recovery. Whether or not other civilizations arise among other peoples remains to be seen. Present economic success indicates that East Asia may be a future center of civilization. However, modern innovations flow predominantly from the creative wellsprings of the West. Whether innovation could be sustained in the absence of Western peoples remains to be seen. There is evidence that this might not happen; intelligence testing of Asians shows a relatively small standard deviation, suggesting a smaller right tail of the IQ distribution and a smaller percentage of innovative individuals.

Although dire predictions about the future are often ridiculed, it is wise to remember Rome—catastrophes can and do occur, and in a globally linked world, the consequences could be shattering. In *The Limits of Altruism*, Garrett Hardin cites Harrison Brown, author of *The Challenge of Man's Future*, as the first person to recognize the vulnerability of the West's advanced civilization. Brown focused on the role of metals in modern civilization and on the technology required to obtain metals. Prof. Hardin summarizes:

"Looking only at the copper component of the problem, we should note that preliterate man managed to create the Bronze Age only because of the ready availability of copper ores assaying greater than 20 percent.... Only the most primitive of means are required to process high grade ores. But now we are reduced to extracting our copper from ores that assay less than 1 percent, and soon we will have nothing better than 0.1 percent. It takes a very sophisticated technology to deal with low-grade ores, a technology that only a large population of technologically advanced people can muster."

Prof. Hardin continues, "Our many technologies form an incredible network of mutual support, mutual dependence. If this network were disrupted... it is doubtful if our kind of technology could ever be rebuilt.... On all counts, it looks as though our civilization, once fallen, will never be replaced by another of comparable quality."

Prof. Hardin suggests two possible causes for the destruction of modern civilization: nuclear warfare and a population crash brought on by exceeding the Earth's carrying capacity. However, genetic submergence of the peoples with the innate ability to sustain civilization will do just as well.

The Roots of Western Order

The *Map of Freedom*, published annually by Freedom House, graphically demonstrates that free forms of government generally track population concentrations of people of European descent, a strong suggestion that freedom has a genetic origin. Although there are exceptions, notably Japan, which lost a nuclear war to the West and had a Western constitution imposed on it, the world of the free is largely the world of the Western European. The partially free include newly emerged Eastern Europeans and a scattering of other nations around the world. Much of Africa and Asia remains in the not free category.

Thomas Jefferson foresaw this. Fearing "importation of foreigners," he wrote in *Notes on Virginia*, "They will bring with them the principles of the governments they leave, or if able to throw them off, it will be in exchange for an unbounded licentiousness, passing, as usual, from one extreme to the other. . . . In proportion to their number, they will infuse into it [the nation] their spirit, warp or bias its direction, and render it a heterogeneous, incoherent, distracted mass."

Because economic inequality between groups inevitably produces envy, stable societies are almost always homogeneous. Multi-ethnic and multicultural societies live on the edge of dissolution. In such cases, the role of government turns to conflict management, as Brent Nelson points out in *America Balkanized*. "Government as conflict management is an emerging theme of public life in the US, a theme which recurrently manifests itself in the concepts of dialogue, mediation, sensitivity, tolerance, and balance. The latter terms are increasingly the shibboleths of American public life. The fiction is maintained that these concepts . . . will produce a final resolution of intergroup conflicts. . . . [T]he reality is something quite other." Laws against "hate crime" and "hate speech" reflect that other reality.

If today's ethnic minorities become a majority it will be beyond the power of Western peoples to control, peacefully by means of the ballot, the destiny of the nations that were once their own. There is no guarantee that protections prevalent in Western societies will be preserved in societies that become non-Western. There is no historical reason to believe that governments based on principles of individual liberty will survive the disappearance of Western peoples.

Post-colonial Africa is enlightening. For the most part, the Dark Continent is reverting to its ancestral ways, suitably updated by the infusion of Western weapons, as evidenced by carnage in Somalia and Rwanda. That this disturbs our heightened Western sense of compassion is understandable. But sentimentality should not blind us to the long term implications for our own survival. Nature's books are being balanced in Africa, and they will be balanced in the West, either by us or by Nature itself. Just as giving food to people who cannot feed themselves simply hastens an inevitable population crash, bringing Third World people into the West simply hastens the transformation of the West into an extension of the Third World.

The European tradition of ordered, self-governing liberty is probably part of our genetic heritage. Throughout the Third World, governments range from anarchy to dictatorship. That too, is surely genetic. Those few non-European countries that appear to be free have generally maintained democracy through intimate contact with the West. If Europeans are marginalized and ultimately absorbed by the Third World, the idealism of Western liberalism that permitted the Third World invasion will have proved to be a lethal genetic flaw.

Few concepts are more ingrained in Western thought than respect for the "rule of law." The West has a history of order that predates the eight-hundred-year-old Magna Carta. Roman Law was supreme in the Mediterranean world for nearly a thousand years. Unique among the peoples of the earth, the people of the West recognize, at least in theory, the subordination of government to individual rights. But laws have been instrumental in bringing on the current crisis. Although there is virtually no popular support for immigration in the Western world, it is everywhere proceeding under laws passed by governments elected by the people.

In the end, laws are no better at ensuring liberty than the people who make and enforce them. Sir Roger L'Estrange said, "The greatest of all injustice is that which goes under the name of law." America's Founders recognized the existence of a natural order to freedom that supersedes laws made by men. Although the American concept of liberty owed much to British and French political thought, the American act of creation, the Declaration of Independence, provided perhaps the best-known expression of "natural law" ever penned. Writing about securing "unalienable Rights" endowed by "Nature and Nature's God," Thomas Jefferson wrote:

"That to secure these rights, Governments are instituted among Men, deriving their just powers from the consent of the governed. That whenever any Form of Government becomes destructive of these ends, it is the Right of the People to alter or to abolish it, and to institute new Government, having the foundation on such principles and organizing its powers in such form, as to them shall seem most likely to effect their Safety and Happiness."

The rights Jefferson identified, "Life, Liberty, and the pursuit of Happiness," were set forth by George Mason in the Virginia Declaration of Rights, ratified on May 6, 1776. Mason's work was the basis for Jefferson's statement, but the Mason version is superior because it eschews Jefferson's poetic nonsense about all men being created equal. Mason's language still stands as a monument of Western political thought:

"[A]ll men are by nature equally free and independent, and have certain inherent rights, of which, when they enter into a state of society, they cannot, by any compact, deprive or divest their posterity; namely, the enjoyment of life and liberty, with the means of acquiring and possessing property, and pursuing and obtaining happiness and safety."

Mason's words are preferable to Jefferson's for two reasons. First, he said that men are "equally free," not "equal." The difference is vast. There is ample evidence that Jefferson understood the difference as well as Mason, but much of the dispossession of Europeans in their own homelands can be traced to exploitation of this egalitarian philosophy by later Western liberals.

Second, Mason states directly the central thesis of natural law: People cannot, by any agreement, deprive their posterity of rights. Natural law is therefore the fulcrum on which rests the case that immigration is genocide. The governments of the West have no right to impose present levels of immigration and race mixing on their people. Nor are we morally bound to accept them.

The Ultimate Moral Principle

Mason recognized the role of "safety" as a motive for the creation of law and government. Others have said the same thing. William Blackstone wrote, "self-defense is justly called the primary law of nature. . . [It] cannot be taken away by the laws of society." Jefferson wrote, "A strict observance of the written laws is doubtless *one* of the highest duties of a good citizen, but it is not *the highest*. The laws of necessity, of self-preservation, of saving our country when in danger, are of higher obligation."

Their message is simple. Laws alone, independent of their survival utility, are not, and cannot be, the underlying basis of civilization. In the end, whoever makes and enforces the laws has the power to determine who lives and who dies. *Survival is the ultimate principle upon which all enduring moral systems must be based.* This is the third, and final, cornerstone of any permanent moral order, for any people who "divest" their posterity of the right to existence will vanish, and their flawed moral system will vanish with them.

All systems of law and government must serve the imperative of survival. Speaking on the eve of the War for Southern Independence, and in the aftermath of John Brown's attempt to incite a slave uprising at Harper's Ferry, President James Buchanan expressed the fear felt by white Southerners who saw their very existence imperiled: "Self-preservation is the first law of nature, and therefore any state of society in which the sword is all the time suspended over the heads of the people must at last become intolerable." Where law and survival were in conflict the Founders took their cue from Cicero: "Laws are silent in the midst of arms."

The West is surrendering the power of life and death into the hands of Third World aliens. In a world ruled by the dual "code of amity, code of enmity," this decision, which was never subjected to systematic scrutiny by an informed electorate, is tantamount to suicide. Sometime in the next century, the sword Western society has suspended over its own head will become intolerable. What our response will be remains to be seen. If there is no response, the long descent into night is sure to follow.

Which Way Western Man?

What would be lost with the passing of Western civilization and its peoples? Two thousand years ago, the Roman historian, Tacitus, wrote in *De Germania* that the peoples of the Germanic tribes possessed a fondness for personal freedom, an independence of spirit, an unusually high status accorded women and a deep affection for the land. These traits have survived twenty centuries. Without the West, will the spirit of individual liberty persevere? The Map of Freedom suggests not. Despite the tendency of liberals to denigrate the only culture on earth that would tolerate their presence, these virtues uniquely characterize only Europeans and their civilization.

Now, the descendants of those same Germanic tribes, the ancestors of much of the white world, and the creators of the only advanced technological civilization the world has ever known, are on the road to extinction. Do Western moral principles require that its creators commit suicide in order to fulfill those principles? *Such a belief is insane.* It therefore follows that if the

West is to survive it must come to grips, as Jean Raspail foresaw, with the profoundly destructive nature of its moral beliefs.

Any enduring moral order must be based on the following principles: 1) a dual code of morality, which is of evolutionary origin, binds the members of ethnic and racial groups together; 2) universal, self-sacrificing altruism in a world in which racial cohesion is elsewhere the norm is lethal; and 3) the imperative of survival and the primacy of self-preservation supersede all laws made by man.

What then, must we do? Raymond Cattell, in his book *A New Morality From Science: Beyondism*, called for a reversal of the universalist creed and creation of many social laboratories where evolution can proceed without harm or subjugation of anyone by anyone else. Wilmot Robertson urged this path as the basis of nationhood in *The Ethnostate*. Richard McCulloch has elevated this principle to a "racial Golden Rule" in *The Racial Compact*.

The only course that gives cohesive groups a chance to survive is ethnic separation. Without separation, the dual code of morality will ensure a long, chaotic period of strife and bloodshed. Eventually, what racial conflict does not finish, miscegenation, diminished birthrates, and physical and psychological displacement will. Personal liberty and individuality, without which Europeans simply cannot exist, will disappear long before the European genetic heritage is completely submerged. Lest this outcome seem remote and therefore of no concern, let the time scale of Rome's decline be always kept in mind. Though those reading this may or may not live to see the collapse of the West, the white children being born today may well suffer it.

Jean Raspail also believed that the end was not far off. In the introduction to the 1985 edition of *The Camp of the Saints*, he wrote, "The Roman empire did not die any differently, though, it's true, more slowly, whereas this time we can expect a more sudden conflagration . . . . Christian charity will prove itself powerless. The times will be cruel."

Louis Veuillot, the 19th century French writer, captured the dilemma facing the West in confronting peoples who do not conform to Western moral principles. "When I am the weaker, I ask you for my freedom, because that is your principle; but when I am the stronger, I take away your freedom, because that is my principle." The West must recognize this appeal for compassion by "the wretched refuse of [the non-Western world's] teeming shore," for what it is: a form of beguiling parasitism that can, by definition, only seduce those with Western moral principles.

In *The Decline of the West*, Oswald Spengler wrote, "One grows or dies. There is no third possibility." The peoples of the West must come to believe in and act in accordance with the only moral principle Nature recognizes: for those who live in harmony with Nature, *survival is moral*. For those who do not, the penalty is extinction. Without this understanding, Western Man, progenitor of law, compassion, technology and a spirit of quest that is unparalleled in the history of the human race, will perish at the hands of those who do not possess the same innate spark. For the sake of our children who are yet to be, let us choose life—by whatever means we must—while the choice is still ours.

This article appeared in the July 1995 and August 1995 issues. Michael Masters has written articles appearing in The Social Contract, Southern Patriot, *and* The Citizens Informer.

Race and the American Identity
by Samuel Francis

In December 1991, as Pat Buchanan announced his candidacy for the Republican presidential nomination, the Republic was edified by the reflections of columnist George Will. Mr. Will quoted from a column by Mr. Buchanan to the effect that "No one questions the right of the Arabs to have an Arab nation, of China to be a Chinese nation. . . . Must we absorb all the people of the world into our society and submerge our historic character as a predominantly Caucasian Western society?" and then proceeded to explain what was wrong with the candidate's reasoning. Mr. Buchanan, he wrote, "evidently does not understand what distinguishes American nationality—and should rescue our nationalism from nativism. Ours is, as the first Republican president said, a nation dedicated to a proposition. Becoming an American is an act of political assent, not a matter of membership in any inherently privileged group, Caucasian or otherwise. The 'Euro-Americans' who founded this nation did not want anything like China or Arabia—or any European nation, for that matter."

Mr. Will's bald assertion that America is a "nation" defined by no particular racial or ethnic identity and indeed by no particular content whatsoever is not unique. The best-known formulation of the same idea is the phrase popularized by Ben Wattenberg, that America is the "first universal nation," and indeed only this year the new Washington editor of *National Review*, John J. Miller, has published a book, *The Un-Making of Americans*, in which he too asserts the universalist identity of the nation and uses that concept as the basis for endorsing virtually unlimited immigration. "The United States can welcome immigrants and transform them into Americans," Mr. Miller writes, "because it is a 'proposition country.'" The proposition by which the American nation defines itself, the sentence fragment from the Declaration of Independence that all men are created equal, means that the "very sense of peoplehood derives not from a common language but from their adherence to a set of core principles about equality, liberty, and self-government. These ideas [Mr. Miller writes] . . . are universal. They apply to all humankind. They know no racial or ethnic limits. They are not bound by time or history. And they lie at the center of American nationhood. Because of this, these ideas uphold an identity into which immigrants from all over the world can assimilate, so long as they, too, dedicate themselves to the proposition."

Nor is the idea of America as a universal nation confined to the contemporary right. Historically, it is based on a core concept of the left, born in the salons of the Enlightenment and underlying the French Revolution's commitment to a universal "liberty, equality, and fraternity"— which was sometimes imposed at the points of rather unfraternal bayonets. Today it continues to inform the American left as well as the right. Bill Clinton himself last year cited the projected racial transformation of the United States from a majority white to a majority non-white country in the next century as a change that "will arguably be the third great revolution in America . . . to prove that we literally can live without in effect having a dominant European culture. We want to become a multiracial, multiethnic society. We're not going to disintegrate in the face of it." More recently, in remarks at commencement exercises at Portland State University in Oregon in June, Mr. Clinton praised the prospect of virtually unlimited immigration as a "powerful reminder that our America is not so much a place as a promise, not a guarantee but a chance, not a particular race but an embrace of our common humanity."

The idea of America as a universal nation, then, is an idea shared by and increasingly defining both sides of the political spectrum in the United States. The fact that the right, in such persons as Mr. Will, Mr. Wattenberg, and Mr. Miller, to name but a few, does share that idea with Mr. Clinton helps explain why the right today can think of nothing better to criticize the president for than his sex life and his aversion to telling the truth. Any substantial criticism of his globalist foreign policy, his defense of affirmative action, his policy of official normalization of homosexuality, his support for mass immigration, and in particular his "national dialogue on race" would involve a criticism and a rejection of the universalist assumptions on which those policies are based.

The common universalist assumptions of both left and right, then, are a major reason for the rapid convergence of left and right in our political life. They are the reason why, to coin a phrase, there is not a dime's worth of difference between them on so many issues and a major reason why we are seeing the emergence, not just of a One Party State in the United States, but also of a Single Ideology that informs the state and the culture. As I discovered myself, those who dissent from the Single Ideology of a Universal Nation or Proposition Country are not allowed to express their views even in self-proclaimed conservative newspapers [As noted previously, Dr. Francis was fired as staff columnist for the *Washington Times* because of his speech at the 1994 AR conference], and it is hardly an accident that Mr. Miller accuses me in his recent book of what he calls "racial paranoia." Prior to his elevation to *National Review*, he admitted that he had "wanted to run [me] out of polite society for months, if not for years." Nor am I the only journalist to discover that you get "run out of polite society" for departing from the Single Ideology of Universalism. Joe Sobran, the *New York Post*'s Scott McConnell, and *National Review*'s Peter Brimelow have all met the same fate for essentially the same reason, though all of them remain in circles rather more polite than the ones I travel in.

But the most casual acquaintance with the realities of American history shows that the idea that America is or has been a universal nation, that it defines itself through the proposition that "all men are created equal," is a myth. Indeed, it is something less than a myth, it is a mere propaganda line invoked to justify not only mass immigration and the coming racial revolution but also the erosion of nationality itself in globalist free trade and a One World political architecture. It also justifies the total reconstruction and redefinition of the United States as a multiracial, multicultural, and transnational swamp. Nevertheless, the myth of the universal nation or proposition country is widely accepted, and today it represents probably the major ideological obstacle to recognizing the reality and importance of race as a social and political force.

In the first place, it is not true, as Miller writes, that the "Proposition" that "all men are created equal" and the ideas derived from it are universal and "not bound by time or history." If that were true, there would never have been any dispute about them, let alone wars and revolutions fought over them. No one fights wars about the really self-evident axioms of Euclidean geometry. Mr. Miller's propositions are very clearly the products of a very particular time and place—late 18th century Europe and America—and would have been almost inconceivable fifty years earlier or fifty years later. Nor have they ever appeared in any other political society at any other time absent their diffusion from Europe or America. They are based on concepts of anthropology and history, including an entirely fictitious "state of nature," a "social contract," and a view of human nature as a *tabula rasa*, that no student of human society or psychology took seriously after the mid-19th century.

Secondly, it is not clear what the proposition that "all men are created equal" means, either objectively or in the minds of those who drafted and adopted it in the Declaration. Assuming that "men" means women and children as well as men, does it mean that all humans are born equal, that they are equal, or that they are created equal by God? If they are born or created equal, do they remain equal? If they don't remain equal, why do the rights with which they are supposedly endowed remain equal, or *do* those rights remain equal? If they are created equal by God, how do we know this, and what does it mean anyway? We certainly do not know from the Old Testament that God created all men equal, because most of it is about the history of a people "chosen" by God and favored by Him above others. Does it mean that God created humans equal in a spiritual sense, and if so, what does that spiritual equality have to do with political and social or even legal equality? Or does it mean that we were created equal in some material or physical sense, that we all have one head and two legs and two arms and so forth? If it means the latter, it is true but platitudinous.

In short, taken out of the context of the whole document of the Declaration and the historical context and circumstances of the document itself, the "equality clause" of the Declaration opens so many different doors of interpretation that it can mean virtually anything you want it to mean. It has been invoked by Christians and freethinkers, by capitalists and socialists, by conservatives and liberals, each of whom merely imports into it whatever his own ideology and agenda demand. Taken by itself, it is open to so many different interpretations that it has to be considered one of the most arcane—and one of the most dangerous—sentences ever written, one of the major blunders of American history.

Yet, if the sentence is taken to imply that race and other natural and social categories are without meaning or importance, it ought to be clear that America as a historic society has never been defined by that meaning. The existence of slavery at the time of the Declaration and well after, and the fact that no small number of the signers of the Declaration were slave-owners and that some parts of Jefferson's original draft denouncing the slave trade were removed because they were objectionable to Southern slave-owners ought to make that plain on its face.

The particularism, racial and otherwise, that made the American people a nation was very clearly seen by John Jay, in a now-famous passage of *The Federalist Papers*, No. 2, that:

"Providence has been pleased to give this one connected country to one united people—a people descended from the same ancestors, speaking the same language, professing the same religion, attached to the same principles of government, very similar in their manners and customs. . . ."

The racial unity of the nation is clear in Jay's phrase about "the same ancestors," and with respect to the US Constitution, although the words "slave" and "slavery" did not appear in the text until the 13th Amendment, the Constitution is, as historian William Wiecik of Syracuse Law School writes, "permeated" with slavery:

"So permeated was the Constitution with slavery that no less than nine of its clauses directly protected or referred to it. In addition to the three well-known clauses (three-fifths, slave trade, and fugitive slave), the Constitution embodied two clauses that redundantly required apportionment of direct taxes on the federal-number basis (the purpose being to prohibit Congress from levying an unapportioned capitation on slaves as an indirect means of encouraging their emancipation); two clauses empowering Congress to suppress domestic insurrections, which in the minds of the delegates included slave uprisings; a clause making two provisions (slave trade and apportionment of direct taxes) unamendable, the latter providing a perpetual security against some possible antislavery impulse; and two clauses forbidding the federal government and the states from taxing exports, the idea being to prohibit an indirect tax on slavery by the taxation of the products of slave labor."

Moreover, Professor Wiecik notes, with respect to the changes in the Constitution after the Civil War,

"Only by recognizing the extent to which the constitutional vision of Lincoln and the Republicans was a departure from the original Constitution can we understand the long struggles through the war, Reconstruction, and after to incorporate black Americans into the constitutional regime. Freedom, civil rights, and equality for them were not the delayed but inevitable realization of some immanent ideal in the Constitution. On the contrary, black freedom and equality were, and are, a revolutionary change in the original constitutional system, truly a new order of the ages not foreseen, anticipated, or desired by the framers."

But even aside from slavery, the persistence of clear and widespread recognition of the reality and importance of race throughout American history shows that Americans never considered themselves a universal nation in the sense intended today. Historian David Potter writes:

"The 'free' Negro of the northern states of course escaped chattel servitude, but he did not escape segregation, or discrimination, and he enjoyed few civil rights. North of Maryland, free Negroes were disfranchised in all of the free states except the four of upper New England; in no state before 1860 were they permitted to serve on juries; everywhere they were either segregated in separate public schools or excluded from public schools altogether, except in parts of Massachusetts after 1845; they were segregated in residence and in employment and occupied the bottom levels of income; and at least four states—Ohio, Indiana, Illinois, and Oregon—adopted laws to prohibit or exclude Negroes from coming within their borders."

Nor were blacks the only non-white racial group to be excluded from civic membership. The first naturalization act passed by Congress under the Constitution in 1790 limited citizenship to "white men," and even after citizenship was granted to blacks through the 14th Amendment, naturalization continued to be forbidden to Asians: to Chinese until World War II, and to Japanese even later. Racial and ethnic restrictions on immigration remained in federal immigration law until 1965, when they were removed, as Larry Auster has shown, after sponsors of the reform assured opponents that removing them would not alter the ethnic and cultural composition of the nation—an assurance we now know to have been false.

As late as 1921, Vice President-elect Calvin Coolidge wrote an article on immigration called "Whose Country Is This?" in the popular women's magazine *Good Housekeeping*. He argued that "There are racial considerations too grave to be brushed aside for any sentimental reasons. Biological laws tell us that certain divergent people will not mix or blend. The Nordics propagate themselves successfully. With other races, the outcome shows deterioration on both sides. Quality of mind and body suggests that observance of ethnic law is as great a necessity to a nation as immigration law." Not only the white but the Northern European racial identity of the nation could thus be publicly affirmed by a leading national political figure in a widely read magazine as late as the 1920s.

What President Coolidge wrote then was by no means exotic or alien. Thomas Jefferson's views of racial equality are probably well known to AR readers. In *Notes on the States of Virginia*, he discussed the significant natural differences between the races, and while he was, at least in principle, opposed to slavery, he was adamantly in favor of forbidding free blacks to continue to live within the United States. Nor did he favor non-European immigration into the Northwest Territory nor into the lands of the Louisiana

Purchase. In 1801 he looked forward to the day "when our rapid multiplication will expand itself . . . over the whole northern, if not the southern continent, with a people speaking the same language, governed in similar forms, and by similar laws; nor can we contemplate with satisfaction either blot or mixture on that surface."

James Lubinskas has written an excellent article in the August 1998 *American Renaissance* on the American Colonization Society, a society that sought the expatriation of blacks to Africa, and which included as members Henry Clay, James Madison, Andrew Jackson, Daniel Webster, James Monroe, John Marshall, Winfield Scott, and many other of the most prominent American public leaders. They may have held different views of slavery and race, but none of them believed that free blacks should or could continue to live in the same society with whites.

Nor did Abraham Lincoln entertain egalitarian views of blacks, and his clearest statements on the subject are to be found in the course of his debates with Stephen Douglas during the Illinois senatorial campaign of 1858. While opposing the extension of slavery to new states, Lincoln repeatedly assured his audiences that he did not believe in or favor civic equality for blacks. In the debate at Charleston, Ill., on Sept. 18, Lincoln said:

"I will say that I am not nor ever have been in favor of bringing about in any way the social and political equality of the white and black races: that I am not nor ever have been in favor of making voters of the free negroes, or jurors, or of qualifying them to hold office, or to intermarry with white people. I will say in addition that there is a physical difference between the white and black races which I suppose will forever forbid the two races living together upon terms of social and political equality, and inasmuch as they cannot so live that while they do remain together there must be a position of superior and inferior, that I as much as any other man am in favor of having the superior position being assigned to the white man."

He repeated this and similar ideas throughout the debates. Lincoln also was strongly in favor of expatriation for blacks and seriously explored the practicality of establishing a black settlement in Central America. Indeed, he proposed what would have become, had it passed, the 13th Amendment to the Constitution permitting federal support for the colonization of blacks outside the country.

In his annual message to Congress in December 1862, in which Lincoln made this proposal, he said:

"That portion of the earth's surface which is owned and inhabited by the people of the United States is well adapted to be the home of one national family, and it is not well adapted for two or more. Its vast extent and its variety of climate and productions are of advantage in this age for one people, whatever they might have been in former ages. Steam, telegraphs, and intelligence have brought these to be an advantageous combination for one united people."

He obviously was thinking, as a unionist, of what he regarded as the inappropriateness of secession, but he was also thinking of the inappropriateness of a different "people" or race inhabiting the same territory, and his remarks are thus a fairly clear expression of what can only be called racial nationalism.

As for Stephen Douglas, he was even more outspoken on the issue of race than Lincoln (the following passage from his opening speech in the debates is from the edition published in 1993 by Harold Holzer, which incorporates into the text the audience responses as recorded by the newspapers of the day, in this case the *Chicago Daily Times*, a Democratic paper):

"For one, I am opposed to negro citizenship in any form. [Cheers—*Times*] I believe that this government was made on the white basis. ['Good,'—*Times*] I believe it was made by white men for the benefit of white men and their posterity forever, and I am in favor of confining the citizenship to white men—men of European birth and European descent, instead of conferring it upon negroes and Indians, and other inferior races. ['Good for you. Douglas forever,'— *Times*]"

Douglas, of course, won the election.

Nor, even after the end of the war, during congressional debates on the 14th Amendment—which today is considered the cornerstone of federal enforcement of egalitarian policies—even then, there was no endorsement of racial equality. Thaddeus Stevens, whom constitutional historian Raoul Berger calls the "foremost Radical" in Congress, was not in the least committed to black voting. He was mainly concerned with perpetuating the domination of the Republican Party. It suddenly began to dawn on the Radicals that with the abolition of slavery, the three-fifths clause of the Constitution, which had limited Southern representation in Congress, was no longer meaningful. The result would be that Southern representation in Congress would be vastly increased to the point that the South, just defeated in the war, would suddenly gain political dominance.

As Professor Berger writes, "Now each voteless freedman counted as a whole person; and in the result Southern States would be entitled to increased representation and, with the help of Northern Democrats, would have, as Thaddeus Stevens pointed out at the very outset of the 39th Congress, 'a majority in Congress and in the Electoral College.' With equal candor he said that the Southern States 'ought never to be recognized as valid states, until the Constitution shall be amended . . . as to secure perpetual ascendancy' to the Republican Party."

The 14th Amendment was passed in order to grant the federal government the authority to enforce the Civil Rights Act of 1866, and the meaning of the language of the amendment is clarified by the debates over the earlier law. The Civil Rights Act was mainly intended to overcome the so-called "Black Codes" imposed on blacks after the end of slavery and the war, and it gave to "the inhabitants of every race". . . . "the same right to make and enforce contracts, to sue, be parties, and give evidence, to inherit, purchase, lease, sell, hold and convey real and personal property, and to full and equal benefit of all laws and proceedings for the security of person and property, and shall be subject to like punishment . . . and no other." In explaining the language of the bill to the House, Rep. James Wilson of Iowa, chairman of the House Judiciary Committee, was explicit about the limits of the bill:

"What do these terms mean? Do they mean that in all things, civil, social, political, all citizens, without distinction of race or color, shall be equal? By no means can they be so construed. . . . Nor do they mean that all citizens shall sit on juries, or that their children shall attend the same schools. These are not civil rights and immunities. Well, what is the meaning? What are civil rights? I understand civil rights to be simply the absolute rights of individuals, such as 'The right of personal security, the right of personal liberty, and the right to acquire and enjoy property.' "

Rep. James Patterson of New Hampshire, a supporter of the 14th Amendment, said much the same. He was opposed to "any law discriminating against [blacks] in the security of life, liberty, person, property and the proceeds of their labor. These civil rights all should enjoy. Beyond this I am not prepared to go, and those pretended friends who urge political and social equality . . . are . . . the worst enemies of the colored race." Republican Senator Lyman Trumbull of Illinois, who drafted the Civil Rights Bill, concurred. "This bill is applicable exclusively to civil rights. It does not propose to regulate political rights of individuals; it has nothing to do with the right of suffrage, or any other political right."

What the framers of the Civil Rights Bill of 1866 and the 14th Amendment were proposing, in other words, was simply to extend to the emancipated black slaves what is generally called "equality under the law," a concept of equality that merely recognizes the equality of citizens and does not rest on any supposition of the natural equality of human beings. Equality under the law demands that the same fundamental civil rights belong to all citizens—what are often called the "Blackstonean rights" of life, personal liberty, and property—and which were generally agreed to be the content of the "inalienable rights" mentioned in the Declaration.

But these basic civil rights were sharply distinguished from "political rights" such as voting or holding office. The Blackstonean rights are fundamental because it is not possible for an individual citizen to function without them—to live without security of being murdered or being abducted or imprisoned or enslaved or having his property stolen. If the black population were not going to be enslaved and not going to be colonized abroad, it was essential that ex-slaves possess these basic civil rights simply in order to function in society; but the Blackstonean civil rights have nothing to do with voting, holding political office, sitting on juries, racial intermarriage, getting a job or being promoted, or school integration, which is what the concept of "civil rights" has come to mean today.

It would be possible to continue with an almost inexhaustible list of quotations from prominent American statesmen and intellectual leaders well into the twentieth century abjuring any belief in the equality of the races or any belief that non-white races should or can have the same political position as whites in the United States. I will not rehearse all of them, but my purpose in what I have said so far is not to invoke all these institutions and ideas about race in American history as a model of what we should seek to restore or because I necessarily agree with all the views of race that have been expressed throughout our history (indeed, some of them are more or less contradictory), but to reinforce two points: First, we are not and never were a "universal nation" or a "proposition country" defined by the equality clause of the Declaration or the bromides of the Gettysburg Address. On the contrary we—Americans in general and our public leaders in particular—repeatedly and continuously recognized the reality and importance of race and the propriety of the white race occupying the "superior position," and indeed it is difficult to think of any other white-majority nation in history in which recognition of the reality of race has been so deeply imbedded in its thinking and institutions as in the United States.

Second, whatever we think of that history and its recognition of race, we have to understand that the current propaganda line about being a universal nation is not only a totally false account of American history but also is a prescription for a total rejection of the American past and the national identity as we have always known it. Racial universalism is not simply an adjustment or a "reform," let alone a continuation of the proper direction of American history, but a revolutionary reconstruction of the American identity.

In a 1996 article and a later book on Thomas Jefferson, historian Conor Cruise O'Brien demands that we eject Jefferson from our national pantheon precisely because of his views of race. O'Brien has a point that is perfectly logical if you accept his premise that America should be, even if it never has been, a universal nation. If indeed we are or should be a universal nation, then Thomas Jefferson must go. If indeed race is a meaningless "social construct" and a device for repression and exploitation as we are commanded to believe, then Jefferson was one of the main architects of and spokesmen for racial tyranny. But let us be aware that Jefferson is not the only god who has to be dethroned. If Jefferson must go, so must George Washington, and indeed, Washington's name has already been removed from a public school in New Orleans because he was a slaveholder.

But Abraham Lincoln has to go as well, and so must Theodore Roosevelt and the leaders of the American Colonization Society and the framers of the 14th Amendment and so must virtually every other president and public leader in American history. You cannot have it both ways: either you define the American nation as the product of its past and learn to live with the reality of race and the reality of the racial particularism and racial nationalism that in part defines our national history, or you reject race as meaningful and important, as anything more than skin color and gross morphology, and demand that anyone, past or present, who believes or believed that race means anything more than that be demonized and excluded from any positive status in our history or the formation of our identity. If you reject race, then you reject America as it has really existed throughout its history, and whatever you mean by "America" has to come from something other than its real past.

That of course is exactly what President Clinton is telling us when he gloats that "we literally can live without in effect having a dominant European culture. We want to become a multiracial, multiethnic society." And that also is what we are being told by contemporary liberalism. In 1997, the *New Republic* published an article by George P. Fletcher, professor at the Columbia Law School, in which Prof. Fletcher argued that "The republic created in 1789 is long gone. It died with the 600,000 Americans killed in the Civil War. That conflict decided once and forever that the People and the States do not have the power to govern their local lives apart from the nation as a whole. The People have no power either to secede as states or to abolish the national government."

The reason the Old Republic died, according to Professor Fletcher, is that it "was grounded in a contradiction" that "glorified the freedom of some and condoned the slavery of others." The new Constitution, he tells us, "begins to take hold in the Gettysburg Address, in which Lincoln skips over the original Constitution and reconstitutes it according to the principles of equality articulated in the Declaration of Independence." As a matter of historical fact, Professor Fletcher is more or less correct. The Civil War did destroy the Old Republic, and the new state that arose from it is defined, at least today, as a universalist and egalitarian regime based on the equality proposition of the Declaration. What he does not tell us, however, is how the new regime can be a legitimate one, since it is, by his own admission, simply the result of victorious military power and not of consent or legal authorization by the representatives of the old regime. It is easy enough to destroy an existing constitutional order, but quite a different matter to construct a new one.

Nevertheless, the significance of Prof. Fletcher's article is that it makes perfectly clear what we are facing from the contemporary supporters of universalism, whether of the left like Prof. Fletcher himself or President Clinton or of the "right" like John Miller. What we are facing and what they are advocating is in no sense a continuation of American history or the American national identity as it has existed throughout our history, but rather a revolutionary reconstruction of the nation, a reconstruction that ruthlessly follows the logic of Mr. O'Brien's exclusion of Jefferson in excluding just about everything else characteristic of the Old Republic. The old identity and everything associated with it have to be excluded because their embrace of non-egalitarian and non-universalist institutions are simply incompatible with the new republic. Once we understand that, most of the universalists' actions, policies, and ideas are perfectly logical. What they are aiming at is precisely what William Wiecik described in a passage I quoted earlier, "a revolutionary change in the original constitutional system, truly a new order of the ages not foreseen, anticipated, or desired by the framers."

And not desired by most Americans today, either, at least not by those white Americans who grasp what is going on. As Peter Brimelow notes in his book on immigration, *Alien Nation*, Americans have never been asked whether they think it's a good thing for their nation to undergo the transition from a white majority to a non-white majority country. They have indeed been lied to about the transition, in being told in 1965 that it wouldn't happen, but until President Clinton embraced it last year, no president has even bothered to mention it.

If white Americans do not desire the transition, they still have a short time to prevent it and to try to salvage what is left of the Old Republic most of them still imagine they live in, and if they do wish to salvage it, they will have to reject, as clearly and firmly as the original Framers did, the universalism and egalitarianism that now threaten to destroy them and their race. Political philosophies and constitutional forms come and go, but nations—peoples and races—remain. Yet without the common blood that made us a nation in the first place, there will be no American nation, no matter what abstractions and forms we vainly invoke.

Samuel Francis is a syndicated columnist. This article is adapted from his remarks at the AR conference held in August 1998, and originally appeared in the December 1998 and January 1999 issues.

━━━◆◆◆━━━

The Evolution of Racial Differences in Morality
by Michael Levin

R eaders of AR will be aware of the well-documented race differences in intelligence and temperament. The mean black score on valid IQ tests is 85, while the white mean is 100 (and some Asian groups outscore whites). Black children adopted into upper-middle class white families fail to attain IQs much above 85, which implicates genes as the cause of this difference. Twin studies and cross-cultural comparisons implicate genes in the greater levels of impulsiveness and aggression also found in blacks.

A less frequently noted point is that these psychological differences suggest race differences in morality. Part of the difference may be due simply to different levels of intelligence. The mean IQ of incarcerated felons is about 90, and Lawrence Kohlberg's extensive research on children found that IQ is correlated with moral development. It should not be surprising that mental ability is linked to moral character, since the latter requires grasping rules and thinking through the consequences of one's actions.

However, different levels of intelligence are not likely to be the sole cause of racial differences in morality. Data reported in *The Bell Curve* show that black and white populations differ in crime and illegitimacy rates even when IQ is held constant. Thus, in one large-scale study, blacks in general were 6.5 times more likely to be incarcerated than whites, but when the comparison was restricted to blacks and whites with IQs of 100, blacks were still 2.5 times more likely to be incarcerated.

Temperament therefore appears to have an effect on behavior that is independent of intelligence. This is intuitively obvious, as aggression easily becomes heedlessness of the rights of others; we should therefore expect black and white standards of behavior to differ.

Examples of this difference abound. "Trash talk," the stream of arrogant banter with which black basketball players seek to intimidate and humiliate opponents, is alien to white ideals of sportsmanship. Likewise, Montel Williams, the host of a television talk show, claimed to have discovered racial bias in a question on an IQ test that asked children what they would do if they threw a baseball through a neighbor's window. The answer scored as correct was offering to pay for the window, but Mr. Williams, who is black, objected that in his old neighborhood a "Sorry, man" would have sufficed. No doubt, Mr. Williams was right that blacks do attach less urgency than whites to compensating damage.

Numerous fights among blacks result from "dissing"—males seeking dominance over each other by shows of disrespect—a practice that indicates disregard for the golden rule. Moreover, it is hard to imagine a more blatant violation of the golden rule than the constant demand for royalties by Martin Luther King's estate whenever his speeches are published—especially when his own plagiarism is justified as "voice merging."

What Morality Is

Evolutionary biology suggests an explanation for race differences in moral values. But first, to begin with a definition: An individual's "morality" is *the rules he wants everyone to follow, and that he wants everyone to want everyone to follow.* Honesty is a moral value for him if he tries to be honest, tries to make his children honest, hopes others will be honest, and encourages others to reinforce honesty. A group's morality is the moral rules its members share.

The clause about "wanting everyone to want everyone" is needed to distinguish moral questions, like honesty, from other "universal" concerns. If you are like most people, you think others ought to be honest. But you may also think everyone should exercise, without considering exercise a "moral" value. The difference between the two is not in their usefulness, since both are useful: jogging is healthful, and honesty facilitates such profitable activities as trade. But honesty, unlike exercise, is advantageous *only if everyone else is honest.* Jogging strengthens my heart whether or not you jog, whereas being honest helps me only insofar as it induces others to reciprocate, allowing me to rely on their words. This is also why it is smart to *be* honest even when tempted to lie—if you are found out, others will feel no obligation to be honest with you.

On the other hand, if everyone else is a liar, honesty only lets others take advantage of you. Therefore, since honesty, self-restraint, and other moral virtues are good ideas only when everyone thinks they are good ideas, you not only want everyone else to be honest, you want everyone to encourage others to be honest, and to ensure that honesty is widespread.

The advantages of honesty and other virtues have a biological dimension. Since moral individuals in a moral community do better than scoundrels, they live longer and have more children. Obeying and reinforcing moral rules is adaptive. If there is any genetic tendency to obey and reinforce moral rules, a tendency to obey and reinforce them and to be susceptible to reinforcement will be passed on to offspring.

However, selection for morality need not have been uniform, since honesty, cooperation, and the other virtues need not have been equally important in all environments. Cooperativeness (like intelligence) was probably more adaptive in the colder, harsher, Eurasian environment in which whites and Asians evolved than in sub-Saharan Africa. Food grows year-round in a warm climate. There is little danger of freezing to death, so it is not necessary to work together to build large shelters. Sexual patterns are also influenced by environment: Since a woman abandoned by her mate has a better chance of supporting herself and her children in a benign environment, there is less pressure on women to evolve a demand for male fidelity, or for males to evolve a strong sense of attachment.

The situation was otherwise in Eurasia, where large game was a dietary staple. Bringing down a cornered mastodon takes cooperation, with each man in his assigned position, ready to respond to shouted instructions. There must be jointly acceptable rules for dividing the kill. And, since females depend on male hunters for their own survival and that of their children, an advantage would accrue to females who chose mates likely to support them for a lifetime. Sexual selection would then mold males more inclined to satisfy the female demand for fidelity.

Environment does not consist merely of natural factors like climate. Since morality is advantageous only when others are moral, a major determinant of the fitness of an individual's "gene for morality" is the character of those with whom he interacts. As Robert Axelrod and William Hamilton put it in their classic study, "The Evolution of Cooperation" (*Science* 1981), "there is no single best strategy regardless of the behavior of others in the population." In fact, seemingly irrational levels of mistrust can become locked into a group. Suppose a mild physical environment has selected for weak cooperative tendencies. A worsening of the environment might make greater cooperation in everyone's interest, but not necessarily more fitness-enhancing, for any honest, helpful mutants who appear will simply be exploited until they die without issue. It is perfectly rational to be indifferent to others when they are indifferent to you.

In short, observed race differences in honesty, sexual self-restraint, and cooperativeness may be due to the fact that these traits did not have the same evolutionary value in Africa that they did in Eurasia. Indeed, since universality and reciprocity are built into the very concept of morals, it is incorrect to talk of "different moralities." It is more accurate to say that individuals of Eurasian descent tend to be more moral than individuals of African descent.

Consequences

Nobody can go back in time to verify whether the races really developed in the way outlined. Still, the hypothesis sketched above is plausible enough, and it may be useful to note some of its implications.

1) Black behavior that is unacceptable by white standards—theft, drug use, preoccupation with sex—is not "sick." It is how traits that were once adaptive in Africa express themselves in Western urban society. This may be part of the reason blacks seem not to experience white laws and standards of personal responsibility as binding, and why black spokesmen are so curiously unapologetic about black crime. They will caution black males that crime is "stupid" (i.e. apt to lead to punishment), and Jesse Jackson may denounce black-on-black crime as harmful to blacks, but they do not say that crime, particularly black-on-white crime, is intrinsically bad.

In one remarkable incident, Edmund Perry, a Harlem teenager recruited on full scholarship to the prestigious boarding school of Exeter, was killed a few weeks after graduation when he attempted to mug a plainclothes policeman. Angry demonstrations ensued, in which blacks complained of Perry's alienation at Exeter. Far from expressing regret over Perry's actions, blacks blamed white society for them. In fact, the difficulties blacks experience in conforming to American society cannot really be blamed on black attitudes *or* white norms, but on the mismatch between the two.

2) Black children cannot be expected to respond as white children do to externally imposed white socialization. If the races evolved different values, black and white children will be receptive to different sorts of training and exhortation, a point with important practical consequences. It is often suggested, for instance, that black children would do better in school if told, as white and Asian children are, that school is important. But black children will not care about grades and the esteem of teachers, no matter how much they are told to, if valuing knowledge is a more weakly evolved norm among blacks. Since black societies never evolved formal education, it would make no sense for black children to be ready to internalize praise of education.

3) Violence will skyrocket when a group acquires a killing technology it did not develop. Groups that have invented such things as firearms without killing themselves off must also have developed sufficient inhibitions about using them. Groups that acquire weapons from outside sources are less likely to have evolved the same level of self-restraint, just as groups that do not discover fermentation are unlikely to develop a tolerance for alcohol, and often fall prey to drinking problems when alcohol is introduced from outside. Blacks may have been unprepared for access to the firearms developed in Western society.

Consider the remarkable increase in gunshot homicides among black men in the last half-century. In 1943 there were 44 handgun homicides in New York City; in 1992, 1,500 black males died of gunshot wounds inflicted by other black males. Since 92 percent of the 2,200 murders recorded in New York that year were committed by blacks, black males must have also killed several hundred non-blacks with firearms as well. The parallel increase in gunshot homicides nationally over the same period is essentially an increase among blacks.

Now, the sheer availability of guns does not automatically mean murder. Guns have been available for centuries to the whites who invented and manufacture them. Every adult male Swiss citizen owns a gun, yet the annual homicide rate in Switzerland is one two-hundredth that of Washington, DC or Harlem. The immediate cause of the rise in homicide has been the sudden availability of guns *to blacks*, who seem ready to resort to firearms in disputes that whites would regard as trivial. (Gunfights over calls in pick-up basketball games are not uncommon in New York City.) It may well be that blacks lack the restraints that would have evolved during the march to the invention of firearms—a possibility that should be considered in any discussion of gun control. If the "gun problem" is really the problem of black access to firearms, forbidding whites to have guns is pointless and unjust.

4) Moral signals may become confused when divergent groups interact. To explain the point with a crude example, suppose that blacks, being less empathetic than whites, must use stronger signals to rouse each others' solicitude. It takes angry shouting to get another black to notice an injury that a

white can be induced to attend to by less strident means. Likewise, a white will take an angry shout as expressing a more serious injury. If these signal patterns have themselves become innate in the two populations, whites will interpret the signals of blacks as if they were coming from other whites, and consistently *overestimate* the seriousness of injuries claimed by blacks.

The tendency of whites to interpret the angrier manner of blacks as if blacks were other whites leads whites to respond to black complaints with inappropriate generosity, thereby reinforcing black anger by teaching blacks that anger is rewarded. The result is intensified demands and further white confusion—a dynamic that may explain the puzzling phenomenon of white guilt, and the indulgence of many whites toward even the most unreasonable black demands.

Neither is Better

The idea that blacks and whites evolved different systems of values says nothing about which values are "better," and each group can be expected to think its values best. Whites will continue to consider blacks "irresponsible" and blacks will, more openly, continue to call whites "up tight." But the practical decisions of life require the adoption of some standards, and a group can use only those standards evolution has given it.

What by white standards is a black deficiency in morality—defined as conformity to the golden rule—explains the persistent unwillingness of the races to associate with each other. People almost by definition prefer the company of those who share their values, so it is no wonder that whites feel more comfortable with whites. Indeed, while blacks—even including Malcolm X—prefer to send their children to white schools and to use the other amenities of white society, blacks nevertheless prefer the company of blacks. The conventional idea is that these preferences are entirely due to "prejudice" that can and should be extirpated by education (i.e. propaganda). But if preference for one's own kind is due to deep-seated differences in values, there seems nothing wrong with it, and there certainly seems no reason for it to be illegal.

Moreover, from their own point of view, whites are *right* to prefer their own company. By white standards, adherence to the golden rule and norms associated with it are the chief criteria of personal merit. Since blacks are on average less likely than whites to adhere to the golden rule—less cooperative, more aggressive, less respectful of property and persons—the average black is, by white standards, not as good a person as the average white. This is perhaps the least politically correct statement it is possible to make, but it is true and must be made. And, put in non-racial terms, it is one that even liberal egalitarians would assent to. Even they would admit to preferring the company of people who are less apt to steal, kill, lie, cheat, and shout them down in a debate.

It is possible to argue on purely philosophical grounds that people should be able to associate with whomever they please. This right, after all, can be enjoyed by everyone, and is itself in conformity with the golden rule. And this right, which implies that whites can "discriminate" in favor of other whites in housing, employment, and the schools to which they send their children, has been contravened by civil rights laws. This was allowed to happen because Americans, who respect freedom but also like to see that freedom is not abused, became convinced by the 1960s that use of the freedom of association to avoid blacks was entirely arbitrary. They became convinced that it could be motivated only by ignorance and hatred, and saw no reason not to forbid actions so maliciously based. Race differences in moral outlook, which people have long sensed, are perfectly good, non-arbitrary reasons for whites to wish to avoid blacks. Perhaps when this is more widely realized whites will once again permit themselves this liberty.

This article appeared in the April 1995 issue. Professor Michael Levin teaches philosophy at City College of New York. He is the author of several books, including Why Race Matters.

Is There a Superior Race?
by Michael Levin

Whether some races are superior to others is a question all those concerned with race must consider, if only because their critics are sure to force them to. Just say that whites are, on average, more intelligent than blacks, and you will be told "Oh, so you think whites are superior to blacks." If you say that Jews are, on average, more intelligent than gentiles you will be lectured that that sort of thinking led to the Holocaust.

Behind all this passionate confusion lie real issues. Academics tend to duck them, from a desire for scientific neutrality or simply to avoid trouble. They will say that race differences in IQ and temperament have nothing to do with questions of value, that the greater intelligence of whites, for example, is just a fact of nature like blood pressure. But very few people view intelligence this way, and I am sure the typical psychologist prefers that his children have IQs of 120 rather than 80. In fact, both views of racial differences are valid. The scientist's "Sgt. Friday," just-the-facts-ma'am approach is basically right, I believe, but at the same time, we must acknowledge that group differences touch people's deepest hopes and fears.

To sort out these issues we must revisit an old riddle common in college philosophy courses: the place of value in the universe. The question is whether justice is "natural" or "conventional"—that is, whether right and wrong, good and bad, beautiful and ugly are objective features of the world, or fictions with no basis in the nature of things. Incidentally, only Europeans have ever reached the level of intellectual abstraction necessary to pose such questions, and the first to do so were the Greeks. They wanted to know whether judgments of good and bad are discovered or invented, whether they are based on reason or on mere projections of human emotion onto the real world. The skeptical view implies that nothing—including one or another race—is inherently better or worse than anything else.

The most eminent ancients—Socrates, Plato and Aristotle—did see value as an objective feature of reality accessible to reason, but they have always had opponents. Socrates' contemporary, Xenophanes, joked that if horses could draw, they would draw their gods as horses. Plato thought that most men failed to understand the existence of objective good. According to him, the Greek-in-the-street thought that all sensible men were profoundly selfish but had reluctantly agreed to limit their pursuit of self-interest to avoid a catastrophic war of all against all. These agreed-upon limits set on selfishness—which are necessary evils—are the laws of justice. They are like traffic rules: It is useful for everyone to agree to stop on red and go on green, but no one imagines that there is something inherent about red that makes stopping when you see it obligatory. (It is a tribute to Greek genius that the hoi polloi had an opinion on so deep a question.)

Although I have great respect for the belief that God determines what is good and what is evil, I'm afraid I must count myself among the skeptics. As I see it, nothing in the world is good or bad, or right or wrong, or better or worse. People, like other organisms, have preferences, some of which are more common in some groups than others, but none is objectively better or worse than any other. They just are.

It is not right or good that a lion catch the gazelle he is after, although a catch will certainly please him, and, as Xenophanes might have added, if lions could talk they would doubtless say that gazelle-catching was "proper" and "what all decent lions deserve." Gazelles, for their part, dislike being caught and would, if given voice, accuse lions of violating their rights. In fact, the universe roots for neither. There is no neutral standpoint from which to rank the lion's evolved appetite for gazelles against the gazelle's evolved aversion to being lunch. It is not possible to say which is right or wrong.

So in my view it makes no sense to say that one race is better or worse, superior or inferior, to another. It makes as little sense as saying that lions are "better" than gazelles.

Before I go into my reasons for this, let me add a few words about that singular value called morality. Man alone has preferences about preferences, his own and those of others. For instance, most of us not only want to be honest and punctual, we want others to be honest and punctual, too. In fact, most of us feel distinctly uneasy about doing things we don't want others to do. This higher-order desire, that our actions conform to general rules that we can also prescribe for others, is the essence of morality. A person is said to be conscientious or principled when he subjects his behavior to the golden rule, the how-would-I-like-it-if-everyone-did-that test.

Concern for morality, like other traits, is not equally distributed. In *Why Race Matters* and elsewhere I cite evidence that, on average, blacks are less concerned than whites about the golden rule. This is clearly suggested by the very high rates of black criminality not only in the United States but around the world. At a more mundane level it is also reflected, for example, in the unwillingness of many blacks to take turns and a tendency of blacks to "talk back" to movies (which displays a lack of sympathy with audience members who want to watch in silence).

Having taught philosophy for many years to a "diverse" student body, I have been able to compare the preferences and actions of different groups by using a classic philosophical conundrum. When I introduce ethics I always ask my students what you should do if a supermarket cashier gives you too much change, and there is no chance of discovery if you pocket it. While I have not kept precise statistics, disproportionately more black students say that "you'd be a fool" to return the money. Many back up their position by saying that the mistake is the cashier's problem. When I ask what they would do if they were the cashier many reply, irrelevantly, that they wouldn't let it happen to them.

Why conformity to universal rules is important to whites may be linked to another Caucasian specialty, the quest for scientific knowledge. The hallmark of scientific explanation is that it follows general rules. Whenever you say that A is why B happened, you implicitly refer to a law of nature. When you say the window broke because the baseball hit it, you have in mind that whenever glass of that sort is struck with a sufficiently great force, it shatters. We find events comprehensible when they fall into general patterns, and we find behavior acceptable only when it obeys rules. It is no coincidence that the race that invented science is also the one pre-eminently concerned with right and wrong.

Having said this, I reiterate that being moral—being concerned with the golden rule—isn't better in any absolute sense than being amoral. It is a preference, neither right nor wrong, that some people feel more intensely than others, and that still others lack altogether.

Skepticism

The basic reason for skepticism about values is that they explain nothing. There are, as I see it, only two grounds for believing in something: It can be observed, or it is needed to explain something else that can be observed. I believe in elephants because I have seen them at zoos. I believe in electromagnetic waves because, if they didn't exist, television could not be explained. Values are not observable—you cannot literally see the goodness of helping a blind man cross the street. Nor is there any phenomenon that requires values to explain it. Nothing in nature happens because it is right; lions chase gazelles and gazelles run away because of natural selection, not because it is "right." Human beings act as they do, not because of right and wrong, but because of their convictions about right and wrong, and I believe these convictions are ultimately explained by natural selection.

So we seem to be back at the Sgt. Friday position, with its corollary that high intelligence and moral concern are not inherently better than dim-witted amorality. There is no progress over evolutionary time, just change—tendencies, for instance, for organisms to display more intelligence, but no direction towards something inherently better.

This position has its attractions, chiefly as an all-purpose reply to inevitable nagging about "racism:" You can doggedly insist on the facts of race and disavow any moral interpretation. But not only will this never satisfy egalitarians, it misrepresents what people ordinarily have in mind when they make comparisons. People do not usually intend some sort of cosmic, absolute judgment when they make comparisons or talk about superiority. Not even the most fanatical users of Apple computers claim that Macs are just better than PCs, period, in the eyes of God. What they have in mind is that Macs are better than PCs according to certain accepted standards like speed and ease of use. Beef is not graded according to some mysterious quality of inherent goodness, but by tenderness and marbling. Of course, accepted standards may change, but so long as the standards in force are clear, there should be no misunderstanding.

In fact, people have four definite standards more or less clearly in mind when they compare human groups, and relative to those standards it is possible to draw conclusions about different races.

1)   The first of these standards is *influence*. The most salient test for ranking individuals is influence: How different would the world be if so-and-so had never been born? (Michael Hart uses this test in his book *The 100*, which is his list of the most important people in history.) Columbus is more important than Joe Blow because the world would have been very different without Columbus, whereas Joe Blow's absence would scarcely have been noticed. This test applies to groups as well as individuals. The Greeks were more important than the Iroquois because they made more difference to the world as a whole.

It is a matter of verifiable fact that the influence of whites dominates mankind. Had blacks never existed, Europe and Asia would be pretty much as they are today. Had Asians never existed, the world would be somewhat different, but still recognizable. But a world in which there had never been Europeans is unimaginable. It is not just that everyone else has been Westernized in the superficial respects that are easy to criticize, like clothing and music. Western science and technology shape mankind's building, trade, transportation, communication and education. Cars are almost everywhere, and where there aren't cars there are bicycles—both Western inventions. People pay bills by check, an innovation of late medieval Europe. They erect large structures according to mechanical principles discovered in the West. Terrorists attack with guns of Western design and explosives mixed according to Western chemistry. Every high school student in the world learns Cartesian co-ordinates, another product of Caucasian ingenuity.

2)   The other side of the coin of influence is *emulation*. Every other culture wants—covets—the control over nature that Western man has achieved by scientific methods of thought. It is important to emphasize this standard, for egalitarians always describe Caucasian influence as "imperialism," as if whites forced it on the rest of the world. Not so; other countries would give a great deal for Western standards of living, infant mortality rates, longevity, productivity and individual freedom. While from a cosmic point of view no culture may be better than another, when all sides agree in prizing the products of one culture, there is from a practical point of view not much to argue about.

This is not to say that other cultures always realize or admit that they emulate the West. They often treat the fruits of Caucasian science as natural resources they are entitled to. Negotiations about sea-bed mining are forever breaking down when backward countries demand that the Western world give them their "fair share" of the world's mineral wealth. They ignore the fact that it takes Western ingenuity and effort to extract it, and that effort and ingenuity deserve to be rewarded. But it is clear that if a magic wand could give the Third World Western skills, Third-World critics of "imperialism" would wave it without hesitation.

Western values are emulated not just collectively, but individually. Everyone admires the traits in which whites excel, chiefly intelligence. Do not be fooled by the esteem in which athletic and sexual prowess are held by some groups. Intelligence may not be valued as highly elsewhere as it is at an American university but there is no culture in which the local equivalent of "bright" is not a compliment nor "stupid" an insult. The picture is fuzzier for traits like law-abidingness, but on the whole Caucasians and Mongoloids excel Negroids in individual traits that members of all three groups prize. In many of these same traits Mongoloids slightly excel Caucasians, while in others—perhaps originality—Caucasians excel Mongoloids.

To repeat, it is a verifiable fact that all cultures agree on the value of certain traits. This is why racialists are always accused of claiming racial superiority when they note the high intelligence of whites. The average person values intelligence, and assumes that other people, including psychometricians and racialists, do too. So when he hears whites described as more intelligent than blacks, he naturally concludes that the speaker is calling whites superior. This, after all, is the inference *he* would draw from the same data. Deep down, even egalitarians view intelligence as an important standard of personal value, so, since *they* would conclude that whites are superior if they admitted to themselves that whites are more intelligent, they foist this view on racialists. Hearing someone say a steak is tender and juicy, you would as a matter of course assume he is praising it. You would be surprised and a little doubtful if he insisted he was only describing the steak's properties.

3)   Closely related to the emulation standard is that of *efficiency*. Given certain goals or ends common to all groups, one group is considered "superior" when its means to those ends are most efficient. "Better" often means "is a better means." Crop rotation, for example, is better than sacrificing to the Sun God, because it produces a bigger harvest. By this means-ends test, Caucasians have created a verifiably better civilization because it more readily secures certain universal goals.

Every group has wanted indoor lighting, for instance. Most have achieved it with dangerous, expensive fire, while whites achieved it with cheap, easily controlled electricity. Every culture has wanted the ability to travel from one place to another. All have attained walking speed—about 3 miles per hour. A few have mastered the horse, allowing them to move at about 10 miles per hour. Caucasian mastery of jet propulsion allows people to travel in comfort at 600 miles per hour.

Of course, the desirability of speed and indoor lighting are not inscribed in stone, and one can imagine a society consciously eschewing them. The Amish still ride carriages rather than drive cars. But since the desire for technological advance is in fact so widely shared, and Caucasians are better at achieving it than anyone else, Caucasians are "superior" in the sense of having developed the best means to certain universal ends.

Technological preeminence is not the only source of Caucasoid means-ends superiority. Let me describe some recent experiments that shed light on how Western moral attitudes create wealth and other generally accepted goods. Western morality is more efficient.

Suppose someone gives me $10, but with the following proviso: I am to offer you any part of that $10, from one cent to $5 to $9.99. You then decide whether or not to take my offer. If you take it, you get what I have offered and I keep the rest. If you reject my offer, the $10 is taken back and we both get nothing. We both know these conditions. What do I offer you? What offer should you accept from me? (There is a real-world parallel: Having discovered there is gold on my land, but being physically weak, I offer you a share of the profits to mine it for me. If you turn me down, the gold stays in the ground and neither of us is any better off. What deal should we strike?)

From a strictly logical point of view, one would expect you to take any offer, down to a penny for you and $9.99 for me. After all, even a lopsided deal like that leaves you a penny richer. However, when this "take it or leave it" game has been tried on Germans, Americans, Yugoslavs, Japanese and Israelis, offers that deviate significantly from $5 for each person are almost always rejected—in effect punished—and no player ever accepts a split as unbalanced as $2.50 for him, $7.50 for the fellow making the offer. What is more, very few players from these countries ever offer a deal significantly more advantageous to himself than $5/$5, perhaps because each player knows that no such offer will be accepted.

The reason for this seems to be a sense of equity, probably innate, that moves players to punish behavior they see as unfair, even at some cost to themselves. This moral indignation, though it may appear irrational and counterproductive, is one of those rules by which sensible men bind themselves for the sake of their own and everyone else's long-run profit. For imagine a society of egotists with no compunction about making lopsided offers in the interest of maximizing short-term gain. No one egotistical enough to feel entitled to a $9.99/1¢ split is likely to settle for the one cent when someone makes that lopsided offer to him, so in such a society few beneficial bargains will be made. In such a society I will offer you one percent of the profits for mining my gold, you will give me a piece of your mind, and we will both remain poorer than we need to be. In a society where everyone has a sense of equity and 50/50 offers are apt to be made, these offers are also apt to be accepted, and everyone will become better and better off. Emphasis on equity leads to mutually enriching bargains.

My sense is that Mongoloid moral systems put less emphasis than Caucasoid on conscience but endorse similar rules of fairness. I would love to see take-it-or-leave-it experiments with subjects of different races, although I cannot imagine such experiments being allowed in the present climate. I would predict that racial differences would be found in the lopsidedness of offers made and in offers accepted, with whites and Asians tending toward a 50/50 equilibrium, with blacks more inclined to make—but disinclined to accept—offers deviating from this midpoint. Please recall the "you'd be a fool" view of keeping incorrect change. This attitude would surely encourage short-sighted, unbalanced offers; would it also lead to the acceptance of such offers (since a penny is better than nothing) or militate against them? I suspect the latter, but I would like some data.

4)   A fourth criterion of group excellence is *power*: When the ordinary person calls one group superior to another, he may mean that members of the first group can be counted on to defeat equal numbers of the second in battle. However unlovely, this is a standard people often have in mind, and there is no doubt that Caucasians predominate. The weapons they have invented would allow easy conquest of the planet, and they would meet resistance only from societies that have managed to imitate the weapons of the West. Nor is there much doubt that, say, a thousand Caucasoid males could organize themselves into a more effective fighting force capable of defeating a thousand Negroids. It is not clear that whites would have equal success against Asians, but again it must be remembered that ever since the Middle Ages, Asian armies have done reasonably well against white armies only by using white inventions. If in our imaginary 1,000-on-1,000 battle each group is restricted to weapons developed by its own society, whites would certainly win every time.

This standard is not as brutish as it sounds, since, for better or worse, military power is the upshot of traits that are admired in their own right: courage, intelligence (to devise better weapons and better treatment for the wounded), discipline, audacity, and concern for the group.

Superiority by this standard also has some interesting demographic implications. The first is that whites may well govern—that is, occupy virtually all positions of power—no matter what ideology is dominant. Blacks and non-European Hispanics may become more numerous in the United States, but even in a democracy they will have to have someone to vote for, and whites will generally manage to be the ones that get into a position to be elected. (We see this with the sexes: there are more female than male voters, but at the national level virtually all leaders are men.) This may explain why whites rule in Brazil, even though the black population is proportionally much larger than in the United States. It is not that blacks think whites are more fit to rule, it's just that the naturally dominant group always does dominate.

Thus, I fully expect that when 2050 rolls around, and assuming (as the demographers assure us) whites become a minority, whites will still rule because they will be better organized. However, at some point they will be unthroned through sheer weight of numbers—perhaps by the 22nd century.

Thus, according to four common criteria—influence, emulation, efficiency and power—whites come out on top, but as I have pointed out, a determined skeptic can reject all four. We can fully expect egalitarians to reject them, at least in public: "What's so great about influence or intellect or the capacity for moral thinking?" I doubt that anyone can mean this question seriously, but it can't be answered except by appealing to other standards egalitarians can also disingenuously challenge. All anyone can do is point out that we *do* care about these things, and ask anyone who doesn't to suggest traits we should care about more.

As I emphasize in my book, the values we have as individuals and as a culture are the ones we can't help but use. While upbringing counts to some extent, our values are the heritage of eons of selection. We are born with them. That is the way we are. One can be objective about one's own values for a few hours in the study, but detachment becomes impossible as soon as the world presses in. Values are like emotions. I know intellectually that the grief I might feel for the death of a son is a biological adaptation—nature's way of making sure I take better care of my other offspring—but realizing that emotions are a trick of neural wiring would not reduce my suffering one bit.

The much touted "wisdom of the East" that teaches the extirpation of emotions is foolish. It can easily counsel an alienation from one's own deepest commitments, and this trivializes life. The Western approach of engagement with the world, with its attendant risks of suffering, is more honest.

Each group therefore finds its own standards best, and judges the rest of the world by them. How could it be otherwise? A group of people that disapproved of its own nature would suffer a spiritual dissonance not conducive to survival, and psychologists tell us that pride in one's ethnic group is a sign of mental health (although this sort of pride is supposed to be reserved for non-whites). By Caucasian standards Caucasians are best.

Critics of white "ethnocentrism," like Capt. Reynaud in *Casablanca*, pretend to be "shocked I tell you, shocked" that whites give the highest grades to white writers, artists, composers, statesmen and inventors. What do they expect? If blacks preferred non-black culture, these same critics would say that whites have taught blacks to hate themselves. In any case, even if ethnocentrism is bad it is inevitable. We have the values we have, and we have no choice but to apply them.

So what should you say if someone asks you whether you believe in racial superiority? Ask him what *he* means by "superior," what standards *he* has in mind. If he can't or won't answer, remind him that the question was his. If he doesn't know what "superior" means, he is as much as admitting that he doesn't know what he is talking about—and if he doesn't know what he is talking about, why should you continue the conversation?

If he says accusingly "You know darn well what I mean," pin him down: Tell him you know what you mean, but not what he means. If you finally elicit a concrete standard from him apply it, but remind him that any aspersions cast are his. For instance, if he says creation of material wealth is a measure of superiority, point out that, yes, white societies are richer than others and therefore better by *his* criterion, and that it is he, not you, who is assuming the value of wealth. This tactic will shame the most shameless egalitarian. In his heart he believes that, by his own criteria, whites (and

Asians) are better than blacks. Since he will never admit this, with luck you can at least get him to go away.

This article appeared in the February 1999 issue.

The Future

— ❧ —

If We Do Nothing
by Jared Taylor

In March 1996, the Census Bureau released its periodic projection of the ethnic makeup of the United States during the next few decades. It reported cheerfully that if current immigration and birth rates hold steady, by the year 2050 the percentage of Hispanics will have increased from 10 to 25 percent, that of Asians from three to eight percent, and that of blacks from 12 to 14 percent. All these increases will come at the expense of whites, who are projected to fall from 74 percent of the population to about 50 percent.

Within 54 years, therefore, whites will be on the brink of becoming just one more racial minority. And because whites are having so few children, they will be an *old* minority. Within just 34 years—by 2030—they will already account for less than half the population under age 18, but will be three quarters of the population over 65. Many of the people reading these words will be alive when these things come to pass.

As usual, the Census Bureau's projections stirred little interest. The *New York Times* did note that the projected changes would represent "a profound demographic shift" and that the future mix of old whites and young blacks and Hispanics might give the debate about Social Security "a racial and ethnic tinge." This seemed to be the most disturbing thing the *Times* could think of.

Why is there almost complete silence about a population shift that, if it takes place, will transform much of the country beyond recognition? Why is there no debate about what this would mean in terms of education, politics, democracy, the jury system, national unity, racial friction, crime, foreign policy, labor productivity, or virtually any other national indicator?

The demographic future of the United States is perhaps the most important question we face, yet it receives no attention. Most whites simply refuse to think about what is happening to their country or about the Third-World future they are ensuring for their children and grandchildren. Those who do think about demographic change have been browbeaten into believing it is inevitable and that resistance would, somehow, be immoral.

What makes the silence so unaccountable is that there is very little mystery about the nature of the changes we can anticipate. Miami and Detroit and Monterey Park, California are good examples of what happens when a city becomes Hispanic, black, or Asian. The details of the transformation are interesting, but it is sufficient to note the obvious: Once the concentration of non-whites reaches a certain level, whites cannot or will not live among them. Except in a few gilded enclaves, there are virtually no whites left in Miami or Detroit or Monterey Park. "White flight" is a universal fact of American life. Liberals may deplore it, but no one can deny it.

In the 1960s and 1970s, whites were generally fleeing blacks, but the great black migrations have largely come to an end, and whites have reestablished distance between the two races. In recent decades, it is massive, non-white immigration that most often drives whites from their neighborhoods, and continuing immigration only hardens the alien character of these places. No one believes that the arrival of yet more Haitians, Guatemalans, Mexicans, Jamaicans, or Vietnamese will somehow restore the former character of South Central Los Angeles or Miami and induce whites to move back.

The process works in precisely the other way. As their numbers increase, non-whites continue to expand into adjacent areas. Whites, many of whom fled their homes in the face of the first incursion, move away once again.

This, then, will be one of the certain effects of demographic change: More and more parts of the United States will become, for whites, essentially uninhabitable. It will be *physically possible* for whites to live with the Mexicans of Brownsville, Texas or the blacks of Camden, New Jersey but such places will be almost as alien and as uninviting as Oaxaca or Mombassa. They will actually be more uninviting. The people of Oaxaca and Mombassa like and admire white Americans, whereas those of Brownsville and Camden have a strong and sometimes violent dislike for whites.

There is much irony in the course on which our nation has been set. Most white Americans can think of any number of communities or neighborhoods in which they might want to live. Not one is likely to have a non-white majority. Likewise, most whites cannot name a single non-white community in which they could bear to live. Furthermore, if one were to ask whites what countries they might move to if given a choice, almost all will mention a European country, Canada, Australia, or New Zealand. All are white. Our country has therefore embarked on a course that will make ever larger parts of it inhospitable, even off-limits, to whites. Eventually the country as a whole could become one in which whites do not wish to live.

At some level, everyone in America understands this. Not even the most deluded white liberals live in Harlem or Watts or South Central Los Angeles, or in any of a thousand other neighborhoods that have been transformed by non-whites. Despite their pronouncements about the vital importance and desirability of integration, virtually no white is willing to take the most obvious step towards making it happen: buy a house in a black neighborhood.

Destroying the Infrastructure

Where it matters most—where they make their homes and rear their children—even the most liberal whites suddenly demonstrate a grasp of reality at odds with what they claim to believe and stand for. Even they have noticed that although the details of non-white dispossession differ according to the part of the country and the people who arrive, something essential is always lost when whites move away.

Blacks frighten even the most ardent integrationists. East Coast blacks, in particular, have the disconcerting habit of physically destroying the cities they move into. Detroit, Newark, the South Bronx, Camden, North Philadelphia, and the South Side of Chicago now have huge expanses of vacant lots and derelict buildings.

Detroit can no longer afford to serve some of its most blighted, sparsely inhabited neighborhoods. It is considering moving out the few remaining people and decommissioning whole sections of itself—shutting off utilities, stopping mail delivery, pulling out bus lines, ending police and fire service, and letting nature take over. There are similarly stark proposals for parts of downtown, where empty skyscrapers tower over deserted streets. Some people want to turn the area into a theme park for urban architecture—like the ghost towns in the West.

Blacks have destroyed cities in several ways. One is arson. Many East Coast neighborhoods never completely rebuilt after the race riots of the 1960s. Today, black youngsters in Detroit, Newark, and elsewhere celebrate Halloween eve—which they call Devil's Night—by burning down as many houses as they can. Other buildings, often charming turn-of-the-century townhouses, become uninhabitable because no one bothers to maintain them. Others are simply abandoned as the decent, responsible blacks flee crime and degeneracy. The result is the blasted, vacant look of so many Eastern black ghettos.

Entire cities have slowly shifted away from the parts that blacks have occupied, as whites build homes and businesses away from the expanding blight. In what were once the centers of important cities, whole chapters of urban history have been wiped away. Not a trace remains of generations of industrious whites who worked hard, reared children, and hoped for a better future.

Hispanics do not ordinarily tear cities down, though the 1992 Los Angeles riots showed that they can sometimes burn and loot their own neighborhoods just as blacks sometimes do. Likewise, the Puerto Rican sections in New York's outer borough can be as menacing as any inhabited by blacks.

Hispanics have a different effect. They bring crime and lower the quality of public schools—reasons enough for whites to move out—but they also bring an alienness blacks do not. Many are willing to live ten to a room, turn garages into bedrooms, park cars in the front yard, keep chickens, and practice a gaudy, Third-World version of Catholicism. But the greatest sign of alienness is Spanish. The airwaves, magazine racks, storefronts, and the very air itself ring with a language most whites do not understand. The occasional passing car marked "Police" rather than "Policia" is a reminder that this is still, theoretically, the United States.

In 1991, the president of a black home-owners association in South Central Los Angeles explained her opposition to a wave of Mexicans moving into a formerly black area: "It's a different culture, a different breed of people. They don't have the same values. You can't get together with them. It's like mixing oil and water." The now-forgotten and long-departed white residents may well have said the same things about blacks.

When Asians arrive in large numbers, their effect is more ambiguous. Some North Asian groups commit fewer crimes than whites, make more money, and do better in school. Others, like the Hmong and the Cambodians, have fantastically high rates of poverty and welfare dependency. However, *it does not matter* whether Japanese or Chinese build societies that are, in some respects, objectively superior to those of Europeans. It matters only that they are *different*.

When large numbers of North Asian immigrants moved into Monterey Park, the long-term white residents did not leave because the newcomers rioted, opened crack houses, covered walls with graffiti, or were rapists and robbers. They moved out because Monterey Park, in countless ways, ceased to be the town in which they had grown up or the town to which they had moved.

The merchandise in the stores and the faces behind the counters changed. So many signs appeared in strange languages that the fire department insisted that at least street numbers be legible to English-speakers. Even city council meetings began to include exchanges in languages other than English. The newcomers reworked zoning laws to permit businesses in what had been residential neighborhoods. Asians bought the little bungalows whites had lived in, bulldozed them, cut down all the trees, and built huge new houses nearly out to the property line.

All these changes and many others—some of them vastly more troubling than issues that are routinely put to the voters to decide—took place without the permission or consent of the whites who had lived there for years. One unhappy resident paid for a billboard that said, "Would the last American to leave Monterey Park please take down the flag."

Once again, the significance of racial change does not lie in the particulars. It lies in the fact of unwelcome, uncalled for, irreversible change. People have every right to expect their children and their children's children to be able to grow up and walk in the ways of their ancestors. They have a powerful, natural desire that their grandchildren be like them—that they speak the same language, sing the same songs, tell the same stories, pray to the same God, take pride in the same past, hope the same hopes, love the same nation, and honor the same traditions. The crucial elements of peoplehood cannot be preserved in the face of a flood of aliens, especially when the central institutions of the nation itself preach fashionable falsehoods about the equivalence of all races, cultures, and peoples.

Most people who grew up in America want to grow old in America, not in some bustling outpost of Mexico or Southeast Asia. They should not have to move to Montana or Idaho in order to grow old with people like themselves. Eventually, of course, if the foreign outposts continue to expand, there will be no refuge in Montana and Idaho either.

This, then, is the effect of racial change at the local level: Whites become refugees in their own land.

What will happen at the national level? We cannot be sure but we can guess. Many non-whites now seem genuinely to believe that equal treatment requires preferences for themselves. It may yet be possible to abolish racial preferences while whites are still a majority, but what will prevent their re-appearance when whites become a minority?

Whites will still have higher incomes than blacks and Hispanics, but this will be seen only as proof of white wickedness and exploitation. Is it so outlandish to imagine outright confiscation of property owned by whites? supplemental taxes for whites? sumptuary laws? exclusion from certain professions? Asians will also be a small but successful racial minority, and their wealth, too, is likely to attract unwelcome government attention.

What sort of foreign policy would a non-white America have? What would it do—or not do—with nuclear weapons? What sort of public health standards would it maintain? How would a Third-World America treat its national parks, its forests, its rivers? So far, only whites have shown much interest in the environment.

In the long term, there is some doubt that a non-white America could even maintain a functioning democracy or any semblance of the rule of law. The record of non-white nations suggests not. Even if our forms of government survive, what fanciful, anti-white readings will a black and Hispanic Supreme Court find in the Constitution? What subjects or opinions will be found to lie outside the protection of the First Amendment?

Not an Ounce of Sympathy

But these will be future concerns. To return to the present, in the United States today, there is not an ounce of public sympathy for whites who escape when the neighborhood turns black or Mexican. The theory is that only ignorant bigots run away from non-whites, but the fact is that people with money never even have to face the problem. As a very clever man once put it, the purpose of a college education is to give people the right attitudes about minorities and the means to live as far away from them as possible.

And, indeed, college-educated, right-thinking people have come up with a whole set of mental exercises for the working-class unfortunates who do not have the money to send their children to private school. The first exercise is to try as hard as possible to believe that aliens and strangers are bearers of a special gift called diversity. We are not being displaced; we are being enriched and strengthened.

Of course, the idea that racial diversity is a strength is so obviously stupid that only very intelligent people could have thought it up. There is not one multiracial anything in America that doesn't suffer from racial friction. Our country has established a gigantic system of laws, diversity commissions, racial watchdog groups, EEO officers, and outreach committees as part of a huge, clanking machine to regulate and try to control racial diversity—this dangerous, volatile thing that is supposed to be such a source of strength. People are so exhausted by this source of strength that they run from it the first chance they get. Families, churches, clubs, and private parties—which are not yet regulated by the government—tend to be racially homogeneous.

Nothing could be more obvious: Diversity of race or tribe or language or religion are the main reasons people kill each other on a large scale. Diversity—within the same territory—is strife, not strength.

Another comical idea is that a "diverse" workforce is somehow a great advantage for business or world trade. This is one of those giant, untested notions that otherwise skeptical people swallow without a gurgle. Ninety-nine percent of the things we buy have nothing to do with "diversity." No one cares whether his computer was assembled by a Chinaman or a Dane or whether his bread was baked by a robot or a chimpanzee.

It does *not* take an Irishman to sell things to the Irish. The world's most successful trading nations today are Japan, Korea, Taiwan, and China, none of which has even heard of "diversity" or "tolerance." American companies are full of blather about multiracial workforces that "look like America"—and are constantly being whipped in their own markets by workforces that look like Yokohama or Shanghai.

At the same time, people seem to be too dazed by this incomprehensible diversity argument to notice that it seems to be only whites who suffer from the paralysis of homogeneity and for whom diversity is going to be such a tonic. No one is urging Howard University, which is overwhelmingly black, to recruit Hispanics or Asians so its students can benefit from racial diversity. No one is suggesting that Mexico should start an immigration program to reduce Hispanics to a minority in a few decades. But if racial diversity is such a great thing for the United States, why not for Mexico, too? Why not for Howard and for all the other "historically black" universities?

If white Americans were pouring across the border into Mexico demanding that their children be educated in English, insisting on welfare, demonstrating for ballot papers in English rather than Spanish, demanding voting rights for aliens, celebrating July 4th rather than Cinco de Mayo, could anyone trick the Mexicans into thinking this was joyous diversity? No. The Mexicans would recognize an invasion when they saw one. They would open fire.

There used to be much talk about "ugly Americans," who traveled overseas expecting to find hamburgers and English-speakers, and who ignorantly deprecated the quaint customs of the natives. We were supposed to be deeply ashamed of them—and they were only tourists! "Ugly Mexicans" and "ugly Haitians" come here *to live permanently*, but we are supposed to be endlessly sensitive to their peculiarities, and revel in the diversity of toadying to their ethnic demands.

"Racial diversity," therefore, is strictly a one-way street. Only whites are ever expected to practice it or benefit from it. The ultimate insult is to expect whites to *celebrate* diversity. This is nothing less than asking them to celebrate their own capitulation, their dwindling numbers and declining influence. The astonishing thing is that so many whites actually do go through the motions of rejoicing in their decline.

Just Deserts

Of course, a few whites refuse to believe that dispossession is a fine thing. For these stubborn cases, there is a completely different argument to justify demographic shift: Whites took America away from the Indians, so it is now someone else's turn. This argument is made by the same people who chant the mantra of diversity, but it implicitly concedes that diversity is a fraud.

Diversity advocates *never* suggest that what happened to the Indians was a good thing. But have Indians not benefited more than any other people in history from the joys of precisely the kind of diversity whites are, today, supposed to welcome? If diversity is to be celebrated, it should be Christmas all year 'round for the Indians. Of course, no one tries to make this point. The you-took-it-away-from-the-Indians argument recognizes that the European conquest of the continent was a catastrophe for Indians and that what is happening now is a catastrophe for whites. It is a catastrophe whites are supposed to accept cheerfully because they took America from its rightful owners.

But this, too, is a completely one-sided argument. The Cherokee, for example, took away the land of an earlier group called the Mound Builders. Why are they known as the Mound Builders? Because the Cherokee exterminated them and no one even knows their name. All that is left of them are their strange earthworks.

If whites are supposed to stand aside while every Third-World tribe marches into the United States because whites took the country from Indians, then the Cherokee should have stood aside for the Europeans—because they took the place away from the Mound Builders.

Needless to say, current orthodoxy holds that for Indians it makes no difference how many people they killed to get the land or how recently; it was theirs to defend with every means at their disposal. Whites, on the other hand, have an unending debt not just to the descendants of the peoples they refrained from exterminating but to every other non-white people on the face of the earth. Just like fairy tales about the joys of diversity, the land-title argument is used exclusively to criticize and demoralize whites.

Successful Societies

What is it, though, that gives rise to movements of peoples and debates about who has rights to the land? It is the fact that whites build successful societies non-whites want to move into. Generous Nicaraguans and Haitians do not come to America eager to share the gift of "diversity" with poor, benighted white people who are about to expire from a galloping case of homogeneity. They come because their societies don't work and they know life will be better here.

The same process is at work in Europe, Australia, Canada, and New Zealand. Whites establish the most desirable societies in the history of man. Desperate people from failed, non-white societies are willing to risk nearly everything—sometimes even their lives—for a chance to live in these societies.

If Europeans had turned North American into a giant pesthole no one would want to come. No one would then have to think up reasons why everyone had the right to come, or why whites actually benefit from being outnumbered and pushed aside by people unlike themselves.

The same is true on a smaller scale. Rarely is it ever said, but in the United States virtually every desirable place to live, work, or go to school is desirable because whites made it that way. Non-whites naturally want access to these places even if they did not—and could not—create them. This is why it is always non-whites who are pushing their ways into white institutions—never the other way around and why all the overblown dramas of "exclusion," "tolerance," "justice," and "racism" are played out on white territory and put whites on the defensive.

Whites are not, of course, clamoring to get into Howard University, live in Harlem, or to move to Guatemala. But if there were something rare and desirable in those places, the non-whites who made them desirable would fight like demons to keep others out.

The sad truth is that, generally speaking, once non-whites have gotten what they want, and have arrived in large numbers in what were previously white institutions or neighborhoods, those institutions and neighborhoods slowly lose the qualities that attracted non-whites in the first place. Whites leave, and the spoor of European man begins to fade. For the most part, Third-World immigrants eventually recreate in the United States the societies they left behind—with all the shortcomings that prompted them to leave home in the first place.

The mystery in all this is not why non-whites want the benefits of white society, but why whites are so willing to hand over to strangers the land of their ancestors—why they appear to be so willing to permit aliens to occupy and transform their nation. Just like every other argument about race in America today, white passivity is based on yet another double standard: Non-whites have powerful and legitimate group interests but whites do not.

Before he was assassinated, Israeli Prime Minister Yitzhak Rabin explained that what mattered most to him as an Israeli was that his country remain at least 80 percent Jewish. No one suggested that Mr. Rabin was a bigot or hatemonger—and of course he was not. He was merely stating the obvious: That if Israel ceased to be predominantly Jewish it would change in irreversible ways that would be intolerable to Jews.

Mexicans, Japanese, Algerians, Senegalese—all non-whites understand that demographic transformation is a national calamity. It is so obvious it need not even be stated. For whites it is just as much a national calamity, and the morality and reasoning of a white who wants America to stay at least 80 percent white are exactly the same as those of Yitzhak Rabin.

The forms of civility, the folkways, the demeanor and the texture of life that whites take for granted cannot survive the embrace of large numbers of aliens. The things whites love most about culture and human society have not survived in Detroit and Miami. It is not considered "nice" to say so; it prompts shouts of "racism" to say so. But it is because the things they love have not survived that whites have moved away from Detroit and Miami. Individually, whites react in an entirely natural way to racial change. *American Renaissance* is unusual only in making explicit what virtually all whites feel but never say.

The crisis that whites face today is that for fear of being called "racists," for fear of being thought not nice, they seem prepared to let their country change in ways that they know will not be an improvement. How can it be good for America—or good for whites—for it to become increasingly like those very parts of the country in which they refuse to live?

Whites are so fearful of the charge of "racism" that they are unwilling even to discuss what they might do to avoid leaving a Third-World nation to their grandchildren. Whites are therefore preparing to pass on to future generations a nation in which they, themselves, might well be unwilling to live.

The colonists did not fight for independence from Britain in order for our generation to turn this country over to Mexicans and Haitians. The Founders did not frame the Constitution to celebrate diversity. Americans did not spill their blood at Gettysburg or in Europe or the Pacific for multiculturalism. And yet, the rightful heirs to what could have been a shining beacon of Western Civilization are giving up their country without a struggle—for fear that to do otherwise would be "racist."

What we are witnessing is one of the great tragedies in human history. Powerful forces are in motion that, if left unchecked, will slowly push aside European man and European civilization and then dance a victory jig on their collective grave. If we do nothing, the nation we leave to our children will be a desolated, Third-World failure, in which whites will be a despised minority. Western Civilization will be a faint echo, vilified if it is even audible. There is no other tragedy that is at once so great, so unnatural, and so unnecessary.

This article appeared in the June 1996 issue.

Fairest Things Have Fleetest Endings

Jean Raspail, *The Camp of the Saints*, (trans.) Norman Shapiro,
The Social Contract Press, 1995, 316 pp., $12.95 (soft cover)

reviewed by Jared Taylor

Fiction can be more powerful than fact. Authors have always lent their talents to causes, often swaying events more effectively than journalists or politicians. Fiction, including virtually everything emitted by Hollywood, has usually been in the service of the left, but occasionally an author declares his allegiance to culture and tradition.

In *The Camp of the Saints*, Jean Raspail goes further and declares his allegiance to his race—though it is an allegiance tinged with bitterness at the weakness of the white man. Originally published in 1973, this may be the first significant racialist novel since the days of Thomas Dixon. It is the story of the final, tragic end of European civilization which falls, like all great civilizations, by its own hand.

The novel is set in the near future in France, where the leftist sicknesses of multiculturalism and multiracialism have undermined all natural defenses. As Mr. Raspail writes of young Europeans:

"That scorn of a people of other races, the knowledge that one's own is best, the triumphant joy at feeling oneself to be part of humanity's finest— none of that had ever filled these youngsters' addled brains, or at least so little that the monstrous cancer implanted in the Western conscience had quashed it in no time at all."

By then, "the white race was nothing more than a million sheep," beaten down by decades of anti-white propaganda. As Mr. Raspail explains, it was "a known fact that racism comes in two forms: that practiced by whites— heinous and inexcusable, whatever its motives—and that practiced by blacks—quite justified, whatever its excess, since it's merely the expression of a righteous revenge . . . ."

This is the state of mind with which the West confronts its final crisis: nearly a million starving, disease-ridden boat people—men, women, and children—set sail from the Ganges delta for Europe. Practically no one is willing to say that this flotilla must be stopped at all costs. Instead, liberals and Christians spout confident nonsense about welcoming their Hindu brothers into the wealth and comfort of Europe.

The thought of this wretched brown mass sailing for Europe is a source of great joy for the World Council of Churches. Its men are "shock-troop pastors, righteous in their loathing of anything and everything that smacked of present-day Western society, and boundless in their love of whatever might destroy it." They are determined "to welcome the million Christs on board those ships, who would rise up, reborn, and signal the dawn of a just, new day . . . ."

One of the few Europeans who recognizes that what has come to be called the "Last Chance Armada" spells the doom of Christendom reproaches a group of anti-Western churchmen:

"There's not one of you proud of his skin, and all that it stands for. . . ."

"Not proud, or aware of it either," replies one. "That's the price we have to pay for the brotherhood of man. We're happy to pay it."

Europe is rife with fifth-column propagandists, products of earlier capitulations. Typical of these is Clement Dio, "citizen of France, North African by blood . . . . [who] possessed a belligerent intellect that thrived on springs of racial hatred barely below the surface, and far more intense than anyone imagined."

Knowing full well that acceptance of the first wave of Third World refugees will only prompt imitators that will eventually swamp the white West, he writes happily about how "the civilization of the Ganges" will enrich a culturally bankrupt continent:

"Considering all the wonders that the Ganges had bestowed on us already—sacred music, theater, dance, yoga, mysticism, arts and crafts, jewelry, new styles in dress—the burning question . . . was how we could manage to do without these folks any longer!"

As the flotilla makes for Europe, school teachers set assignments for their students: "Describe the life of the poor, suffering souls on board the ships, and express your feelings toward their plight in detail, by imagining, for example, that one of the desperate families comes to your home and asks you to take them in."

The boat people steam towards the Suez Canal, but the Egyptians, not soft like whites, threaten to sink the entire convoy. One hundred ships turn south, around the horn of Africa—towards Europe. The refugees run out of fuel for cooking and start burning their own excrement. Pilots sent to observe the fleet report an unbearable stench.

A few deluded whites have boarded the ships in Calcutta and sail along with "the civilization of the Ganges," dreaming of Europe:

"Already they saw it their mission to guide the flock's first steps on Western soil. One would empty out all our hospital beds so that cholera-ridden and leprous wretches could sprawl between their clean white sheets. Another would cram our brightest, cheeriest nurseries full of monster children. Another would preach unlimited sex, in the name of the one, single race of the future . . . ."

The Hindus tolerate these traitors until almost the end of the voyage and then strangle them, throwing their naked bodies overboard so that they drift onto a Spanish beach as the armada heads for the south of France. The boat people have no need for guides of this kind, from a race that has lost all relevance:

"The Last Chance Armada, en route to the West, was feeding on hatred. A hatred of almost philosophical proportions, so utter, so absolute, that it had no thoughts of revenge, or blood, or death, but merely consigned its objects to the ultimate void. In this case, the whites. For the Ganges refugees, on their way to Europe, the whites had simply ceased to be."

Finally, on the morning of Easter Sunday, the 100 creaking hulks crash onto the beaches. The local inhabitants have abandoned all thought of taking in a family of Hindus, and have fled north. Many of the fashionable leftist agitators have likewise left their editorial jobs and radio programs and disappeared, with their gold bars, to Switzerland. The army has been sent south to prevent a landing, but there are doubts as to whether whites can be made to slaughter unarmed civilians.

As one government official explains to another, "[D]on't count on the army, monsieur. Not if you've got . . . genocide in mind."

The other replies: "Then it just means another kind of genocide . . . . Our own."

At the last moment the French President is unable to give the order to fire. He urges the troops to act according to their consciences. They throw down their rifles and run.

Bands of hippies and Christians, who have come south to welcome their brown brothers also turn and run as soon as they get a whiff of the new arrivals. "How could a good cause smell so bad?"

The few remaining whites with any sense of their civilization find they can communicate practically without speaking: "That was part of the Western genius, too: a mannered mentality, a collusion of aesthetes, a conspiracy of caste, a good-natured indifference to the crass and the common. With so few left now to share in its virtues, the current passed all the more easily between them."

A handful of citizens drive south with their hunting rifles on suicide missions to do the job their government is unable to do. One of these, ironically, is an assimilated Indian. As he explains to another band of citizen-hunters, "Every white supremacist cause—no matter where or when—has had blacks on its side. And they didn't mind fighting for the enemy, either. Today, with so many whites turning black, why can't a few 'darkies' decide to be white? Like me."

The Indian is killed, along with his white comrades, in an attack by fighter-bombers sent by the French government to put down resistance to the invasion. Soldiers who were unable to kill brown people make short work of "racist" whites.

All over France non-whites take the offensive. Algerians on assembly lines rise up and kill their white bosses. African street cleaners knock on the doors of de luxe Paris apartments and move in. A multiracial government, including a few token whites, announces a new dispensation.

Capitulation by the French means capitulation everywhere. Masses of ragged Chinese pour into Russia, whose troops are likewise unable to fire on hungry civilians. Huge fleets of beggars set sail from every pestilential southern port, heading for Europe, Australia, and New Zealand. The same drama unfolds In the United States. "Black would be black, and white would be white. There was no changing either, except by a total mix, a blend into tan. They were enemies on sight, and their hatred and scorn only grew as they came to know each other better." Americans lay down their arms just as the French do.

Raspail hints here and there at what the new Europe will be like: "At the time, each refugee quarter had its stock of white women, all free for the taking. And perfectly legal. (One of the new regime's first laws, in fact. In order to 'demythify' the white woman, as they put it.)"

The first provisional government also has a Minister of Population—a French woman married to a black—to ensure a permanent solution to the race problem. After all: "Only a white woman can have a white baby. Let her choose not to conceive one, let her choose only nonwhite mates, and the genetic results aren't long in coming."

And so ends the saga of Western man, not in pitched battle, not in defeat at the hands of superior forces, but by capitulation.

Even after a quarter century, the novel is astonishingly current. It was written before Communism collapsed, and the new French revolution is spiced with anti-capitalist slogans that now sound slightly off-key. One might also complain that a few of the characters verge on caricature. Nevertheless, the central tragedy—suicidal white weakness—is brilliantly portrayed and could have been written in 1995.

Mr. Raspail obviously loves his culture and his race, and wrote in the afterward that although he had intended to end the book with a spasm of white self-consciousness that saves Europe, the final catastrophe seemed to write itself. Perhaps he could not, in good faith, write a different ending. In the preface to the 1985 French edition he observed:

"[T]he West is empty, even if it has not yet become really aware of it. An extraordinarily inventive civilization, surely the only one capable of meeting the challenges of the third millennium, the West has no soul left. At every level—nations, race, cultures as well as individuals—it is always the soul that wins the decisive battles."

The Camp of the Saints puts the white man's dilemma in the most difficult terms: slaughter hundreds of thousands of women and children or face oblivion. Of course, a nation that had the confidence to shed blood in the name of its own survival would never be put to such a test; no mob of beggars would threaten it.

The story that Mr. Raspail tells—the complete collapse of Western man even when the very survival of his civilization so clearly hangs in the balance—may seem implausible to some. And yet, what whites do in *The Camp of the Saints* is no different from what they have done every day for the past forty years. The only difference is that the novel moves in fast forward; it covers in months what could take decades.

Whites all around the world suffer from Mr. Raspail's "monstrous cancer implanted in the Western conscience." South Africans vote for black rule. Americans import millions of nonwhites and grant them racial preferences. Australians abandon their whites-only immigration policy and become multicultural.

Even if he did not actively cooperate in his own destruction, time works against the white man. As Mr. Raspail writes in the afterward, "the proliferation of other races dooms our race, my race, irretrievably to extinction in the century to come, if we hold fast to our present moral principles." No other race subscribes to these moral principles—if that is really what they are—because they are weapons of self-annihilation.

Mr. Raspail's powerful, gripping novel is a call to all whites to rekindle their sense of race, love of culture, and pride in history—for he knows that without them we will disappear.

This review appeared in the June 1995 issue.

Closed Minds Are an Open Book

Roberto Suro, *Strangers Among Us: How Latino Immigration is Transforming America*, Alfred A. Knopf, 1998, 349 pp., $26.95

reviewed by Thomas Jackson

This book's premise is all in the subtitle: Hispanic immigration is transforming the United States. But unlike the countless books and articles that would have us celebrate transformation, *Strangers Among Us* sounds the alarm. Hispanic immigration is causing big problems and they are getting worse:

"[T]he outcome [of how we handle these new immigrants] will determine whether the nation's cities work or whether they burn."

"Latino immigration could become a powerful demographic engine of social fragmentation, discord, and even violence."

Because of the surging number of Hispanics, "the size of America's underclass will quickly double and in the course of a generation it will double again."

"The choice [of making immigration a success] is still possible, but the opportunity is rapidly disappearing."

So, do we have here another Peter Brimelow-style argument for restriction? Well, no. Roberto Suro, a half Puerto Rican-half Ecuadorean reporter for the *Washington Post* says that the crisis is proof we are *neglecting* the millions of Hispanics now pouring into the United States. It is to spur us to ever-greater acts of liberalism that he describes the failures of Hispanic immigration and the dangers that loom ahead.

This is a risky game for a liberal to play. The very picture of Hispanic failure Mr. Suro paints in the name of better schools, more jobs, more effective assimilation, etc. is the very one a restrictionist would use to argue that Third World immigration should stop right now. This book, therefore, is built around a gaping logical flaw. It is a readable, honestly-drawn, sometimes agonized portrait of the major Hispanic immigrant groups in the United States, but not once does it consider the most obvious solution to the problem of Hispanic immigration: end it. It is like discovering that the house has a leaky roof, and then devising ingenious and complicated ways to channel the water around the furniture and away from the clothes closets. Why not just fix the roof?

Mr. Suro, like so many others, seems to think Hispanic immigration is an irresistible force of nature like an earthquake or hurricane. We can prepare for it and try to deal with its consequences but there is no hope of stopping it. Indeed, the last words of the book's first chapter, in which Mr. Suro introduces the problem, are "they will keep coming."

Portaits of People

Most of the book is a report of what Mr. Suro has found while roaming, notebook in hand, among his fellow Hispanics. But he has also done some research, and keeps dropping interesting little facts into the narrative: During one 15-year period, half of the entire population of the town of San Cristobal, Guatemala, moved to Houston. The fertility of Hispanics is three times that of other groups, and Hispanic mothers have even less education than blacks. The average California household headed by a native pays $1,178 per year in state and local taxes to pay for services for immigrants, legal and illegal. Three quarters of immigrants from Mexico never made it through high school.

Mr. Suro is a good reporter and his portraits are vivid. The only trouble is that what he shows is not what most people want for America.

What most disappoints Mr. Suro is the downward mobility of so many Hispanics. Other immigrants start out the with a substantial income gap compared to natives, which they narrow over time. Not Hispanics. Their gap widens.

The first generation often has a stolid, peasant work ethic and is grateful to trade the hard scrabble life south of the border for a minimum-wage job and a garage converted into an apartment. The children are different: "With no memory of the rancho [subsistence farm], they have no reason to be thankful for escaping it. They look at their parents and all they see is toil and poverty."

Disaffected children go on to assimilate the worst of America—essentially black behavior. Many, says Mr. Suro, are "racing ahead of their parents in absorbing American ways but are turning into unemployable delinquents as a result." He regretfully describes one young U. S. citizen this way: "He could have remained in Mexico and become a very different person, but now, like the rest of the night people [who hang around the barrio doing nothing], he walked a walk and talked a talk that had been largely plagiarized from the black ghetto."

Central Americans share the same fate. Many of them "learned how to become gang bangers from their Mexican and Mexican-American neighbors who had been at it for a long time . . . ." Mr. Suro concludes that "the chances for downward mobility are greatest for second-generation youths who live in close proximity to American minorities . . . ."

And so it is that in many Hispanic communities, every succeeding generation is less likely to graduate from high school or get a job, and more likely to run drugs, go to jail, have illegitimate children or go on welfare. Not surprisingly, some parents and grandparents now regret coming to a country that has turned their sons and daughters into thugs and whores. A few, says Mr. Suro, are even going home, where they will be poor but will have children they can be proud of.

The least successful Hispanic immigrants have been Puerto Ricans, many of whom have not even managed to rise much above the level of life back in the Third World. In New York, many live on vacant lots in thrown-together shacks just like the ones they left behind: "Men with no work sit and play dominoes and tend little gardens as if they were back on their island and the whole migration had simply taken them back to where they were fifty years ago." New York's Puerto Ricans are actually worse off than the city's blacks. They are more likely to be on welfare, and only 50 percent have a high school diploma (as opposed to 66 percent for blacks.)

Mr. Suro marvels at how quickly Hispanics degenerated to the point that during the 1992 Los Angeles riots after the first verdict in the Rodney King beating case, more Hispanics than blacks were arrested for arson and looting. "L.A's blacks had taken a journey of centuries—from Africa, through slavery, out of the rural South, and into urban poverty—to reach that kind of rage," he writes. "The Latinos who took to the streets had accumulated enough bitterness to reach critical mass in less than a decade." As a young man in South Central Los Angeles explained to him, "To most people here, this is still a foreign place that belongs to someone else."

Indeed, Hispanic immigration cannot help but keep foreigners foreign. Most are a different race from the majority. They come in large numbers and create ghettos. They can easily go home and revive nationalist sentiments. The Dominicans of New York, says Mr. Suro, are just one more typical group. They never considered the United States their home, and the 330,000 that had piled into New York City by 1990 went through "the classic process of assimilation, but in a downward cycle."

(A study that came out after this book was published puts the current Dominican population in New York at 500,000. From 1989 to 1996, the Dominican per capita income dropped 23 percent in inflation-adjusted terms to $6,094, and the poverty rate rose from 37 to 46 percent. The Dominican Republic is sending losers to America. The ones who come are half as likely to have a college education as the ones who stay. Within just two years there could well be 700,000 Dominicans in New York City.)

Mr. Suro is not even satisfied with the Cubans of Miami. He rightly describes them as the richest Hispanic enclave in the United States—a barrio with country clubs—but "it remains a place apart from the rest of the country." And poverty alone does not explain why Hispanics are separate: "Rich Latinos remain ambivalent toward America just as much as poor ones. In fact, wealth may make it even easier to avoid full engagement with the new land . . . ." Mr. Suro quotes one of the gilded young men who attend a snooty private school for upper-crust Miami Cubans: "Our parents had to hassle with Anglo society, be we don't. This is our city."

Mr. Suro notes that Hispanics have not closed ranks with blacks to fight for "equality," and other redistributive schemes. He finds that Hispanics don't like blacks, and complain that they are lazy and crime-prone. All this is disappointing to him but he concedes that the historic experience of Hispanics is different from that of blacks and thinks this may explain why there is no rainbow coalition: "The logic and the mechanism of civil rights law developed as a solution to the plight of African-Americans, and it was never particularly well suited to Latinos."

Mr. Suro reluctantly acknowledges that race is the great divide. Even when they are forced to live close to blacks, most Hispanics try to ignore them. The only real exceptions are the young men—who fight them. They "call themselves raza and march forward as ethnic Mexicans to do battle against American blacks." If anything, Hispanics seem even more likely than blacks to form gangs, and turf battles are small-scale race wars.

"Solutions"

So, what is to be done about Hispanic immigration. Though Mr. Suro thinks white America has not done enough to assimilate new immigrants, he cannot deny that Hispanics are largely responsible for their persistent status as outsiders: "[T]his country's Latinos must answer a basic question about who they want to be." Mr. Suro very much wants them to be Americans and is pained that they remain so alien. He wants them to learn English, and he even wants them to oppose illegal immigration—to put respect for American law over ethnic solidarity.

Mr. Suro admits that he is asking Hispanics to "put the whole question of group identity in a new light." They must think of themselves as Americans with a stake in an English-speaking country with Anglo-Saxon institutions. Then they will oppose illegal immigration and turn their backs on south-of-the-border kinfolk who keep sneaking into the country.

But is this possible? Mr. Suro concedes that "more than half of the entire Latino foreign-born population of the United States has had some direct experience of illegality." He notes that many neighborhoods and even households are a mix of legals and illegals. How realistic is it to think Hispanics are going to repudiate their friends, co-workers, or even family just because they don't happen to have papers?

Moreover, Mr. Suro completely ignores the *reconquista* element of Hispanic immigration, the zealots who want to "retake" the Southwest and drive out whites. The last thing these people will do is think of themselves as "Americans."

Therefore, Mr. Suro's "solution" to the problem of Hispanic immigration—more liberalism and an effort by Hispanics to renounce their ethnicity—is pure fantasy. Americans are tired of uplift programs that don't work, and the past 40 years have shown how illusory is the idea of a race-unconscious America. One might take Mr. Suro more seriously if he added to these recommendations a call for a halt to further Hispanic immigration. But, no. He looks forward to more and more. Anyone who suggests that Hispanics are going to set aside race and foreign loyalties while yet more millions march into the country has either fooled himself or is trying to fool his readers.

This book, therefore, is an excellent example of the incoherence that characterizes any social question that touches on race. Mr. Suro could hardly be more compelling when he describes the failure and degeneracy that has often followed Hispanic immigration.

After detailing the dead-end lives of so many Puerto Rican immigrants, he returns to his central theme:

"Like the Puerto Ricans, many of today's Latino newcomers arrive with little education and not much in the way of technological job skills. The main difference is one of scale. The Puerto Rican migration was small enough so that the primary victims of the disaster were the Puerto Ricans themselves. Today's Latino migration is so much larger and more widespread that the entire nation will suffer grievously if the Puerto Rican fate is repeated."

There is one sure way to avoid more suffering: Stop the immigration. This is so obvious that not even intellectuals and policy-makers can fail to see it. But until Americans can shake off the mental paralysis that falsifies every discussion of race and immigration, they will be unable to take the most basic steps necessary to save their country.

This article appeared in the August 1998 issue.

Towards Renewal and Renaissance
by Fr. James Thornton

I am greatly honored to have been invited to address this assembly of men and women who seek some deliverance from the contemporary dilemma surrounding the question of race. This question has bedeviled our poor country for the better part of two centuries, and has brought about in our history expenditures in human lives and treasure of tragic proportions. Of late, it threatens thoroughly to overwhelm us and transform this nation, totally and permanently, into a national and social entity radically dissimilar from that represented by the past four hundred years of our history.

We have come to think it curious that a committed Christian would have an opinion on the subject of race not consonant with the prevailing and rather rigorously invoked view, and would express that personal opinion in a public forum. For in these closing years of the twentieth century, Christianity has come to be looked upon by some as a religion for the fainthearted and the perfidious, as a kind of fifth column within our European culture, and as one of the seeds of European man's own destruction. Needless to say, I do not agree with that view.

Yet, I would be the first to admit that among those who call themselves "Christians," and especially within the leadership councils of certain official, mainstream, ostensibly Christian groups, there are multitudes of spiritual charlatans and cultural Bolsheviks. Just as the early Church was disturbed by heretical offshoots that amalgamated elements of Christianity with some of the more bizarre forms of paganism, so in our day do we witness the proliferation of heretical, sectarian modes of thought. These are perfectly described by the Russian Orthodox philosopher and sociologist Pitirim Sorokin in these words:

". . . a wild concoction of a dozen various 'Social Gospels,' diversified by several beliefs of Christianity diluted by those of Marxism, Democracy, and Theosophy, enriched by a dozen vulgarized philosophical ideas, corrected by several scientific theories, peacefully squatting side by side with the most atrocious magical superstitions."

What he refers to, of course, is the World Council of Churches kind of Christianity—that artificial, ideological, politically correct substitute for the original product. It is, indeed, the very antithesis of traditional Christianity.

I contend that our magnificent European culture, stretching across the North American continent eastward through Europe to the Urals (and incorporating some outlying areas such as Australia and New Zealand), is one of the matchless and wonderful gifts of Christianity, of Christian teaching, of Christian civilization. We need only think for a moment of buildings such as Notre Dame, Chartres, Justinian's Hagia Sophia, San Marco in Venice, San Vitale and Sant' Apollinare in Ravenna, and Dormition and Annunciation Cathedrals in Moscow; works of architecture of matchless beauty; buildings, all of them, that still, even in this age of skyscrapers, produce gasps of awe from those blessed to visit them.

We need only think, too, of the literature of the Christian European peoples—Dante, Shakespeare, Milton, Cervantes, Schiller, Goethe, Dostoyevsky—of the music—Bach, Handel, Mozart, Beethoven, Berlioz, Bruckner, Rachmaninoff—and of the great works of art—Fra Angelico, Titian, Raphael, Michelangelo, Dürer, Rembrandt, Rublev. I mention only a few names from each field. The point is that virtually all of the works of creative genius of the past 2,000 years, all that we admire as monuments of European high culture, all of those things that nurture the spirits of refined men and women, come from Christian civilization.

Pre-Christian, ancient Mediterranean civilization, with its own great accomplishments in philosophy, law, sculpture, architecture, and so forth, had by the second century of the Christian Era reached an impasse. The tremendous edifice erected by the ancients was rapidly crumbling by then, and was in danger of being lost forever. But this did not happen. Christianity took dying Greco-Roman civilization, perfected and transformed it to a remarkable degree, and imparted new life to it. In the West this was done under the auspices of barbarian tribes who very slowly absorbed aspects of the dying pagan civilization they found, and who, though they possessed no real understanding of this civilization for a long time, after some centuries of comparative darkness gave birth to Western European civilization.

In the East the process was different. The Empire, and Greco-Roman civilization, lived on under New Rome, under Constantinople. What took place there was, in the words of the renowned scholar Father Georges Florovsky, "a conversion of the Hellenic mind and heart" or, to put it another way, the "Christianization of Hellenism." And the achievements of the resulting Eastern European Christian civilization—first in Byzantium and then in Old Russia—are incomparable. So Christianity, far from the "culture destroyer" or "culture distorter" of Nietzsche, et al., was a premier culture preserver and profound culture creator. Both in the Eastern and Western halves of Europe, civilization and culture sprang forth from Christianity; they *are* Christian.

What interests us here today is the culture sickness that seems to have infected European mankind over the whole of the globe, a sickness that seems slowly to be pulling us downward towards some terrible void. It is only by understanding this larger sickness that we can begin to grasp the dimensions of the peculiarly racial sickness that is the subject of this gathering.

I suggest that we have come to this melancholy state precisely because the old traditions of European Christian civilization have been lost. Were Christianity as vital today as, say, 1,000 years ago, or 500 years ago, or even 150 years ago, the state of affairs in which we now find ourselves would be impossible. What brought us to this unhappy condition? Why is the way of life of our American and European forebears dissolving around us?

Many men have analyzed this question; to name only a few, Juan Donoso Cortés, Friedrich Nietzsche, Konstantine Pobiedonostev, Jacob Burckhardt, Oswald Spengler, José Ortega y Gasset, and the twentieth-century American Richard Weaver. All grasped that our way of life was at grave risk, that those concepts and ideals which we value so highly were in danger.

Insofar as precise diagnosis is concerned, many would disagree with the others. Some were Christians and some were not. Nietzsche contended that Christianity had exhausted itself and that a new system of morality should replace it, for the sake of the survival of civilization. Spengler believed that the fate of Europe was inevitable, that European man had lived out his natural, allotted span of time and now must face his doom. Others, like Sorokin, held out the hope that civilization might regenerate itself through a spiritual awakening and live on for many hundreds of years to come. I will not argue the precise merits of each of these points of view, though I will now briefly discuss a few of them.

In re-reading the nineteenth-century Swiss historian Jacob Burckhardt's *Reflections on History*, I was struck by his extraordinary insights into the pathologies that were then beginning to attack European civilization. Those pathologies are no different today, though they have advanced to a critical stage. Those familiar with Burckhardt know that he speaks of the interaction within societies between three primary institutions: Church, State, and Culture. The terms Church and State require no definition, but Burckhardt's use of the word Culture requires some elucidation.

Culture, in Burckhardt's scheme, is very broad and encompasses just about everything not included in the first two. In Burckhardt's words, "[culture's] total external form . . . , as distinguished from the State and religion, is society in its broadest sense." Now, history after the rise of Christianity is the record of a long rivalry between Church and State. Both tend, however, to be very conservative forces and, though they compete for power, both inhibit Culture, which tends to be revolutionary. The most revolutionary of the forces within Culture is money-making, that is, the economy.

From the time of Constantine until the French Revolution, Church and State acted successfully to keep Culture circumscribed, particularly its money-making component. Since the time of the French Revolution, the prestige of both Church and State have suffered and Culture has broken free, so to speak. The State has now become the instrument of Culture, and to some extent the Church too. Economic Man, in both his capitalistic and Marxian incarnations, sits triumphant, bestriding the whole globe.

Burckhardt writes, "We need not wish ourselves back into the Middle Ages, but we should try to understand them. Our life is a business, theirs was living. The people as a totality hardly existed, but that which was of the people flourished." He goes on to warn of "the vast increase in the power of the State over the individual, which may even lead to the complete abdication of the individual, more especially where money-making predominates to the exclusion of everything else, ultimately absorbing all initiative." And, ponder these prophetic words from Burckhardt: "Money-making, the main force of present-day culture, postulates the universal State, if only for the sake of communications . . . ." To Burckhardt, unrestrained money-making, the obsession with materialism, the "bourgeoisification" of the spirit of European man, are dangerous things.

So long as Church, State, and Culture interacted with one another in an organic fashion, curbing one another and thereby holding back certain darker human proclivities, then our European civilization remained essentially healthy. Once these institutions were uncoupled from one another, thanks to the forces loosed by the Enlightenment, the foundations of the structure of our civilization began to disintegrate.

Contemplate, for a moment, the reality of contemporary television, radio, films, entertainment, music, advertising, painting, sculpture, and so on—all powerful elements of a culture without restraints. Consider how our present culture sickness undermines the authority of the traditions of society, of family, of morality, of religion, of nation, of language. Rightly is it said that the great crisis of our age is a crisis of the breakdown of authority. Our modern commercial, hedonistic society denies the father authority over his family, the parent authority over his child, the law authority over miscreants, the priest authority over his flock, the Church authority over sinners, man authority over the living things of the Earth, and God authority over His creation.

More than likely, such propensities are intrinsic characteristics of the commercial way of thinking that makes money the king of all and the final arbiter of right and wrong, that atomizes the community, that transforms citizens into consumers and units of production. They are innate in an economic-rationalist mode of thought that teaches that materialistic self-interest is the engine of human history and human society, that holds that men do live by bread alone.

If money is king and money-making the ultimate criterion, if materialistic self-interest is the engine of history, if men do live by bread alone, then what utility is there in the preservation of the unique civilization of European man? Does not some sort of "global village" with a world culture make far more economic sense? The more uniform the habits, tastes, and mores of the peoples of the world, the easier to do business, the easier for some to make money.

It is expressive of our current predicament that such discourse as is now allowed in the matter of Third-World immigration to North America revolves exclusively around economic arguments—the economic advantages or disadvantages of immigration. A young American, supposedly a conservative, recently told me that he does not believe that Third-World immigration is a problem and that if we can simply stimulate the economy to grow more quickly, such growth will solve all concerns about immigration. Would that the things of this world were that easy!

"The American Dream"

Today, terms such as "the American Way of Life" and "the American Dream" are almost exclusively associated with a successful business mentality; they are formulated in materialistic, even hedonistic, terms. That type of thinking dominates our nation, and much of today's world. Ask even most modern "conservatives" in America and Europe what they stand for, and the glories of our economic system and our prosperity will form the dessicated heart and soul of their ideological analysis—the so-called conservative philosophy will be shot through with materialism, although there is nothing conservative in the commercial *Weltanschauung*. By its very nature, the unfettered money-making mentality tends always to wreak havoc on traditional relationships within society, the traditional hierarchy and patriarchy of European custom, the traditional family, traditional religion and morality, and the traditional ways of life.

Is it any wonder, since successful money-making has become the ultimate criterion for our society, that education has become a kind of glorified job training and that to make education into job training, traditional curricula—from classical languages and history to philosophy and great literature—have been largely abandoned? One can become prosperous with an MBA, but probably not with an MA in classical Greek or Ancient History.

Is it any wonder that entertainment, literature, films, and the like have become the domain of degenerates whose products flow straight to our youth from moral and intellectual cesspits? There are vast sums of dollars to be made from such cultural sewage, and men become rich thereby. Since becoming rich is considered the supremely admirable quality these days, such men are admired above all others.

Is it any wonder that rock "music" has supplanted nearly all other musical forms? Rock "music" and its multiform appurtenances, are the very quintessence of decadence. Rock music celebrates primitiveness, is soddened in nihilism, and luxuriates in barren, loveless sexuality. It is a musical lowest common denominator and so possesses colossal appeal today. Such music generates huge revenues, so much so that it is one of America's great export products. More importantly, perhaps, it represents the negation of genuine musical culture, which draws its inspiration from particular national cultures, and represents its replacement with the artificial, rootless, pseudo-culture of internationalism. It is the perfect music for the new world order, the perfect accompaniment for life in a "global village."

Is it any wonder that illegal drugs are a source of spreading chaos and tremendous pain in contemporary American and European societies? I believe that it may be declared with confidence that our current money-oriented society will never take decisive action against the drug barons at home and abroad who have done so much to corrupt our society in the past thirty-five years. The corruption already touches the upper echelons of both major political parties, and so apart from certain gestures and political posturing about the issue, nothing will be done.

Finally, is it any wonder that enjoyment of the "good life" by most ordinary citizens necessitates such drastic limitations on family size that in virtually every nation of the European world, birthrates have fallen considerably below replacement level? Thanks to money-mindedness and hedonism, we are a dying breed.

If obsession with money and the commercial worldview have brought us near collapse, it can come as no surprise that, with regard to questions surrounding America's racial dilemma, short-term economic considerations supersede all other considerations. When one contemplates the kind of well-ordered society we had 50, or 60, or 80 years ago, the conclusion is inescapable that for primarily the economic enrichment of certain groups and individuals, the country is being systematically strip-mined, culturally speaking.

Rightly did Solzhenitsyn speak of our heritage being trampled upon by the party mob in the East and the commercial mob in the West. This is sensed by many ordinary citizens who for good reason feel threatened by the societal revolution that has overtaken us in the past forty years. Whatever hope we have seems to reside with ordinary Americans, especially those of the lower middle-class who no longer enjoy so great a measure of material prosperity as heretofore. Though they are confused by a continual spate of propaganda from the mass media, nevertheless they know in their hearts—at the deeper levels of their consciousness—the source of their gathering troubles. To bring these people to a realization of their priceless Christian European heritage, and its source, is therefore essential for the resurrection of this country and of the West.

Healthy Cultures

I wish here briefly to mention another diagnostician of our current time of troubles, the sociologist Pitirim Sorokin. Sixty years ago, Sorokin wrote that healthy cultures are integrated unities. Art, architecture, music, literature, philosophy, ethics, morals, government, and religion are all interrelated with one another. Useful elements may be drawn from foreign cultures, so long as they do not contradict the unity of the host culture, and so long as they are modified and digested, so as to become wholly a part of that unity.

Until relatively recently, our own European culture was just such a unity, consistent throughout the multiplicity of its elements. Drawing that which is valuable from other cultures (for instance, Hindu-Arabic numerals), it digested these things, so that they became completely part of its unity. The values of this healthy culture were still strong, its creativity still vigorous, its "soul" still undefiled. That which was intrinsically contradictory it rejected, since, as a healthy entity, it was highly selective and discriminatory.

Now, however, the picture has changed. Our society is no longer healthy, but is sick or perhaps dying. While still robust, still believing in itself, its genius created a grand civilization. This creativity, however, has now been lost. It can no longer discriminate between the useful and dangerous, and, consequently, everything pours in and takes root in our unhealthy culture, often to the exclusion of the healthy, formerly unified elements.

As the flood of undigested, foreign elements becomes greater and greater, the host culture becomes more distorted, more sickly, and less able to protect itself. Thus, the host culture undergoes disintegration, at times more slowly and at other times more rapidly. We may observe all of this in our contemporary culture which, in its variety of undigested elements, is utterly astonishing. Literally everything and anything can be found within it, each loudly competing for our attention and allegiance. All possess "rights" equal to those of every other, and all enjoy equal tolerance by society. Between that which is venerable and native, and that which is new and foreign, there are absolutely no distinctions. So it is with a society that has lost faith in the source of its greatness; so it is when a living ideal no longer exists to inspire it.

Interestingly, Richard Weaver writes similarly in his book, *Visions of Order*. He observes that the spirit of a culture "always operates positively by transfiguring and excluding. It is of the essence of culture to feel its own imperative and to believe in the uniqueness of its worth. . . . Syncretistic cultures like syncretistic religions have always proved relatively powerless to create and influence. . . . Culture derives its very desire to continue from its unitariness."

I have given you some thoughts, borrowed from some great thinkers of the nineteenth and twentieth centuries, touching on one or two aspects of our crisis. I have striven to show that the racial dilemma does not exist in isolation, but is part of a whole matrix in which we are bound, which is itself the consequence of evil choices made by our forebears long ago.

I wish now to say a few words specifically on the question of race. One of the most valuable sociological attributes of traditional Christianity since its founding two thousand years ago has been its recognition that human beings are not equal. Christianity, it is quite true, holds that all men are equal when standing before the throne of God at the Last Judgment. But, apart from that, the doctrine that human beings are, or should be, equal in a worldly sense appears nowhere in Christian teaching. That human beings are intellectually equal, or that such differences as do exist in individuals or groups are rooted, for example, in economic deprivation, would have been preposterous notions to most traditional Christian thinkers and teachers of past ages. That all cultures or peoples of the world are equally suitable as bearers of high Christian civilization would have been a laughable proposition to these men.

No, traditional Christianity believes that healthy societies are socially diverse and that a healthy society is organized hierarchically, with different orders and classes and with the differing material conditions and privileges appropriate to those orders and classes. We see this in the very organization of the Church itself, with its many distinct levels: clergy and laity; Archbishops, Bishops, Archpriests, Priests, Deacons, Subdeacons, and so forth. The levels of responsibility attained correspond to the special God-given gifts of each, in accordance with the needs of the Church. Certainly, that elaborate, consciously hierarchical organization, entwined by the symbols of sacred mystery and blessed by the Church, is evident in every Christian society, from that of Constantine and Justinian all the way down through the centuries to that of Nicholas II. It was true in Western Europe as well as Eastern Europe.

The Fathers of the Church taught that just as the spiritual world is organized hierarchically, so too should be the earthly world; any other kind of societal structure was regarded as something demonic, in that it promotes spiritual and societal disorder. The Fathers believed that God abhors chaos, that in a Christian society the earthly order should properly reflect the heavenly order, and that egalitarianism and rule by the mob—that is, rule according to the whims and lusts of the herd—are injurious to the morals of Christians and to the fabric of the Christian community. Clearly, if the Christian ideal is that human society is constituted in aristocratic, hierarchical fashion, and if this kind of constitution is regarded as something of divine origin, so it is implicit in such theories of organization that men are not created equal insofar as their innate abilities are concerned. Christianity is clearly not a religion of earthly egalitarianism.

Our own country is rooted in a somewhat different philosophical tradition, but even here no objective scholar would dispute that the Founders of this nation, most of whom were Christians, did not believe in the inherent equality of individual men or of races, apart from the idea that free men should be equal in the eyes of the law. In no other sense were men born equal. Certain it is that insofar as this country was traditional in its religious beliefs, it strongly believed in the superiority of its European-derived way of life. There could be no question of overthrowing that order.

John Baker, in his volume, *Race*, suggests that a marked sense of racial differences has existed in mankind for thousands of years, certainly during all of recorded history, and very likely in pre-historic times. Italian sociologist Corrado Gini writes similarly, showing how all ethnic or racial groups exhibit a strong consciousness of human ethnic differences with a preference for their own. Today, some, most notably Marxists and liberals, may decry this inclination which seems to be intrinsic to human nature, yet it is nonetheless an indisputable fact of man's existence. Towards the Canaanites, the ancient Hebrews showed, as Baker puts it, a "marked disrespect." Virtually all outsiders, according to the reckoning of the ancient Greeks, were barbarians. Even among certain primitive tribes of Africa, there is evidently a belief that some of the even more primitive tribes are inferior. Until fairly recently, especially the last fifty or sixty years, these facts did not appear to trouble Christians.

Everyone here probably has some familiarity (directly or indirectly) with the writings of Joseph Arthur, Comte de Gobineau. Gobineau, in his *Essay on the Inequality of the Human Races* makes clear that he believes that different races of men have been blessed by God with different attributes and that certain races of men are exclusively responsible for the creation and maintenance of high culture and civilization. The important matter for me is that this author was a devout Christian, and accepted as a matter of course that, a) men, and ethnic groups of men, are not equal in their inherent abilities, and, b) that all men, from the most noble to the most primitive, have within themselves a divine spark, the *Imago Dei*, that entitles each to the special dignity reserved for children of God. Each is unique in his abilities, in the gifts that God has bestowed on him—and this is true also of ethnic groups—but all are human and all possess a dignity appropriate to humankind.

In Gobineau's own words, "I believe, of course, that human races are unequal; but I do not think that any of them are like the brute, or to be classed with it." To the theory that some human races are simply bipedal beasts, Gobineau responds: "I absolutely reject such an insult to humanity . . . ." Though some of his friends and some other writers disagreed with him, Comte de Gobineau was never chastised by his Church for his widely published belief in the inequality of the human races. So far as I can determine, he remained a faithful communicant of the Roman Catholic religion until his death in 1882.

Alexis Carrel, author of one of the most widely read works of nonfiction in the 1930s and 1940s, *Man the Unknown*, was also a devout Roman Catholic. Carrel was a surgeon and biologist, who won the Nobel Prize for physiology and medicine in 1912, and the Nordhoff-Jung Prize for Cancer Research in 1931. Reading *Man the Unknown*, it is clear that the author entertains no notion of the equality of the human races. He writes: "Man is the hardiest of all animals, and the white races, builders of our civilization, the hardiest of all races. . . . The great white races owe their success to the perfection of their nervous system—a nervous system which, although very delicate and excitable, can, however, be disciplined. To the exceptional qualities of their tissues and consciousness is due the predominance over the rest of the world of the peoples of western Europe . . . ."

This forthright statement caused not the slightest ripple of controversy when it was published in 1935, nor did it do so in subsequent editions of his book published even in the immediate postwar years. As recently as that, men seemed able to discuss and debate things, and to disagree with one another, without resorting to hyperbole, *ad hominem* attacks, hysteria, and defamatory labelling. Intelligent men were still able to focus their minds on facts and issues and to think and express themselves rationally. In the 1960s, Father Joseph T. Durkin, S.J., honored the memory of Carrel in his highly laudatory biography entitled *Hope For Our Time*, in which he discusses Carrel's deep religious faith. Dr. Carrel, he writes, was a Christian believer through and through, though at times rather singular in his expressed opinions.

My third example is the Russian Orthodox sociologist and philosopher, Pitirim Sorokin, from whom I have already drawn several quotations. On the last page of Part One of John Baker's book, *Race,* the author pays special tribute to Sorokin for a chapter on the racial question in Sorokin's work, *Contemporary Sociological Theories,* which appeared in 1928. About this work, Baker writes that, "Sorokin's chapter is well worth reading today, as a reminder of what was still possible before the curtain came down."

In this work, as well as in an earlier work entitled *Social and Cultural Mobility,* Sorokin discourses at considerable length on differences in cognitive ability between Europeans and some non-Europeans. Considering about twenty-five separate studies of the subject of IQ and race that had been completed and published up to the middle of the 1920s, Sorokin concludes that, "the difference in the cultural contributions and in the historical role played by different races is excellently corroborated by, and is in perfect agreement with, the experimental studies of race mentality and psychology." That heredity is a crucial factor in the development of complex forms of civilization, Sorokin asserts, "may scarcely be questioned by any serious investigator of facts."

I have mentioned two prominent Roman Catholics and one Orthodox Christian. I shall also briefly mention a Protestant Christian, Thomas Carlyle. One of the great essayists and historians of the last century, Carlyle was a Calvinist. In his early years he served as a minister of the Scottish Kirk, and though he later gave up the ministry in disagreement with certain of the dogmatic pronouncements of his Calvinist ancestors, it is written that "he was and always remained in profound sympathy with the spirit of their teachings." Anyone who knows the essays of Thomas Carlyle knows also that he was not a believer in the equality of the human races. In fact, he wrote somewhat harshly on the subject.

Inasmuch as he wrote on this subject at the end of the first half of the nineteenth century, perhaps his thinking is not so remarkable. Nearly all educated men, Christian or non-Christian, believed similarly at that time. But the point is that, insofar as I am aware, the published beliefs of Carlyle were not condemned at the time by the leaders of his Church. Nor, in this century, have the published beliefs of Drs. Carrel or Sorokin been condemned by the leaders of their respective Churches.

It may be argued that the evidence I have just presented is purely anecdotal and that Christian spokesmen representing the opposite viewpoint could also be assembled. Doubtless that is true. But my response to that must be that scientific findings with regard to the equality or inequality of human beings in cognitive ability in fact is not a subject on which there exists any Christian dogmatic teaching whatsoever. Those mainline sectarian groups that have attempted to create such dogma in recent years represent not authentic traditional Christianity, but a blend of decadent, rationalized Protestantism and Marxism.

With respect to what I have just said, I must also add a caveat that the formulation of secular, procrustean ideologies based on race, especially those that deny the innate dignity of all men, or promote the unjust or inhumane treatment of persons on account of their race, would indeed run contrary to Christian teachings and would rightly be opposed by traditional Christians.

Since the late nineteenth century, science has grappled with the subject of racial differences and, apart from pockets of inveterate ideologues within the scientific community, it is now generally acknowledged by scientists in relevant fields that the accumulated evidence has become overwhelming that such differences do exist. (It is interesting that in 1928, Sorokin regarded the evidence as overwhelming even then.) Findings related to genetically determined differences in intelligence and temperament among the various races of mankind are slowly coming to be accepted within scientific circles, despite formal and informal barriers now frantically being reared by Marxists, crypto-Marxists, ignorant journalists, and cowardly politicians.

In many so-called free countries of the West (in Canada and England, for example), it is now illegal (at least to some extent) to discuss such scientific findings publicly or to publish them in most periodicals or in books. In the United States, though it is not yet illegal, those who do muster the courage to discuss such findings publicly, often find themselves subject to informal sanctions; commonplace now is character assassination in articles printed in the daily press, written by uncouth journalists—those masters of inferential falsehood. Also commonplace are threats of physical violence against the person, family, and property of the politically incorrect speaker or writer, various kinds of mob actions, and, of course, threats to the person's livelihood.

Thought control thus comes in several forms: at one end of the spectrum we have the Gulag of the old USSR, at the other end the more informal processes of thought control favored in this country, and somewhere in between the harsh laws now in force in Europe and Canada. In any case, the Orwellian intent and thug mentality are identical, only the methods and degree differ slightly. And I would add it is questionable how much worse it is being confined to a concentration camp for a thought-crime (as in the old USSR), as opposed to being ruined financially and professionally, lied about in the press, unjustly held up to public ridicule, and subjected (along with one's family) to mob violence and terror for the same variety of thought-crime.

One would hope that in the journalistic profession a man of conscience and courage, a man of elementary decency, would occasionally step forward to remind his colleagues of their duty in a free country. Alas (though I can think of one or two exceptions) such men seem to be almost as scarce here as in Stalin or Brezhnev's Soviet Union. Liberal journalists and their political allies justify the evil they do by pretending that they oppose what they call (in the cant of our age) "hate," "prejudice," "racism" and the like.

The plain truth is, however, that their madness has generated a sociological disaster and human misery of appalling dimensions, in the cities of the United States, primarily among racial minorities—from whom, despite their endlessly repeated slogans, the liberal journalists and politicians assiduously shield and segregate themselves and their families. Their experiments threaten in the next century to generate horrors which, by comparison, will make our current difficulties seem trifling. "Great humanitarians," these men who think of human beings as laboratory specimens! May God protect us all from their further depredations!

Even to attempt to extricate ourselves from the morass in which we now sink will require a major miracle—the renewal of our courage and of our belief in the preeminence of our way of life. The civilization of the European peoples around the globe must return to its roots if it is to accomplish that miracle, if it is to save itself. Those roots are traditional Christianity. Father Joseph Koterski, in a recent article in *Modern Age*, states that all civilization arises out of religious belief, that culture comes from cult, and that a renewal of our commitment to traditional religion would be the "best strategy for the renewal of high culture amid the collapses of order now being experienced in a largely post-Christian era." I could not agree more.

Father Koterski goes on to make another important point: "But this is not to say with the skeptics that that high culture is itself the goal and religion a more or less convenient means. . . . Rather, culture itself has a further purpose: to enable human beings progressively to discover the deepest truth about themselves as human, that their real fulfillment resides in reverence for the Transcendent God in whose image they are made." The aim of religion is not the creation of culture, but the culture it creates assists religion in achieving its ultimate goal.

Grotesque attempts have been made to obviate the need for a return to traditional Christianity by the substitution of secular ideologies. Such attempts have been catastrophic. In the last century Nietzsche postulated a coming new moral system that would replace Christianity—such systems were attempted in this century and brought about an even more dramatic erosion of the position of European man and his civilization, as well as the deaths of tens of millions of human beings in wars and revolutions. Apart from traditional Christianity, there is no alternative path, in my judgment, which will lead us to the successful revitalization of our civilization. For 2,000 years the soul of European man has been Christian. Remove that soul, and we now know that European civilization becomes sterile and soon dies. European civilization is Christian. If we recognize that, we begin the mighty endeavor that will lead us to renewal and renaissance.

This article appeared in the August 1996 issue. It is the text of a speech given at the 1996 AR Conference, held in Louisville, Kentucky. Fr. James Thornton is a priest in the Greek Orthodox Church.

A Certain Trumpet
by Sam G. Dickson

The title of my remarks is drawn from *First Corinthians*, Chapter 14: "For if the note of the trumpet be uncertain, who shall prepare himself for the battle?" At this conference we have had speakers who have served as trumpeters, sounding a clear and certain note, and the battle to which the trumpet calls is likely to be the decisive one for our people.

As most of you know, the militant advocates of racial equivalence and racial integration tried to prevent this conference from taking place. It was their intention to prevent our ideas from being heard, and to keep in place an iron curtain sealing off any discussion of racial differences. Their campaign failed and, I would note, their failures have not been limited merely to one momentary failure here in Louisville. Their failures have been consistent.

When the theory of racial egalitarianism had not yet been put into practice, it did not have the disadvantage of a track record that could be examined to test the validity of their hypotheses. Thoughtful people—those who opposed the integration of the school systems in the 1950s and other subsequent proposals to force racial mixing—predicted correctly that these policies would fail. However, they had no examples to point to as proof of the inevitable failure of racial egalitarianism.

The advocates of integration had the advantage of a theory that appealed to human emotion and that promised to accomplish great things. We were told when the liberal program was in its infancy and was then called "desegregation," that if the races were mixed and white control of our society removed, poverty would be abolished. Blacks would rise to the academic levels of whites. Crime rates would drop. Schools would improve. As blacks were elevated academically, welfare would decline. Since the theory had not been put to the test, such prospects were very alluring.

Despite the warnings of such men as Lothrop Stoddard, Madison Grant and Carlton Putnam, the racial liberals had their way. They triumphed—temporarily, of course—but they triumphed. The policies they advocated have been implemented all across America, and indeed throughout the entire European world. In every case they have failed. Who can name an integrated community that has succeeded? Where has integration led to greater prosperity, higher academic standards, reduced welfare and less crime? "Success" exists only in the imaginations of liberals, who are always willing to try their failed experiments yet again.

It is perhaps significant that the liberals themselves speak of their policies as "experiments," yet they are unable to draw any lessons from the results. As each liberal program fails for the umpteenth time, the liberal diverts his gaze and focuses on the horizon where he sees his utopia hovering somewhere out there; where everyone of every race and hue will be exchanging comments in their bathrooms—as they do on television—over the wonders of respective brands of toothpaste or shampoo.

The fact that the liberal racial program has failed consistently for 40 years does not phase or deter the liberal. He remains convinced that he is only one more civil rights law, only one more government program, only one more Supreme Court decision away from reaching his dream. The liberal reasons: "It didn't work in Miami, but we are going to make it work in Jacksonville. Maybe it didn't work in Atlanta, but we are going to make it work in Louisville."

The only concession the liberal seems to make to the reality of his program's terrible record is that he cleverly gives the same policy different names. We note that the egalitarian product has been constantly repackaged, as the public comes to associate the name with its failed results. Thus does the name keep changing, from "desegregation" to "integration" to "multiculturalism" to "diversity."

What is truly appalling is how slow this country is to catch on to the failure of the experiment. It took the United States only about a decade to recognize that Prohibition was unworkable. Prohibition was correctly described by Herbert Hoover as "the noble experiment," but it failed. The country soon realized that the costs of Prohibition outweighed the benefits. And unlike desegregation/integration/multiculturalism/diversity, Prohibition could show some successes. Alcoholism and its attendant tragedies declined. Nevertheless, Americans by and large, after only one decade, recognized that the cost to society in the form of organized crime outweighed this benefit, and that Prohibition should be abandoned.

Today, Americans seem to be slow learners.

When the grip of the Communists began to slip in the Soviet Union a few years ago, opponents of that cruel system, who had previously been silenced by the secret police finally were able to demonstrate openly their disdain for the failed Marxist state. In the first anti-Communist demonstration in Red Square in Moscow, Russians marched with placards bearing a wise and clever slogan: "70 years on the road to Nowhere!"

I could not help but notice the absence of any similar slogan or demonstration here in the United States two years ago on the 40th anniversary of *Brown v. Board of Education*. Where were the demonstrators bearing signs reading, "40 years on the road to Nowhere!"?

One also wonders how it is that our people ever succumbed to the nonsense of racial equality. People have known the truth about race for centuries. They did not need the research of Arthur Jensen or Philippe Rushton. The truth about race was obvious to virtually all people until very recent times. Now is it not odd that the burden of proof has been shifted to us to prove a negative—that the races are not equal?

Two clear examples come to mind immediately to show how preposterous is the liberal position. The first is the evolution argument. Most liberals believe in evolution, as do I. Yet the position of a liberal who believes in evolution can be summed up as follows:

"After a period of hundreds of thousands of years, evolving under different climatic conditions, encountering different challenges such as the Ice Ages, suffering different epidemics, subjected to different catastrophes and good fortune, all races magically ended up equal."

It would appear unlikely and hard to believe that after such an enormous length of time and under such different circumstances every group would end up at the same point, but this is the theory the liberal has to sell to intelligent people. Astonishingly, they seem to buy it.

The other example of a liberal position that seems impossible to defend is the view that the human brain is the sole exception to the laws of heredity. It is now indisputable that heredity governs many facets of human life. It is admitted even by the liberal that heredity governs height, eye color, and hair color. The liberal will concede that heredity governs all forms of plant and animal life. Nor will it be disputed that it governs every organ of man—except for the human brain.

The egalitarian's position may be summarized as follows:

"All creation, including plant and animal life, is subject to the laws of heredity. Every organ of the human species is likewise governed by the laws of heredity. The human brain stands alone as the only object of creation whose functioning is unaffected by heredity and is controlled strictly by environment."

Amazingly, this goofy theory prevails in our greatest universities, and its opponents have to explain scientifically why such a preposterous theory is fallacious. And those who refute the theory of racial equality have to do so at the risk not only of their financial security, but sometimes even of their physical safety.

This situation has been brought about in part by the strategic use of guilt. The only people who outperform Christians in the business of guilt are liberals. And I will concede that when liberals decry the white race as the cancer of history, they are right about one thing: It was our race that gave the world liberalism and for that we should feel guilty.

White Racial Weaknesses

Our race has many fine qualities. We have given the world great things—a magnificent literature, incomparable music, the world's greatest architecture, the breakthroughs in science and medicine that have made humanity's lot so much better. But while we may take pride in the achievements of our race, we would be foolish not to recognize that our race also has its peculiar weaknesses.

We are already able to warn individuals of genetic susceptibilities they may carry. We will soon be able to determine, for instance, if a child has the genes that dispose him toward alcoholism or Alzheimer's disease. We would be similarly advised to look at ourselves to see if there are any peculiar weaknesses we have as a race that put our survival at risk. Specifically, we need to determine if there are any particular factors that make whites vulnerable to the preposterous but fatal theory of racial equality and even equivalence—the theory that whites could be displaced, without much loss, by people of any other race.

One notes at the outset a peculiar phenomenon—the more gifted and well educated a European is, the more likely he is to succumb to this fantasy. It is a commonplace observation that the average truck driver in America has a far better understanding of race than the average professor. Anyone who has talked with cab drivers in London knows that they have a much better grasp of racial problems in England than does Prince Charles with his Cambridge education.

We can partly excuse the academic and the Prince of Wales because of their relative lack of exposure to racial realities. Certainly, Prince Charles knows little more about race than what he has been told. But how is it that the leading minds of our people have succumbed to the fallacy of egalitarianism? Observations of this kind are admittedly speculative, but I think the explanation lies in our genetic weaknesses, weaknesses that are the unfortunate "other side" of our virtues.

The excessive sense of "fair play" of which Mr. Taylor spoke in his talk can be a severe and crippling weakness in the struggle for self-preservation. Blacks are, I believe, less hampered by such feelings. For example, they vote far more intelligently than whites. Whites vote to please their college sociology professor, their newspaper editor, their priest, or their fellow yuppies. Whites therefore do not vote for what is good for themselves, their people, their progeny, or their country. Blacks are not so befuddled. They go to the polls in election after election and return an overwhelming vote for candidates and policies that favor them, their race, and their children.

Only a tiny number of whites are able to think coherently about their survival as a group. Even we in this room are often unable to think consistently; we must concede that we, too, can be victims of liberal guilt feelings foisted upon us. Recently, *American Renaissance* published an elegant essay in two parts written by Michael Masters[1], explaining in most convincing terms why it is moral for whites to survive, why it is moral to resist the forces that are reducing us to a racial minority here and, eventually, even in Europe.

One would think that even an amoeba would know that survival is better than death! With our people, however, one has to argue them into surviving. This situation is comparable to being sent onto the playing field, huddling with the team, and having to explain the exciting new idea that it is better to win than to lose. It is breathtaking, absolutely breathtaking, that our race is so tripped up in abstractions about racial equality and equivalence that we can now be objective about our own survival. To have to argue the men and

---

[1] See "The Morality of Survival" on page 241.

women of our race into survival is like going hunting and having to carry the hound.

It could even be said that the prevalence of such fuzzy thinking about racial survival is an argument in favor of those who dispute the theory of evolution and believe in creation. The scientists among us are forced to explain how genes that permit abstract speculation about our own survival could possibly have survived the millennia. One would think that the genes of people this befuddled would be found only by scientists doing DNA research on the fossilized dung of saber-tooth tigers!

Squanto and Ephialtes

When I was a child, my parents were not great believers in television. The first television program we were allowed to watch was the coronation of Queen Elizabeth, which we were marched up the street and ordered to sit and watch. Since I had thought from what my friends had said that TV was some sort of sinful treat, I was surprised to see what appeared to be nothing more than another boring church service, with adults walking around in robes and reading the Bible.

The lack of television meant that I did a lot of reading, much of which was from the tales of antiquity and novels by the Victorian writer, G. H. Henty. One of these stories was that of the pass at Thermopylae. Like generations of Europeans before me, I sentimentally identified with the men of Sparta who died "obedient to her laws." One main character in that story, however, fails to stick in most people's memory. You will remember that a Greek shepherd showed the Persians a mountain path around the pass by which they could ambush the Greeks from the rear. That man was Ephialtes the Malian.

As a child I read about Ephialtes and imagined that he must have been the most shocking sort of out-and-out traitor. However, in my old age, having had much experience with liberals, and especially with Christian liberals who believe that Christianity enjoins more concern for other groups than for our own, I have changed my image of Ephialtes the Malian. I no longer see him as simply a traitor, pure and simple, but as a much more complicated psychological type.

I see him looking at the Persian "immigrants" as they come to take his people's homeland. I hear him saying, "Oh, look! Here come those poor Persians looking for a home. I bet they have interesting things to eat. Maybe they will open up a Persian restaurant. We'll have diversity. Why, look at that one there; he might want to marry my daughter. Poor things. They look hungry and thirsty. Maybe I can help them. It's what Zeus would have us do."

Likewise I thought for some time that only our race produced renegades like Ephialtes. However, I then recalled the story of little Squanto. Some of you will remember Squanto, the kindly Indian boy who showed the Pilgrims how to fertilize their corn by planting a little fish in the ground with each corn seed. Most of us were told the Squanto story in 5th or 6th grade, as the schools were already softening us up for multiculturalism and laying the ground work for guilt feelings we were supposed to have for mistreating the noble, kindly Indians, especially when whites should have been grateful to clever Squanto for teaching them how to plant crops.

In the light of later history, it certainly seems that Squanto and his female predecessor, Pocahontas, were both unlucky draws of the cards for the Indians. When one reflects that the Indians generally sired brave heroes like Geronimo and Sitting Bull, who defended—albeit without success—their people's patrimony, how unlucky for them that at the precise moment when they most desperately needed a Geronimo or a Sitting Bull they got a Squanto and a Pocahontas!

Our own race has gone from a situation in which our equivalent of Squanto, Ephialtes the Malian, was the rare exception to one in which we have almost nothing but Squantos in churches, schools, colleges, newspapers and labor unions helping the alien colonizers plant the corn. I wonder if any of them ever reflect on how the descendants of Geronimo and Sitting Bull today—cooped up on reservations, having lost their native languages and culture—must gnash their teeth and curse the day when Squanto and Pocahontas were born.

If a fate for our people different from that of the Indians is to be avoided, it will require brave and intelligent leadership. When I was a child, one of my favorite chapters of history was the story of the Spanish Armada. I read and reread the G. H. Henty novel on this episode in British history, *With Drake in the Armada.*

Most of you remember the story. In the time of Queen Elizabeth, England was a poor little island on the fringe of Europe. It was one of the last citadels of freedom left, as the Spanish Empire had crushed nation after nation beneath the weight of royal absolutism and the Inquisition. Everyone knew that there would eventually be war between the colossal empire of Spain and little England. For years the government of Queen Elizabeth had scrimped and saved, pouring what little revenue was available into preparing the fleet for the inevitable war and into succoring the hard-pressed Dutch patriots. Every loyal Englishman knew how high the stakes were, because he could see across the Channel what the results of Spanish despotism were.

At last, after years of waiting, came the long anticipated declaration of war from Spain. The greatest fleet in human history was preparing to sail. All the forces of Spain, the Inquisition, and the Counter-Reformation were descending upon England. Every Englishman knew what the fate of his country would be if that Armada were ever able to escort to an English port the Duke of Parma with his dreaded Spanish *tercios*, the unrivaled Spanish military formations that had never known defeat on land. No nation had ever stood up to the Spanish infantry. The only hope was to imitate the Dutch, who had opened the dikes, flooded their land, and defended themselves at sea. At all cost the Armada had to be stopped.

All during the spring and summer the sentinels had stood on the rocky promontories along the southern coast of Britain, straining their eyes south for the first sight of the Spanish sails. Finally, the word came to The Lizard, the southernmost point in Britain, that the Armada had been sighted and was now bearing down on the little island. The bonfire was lighted at The Lizard and then as planned all across southern England bonfire after bonfire was lighted as signals to send word to London and the Queen that the Armada was coming.

The Queen, knowing the mortal threat to England's very survival, made a royal inspection of her army, gathered at Tilsbury for the nation's defense. After riding slowly through the ranks, she made a magnificent declaration to the men, which was met with a thunderous ovation. It still speaks movingly—or should—to every Anglo-Saxon wherever he lives.

"My loving people, I have been urged by some to take care how I expose myself to armed multitudes for fear of treachery [there had been assassination attempts]. But I do not desire to live to distrust my faithful and loving people. Let tyrants fear their people. I have always so governed that, next to God, I have placed my chiefest strength and safeguard in the loyal hearts and good will of my subjects. Therefore, I come amongst you at this grave hour as you see, being resolved in the midst of the heat of battle to live or die amongst you all for my God, for my kingdom, for my people and in defense of their religion and liberty. I know I have the body of a weak and feeble woman but I have the heart and stomach of a king, and of a king of England too, and think foul scorn that Parma or Spain, or any prince of Europe should dare to invade the borders of my realm; to which, rather than any dishonour shall grow by me, I myself will take up arms."

One can imagine the impact of this proclamation on the English. Spain was defeated by the superior seamanship of the British sailors as well as by a stroke of good luck in the form of favorable weather (the "Protestant Wind"), which scattered the Armada at a crucial moment.

Today, as an adult, having read more widely, I know that the story is not quite so pat as this. While England was freedom's hope, her freedom was not all that it could have been. Catholics and the Irish did not enjoy that freedom, although in time they would come to do so. Nevertheless, I do not regret having enjoyed a boy's view of such events, free of qualifications.

The Drakes of Today

As a boy I dreamed of being involved in such a cause. I would read such stories by Henty and other writers and I would imagine what it must have been like to have sailed with Drake. I never dreamed, however, that during my own lifetime there would arise an issue the stakes of which would dwarf to insignificance the stakes at issue in the battle between Sir Francis Drake and the Spanish Armada. Today we stand at a turning point in the history not merely of our country or even of our race, but of civilization itself.

Most of us can see three worlds. We can look back to the world of the America-that-was, the America of our childhood—which is a laughing-stock to liberals—the "Eisenhower era" America. That America was already not what it had been earlier or should have been. It already bore within itself the seeds of its own decline. Nevertheless, we remember it with fondness as a happy America of safety and confidence. That America is gone. It will never return.

When we look forward, there are two worlds in the future. We see one world in the chasm and one at the summit. Our species can take the road to either of these worlds. If we continue on our present course, we will use our marvelous scientific advances to encourage the procreation of the sorriest sort of our species and drag ourselves down into a debased humanity.

Or we could use the knowledge science has given us to carry our people and humanity to greater heights than have ever been dreamed of. We have it in our capacity to bring forth brilliant people who will be free of hereditary physical and mental diseases, people who will surpass the great geniuses of Pericles, Shakespeare, Goethe, and Tolstoy.

If we continue our present dysgenic policies (for we do have a national genetics policy—a policy of subsidizing the incompetent at the expense of the competent), we can continue to increase the number of problem causers and diminish the number of problem solvers with each generation. This policy can be pursued until we have debased the human race and are bereft of genius.

If we are to pursue the path to a higher, greater humanity, it may be in no small measure due to the work of many of you in this room today. We are the Drakes and his seamen of this later age. It is up to us. No one else is going to do it, not even among conservative groups not represented here today.

For our opponents are not limited to liberals. Indeed, some liberals, a very few, are not totally lost to the cause of the survival of our race and the development of our species. Some liberals, who see the cessation of immigration as the *sine qua non* of a sensible environmental policy, can be welcome allies. Most liberals are quite otherwise. But while we condemn liberals, let us not forget that many conservatives are equally if not more to blame for our circumstances.

On the right you find many "responsible conservatives," like the Bill Bennetts, the Ralph Reeds, the Jack Kemps. You find many people on the right who believe that it is immoral to work for the survival of our race. Such conservatives firmly believe that it makes no difference if whites are displaced by non-whites. Admittedly, this is a strange mind-set, the "anti-racist" conservative, but it is a common problem. Indeed, such people are more dangerous to us at this stage than liberals. Through such conservatives the establishment is able to choke off debate on the crucial issue of race. The thought control begins with those conservatives who are in essential agreement with liberals when it comes to race.

Leadership on the race issue will have to come from the Right. Although there are some few liberals who may come to our cause, they will always be a minority. The Left can never part from its commitment to egalitarianism, which is the warp and woof of Leftism of all stripes. It has been the Right, which historically has accepted the fact of human inequality. A belief in the inequality of individuals and of races was the faith of the American Right from Jefferson, to John Randolph, to John C. Calhoun right down to the Taft Republicans and Southern statesmen like Senator Richard B. Russell only several decades ago.

Only in the last decades has the leadership of the Right been usurped by those who call themselves "conservatives," but who are actually committed egalitarians. The establishment has succeeded in coopting the legitimate Right and replacing it with an opposition that opposes nothing of consequence.

Jack Kemp or Ralph Reed appear as purported conservative spokesmen yet they promote egalitarianism and denounce opposition to the establishment's racial program as "evil." The unsuspecting white who looks upon them with a measure of trust is confused and misled into accepting the idea that it is somehow immoral to oppose the reduction of whites to a minority. This is especially true because the leftist view on race being promulgated by Mr. Kemp and Mr. Reed is seasoned with free enterprise economics by the former and a shallow, trendy theology by the latter.

It is up to us to break through the Iron Curtain imposed on the honest discussion of racial issues and it is time to get on with the task. When Joan of Arc finally found someone who offered to lead her to the King of France, he asked her when she would like to go. She replied, "Better today than tomorrow. Better tomorrow than later yet." How then are we to get on with the task which history has laid before us? First by having the trumpet sound a certain note, "for if the note of the trumpet be uncertain, who shall prepare himself for the battle?" If we are unequivocal and unwavering in our message, our people will respond to the call.

Our message must be clear and uncompromising—not hysterical or overstated, but certainly clear and uncompromising. We must never waver or falter. We must without qualification stand for what we believe and hold our positions even under the fiercest fire. In the words Shakespeare put into the mouth of Henry the Fifth, "he which hath no stomach to this fight, let him depart . . . . We would not die in that man's company that fears his fellowship to die with us." Those conservatives who cannot or will not take a principled stance in defense of the historic conservative truths about race should retire to their homes and leave the field to those who can. After all, what could be more worthy of being conserved than the very genetic survival of our people?

Let the fair weather patriot and the sunshine soldier depart. We will not depart. We will not be silenced by media denunciations. We will not be bullied by threats of financial reprisal. We will not be silenced by appeals to

guilt offered in the guise of Christianity. We are resolved to fight these issues out to their ultimate conclusion so that we can say, with the men who
sailed with Nelson at Trafalger, "Thank God we have done our duty!" As
Rudyard Kipling said: "The strength of the wolf is the strength of the pack,
and the strength of the pack is the strength of the wolf." Each of us adds his
individual strength to our cause and each of us is strengthened by the
strength of our cause.

To plagiarize William Lloyd Garrison in *The Liberator*, many will object
to the severity of our language, but is there not cause for severity? We will
be as harsh as truth and as uncompromising as justice. We are in earnest. We
will not equivocate. We will not excuse. We will not retreat a single inch.
And we will be heard.

This article is adapted from a speech delivered at the American Renaissance *conference held in Louisville, Kentucky in 1996. It appeared in the
May 1997 issue. Sam G. Dickson is a lawyer who lives in Atlanta, Georgia*

Twelve Years of American Renaissance
by Jared Taylor

With this issue, *American Renaissance* marks 12 full years of publication. Our readership has never been larger nor our reach greater, but the crises the inaugural issue was launched to combat remain as acute as ever. We can look back with some satisfaction on what AR and other activists have achieved during the past 12 years, but any successes are only the smallest beginnings of a struggle that will continue for decades.

What does AR stand for? What must whites do if they are not to lose their peoplehood and their civilization? And from the perspective of more than a decade of advocacy, are we any closer to achieving our goals? Perhaps it is time to reflect on some of these questions.

Racial Consciousness

AR's purpose has always been to recall to whites their legitimate and even noble interests *as a race*, to reinstill in them a consciousness of race without which they cannot survive as a race. It is to remind whites that they are not isolated individuals but a people with common goals. It is to resurrect the pride and sense of destiny that were once ours, and that gave rise to our greatest achievements.

But what does it even mean to survive or to prosper *as a race*? Most whites have only confused and contradictory ideas about this, while virtually every non-white instinctively understands the importance of racial solidarity. Non-whites feel a powerful tie of race loyalty that requires neither instruction nor reflection, and they support explicitly racial goals that can be achieved only at the expense of others. Whites have an uneasy awareness that non-whites stick up for each other, but most have no idea what this means for whites, and have learned to think it is wrong for whites to do the same.

Blacks and Hispanics, for example, consistently call for more power, representation, and privileges for their own groups. They clamor for "affirmative action," political appointments, safe electoral districts, and official recognition of their distinctive celebrations and characteristics. They have established large, well-funded organizations to make demands that are emphatically racial. They do not call for *better* judges or legislators, but for *black* judges or *Latino* legislators. A black or Latino is automatically better because he will fight for their narrow racial interests.

Only the most unusual non-whites even pretend to work for the country as a whole or to consider the interests of other racial groups. When non-whites do call for "fairness" or "justice" it is almost always an attempt to make a narrow, racial demand look like a principled appeal. For non-whites, America is like a football game, but with skin color instead of uniforms. They know which side they are on, and take the support of their teammates for granted. That is why non-whites are so angry when one of their own reaches a position of authority but refuses to carry the ball. Most blacks hate Supreme Court Justice Clarence Thomas more than they hate any white man, because to them he is a traitor. He wears the uniform but does not play for the team.

Judges and legislators are, of course, just the beginning. Non-whites want more firemen, teachers, policemen, editors, bureaucrats, fat cats, politicians, movie stars, holidays, and festivals. They want America to reflect *them*, to be more like *them*, to celebrate and glorify *them*. If these gains come at the expense of whites it only makes the triumph that much sweeter.

Non-whites close ranks around their own, no matter how criminal or degenerate. Blacks, especially, like to riot when some thug gets rough treatment at the hands of a white policeman. This is the classic spark for arson and violence, from the pitched battles of the 1960s in Newark and Detroit to the mayhem in Cincinnati in April a year ago. An insult to one—even a hardened criminal—is an insult to all, and a benefit for one is a benefit for all.

As their numbers rise even Asians, who have generally been quiet about group interests, have begun to assert them more vigorously. When the immigrant Taiwanese nuclear physicist Wen Ho Lee was charged with espionage in December 1999, Asians of all nationalities rallied to his defense, and there are now publications like *Monolid* that cultivate resentment against whites. Wherever Asians gather in sufficient numbers they will assert racial interests, but will never do so as crudely as blacks and Hispanics because Asians can often succeed on their own merits.

Robert Frost once defined a liberal as someone who cannot take his own side in an argument. When it comes to racial arguments, whites are so liberal they do not even realize they have a side. They are a perfect example of unilateral disarmament. They have abandoned and even condemn every sign of loyalty to their own group while they encourage solidarity and group loyalty among the members of every other group.

Before the age of "tolerance" and "sensitivity," whites had a clear grasp of their group interests. They kept non-whites out of the country through restrictive immigration laws. They prevented them from voting. They maintained the quality of their schools and neighborhoods by restricting non-white access. Their vision of the United States took for granted its European, Western character, which they never imagined could be transformed by mass immigration and claims of "multiculturalism." This conviction of the essential "whiteness" of America was central to American thought from colonial times until only 50 or 60 years ago. Virtually all whites had the instinctive racial consciousness of the kind non-whites express so aggressively today. It is only by rekindling this sense of solidarity, loyalty, and pride that we can hope to see a real American renaissance, and it is from this vision that AR takes its name.

Whites still have a residual racial consciousness that only requires cultivation. People of all races start out with healthy feelings of racial loyalty, which are evident in every integrated school in America. Blacks, Hispanics, and whites can be assigned mixed seating in the classroom, but at lunch time and on the playground they separate by race. Self-segregation persists generation after generation in the face of every effort to combat it. There are school districts like those of Shaker Heights, Ohio, and Montclair, New Jersey, that go to absurd lengths to spread blacks, whites and Hispanics evenly through every class, extra-curricular activity, and position in student government. It makes no difference; left to themselves the children sort themselves out by race.

Left to themselves, adults do the same. Gary Orfield of Harvard and William Frey of the University of Michigan are always publishing hand-wringing articles about the return of segregation. Prof. Orfield gets press attention every year when he warns that today's blacks and Hispanics go to school with fewer whites than the year before. He blames increasing residential segregation and the end of court-ordered busing. Prof. Frey writes frequently about the most recent kind of white flight, in which whites are abandoning those parts of the country that receive the most immigrants. And although people seldom write scholarly papers about it, anyone can see that church services and private gatherings are almost always segregated.

This, then, is the great white paradox: Whites claim to adore "diversity," but they make every effort to avoid it. They make every important decision in their lives—where to live, whom to marry, where to send their children to school, whom to choose as friends, which church to attend—as if it were made for racial reasons, but deny that race had anything to do with it. As one wag put it, in their mating and migratory habits, liberals are no different from members of the Ku Klux Klan.

Unlike non-whites, who understand their interests and work together consciously to promote them, whites express their racial interests only as individuals. Their choices reflect their deep desire not to be part of a darkening, alien America but they refuse to admit they are fleeing the rising tide of color. They would say, instead, that they are protecting their families from crime and bad schools. Crime and bad schools would hardly be a problem were it not for blacks and Hispanics, and if whites defended their collective interests as actively as other races defend theirs, we would close the country to non-Europeans, expel all illegals, and repeal the anti-discrimination laws that make it impossible to maintain the character of neighborhoods and institutions. Because whites will not act as a group, because they are left to solve the daily problems of "diversity" only as individuals, their sole strategy is flight. They are displaced piecemeal, until even the most stubborn hand over to aliens the homes and schools their ancestors built.

How can we bring this suppressed racial sentiment to the surface? How can we persuade whites of the legitimacy, the necessity, the urgency and morality of acting together as a race?

The first step—and this is one all readers can take—is to break the silence. Most people do not have original ideas; they only absorb the ideas around them. The racial ideas that circulate in this country are unnatural and destructive, but they are in the ascendancy, and only the most remarkable people can single-handedly face down the zeitgeist. This is why it is so important to shine even the faintest ray of light into the darkness. It may illuminate the one obscure stumbling block that has prevented someone from understanding our crisis. What whites are told to think is so contrived, so obviously false, so contrary to their interests, that sometimes the scales fall from their eyes after only a little instruction. Likewise, there are some whites who have kept healthy racial feelings alive despite the zeitgeist, but think they are alone in doing so.

AR has received many letters and e-mail messages from people who say they had feared they were the only people left in America who thought as they did, and are relieved to discover they are not alone. As one woman put it, "Thank, God. Now I know I'm not insane." Of course, she is not insane. Racially conscious whites are the only sane ones. And yet, when whites see glorification of multiracialism and miscegenation everywhere, when they see the most alien and disconcerting immigrants held up as lovable examples of "diversity," when they hear the failings of non-whites everywhere blamed on white wickedness, when every politician and commentator tells them they must celebrate the transformation of their country into a jabbering outpost of the Third World, it is very hard not to deny the evidence of their senses and to go along—at least outwardly—with lies and nonsense. For some, AR has been a lifeline.

Of course, it is because the prevailing racial message is so unnatural and destructive to whites that those who promote it are so intent on quashing dissent. "Watchdog" groups such as the Anti-Defamation League and the Southern Poverty Law Center invariably describe AR as "dangerous," and would love to see us disappear. If AR is dangerous it is only because it is right, because it makes sense, because it cannot be refuted. It is the highest compliment for AR and other racially-oriented publications to be described as dangerous.

Still, there are only a few whites with fully-formed racial consciousnesses, just waiting to learn they are not alone. Most whites cling to conventional, self-destructive thinking because it is all they know. Even when the views propounded by every respected institution are shown to be wrong, it still takes an independent turn of mind to reject them. People do not happily give up fashionable fantasies about equality and harmony in exchange for the disagreeable facts of inequality and friction, and those facts must be put before them repeatedly and persuasively. This is why AR actively seeks out speaking engagements and radio and television appearances. It is our belief that every calm, well-considered racial argument plants a few seeds of dissent. As the editor of AR, I have been a guest on hundreds of radio programs, and these often bring in new subscribers.

Fortunately, argument is not the only thing that changes people's minds. The most persuasive arguments for our side are the simple facts of demographic change. As aliens spread into every corner of our country, more and more whites find that reality is far different from media-driven fantasy. When I first began to speak on radio, callers overwhelmingly opposed what I said. Not anymore. Now, even "conservative" talk show hosts are surprised by the level of support for the AR point of view.

Although callers sometime mention that they are AR readers, we do not pretend that AR has had any but the slightest role in changing the way Americans think. It is the constant racial double standards, the destruction of neighborhoods, the demonizing of whites, and the alien and unpleasant behavior of the newcomers that are waking up more and more people. The truth can be denied for only so long. Whites can run away only so many times. Eyes are constantly being opened, and the change in the way I am received as a radio guest is one of the most encouraging developments since AR began publishing.

Another reason racialist ideas are better received is that compared to a dozen years ago, there are far more voices of active white dissent. Besides AR, there are the *Citizens Informer*, the *Nationalist Times*, *Middle American News*, and *The Occidental Quarterly. The Truth At Last,* and the publications and broadcasts of the National Alliance also openly attack racial conventions, although they come with a harshly anti-Jewish message.

Ten years ago, it would have been impossible to find a public meeting devoted to white racial consciousness, but they are now commonplace and well attended. Every two years, *American Renaissance* holds conferences at which racially-oriented academics, journalists, and clergymen address several hundred people. The Council of Conservative Citizens also attracts large audiences to its meetings. Gatherings of this kind sometimes get media coverage, and have even been broadcast by C-SPAN.

Today, there is no end of Internet web sites offering every possible dissenting view on race and immigration, from environmentalist reasons to oppose a growing population to outright National Socialism. For any white person with a computer, powerful arguments against orthodoxy are just a few keystrokes away. This deeply disturbs the purveyors of lies and foolishness. There is a constant outcry about the dangers of "hate" on the Internet— meaning any opposition to the demonization and displacement of whites— but no one is worried that Marxism or Maoism, for example, are making a comeback via the Internet. Free speech is "dangerous" only when it is plausible, and this is what distinguishes racial dissent from Communism or tree worship or *feng shui*, or any other body of thought outside the mainstream. We have history, science, tradition, morality, and human nature on our side, which makes our positions impossible to refute.

At this point only a small number of whites fully understand our racial and civilizational crisis, but many have lost patience with the demands of non-whites. For decades, whites quietly put up with "affirmative action," but lawsuits and referenda have beaten it back, and systematic racial preferences may be only a Supreme Court decision away from extinction.

There are other signs of resistance. In the aftermath of the Sept. 11 attacks, the city of New York considered building a bronze statue of the three firemen who raised the flag over the ruins of the World Trade Center—except that instead of the three whites, the statue would be of a white, a Hispanic, and a black. This proposal was swept away by a mighty blast of outrage. In a show of backbone I would not have expected ten years ago, whites flatly rejected this falsification of history.

Likewise, whites do not conceal their contempt for the idea of reparations to blacks for slavery. I was recently on perhaps a dozen radio programs devoted to this subject, and was encouraged by the essentially unanimous white view that reparations would be larceny. Several whites predicted violence if Congress gave money to blacks. Although the mainstream media do not acknowledge it, there is smoldering resentment among whites that could burst into flame over a new round of handouts. A dozen years ago, demands for reparations were not met with outright derision.

There has also been great progress in the scientific study of race and genetics. The dozen years since AR began publishing have seen the appearance of *The Bell Curve*, *The g Factor*, *Why Race Matters*, *Race, Evolution, and Behavior*, and a whole series of pioneering books by Richard Lynn. The famous 10-year study by Sandra Scarr and Richard Weinberg that was to prove that black children adopted by whites would grow up as smart as whites proved the opposite. Increasingly, if only for medical reasons, scientists are setting aside the silly idea that race is a "social construct," and although the Human Genome Project has prompted absurd pronouncements about the meaninglessness of race, it is steadily revealing the profound importance of the kind of small genetic differences that distinguish the races. The gene variations that code for intelligence and other characteristics are already being found. It will inevitably be discovered that they are not distributed equally among all races, and these data will become public knowledge despite every attempt to suppress them. Every new study is another arrow in our quiver.

The myth of racial equality—of racial equivalence, really—has been one of AR's permanent targets. It is disastrous for at least three reasons. First, it supports the view that anyone can become American. Even after 300 years, the mass of blacks are still not Americans in the sense whites are, and Hmong, Bolivians, and Mexicans are yet more proof that race is an almost insuperable barrier to assimilation. Second, myths about race encourage interracial sex and miscegenation, which often put white women at the mercy of violent non-whites and further reduce our numbers.

Finally, liberals love to blame the failures of blacks and Hispanics on white "racism," and though fewer and fewer whites accept this blame, the image of wicked whites oppressing noble people of color is still a potent weapon against us. Comparative data from the Human Genome Project will eventually exculpate us completely, but until that day we must continue to use the nearly as conclusive data gathered by researchers like Arthur Jensen,

Philippe Rushton, Richard Lynn, Michael Levin, Linda Gottfredson, Charles Murray, and Robert Gordon. The facts and arguments support us; the challenge is to make them better known.

The social sciences as a whole are finally turning away from the "blank slate" theory that there is no such thing as human nature and that all behavior is learned. Even the worst fanatics are grudgingly conceding that men and women are different, that some children are smarter than others, that genes set limits on what the environment can change. Myths of racial equivalence were a natural extension of the blank slate theory, and the return of a common sense understanding of heredity and human nature will eventually illuminate the question of race as well.

Immigration Control

Immigration is the greatest world-wide threat to our race. With perhaps the single exception of Iceland, every white country is besieged by non-white immigrants. Whites have built the most successful societies in human history, and non-whites from failed societies are flooding into them. Once non-whites arrive in large numbers, especially once they have become naturalized citizens, it is very difficult to remove them. In any democratic society, where elections are often nothing more than racial head counts, once non-whites reach a certain percentage of the population there is no longer any realistic hope of preserving our race and civilization except in activist enclaves. A constant flow of non-whites into our lands threatens our very survival as a people.

To cut immigration is therefore the most urgent practical measure we can take, and AR applauds any immigration-control group, no matter what its orientation. In the current "anti-racist" intellectual climate it may be that organizations like Numbers USA, which stresses only the strains that additional people put on our resources and infrastructure, will be the ones that win enough support to change policy. We should endorse any arguments that work.

There are now countless grass-roots immigration-control groups, and more come into existence all the time, and no matter how "anti-racist" a position their leaders take, racial consciousness runs strong among the activists. Recently, I spoke to a regional group that officially opposes only *illegal* immigration. The organizers were worried I might say something "racist," but as I got acquainted with the activists it was clear they feel as I do: They don't want large numbers of non-whites changing their country. I gave a talk little different from one I would give to an AR audience, and received a standing ovation.

Immigration control is an almost exclusively white concern, and would be nothing like the issue it is if all the newcomers were handsome, high-IQ, English-speaking white people. Although there are exceptions, almost all immigration-control activists—even the occasional black or Hispanic activists—do not just see people; they see race.

It is in Europe, however, that immigration control has had the most success in the past 12 years. There is hardly a European country that does not have an explicitly nationalist party that calls for strict limits on immigration. Most Europeans are almost as terrified of charges of "racism" as we are, but parties in France, Denmark, Switzerland, Belgium, Italy, Austria, and Holland now campaign openly to preserve their national cultures and populations—and win votes for doing so. Progress has been slower in Germany and Britain, but the successes of European nationalist parties are pushing "mainstream" politicians in a sensible direction. Nationalists have held cabinet positions in Italy and Austria, and it is only a matter of time before a staunch nationalist heads a coalition government or even wins an outright majority.

These parties are seldom openly racialist, but they do not have to be. An appeal to the Danes that their nation remain Danish is difficult to criticize as "racist," even though its practical effect is to keep out non-whites. European nationalists are probably very much like American immigration activists: Racial sentiment lies just below the surface.

Europeans have a number of advantages over us in the struggle to preserve their people and civilization. "We are a nation of immigrants" is a slogan that has no effect on them, nor can they be attacked for perpetuating "the legacy of slavery." They did not displace native populations within the last few centuries, and the smaller countries did not even have overseas empires. Europe therefore has much better defenses against the guilt-mongering that paralyzes so many American whites. Although no nation in Europe has achieved the decisive political and psychological breakthrough that would completely remove it from danger, that day will come. Just as Austria faced a period of clumsy European Union sanctions when Jörg Haider's Freedom Party entered a ruling coalition, any nationalist European government will have to weather a storm of outrage, but the first nationalist government could be the first domino. It may not be long before American activists look across the Atlantic not only for inspiration but for material support.

People often ask if there is still any hope for a white America. No one can answer that question. Sometimes social change is surprisingly quick. Ten years before the fall of the Soviet Union hardly anyone would have predicted it would crumble so quickly. There had been years of growing disaffection, just as racial disaffection grows in America, and collapse in one quarter led to collapse in all quarters. Could there be a similar collapse of racial myths in America? It is impossible to know, but if there ever is a collapse it will be because racial activists have been systematically undermining the foundations.

Ultimately, the odds of victory are not a preoccupation for those who know their cause is just. We fight for our children, in the name of our ancestors. We fight so that generations to come will walk in the ways of their forefathers, so that they will live as men and women rooted in the West rather than as waifs without loyalty or destiny. We fight so that our grandchildren will be the unmistakable descendants—biologically, culturally, and spirituially—of our grandparents. Like all who fight with conviction, we fight for what we love, and if there is justice in this world we will surely win.

This article appeared in the November 2002 issue.

Note to readers:

Anyone with an interest in reading more about the subjects covered in this book will find an extensive archive of *American Renaissance* on the AR web page, www. amren.com, as well as other material that has not appeared in the print publication.

Readers who would like to subscribe to AR can likewise find details on the web page or may call (703) 716-0900. In the United States, the cost of 12 monthly issues is $24.00. The electronic version, which contains the same information in PDF format, costs $15.00. Please make checks out to 'AR,' and mail to: Box 527, Oakton, VA 22124.